ENVIRONMENT, NATURAL SYSTEMS, and DEVELOPMENT

ENVIRONMENT, NATURAL SYSTEMS, and DEVELOPMENT

An Economic Valuation Guide

Maynard M. Hufschmidt
David E. James
Anton D. Meister
Blair T. Bower
John A. Dixon

THE JOHNS HOPKINS UNIVERSITY PRESS
Baltimore and London

The Johns Hopkins University Press, Baltimore, Maryland 21218
The Johns Hopkins Press Ltd., London

Library of Congress Cataloging in Publication Data
Main entry under title:

Environment, natural systems, and development.

Prepared by a team of experts assembled at the
East-West Environment and Policy Institute.
 Bibliography: pp. 321–27
 Includes index.
 1. Environmental policy—Cost effectiveness—Addresses,
essays, lectures. 2. Economic development projects—
Cost effectiveness—Addresses, essays, lectures.
I. Hufschmidt, Maynard M. II. East-West Environment and
Policy Institute (Honolulu, Hawaii)
HC79.E5E573   1983   363.7'05   82-17237
ISBN 0-8018-2930-5
ISBN 0-8018-2931-3 (pbk.)

Contents

Chapter 1.   INTRODUCTION   1

Chapter 2.   INSTITUTIONAL AND PLANNING CONTEXT   12

Chapter 6.   ENVIRONMENTAL QUALITY VALUATION FROM THE BENEFIT SIDE   170

Chapter 7.   ENVIRONMENTAL QUALITY VALUATION FROM THE COST SIDE   261

**Chapter 8.   MULTIACTIVITY ECONOMIC-ENVIRONMENTAL
QUALITY MODELS   286**

List of Figures

List of Tables

Foreword

The Environment and Policy Institute (EAPI) was established at the East-West Center in October 1977 to study the variety of policy objectives that rely on or affect the natural environment. Experts, practitioners, and students from the United States, Asia, and the Pacific come together under the auspices of the EAPI to do research, exchange information, synthesize new approaches to mutual problems, and develop educational materials.

A major program of the institute is "Natural Systems Assessment for Development," in which methods are being devised for identifying, quantifying, predicting, and evaluating the natural resource and environmental quality factors that are important to economic activities. Assessment is viewed as a practical aid to decision makers, as a complement to the conventional package of engineering, economic, and sociopolitical analyses. The methods sought are systematic and comprehensive, including the recognition of appropriate development opportunities using natural systems as well as warnings against unacceptable degradation of sustainable production capabilities.

Urgencies and exigencies of economic development dominate policy making and decision making. Immediate gains carry high political and economic rewards, even when the development activity may degrade the renewable resource base. Management for sustained productivity must still meet financial goals of investors. Conservation of natural systems will, to some extent, necessarily be rationalized on the base of social objectives that cannot be quantified and monetized. Recognizing these facts of development, the EAPI program proceeds on the thesis that more explicit and thorough research and analysis can enhance the management of natural systems. A more complete understanding of the structure and function of ecosystems will improve chances of project success and longevity. Careful internalization of benefits and costs will improve choices among alternative schemes and technologies. Uncertainty can be reduced, and fewer decisions will then rest upon subjective argumentation.

The program is producing two closely related sets of training and information materials. The first in sequence of analysis is a handbook, *Natural Systems Information for Planners* (scheduled for publication in late 1983). Each chapter addresses a concern for changes in the renewable resource base that may create hazards to the success of economic development activity: for example, soil erosion, air and water pollution, insect pest outbreaks, or loss of watershed protection. The unwanted consequences are described in concise, nontechnical language in order to alert the planner and provide guidance in how to avoid or ameliorate them as development projects are carried out. The handbook shows how to quantify the status and trends of natural systems in physical, chemical, and biological parameters wherever possible.

The second activity for multinational collaboration concerns techniques for the economic valuation of these natural systems changes and their effects on human health and welfare. This book is the major product of this part of the program.

In late 1977, the International Institute for Environment and Development was completing a study of multilateral aid agencies (e.g., the World Bank and the Asian Development Bank). Researchers at the EAPI became aware that a major conclusion of that study (subsequently published in 1979 in *Banking on the Biosphere?*) was the urgent necessity to develop and introduce new forms of analysis and accountancy—credible means of assessing and including indirect and longer-term benefits and costs of development projects. Staff and visiting experts considered that a response to this challenge was of immediate importance and could be accomplished with the style and resources of the East-West Center. A more tentative assumption was that innovative valuation techniques would be applicable in developing countries—they were still not widely used in the industrialized world.

The essential intellectual leadership for the preparation of the *Guide* was found in Professor Maynard M. Hufschmidt, who accepted an appointment as fellow in the summer of 1978 and returned in June 1979 to commit his full energies to the project for the next three years. A network of American and Asia-Pacific collaborators was assembled. The contributions of the major authors must be regarded as labors of professional pride—most of the available funds were spent to bring knowledgeable people together, not for generous stipends. The result is a compilation that is already highly rewarding to those who participated in the several conferences and workshops. The next step after publication and distribution of this book is the reception of feedback from economists and planners who are in the day-to-day business of development. The Environment and Policy Institute invites comments on the *Guide* and inquiries about its continuing program.

RICHARD A. CARPENTER
Program Coordinator

Preface

This guide is the result of two years of work on applied benefit-cost analysis at the East-West Environment and Policy Institute by a multinational team of economists and natural resource-environmental quality professionals. Soon after the establishment of EAPI in 1977, it became increasingly evident that many important natural-systems and environmental quality values were not being given adequate consideration in development planning and decision making in developing nations. This deficiency arose, in part, from the inability to express the natural systems effects of development in monetary terms that are familiar to and persuasive with decision makers responsible for allocating scarce resources in capital and operating programs and budgets.

At a planning conference held at the East-West Center in September 1979, participants recommended that EAPI prepare a training guide to show how techniques of economic analysis and valuation could be used in actual planning situations in both developed and developing countries. Work on the guide and a set of related case studies of valuation techniques began with a planning workshop held at the East-West Center in May 1980. At a second workshop held one year later, a draft of the guide was reviewed intensively by twenty scholars and professionals from the United States and eight Asian-Pacific countries and representatives of the World Bank, the United Nations Environmental Program, and the U.S. Agency for International Development. The principal authors thereupon made major revisions in the guide based on comments and suggestions from workshop participants.

The basic outline, format, and schedule for preparation of the guide were undertaken by Dr. David James, Economist, MacQuarie University, North Ryde, Australia; Dr. Anton Meister, Economist, Massey University, Palmerston, New Zealand; Mr. Blair Bower, Economist-Engineer, Arlington, Virginia, U.S.A.; and myself. Chapters 1 and 2 of the guide were written by me, Chapters 3, 7, and 8 by David James, Chapters 4 and 5 by Blair Bower, and Chapter 6 by Anton Meister and Dr. John Dixon, Economist and Research Associate at EAPI. Valuable contributions to the outline and substance of the guide were made by Richard Carpenter, Coordinator for the Natural Systems Assessment for Development Program at EAPI; Dr. Charles Pearson, Economist, School of Advanced International Studies, The Johns Hopkins University, Washington, D.C.; Eric Hyman, Joint Doctoral Research Intern, EAPI; and Dr. Kem Lowry, Assistant Professor, Urban and Regional Planning Program, and Dr. Hiroshi Yamauchi, Professor of Agricultural and Resource Economics, both at the University of Hawaii, Manoa campus. Final substantive revision of the manuscript was undertaken by me with the help of Dr. Dixon and Dr. Somluckrat Wattanavitukul, Economist and Research Associate at EAPI. Final editing was the work of Norma Gorst. Coordination of preparation of the final manuscript was undertaken by Sheryl Bryson, EAPI Publications Officer.

Typing of the various drafts and reproduction of the final version was the responsibility of Joan Nakamura, secretary of EAPI. The devoted and cheerful performance of Joan and her staff in discharging these important responsibilities is very much appreciated.

Overall support for the extensive work involved in preparation of this guide was provided by the EAPI staff, by Richard Carpenter, and by Dr. William Matthews, Director of EAPI.

MAYNARD M. HUFSCHMIDT

ENVIRONMENT, NATURAL SYSTEMS, and DEVELOPMENT

1

Introduction

Economic development in both industrialized and developing countries relies crucially on natural resources and on the productivity of natural systems. Economic development implies sustained increases in welfare derived from conventional goods and services, the production of which often requires natural resources and productive natural systems. Moreover, the environment directly provides services that contribute to increased welfare as implied by economic development.

At the same time, economic growth often is accompanied by increasing stress on natural systems and significant adverse effects on environmental quality. The central issue, then, is to conduct development activities in a fashion that preserves the long-run productivity of natural systems for sustained development and that minimizes deterioration in environmental quality.

Unfortunately, experience in both the developed and developing worlds demonstrates that on many occasions economic development activities have not shown sufficient concern for maintaining natural systems and environmental quality. This is due in part to the view that economic growth and environmental quality are alternatives—deterioration in environmental quality is viewed as a necessary cost of rapid economic growth. This view is misleading. Deforestation and the resulting soil erosion undermine the agricultural base of an economy and reduce long-term growth prospects. Pollution of coastal waters can destroy commercial fisheries and can also check economic growth. Air pollution affects human health with a resultant loss in productive effort as well as direct welfare losses to individuals. Even when deterioration of environmental quality does not lead to reduced capacity to produce conventional goods and services, natural-systems services that are consumed directly, such as recreation, are affected and the objective of development—improved human welfare—is undermined. For these reasons, it is of utmost importance that the effects on natural systems of development projects and programs be carefully analyzed. Such analysis is not a luxury, but must

1

become an essential part of project formulation and evaluation if protection is to be provided to the natural-resource base that sustains human welfare.

The basic premise of this guide is that a collection of already existing analytical approaches and techniques, including benefit-cost analysis, can be used to incorporate environmental quality concerns into the economic analysis of projects, programs, and development strategies. Until now, these techniques have not been used widely and systematically for economic analysis of development projects and programs. Although there have been rapid advances in environmental and natural-resource economics and in environmental management techniques, primarily in industrialized countries, and although there have been major advances in project evaluation in developing countries, the two strands have evolved separately. Now the time has come to pull the strands together and show how these techniques can assist in incorporating the dimension of environmental quality into development planning.

The terms *natural systems* and *environmental quality,* as used in this guide, refer to the physical-chemical-biological environment. Taken together, the terms are synonymous with the general term *environment* as used in much of the environmental literature. The term *natural systems* refers to ecosystems of various types—aquatic and terrestrial—in various types of use—agricultural, fisheries, forest, grazing, and water resources. The objectives of natural-systems management are the maintenance of the renewable resource base and of ecosystem productivity, and the preservation of species and habitats. The term *environmental quality* refers to the state of the air, water, land, and human artifacts as affected by human activities. The concern here is with the effects of changes in the state of the environment on receptors, including humans, plants, animals, and materials.

BENEFIT-COST ANALYSIS

This guide presents a number of different analytical techniques and approaches with a view toward their practical application to development projects and programs. Although benefit-cost analysis receives the most attention, other techniques, including input-output analysis, mathematical programming, and simulation, are also discussed. In all cases, the purpose is to show how the technique can be used to improve environmental quality management rather than to give a comprehensive exposition of the technique.

Benefit-cost analysis is a systematic method of identifying and measuring the economic benefits and costs of a project or program. The benefits of a project are the values of incremental outputs of goods and services, including environmental services, made possible by the project, and the costs are the values of the incremental real resources used by the project. Both project costs and benefits are appropriately discounted over time to make them commensurate. The intellectual roots of benefit-cost analysis lie in neoclassical welfare economics as explained in Chapter 3. The historical development of benefit-cost analysis has strong ties to water-resource development projects.

History

Benefit-cost analysis (also called cost-benefit analysis in the literature) was developed in the United States in response to a legal requirement imposed in 1936 on water-resource projects of the federal government (U.S. Flood Control Act of 1936). Efforts to implement this requirement, started by the National Resources Planning Board in the late 1930s, led to the preparation of the ''Green Book'' by a federal interagency committee composed of representatives of the major water-resource agencies (U.S. Federal Interagency River Basin Committee, Subcommittee on Benefits and Costs 1950). This report codified the general principles of economic analysis as they were to be applied in formulating and evaluating federal water-resource projects. The authors, some of whom were professional economists, drew on the then-emerging field of welfare economics as a theoretical base for the ''Green Book'' (Little 1957).

Application of these principles raised controversial issues in the executive branch and in Congress during the 1950s, and a number of academic economists became interested in these issues. The year 1958 was noteworthy for the publication of three influential books on benefit-cost analysis (Eckstein, Krutilla and Eckstein, and McKean). This was followed in the early 1960s by the influential book on water-resource systems (Maass et al. 1962) and the first extensive report about applying benefit-cost analysis to substantive areas other than water resources (Dorfman 1965). The use of benefit-cost analysis soon spread to other countries, especially to the United Kingdom, and to other sectors including highway transportation, urban planning, and environmental quality management. In 1965, the first economic review article on benefit-cost analysis carried ninety citations, largely from the United States and the United Kingdom (Prest and Turvey). The literature and applications of the approach have continued to expand rapidly (Mishan 1976).

Hammond (1958) was one of the first analysts to apply the principles of benefit-cost analysis to pollution control. The major advances, however, were made at Resources for the Future (Kneese 1962; Kneese and Bower 1968; Kneese, Ayres, and d'Arge 1970). Since then, environmental economics has become a recognized field of specialization in the economics discipline, with its own journal, the *Journal of Environmental Economics and Management,* which started in 1974. A 1976 review of the field of environmental economics contained 147 literature references (Fisher and Peterson). The related field of natural-resource economics also expanded significantly during this period, with important contributions by Ciriacy-Wantrup (1952), Scott (1955), Barnett and Morse (1963), and Herfindahl and Kneese (1974).

Benefit-cost analysis was broadened in the 1960s to accommodate equity-income distribution issues and situations of unemployment and underemployment (Maass et al. 1962; Weisbrod 1968; Haveman and Krutilla 1968). In the early 1970s, techniques were developed to deal with income distribution, unemployment, and foreign exchange issues in investment planning in developing countries (UNIDO 1972; Little and Mirrlees 1974; Squire and van der Tak 1975; Helmers 1979). The World Bank has adopted simplified versions of these techniques in its procedures for benefit-cost analysis of proposed investment projects. More than forty years of experience in applying benefit-cost analysis to water-resource developments have accumulated, as have about twenty years of experience in other sectors, such as transportation, urban development, electric power, and health, education, and welfare. Extensions of the techniques to natural-resource systems and environmental quality management and to social issues, such as equity, income distribution, and unemployment, have increased significantly over the past fifteen years. These extensions have resulted in a valuation approach that recognizes the reality that most public policy decisions have multiple objectives and embrace social goals that are much broader than mere economic efficiency.

Recent Applications to Natural Systems and Environmental Quality

The great expansion of interest in environmental and natural-resource economics has led to many applications of benefit-cost analysis and related techniques to the valuation of natural systems and environmental quality. These applications have been most numerous in North America and in Western Europe (Hufschmidt and Hyman 1982).

In general, such applications attempt to extend the theoretical concepts and measurement techniques of applied welfare economics and microeconomics to the valuation of those nonmarket goods and services that characterize many natural-systems and environmental quality effects. Although some early applications were ad hoc in nature, often without adequate theoretical foundation, many recent studies have effectively combined theory and empirical measurement techniques (Mäler and Wyzga 1976; Freeman 1979).

As described in detail in Chapter 3, valuation techniques for natural-systems and environmental quality effects can be classified broadly as market oriented and consumer-survey oriented. Within the market-oriented category, costs and benefits can be valued by using actual market or surrogate market prices. Valuation based on actual market prices, although not without problems, represents a straightforward application of standard benefit-cost analysis techniques. Much more difficult are valuations using surrogate markets and survey techniques. Much creative work has been done, however, in developing applications that are theoretically sound and feasible in practice. The travel-cost approach, discussed in Chapter 6, is an example of such an application.

Related economic and systems analysis techniques that have been applied with some success to natural systems and environmental quality include input-output models, mathematical programming, and simulation models. These are discussed in Chapter 8.

Economic analysis thus holds great promise for improving environmental quality management. At the same time, one must have modest expectations. There are two principal reasons for this. First, economic valuation relies critically on understanding and measuring the physical, chemical, and biological effects of development activities—in general, economic valuation is the last step in the analysis. Second, available conceptual and empirical methods for placing monetary values on nonmarket goods and services are quite imperfect. For example, it is difficult to value human life and the damages to human health, because even when the effects of air pollution on human health are known, there is no general agreement among economists on how to value damages to health. There also are aspects of environmental quality and natural systems that are important to society but that cannot be readily valued in economic terms. For these reasons, this guide should be viewed as an initial attempt to improve the valuation step in environmental quality management, not as a final effort.

Applicability in Developing Countries

The extensive development of these applications in North America and Western Europe gives promise that they can be adapted for use in developing countries. One purpose of this guide is to help advance the process of adaptation. In considering the opportunities as well as the problems of adaptation, one important factor is that the basic principles of the techniques are applicable in all types of economies—rich or poor, East or West, and centrally planned or market oriented. But the specific applications of the techniques presented in this guide must take account of these differences in income level, types of economy, levels of development, character of natural systems and environmental quality problems, and prevalence of markets.

Developing countries are at the crossroads of social choices regarding economic development, natural-resource use, and environmental quality management. Social choices may create or contribute to natural-system or societal imbalances or redress them through mitigation and compensation. Examples of natural-system imbalances include degradation of range and pasture quality, nutrient losses, erosion, sedimentation, spread of pathogens and vectors, deterioration in water quality through biological or mineral contamination, deforestation, and the extinction of living or abiotic features of the environment. Air and water pollution in urban areas are also examples of such environmental quality imbalances.

Human social and economic imbalances are reflected in the contrasts between the rich and the poor, the present and the future, and the city and the country, and among different social groups. The connections between natural-system and environmental quality imbalances and social and economic imbalances are strong. On the one hand, extensive rural poverty and severe population pressures create environmental stress on agricultural resources, including mining soil of its nutrients, cultivation of ecologically fragile lands, and salinization of soil through improper irrigation. Urban poverty is associated with the problems of unsanitary water supplies, inadequate sewage disposal, congestion, noise, air pollution, and loss of amenities. On the other hand, natural-system and environmental quality imbalances themselves can contribute to poverty and a widening gulf between rich and poor. To some extent, environmental problems are the result of unsatisfactory economic performance, and the solution may lie in economic growth. But economic growth increases environmental disruption in the extractive sectors and pollution from the transport, processing, and consuming of goods and services. In that light, growth must be balanced, with due regard for maintaining environmental quality.

It follows that the income distribution dimension of environmental quality deterioration and of programs for environmental improvement is crucial in developing countries where inequality among regions and groups is a pressing problem. The problem must be considered in two parts. Who benefits and who loses if environmental deterioration is permitted to go unchecked? These gains and losses often are perceived differently by affected groups. Also, who are the beneficiaries and who bears the costs if extensive expenditures are made for preserving environmental quality? Benefit-cost analysis should not stop with efficiency, even if efficiency includes environmental quality effects, but should at least identify the gainers and losers.

Because developing countries are at a critical point in natural resource and environmental management, they have the opportunity to avoid costly mistakes often made in industrialized countries and can reduce total social costs by anticipatory rather than remedial actions. Some specific problems facing developing countries in the planning and management of natural systems and environmental quality are:

1. Inadequacies in monitoring and enforcement of existing environmental protection laws and regulations;
2. Extensive poverty that puts a premium on current income-producing activities to the detriment of long-term protection of natural systems;
3. Scarcity of financial resources in relation to current needs, which constrains the willingness to protect natural systems;
4. The often perverse distributional effects of environmental quality plans and programs, which may worsen the existing inequitable distribution of income;
5. Difficulty in controlling the environmental quality effects of private sector and public sector development activities, which limits the effectiveness of public programs for environmental quality management;

6. Inadequacies in the technical, economic, and administrative expertise available for the planning and implementation of environmental management programs;
7. Widespread market failures, which require extensive use of shadow prices to replace market prices;
8. Minimal participation in environmental quality planning, either by the general public or by many affected governmental agencies, which reduces the effectiveness of implementation;
9. Inadequacies in environmental, economic, and social data, including difficulties in data collection and processing and lack of knowledge of past trends and baselines, which limit the quality of analysis;
10. Wide diversity of cultural values, which increases the difficulty of social evaluation of environmental quality effects.

Many of these problems are shared by industrialized nations. The major difference, however, is the degree to which these problems occur in developing countries.

With limited resources relative to development and natural-systems maintenance needs, developing countries face greater challenges in future environmental quality management than industrialized countries have in the past.

CONCEPTUAL FRAMEWORK

Benefit-cost analysis, including its application to natural-systems and environmental quality valuation, is a technique that can help decision makers make more rational decisions about the allocation of scarce resources. Accordingly, the technique is used necessarily as part of a planning and decision-making process that takes place in a specific institutional context—with local, regional, national, or international characteristics. The goal is to apply benefit-cost analysis to natural-systems and environmental quality effects and to environmental-quality management measures designed to reduce or counteract adverse effects. To this end, such effects and measures must be expressed in specific physical terms—quantitatively, if at all possible. The determination of such physical changes in natural systems and subsequently in receptors is a necessary but complex and difficult task. In general, as shown in figure 1.1, it is necessary to undertake a series of studies and analyses that begin with an analysis of an *activity*—an industrial plant, irrigation project, or forest management program—that generates *residuals* in gaseous, liquid, or solid form, which in turn affect the natural system and ambient environmental quality. Ambient environmental quality in turn affects *receptors,* which may be humans, plants, animals or materials. The physical effects on receptors, effects which may be beneficial or adverse, are then subjected to economic *valuation*. Only after these physical effects are determined can benefit-cost valuation techniques be applied.

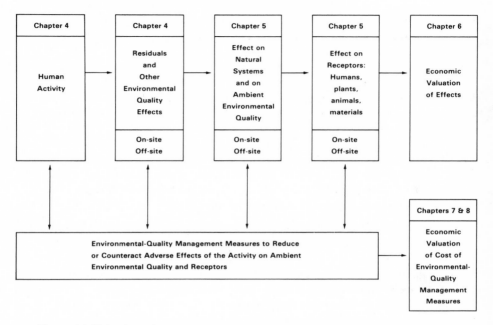

Figure 1.1 Valuation of natural-systems and environmental quality effects and of environmental quality management measures.

Figure 1.1 also depicts the relationship between the formulations of environmental-quality management measures and the economic valuation of the cost of the measures.

ORGANIZATION OF THE GUIDE

The chapters in this guide are organized according to the conceptual framework just described. Following this introductory chapter, Chapter 2 treats the institutional and planning context with special reference to developing countries. The complexity of institutions and planning processes is emphasized, and the important roles of international aid agencies and the private sector are pointed out. Clearly, the specific local institutional and planning context is an important factor influencing the opportunities for and limitations on the application of these techniques in both developed and developing countries.

Chapter 3 includes a concise summary of the basic principles of benefit-cost analysis and its extensions to environmental quality and natural-systems valuation. The discussion of the underlying theory, including assumptions and value judgments, allows the reader to consider the applicability of specific techniques to both developed and developing countries and to various economic systems, ranging from centrally controlled, nonmarket economies to predominantly market economies.

Chapter 4 is concerned with the problems of analyzing activities (the first box in figure 1.1) by (1) determining and measuring how a specific activity—a power plant or an irrigation project—generates residuals and other environmental quality effects (the second box in figure 1.1) and by (2) analyzing the factors that influence their generation. A thorough understanding of the activity that generates residuals is essential if cost-effective and feasible environmental quality management measures are to be developed.

Chapter 5 takes up the analysis of the effects of residuals on natural systems, on the quality of the ambient environment—air, water, and land—and on receptors, including humans, plants, animals, and materials. (These steps are depicted as the next two boxes in sequence in figure 1.1.) A crucial distinction is made between on-site effects of an activity, such as deterioration of a forest because of poor management, and off-site effects, such as downstream sedimentation beyond the forest boundaries, caused by such poor management. The emphasis in this chapter is on the analytical approaches required to develop specific quantitative information about natural-systems and receptor effects that can provide a realistic and scientifically valid basis for economic valuation.

Chapter 6 presents the various market, surrogate market, and survey techniques for valuation of environmental quality and natural-systems effects. Discussion of the techniques is related to the theory presented in Chapter 3. Specific examples of application are drawn from cases in developing as well as developed countries.

Chapter 7 follows with a presentation of economic valuation from the cost side, including a discussion of the cost-effectiveness approach to environmental quality management and techniques for valuing replacement and defensive measures.

Finally, in Chapter 8, the techniques of input-output analysis, mathematical programming, and simulation are presented as methods by which complex economic-technologic interactions can be traced through the relevant systems.

The sequence of the chapters is based on the idea that the application of benefit-cost analysis, especially the valuation of environmental quality effects, comes only after one has obtained a good knowledge of the basic theories, management contexts, and natural-systems analyses. Given this logical framework, this guide is important as a total package. It has been written for a wide readership: professionals, planners, practitioners, trainers, and teachers. Some will have a strong economics background; others, a strong natural-systems background; still others, a multidisciplinary background. To accommodate the variety of readers, each chapter is largely self-contained. Therefore, a person with a strong economics background can skim or even skip Chapter 3 and concentrate on Chapters 4 and 5 before reading Chapters 6, 7, and 8. The converse holds for a person with a strong natural-systems background.

It is not possible to provide a specific guide for each type of reader. The chapters and subsections have been labeled carefully so that anyone can readily identify the sections of greatest interest. Because this is a long report, readers should be selective in their use of it, realizing, however, that the level of difficulty varies among the different chapters.

REFERENCES

Barnett, H. J., and C. Morse. *Scarcity and Growth: The Economics of Natural Resource Availability.* Resources for the Future. Baltimore: Johns Hopkins Press, 1963.

Ciriacy-Wantrup, S. V. *Resource Conservation Economics and Policies.* Berkeley and Los Angeles: University of California Press, 1952.

Dorfman, R., ed. *Measuring Benefits of Government Investments.* Washington, D.C.: Brookings Institution, 1965.

Eckstein, O. *Water-Resource Development: The Economics of Project Evaluation.* Cambridge, Mass.: Harvard University Press, 1958.

Fisher, A. C., and F. M. Peterson. "The Environment in Economics: A Survey." *Journal of Economic Literature* 14, no. 1 (March 1976):1–33.

Freeman, A. M. III. *The Benefits of Environmental Improvement: Theory and Practice.* Baltimore: Johns Hopkins University Press, 1979.

Hammond, R. J. *Benefit-Cost Analysis and Water Pollution Control.* Stanford, Calif.: Stanford University Press, 1958.

Haveman, R. A., and J. V. Krutilla. *Unemployment, Idle Capacity and the Evaluation of Public Expenditures.* Baltimore: Johns Hopkins Press, 1968.

Helmers, F.L.C.H. *Project Planning and Income Distribution.* The Hague: Martinus Nijhoff, 1979.

Herfindahl, O. C., and A. V. Kneese. *Economic Theory of Natural Resources.* Columbus, Ohio: Merrill, 1974.

Hufschmidt, M. M., and E. L. Hyman. "A Survey of Economic and Related Approaches to Analysis of Natural Resource and Environmental Aspects of Development." In *Economic Approaches to Natural Resource and Environmental Quality Analysis,* ed. M. M. Hufschmidt and E. L. Hyman. Dublin: Tycooly International, 1982.

Kneese, A. V. *Water Pollution: Economic Aspects and Research Needs.* Washington, D.C.: Resources for the Future, 1962.

Kneese, A. V., and B. T. Bower. *Managing Water Quality, Economics, Technology, Institutions.* Baltimore: Johns Hopkins Press, 1968.

Kneese, A. V.; R. V. Ayres; and R. C. d'Arge. *Economics and the Environment: A Materials Balance Approach.* Washington, D.C.: Resources for the Future, 1970.

Krutilla, J., and O. Eckstein. *Multiple Purpose River Development: Studies in Applied Economic Analysis.* Baltimore: Johns Hopkins Press, 1958.

Little, I.M.D. *A Critique of Welfare Economics.* 2d ed. Oxford: Oxford University Press, 1957.

Little, I.M.D., and J. A. Mirrlees. *Project Appraisal and Planning for Developing Countries.* New York: Basic Books, 1974.

Maass, A. A.; Hufschmidt, M. M.; Dorfman, R.; Thomas, H. A., Jr.; Marglin, S. A.; and Fair, G. M. *Design of Water-Resource Systems.* Cambridge, Mass.: Harvard University Press, 1962.

Mäler, K. G., and R. Wyzga. *Economic Measurement of Environmental Damage.* Paris: Organization for Economic Cooperation and Development, 1976.

McKean, R. *Efficiency in Government through Systems Analysis.* New York: Wiley, 1958.

Mishan, E. J. *Cost-Benefit Analysis.* New York: Praeger, 1976.

Prest, A. R., and R. Turvey. "Cost Benefit Analysis: A Survey." *Economic Journal,* 75 (December 1965):683–735.

Scott, A. *Natural Resources: The Economics of Conservation.* Toronto: University of Toronto Press, 1955.

Squire, L., and H. van der Tak. *Economic Analysis of Projects.* Baltimore: Johns Hopkins University Press, 1975.

Weisbrod, B. A. "Income Redistribution Effects and Benefit-Cost Analysis." In *Problems in Public Expenditure Analysis,* ed. S. B. Chase, Jr. Washington, D.C.: Brookings Institution, 1968.

United Nations Industrial Development Organization (UNIDO). *Guidelines for Project Evaluation.* New York: United Nations, 1972.

U.S. Federal Interagency River Basin Committee, Subcommittee on Benefits and Costs. *Proposed Practices for Economic Analysis of River Basin Projects.* Washington, D.C., 1950.

U.S. *Flood Control Act of June 22, 1936, Section I.* (49 U.S. Stat. [1936]).

2

Institutional and Planning Context

Plans and decisions relating to environmental quality and natural systems in developing countries are made in complex *institutional contexts* that have little resemblance to idealized models of the planning process or to formal organizational structures of governments. The institutional context of a particular developing country is the product of a number of important factors. These include:

1. The historical circumstances surrounding the emergence of concern for natural systems and environmental quality;
2. The mix and relative weights of national objectives such as economic development, equitable distribution of income, regional and rural development, national self-sufficiency, environmental quality, and maintenance of the productivity of natural systems;
3. The stage of economic and social development of the country;
4. The nature of the cultural traditions and values of the society;
5. The nature of the socioeconomic system, ranging from a command economy with dominance of public ownership of the means of production, through various degrees of mixed public-private ownership and control, to a predominantly private enterprise economy;
6. The nature of the political and governmental system, including strong, centralized, executive control; shared executive-legislative control through a parliamentary or U.S. type of legislative system; or a federal system with power shared between central and provincial levels;
7. The nature and relative importance of international economic links as reflected by activities of multinational corporations and bilateral and multilateral aid agencies, such as the U.S. Agency for International Development (U.S. AID), the World Bank, other development banks, and specialized agencies of the United Nations.

Practical applications of the techniques for analysis and valuation of natural systems and environmental quality clearly must work within a particular context.

MULTIPLE OBJECTIVE NATURE OF DECISIONS

Even more than in developed countries, environmental quality programs and objectives in developing countries have only a secondary status in comparison with national and regional economic development and, in some cases, the objective of meeting basic human needs. Following World War II, the first thrust of developing nations was toward economic development in the classic Western form of industrialization, urbanization, agricultural development for export markets, and provision of major infrastructure. In this they followed the leadership of developed countries, multilateral aid agencies, and the United Nations. Experience with this approach over more than a decade revealed serious limitations, especially in dealing with endemic poverty. This led to the addition of programs directly addressed to income redistribution, rural and village development, and the meeting of basic human needs for housing, nutrition, sanitation, and health services. Prior to the Stockholm Conference on the Environment in 1972, most developing countries had placed little or no emphasis on the problems of natural-resource deterioration and degradation of air, water, and land quality. Although some advances have been made since the early 1970s in the priority given to environmental quality problems, in most developing countries today the greatest weight is still placed on objectives for economic development, promotion of exports, reduction of poverty, and fulfillment of basic human needs, including food and shelter.

Within such a context, it is especially important that environmental quality and natural-systems analysis and valuation stress the positive role they can play in long-range sustainable economic development and natural-resource management. It is also crucial that valuation techniques analyze environmental quality and natural-systems effects in economic terms that can be accommodated in the calculus of economic development.

PLANNING AND DECISION-MAKING CONTEXT

Environmental quality and natural-systems problems arise in a wide variety of planning and decision-making contexts in the public and private sectors of developing countries. Although there is no typical context, many of these can be identified in two important dimensions: (1) the level of planning and decision making and (2) the nature of the planning and decision-making process. Ideally, natural-systems and environmental quality analysis and valuation should be integral parts of the planning and decision-making process at all levels of planning. In practice, they are often absent or, at best, present only as afterthoughts once plans and projects have been formulated and major decisions made.

Levels of Planning

Within a developing country, there are at least four distinct planning and decision-making levels (fig. 2.1). There is two-way interaction between the various levels.

The Project Level.   The most basic level is the *project*. A project is defined as a relatively self-contained combination of activities that may consist of a number of physical facilities, management measures, and implementation incentives designed to achieve one or more objectives. Examples are (1) construction and operation of a water-storage reservoir designed to provide irrigation water, electric energy, and flood damage reduction; (2) a forest management scheme for a specific land area designed to produce forest products; (3) a fossil-fuel electric power plant to provide electric energy; and (4) a wastewater treatment plant to improve the water quality of an urban area and adjacent regions. Effects on natural systems and receptors are perceived most directly and measured most readily at the project level, especially in the short term. Valuation of such effects at the project level thus are better grounded on actual physical data than at higher levels of management.

The Regional Level.   At the regional level, planning involves analysis leading to decisions on a number of interrelated projects that typically comprise a plan and on an associated program for undertaking the projects over a period of several years. Examples are (1) a forest management program for a specific region, which may include a number of interrelated projects, such as reforestation, harvesting, fire prevention, and management of access, linked in both time and space to produce a time stream of products and services; (2) a river-basin development program consisting of a number of interrelated water management projects, such as dams, canals, power plants, irrigation works, wildlife management schemes, and erosion reduction measures to serve a number of different purposes including agricultural development, energy production, flood damage reduction, and fish and wildlife management; and (3) a broad regional development or redevelopment program, which might include urban development, industrialization, and tourism along with agricultural and other natural-resources development of a specific area.

Analysis of natural-systems and environmental quality aspects of such regional plans and programs must necessarily be based on information developed at the project level. Cumulative and indirect effects that become manifest only over several years can be aggregated at the regional level from project-level data. Valuation of such effects at the regional level thus can reflect complex spatial and temporal relationships.

The Sectoral Level.   The sectoral level typically involves the management plans and programs of a specific mission-oriented ministry at the national or provincial level. A sectoral plan and its associated program usually consist of a set of separable projects distributed geographically over the nation or province and scheduled for undertaking over a period of years. Typical examples include (1) the national highway transport sector that has a plan and

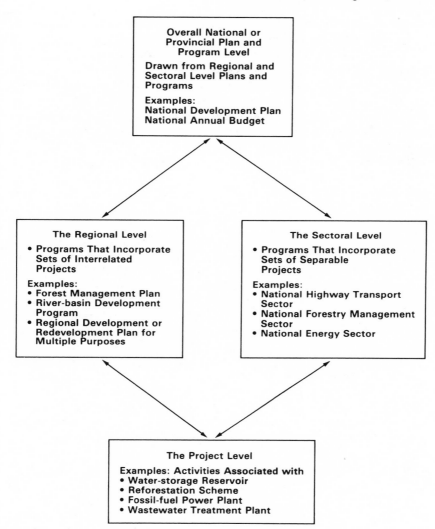

Figure 2.1 Illustrative levels of planning and decision making in a developing country.

program for construction and maintenance of a national network of highways, in which specific highway segments are included as separable projects; (2) the national or provincial forestry management sector with an overall forestry policy, plan, and program consisting of separable public forest management projects along with general regulations, incentives, and other policies affecting privately owned forests; and (3) the national energy sector that involves a plan, program, and policies for energy production and use, consisting of a number of discrete projects that may involve oil, natural gas, coal, nuclear energy, bio-fuels, and other solar energy sources.

Environmental quality and natural-systems aspects of sectoral programs necessarily involve knowledge of effects at the project level. Accordingly, overall development policies and programs established at the sectoral level require the aggregation of such project-level environmental quality and natural-systems effects at the sectoral level. For example, valuation of the air quality effects of a specific energy policy or program can thus be done at the aggregate sectoral level.

Overall Plan and Program Level. The overall plan and program level, which is often located in the national organization of government, is where national objectives are formulated and passed on to the regional, sectoral, and project levels. Activity at this level also involves combining and adapting the management plans and programs of the sectoral and regional levels into an overall plan and program, with an associated set of policies. Examples of this level in action are (1) the national long-range development plan, with an associated set of objectives, typically prepared for a five-year period, along with its financial and policy commitments; and (2) the national annual budget, which often consists of both investment and routine operating subbudgets. Both the long-range plan and the annual budget are usually subdivided into regional and sectoral units, each of which may be further subdivided into project units. At this level, environmental quality and natural-systems effects may be revealed only in very general terms; that is, by generalization from a few specific cases. Ideally, such effects should represent an aggregation of specific effects of the individual projects that comprise the overall plan and annual budget. At this national level, the environmental quality and natural-systems consequences of any specific development plan, or variant of it, could be traced through the entire economy by use of national and regional input-output models as discussed in Chapter 8. Valuation of environmental quality and natural-systems effects at this level necessarily must be done in a macroeconomic context.

The Private Sector. The private sector often plays an important role in one or more of the four levels just discussed. Frequently, the private sector proposes to undertake specific projects—an industrial plant, a mining scheme, or a timber-harvesting activity—that have important effects on natural systems and environmental quality. These projects may or may not be elements in the government's sectoral, regional, or national plans. Sometimes, however, private projects comprise significant portions of sectoral or regional plans and even of the overall provincial and national plans and programs, particularly when promoting exports is an important objective.

The Planning and Decision-making Process

In a general sense, projects and sectoral and regional programs are the outcomes of some planning and decision-making process. This process may be highly organized, as is true for projects seeking World Bank financing, or it may be informal and ad hoc, as with small or locally generated projects.

A simplified version of an idealized planning and decision-making process is shown in figure 2.2. (Although an actual planning process may not conform strictly to this idealized model, most processes contain some version of these steps.) In this general scheme, the process begins with (1) the perception and definition of a problem, need, or opportunity and is followed by (2) the specification of the basic social objectives and the development of associated

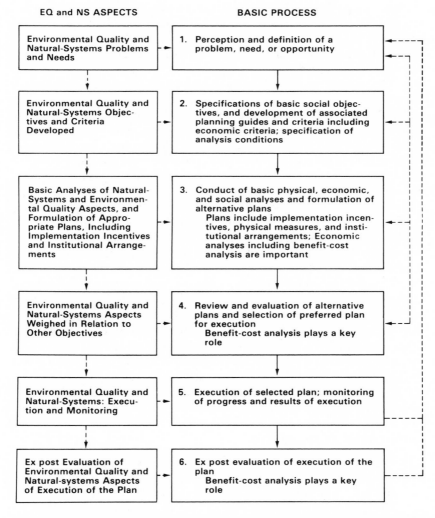

EQ and NS ASPECTS   BASIC PROCESS

| Environmental Quality and Natural-Systems Problems and Needs | 1. Perception and definition of a problem, need, or opportunity |

| Environmental Quality and Natural-Systems Objectives and Criteria Developed | 2. Specifications of basic social objectives, and development of associated planning guides and criteria including economic criteria; specification of analysis conditions |

| Basic Analyses of Natural-Systems and Environmental Quality Aspects, and Formulation of Appropriate Plans, Including Implementation Incentives and Institutional Arrangements | 3. Conduct of basic physical, economic, and social analyses and formulation of alternative plans Plans include implementation incentives, physical measures, and institutional arrangements; Economic analyses including benefit-cost analysis are important |

| Environmental Quality and Natural-Systems Aspects Weighed in Relation to Other Objectives | 4. Review and evaluation of alternative plans and selection of preferred plan for execution Benefit-cost analysis plays a key role |

| Environmental Quality and Natural-Systems: Execution and Monitoring | 5. Execution of selected plan; monitoring of progress and results of execution |

| Ex post Evaluation of Environmental Quality and Natural-systems Aspects of Execution of the Plan | 6. Ex post evaluation of execution of the plan Benefit-cost analysis plays a key role |

Figure 2.2 Simplified version of a project or program planning and decision-making process, showing environmental quality and natural-systems aspects.

planning guides, criteria, and conditions for analyses. Then follow (3) the basic physical, economic, and social analyses and the formulation of alternative plans and (4) the review and evaluation of these plans by the decision makers, leading to selection of a preferred plan for execution. The final steps are (5) the actual execution of the adopted plan, which involves detailed design, construction, operation, and monitoring of progress, and (6) the ex post evaluation of the executed plan relative to the original objectives.

Note several points about this simplified process. First, regardless of the level or nature of the problem—for example, whether it is a national energy program or a project-level irrigation scheme—environmental quality and natural-systems aspects need to be considered from the very start (entries at the left of figure 2.2).

Second, benefit-cost analysis, including valuation of environmental quality and natural-systems effects, enters the process early in plan formulation (step 3) and continues throughout the review, evaluation, and execution (steps 4, 5, and 6).

Third, an essential feature of the alternative plan formulated in step 3 is the inclusion of "implementation incentives"—the means for obtaining or achieving the installation and operation of the physical and other measures of the management plan. Clearly, the project benefits of a plan can be achieved only if the plan is successfully carried out. For example, a management plan that calls for the reduction of liquid effluents by specific amounts in a specified time also must include a set of implementation incentives—subsidies, effluent charges, standards, legal sanctions, monitoring, and inspections—to ensure that these reductions are made by a specific time and that they are maintained. A corollary feature of each alternative plan is the specification of the institutions—public and private—that will have the authority and responsibility to impose implementation incentives and carry out other tasks of management.

Finally, the process involves frequent feedback of information from later steps to earlier ones. Thus, for example, information developed during the formulation of alternative plans (step 3) may help to redefine the problems and reformulate the objectives and associated criteria (steps 1 and 2). The continuous monitoring function of step 5 and the evaluation function of step 6 will be primary sources of information—to be returned to earlier steps of the process.

Context of the Problems

Problems of environmental quality and natural systems arise in a number of different contexts (fig. 2.3). The first category is the typical economic development project—an irrigation project or an industrial plant. The environmental quality objectives associated with an irrigation project, for example, are (1) to maintain the long-run productivity of the transformed natural systems,

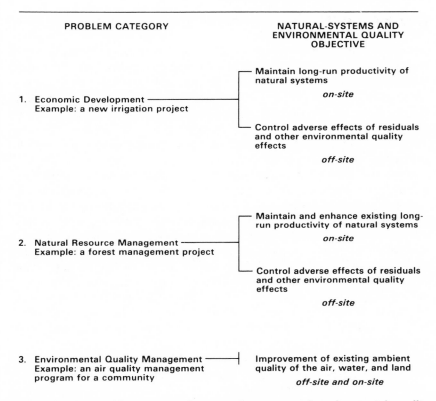

PROBLEM CATEGORY

NATURAL-SYSTEMS AND
ENVIRONMENTAL QUALITY
OBJECTIVE

1. Economic Development
    Example: a new irrigation project

— Maintain long-run productivity of
natural systems

on-site

— Control adverse effects of residuals
and other environmental quality
effects

off-site

2. Natural Resource Management
    Example: a forest management project

— Maintain and enhance existing long-
run productivity of natural systems

on-site

— Control adverse effects of residuals
and other environmental quality
effects

off-site

3. Environmental Quality Management
    Example: an air quality management
    program for a community

Improvement of existing ambient
quality of the air, water, and land

off-site and on-site

Figure 2.3 The problem context for natural-systems and environmental quality analysis.

for example, the on-site irrigation system; and (2) to control the adverse off-site effects of residuals from the irrigation system. Note that economic development projects can be carried out by the private sector, the public sector, or jointly.

The second category is concerned with effective public and/or private management of existing renewable natural resources, such as forests, fisheries, and grazing lands. The problems here are to maintain existing long-range on-site productivity and to control adverse off-site effects.

The third category is concerned with improving the existing quality of the ambient environment—air, water, and land—by controlling residual discharges and other environmental quality effects from existing public and private developments—urban, industrial, commercial, and transportation. In this case, off-site effects may be of greater significance than on-site effects. Also, this category is the concern primarily of the public sector.

ORGANIZATIONAL AND ADMINISTRATIVE STRUCTURE

Governmental organizational and administrative structures vary in detail from country to country, especially concerning how natural-resource management reponsibilities are executed and environmental quality interests are accommodated. Also, formal structure is only a part of the complex government and private sector milieu within which decisions are made. In general, however, typical structures can be identified within which development planning and management takes place and where environmental quality and natural-systems aspects are accommodated.

Generally, there are two broad types of governmental structure: the unitary national governmental system and the federal system. The *unitary system* has complete policy and administrative purview of domestic, foreign, and defense sectors as well as overall national planning, finance, taxation, and budgeting responsibilities. Administrative delegation of authority to regions or communities may occur, but policy and budgetary control is with the central government. In contrast, under the *federal system* the states or provinces share authority and responsibility over domestic programs with the central government and often play the dominant role. They may have independent taxing, borrowing, or budgeting authority. Typically, the central government retains exclusive authority only over international relations, national defense, and national planning.

In a federal system, authority to undertake economic or natural-resource development projects and programs typically is shared by the provincial and national levels. This means that assessment and valuation of environmental quality and natural-systems aspects of development can occur at both levels. In the People's Republic of China, for example, environmental protection agencies have been established at the provincial level, whereas overall policy with respect to environmental protection is lodged in the central government.

Regardless of the level of government—national or provincial—a typical organization of government for economic and natural-resource development might take the form shown in figure 2.4. Primary responsibility for undertaking economic development programs and for managing natural resources is in the hands of sectoral agencies or ministries—public works, agriculture, energy, industry, transport, forestry, public health—and purview over national planning and finance, including taxation and budgets, is directly under the chief executive. Legislative and judicial arms of government are closely linked with the executive branch at the top of the governmental structure.

Environmental quality as an objective of government may be accommodated in this typical structure in a variety of ways. As shown in figure 2.4, there may be a specific sectoral agency with responsibility for some aspects of environmental quality; the Environmental Protection Agency in the United States is an example. Alternatively, this responsibility may be in the Ministry of Health. Usually, there are one or more sectoral agencies concerned with

21

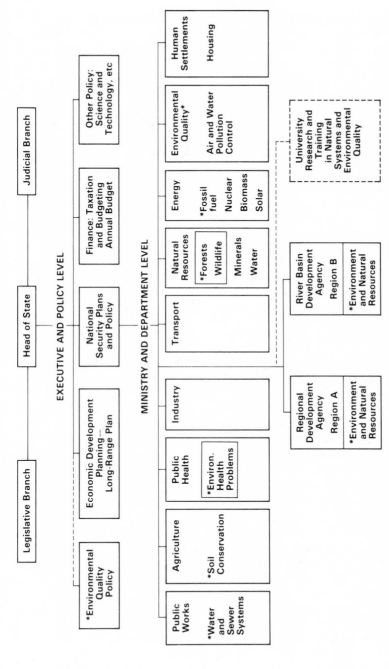

*Indicates possible location of major environmental quality and natural-resource activities.

Figure 2.4 Typical organizational structure of a national government showing locus of environmental quality and natural-resources activities.

natural resources—forestry, minerals, energy, water—although these agencies typically have a developmental rather than an environmental quality orientation. There also may be an overall environmental quality policy agency—at the same level as the economic planning and budgetary agencies—at the chief executive level. The U.S. Council on Environmental Quality during the 1970s and various interministerial committees are examples of this type. Environmental assessment and evaluation staffs also may be organized within the sectoral agencies, with responsibility for preparation of environmental impact analyses of sector projects. In addition, univerities may have research and training responsibilities in the fields of natural systems and environmental quality.

Clearly, the environmental quality and natural-resource considerations of government and the private sector are so pervasive that no neat organizational or administrative "solution" exists. Assessing the effects of projects and programs on natural systems and receptors and valuing these effects necessarily must take place at many different points and levels in the organizational structure. It follows that each sectoral agency and each project planning team should have access to such assessment and valuation capability. This need is supported by the requirements of foreign aid agencies for environmental assessments and valuations.

External Aid Organizations

An additional consideration in development planning and implementation is the important role played by the external aid organizations, including especially the World Bank, the regional development banks, U.S. AID, and specialized agencies of the United Nations such as the United Nations Environmental Program, the World Health Organization, the Food and Agricultural Organization, and the United Nations Development Program. These agencies provide loans and grants for development projects and programs as well as technical aid to a large variety of programs and activities, including natural resources and environmental quality.

Most of these agencies require substantial information about environmental quality and natural-systems effects as part of the application for financial aid for development projects. AID has had formal procedures for analysis of environmental quality effects of development activities since 1976. The original AID procedures were patterned after the requirements of the U.S. National Environmental Policy Act. On the basis of field experience, they were revised in 1980 to achieve greater flexibility, reduce opportunities for delay, provide for early identification of key environmental issues, and help build environmental quality analysis into project formulation.

The World Bank has been formally concerned with the environmental quality effects of its activities since it established an environmental office in 1970. Throughout the years, it has strengthened its procedures and analytical capability to deal with the environmental aspects of development. The bank has a well-developed set of environmental quality policies and practices and has exercised considerable leadership on environmental issues in the international development community (Stein and Johnson 1979). It has built environmental analysis into each step of the "project cycle," which consists of the procedural steps that a project proposal follows from initial identification of a project to its completion and post audit.

As of 1979, the regional development banks and other international aid agencies, such as the United Nations Development Program (UNDP), also were beginning to incorporate environmental quality aspects into their assistance policies and procedures. The February 1980 Declaration of Environmental Policies and Procedures by the nine multilateral development agencies along with UNDP has served to strengthen the activities of these agencies in providing more and improved environmental quality of their development activities.

It appears that one of the most effective means of promoting economic valuation of the natural-systems and environmental quality aspects of development is through the programs and activities of the external aid organizations. For example, their current requirements for benefit-cost analyses of development projects could be extended to apply to environmental quality and natural-systems aspects. Also, their training programs, such as those of the Economic Development Institute of the World Bank, can incorporate materials on economic valuation of these aspects.

REFERENCE

Stein, R. E., and B. Johnson. *Banking on the Biosphere?* Lexington, Mass.: Heath, 1979.

3

Principles and Environmental Quality Extensions of Benefit-Cost Analysis

THE PURPOSE OF BENEFIT-COST ANALYSIS

No country has unlimited supplies of land, labor, capital, and managerial expertise. Although resources can be combined in many different ways to produce goods and services of various kinds, production possibilities over any given period of time will always be restricted. Every society is thus forced into making decisions about the best use of its resources. Benefit-cost analysis represents an application of modern welfare economics and is directed toward improving the economic efficiency of resource allocation. As far as possible, the economic values of society itself are relied upon to evaluate specific proposals. Value judgments by the benefit-cost analyst should be kept to a minimum and, where required, should be described explicitly to society's decision makers.

Any new project, program, or policy proposed by a society will lead to benefits and costs. To evaluate the absolute and relative worth of projects, programs, and policies, some basis for comparison is needed. The common measuring rod for benefit-cost analysis is monetary value. This does not mean that benefit-cost analysis need be restricted to items that are actually bought and sold. The assumption is made that actions that contribute to positive increases in a society's economic welfare can be represented by the equivalent monetary value of goods and services the society is prepared to relinquish in exchange. Conversely, adverse effects on economic welfare can be measured in terms of the monetary equivalent of goods and services that would be needed to compensate the society for the harm done. This is a basic value judgment of benefit-cost analysis.

General agreement exists among Western economists that maximum economic efficiency in resource allocation can be attained by a perfectly operating market system (Baumol 1972). Market prices act as indicators of value and guide the use of resources. Economic decisions are made on a decentralized basis by individual consumers and firms. In economic systems based largely on centralized planning, values of resources and commodities are measured in terms of imputed, or "shadow," prices (Lange and Taylor, 1938, Lerner 1944). In principle, with given resources, methods of production, and social economic goals, the conditions for maximum economic efficiency will be the same for both types of economic system. Optimal market prices and shadow prices will be identical.

Elements of both systems will be found in every country's economic framework. Western economies, as typified by Organization for Economic Cooperation and Development (OECD) countries, rely mainly on private markets to allocate resources, but goods and services supplied by governments also enter their market systems. Some goods supplied by government may be priced to reflect resource scarcities accurately, while others may be supplied free or at some arbitrary price. Market prices do not always properly reflect *economic* as distinguished from *financial* values. Benefit-cost analysis is based on values measured in socially desirable prices (Pearce 1978). Such prices frequently take the form of imputed, or shadow, prices. These are obtained by adjusting, where necessary, actual market prices and by deriving appropriate economic values where markets do not exist. Shadow prices often are used in centrally planned and developing economies to assist resource allocation decisions. As will be shown later, economic values of environmental quality may need to be measured in terms of imputed prices, in both centrally planned and free market systems.

SOURCES OF VALUES

Economic Efficiency and Monetary Values

Benefit-cost analysis is based on neoclassical economic theory, which emphasizes the philosophy of individual consumer sovereignty. Social economic welfare is assumed to be the sum of the self-expressed welfares of all individuals in a society. Under the *Pareto welfare criterion*, the allocation of resources will be economically efficient when it is impossible to make one individual better off without making some other individual worse off (van de Graaf 1957, Baumol 1972).

A fundamental assumption of benefit-cost analysis is that the degree of satisfaction or level of economic welfare experienced by individuals can be measured in terms of the prices they were prepared to pay for the consumption* of goods and services. In many instances, individuals consume goods and services without actually paying for them, but prices that individuals would be willing to pay can, in principle, be imputed from observed behavior,

---

*The term *consumption* is used throughout this chapter to conform with its general use in economic literature. Note, however, that material goods are not "consumed"; rather, they are ultimately transformed into material or energy residuals.

from survey data, or by other means. Also assumed is that social welfare can be measured in monetary terms by adding individual monetary values.

The Pareto criterion is inapplicable when a change in resource allocation makes some individuals better off and others worse off (Cooper 1979). Benefit-cost analysis, however, is based on the concept of a potential Pareto improvement. Under this approach a change is economically desirable if, in principle, the gainers can compensate the losers. For this to occur, the increase in total monetary benefits must exceed the change in total monetary costs. Even if actual compensation is not paid, the increase in net monetary benefits is judged desirable because of economic efficiency. Value judgments clearly are required in assuming that the monetary equivalents of welfare for different individuals can be added and compared and that any change in income distribution is still acceptable. Under the assumption of benefit-cost analysis stated above, a society will be economically efficient in its use of resources when net monetary social benefits—that is, the difference between total monetary benefits and total monetary costs measured in socially desirable prices—are maximized.

Individual Economic Welfare

Utility Theory.   The satisfaction an individual receives by consuming economic goods and services is termed *utility*. Within a certain range of consumption, the more one consumes, the higher is one's total utility level. In figure 3.1, total utility is shown on the vertical axis, and increasing quantities of a good X consumed per unit of time are on the horizontal axis. Total utility rises at a declining marginal rate. A saturation point X_s may be reached, after which total utility declines.

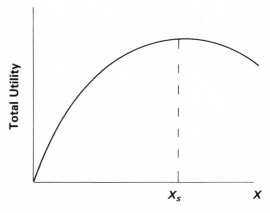

Quantity Consumed per Unit of Time

Figure 3.1 Typical total utility function of an individual.

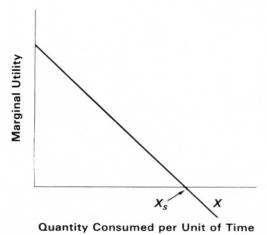

Quantity Consumed per Unit of Time

Figure 3.2 Typical marginal utility function of an individual.

The individual's marginal utility function for good X can be represented graphically, as in figure 3.2. Marginal utility is the rate of change of utility associated with a small unit increase in the quantity of X consumed per unit of time. It is represented by the slope of the total utility curve. Typically, marginal utility is at first positive and declining; it reaches zero at X_s and then becomes negative.

Utility itself cannot be measured in absolute terms. Information about the nature of marginal and total utility functions of individuals must be obtained from "revealed preferences," that is, empirical data describing the individual's consumption behavior or preferences under different economic circumstances. Western economic thought contends that the most reliable information is obtained by allocating the individual a certain sum of money in each time period and allowing the individual to express preferences, or willingness to pay, for goods and services in terms of money prices. This leads to the concept of an individual demand curve.

Individual Demand. With a fixed money income and with constant market prices for all other commodities, the individual's willingness to pay for good X can be observed by varying the price of X and observing the changes in the quantity of X consumed in different time periods. In consuming a given quantity of good X, one will be willing to pay a price reflecting one's marginal utility at that consumption level. By observing the variation in the quantity consumed, the individual's willingness to pay—based on the marginal utility function—can be determined. This yields an individual demand curve for X (fig. 3.3). Because the marginal utility curve slopes downward to the right, so does the demand curve. This demand curve is known as a *Marshallian demand curve* (after the British economist Alfred Marshall) and would be ob-

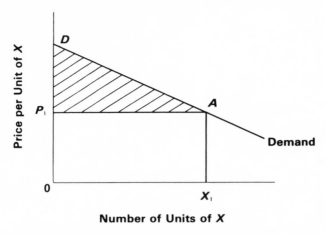

Figure 3.3 Individual demand curve for good X.

servable in a free market system, although, conceptually, such curves exist in any economic system.

Consumer's Surplus. Suppose that in figure 3.3 the individual were supplied the quantity $0X_1$ of good X. The marginal valuation of X would be $0P_1$. To buy $0X_1$ of X, the monetary outlay would be price multiplied by quantity consumed, or the area of the rectangle $0P_1AX_1$. Total willingness to pay, however, clearly exceeds this amount, for it comprises the sum of all of the marginal valuations of X from 0 to X_1—that is, the area of the region $0DAX_1$. This area is a representation of the total utility level and would appear as a gross or total benefit in a benefit-cost calculation. The area of the shaded region DAP_1 is known as (Marshallian) consumer's surplus and measures the maximum willingness to pay over and above the actual cash cost of consumption. Consumer's surplus should always be added to the market value of goods and services consumed to obtain a proper estimate of total economic benefits.

Social Economic Welfare

Market Demand and Social Benefits. In market-based economies, provided that the prevailing distribution of income is acceptable and markets operate perfectly, social benefits can be measured in terms of market demand functions. The market demand curve for a particular good can be found by adding together horizontally the individual demand curves for it. A market demand curve for good X is shown in figure 3.4. The quantity of X consumed is $0X_1$ at a market price of $0P_1$. The total willingness to pay is equal to the area of the region $0CDX_1$, comprising cash outlays of $0P_1DX_1$ and consumer's surplus CDP_1.

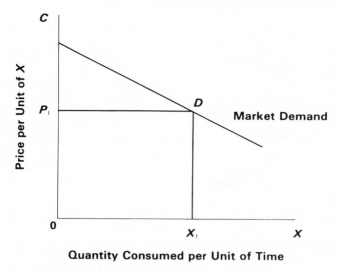

Figure 3.4 Market demand curve for good X.

Market Supply and Social Costs. To generate social benefits, resources must be used, and costs rise accordingly. Using any scarce resource in a particular way will always involve a cost whether or not it is reflected in market prices. This cost is measured most accurately as an opportunity cost, that is, the economic value of the resource in its next best alternative use. For example, steel used in constructing transport facilities is unavailable for use in constructing a petrochemical plant. In a properly operating market system, the prices of goods supplied will reflect the marginal opportunity costs of all resources used in production.

The market supply curve for good X is shown in figure 3.5. For technological reasons as well as for reasons of resource scarcity, the marginal cost of production increases as larger quantities of X are produced in a given time period. To cover incremental costs of production, producers charge a price equal to marginal cost. Thus, the supply curve slopes upward. The total cost of resources needed to produce a given quantity $0X_1$ of good X is equal to the sum of the marginal production costs from 0 to X_1—that is, the area $0FGX_1$ under the supply curve.

If producers receive a price $0P_1$ when supplying $0X_1$ to the market, their total cash receipts will be $0P_1$ times $0X_1$, or the area of the rectangle $0P_1GX_1$. These clearly exceed total production costs. The extra benefits accruing to producers, the shaded region P_1GF, are known as producer's surplus.

Maximization of Social Economic Welfare. In producing and consuming any good X, society will, under all the previous assumptions, maximize its economic welfare by maximizing net benefits—namely, the difference be-

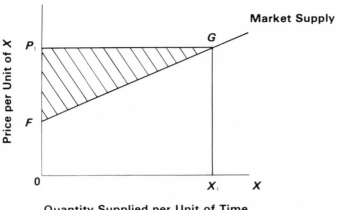

Quantity Supplied per Unit of Time

Figure 3.5 Market supply curve for good X.

tween total monetary benefits and total monetary costs. This is shown in figure 3.6(a) where the marginal benefits and marginal costs represented by the slopes of the total benefit and total cost curves are equal. The optimal consumption and production level is $0X_3$. Exactly the same result would be obtained by a perfect market system, as shown in figure 3.6(b), where the market supply and demand curves intersect. The price that clears the market is $0P$. Net economic benefits are measured by the area between the market supply and demand curves comprising the sum of consumer's surplus (area of region I) and producer's surplus (area of region II). Net benefits equal the difference between the total willingness to pay for good X and the total costs of production at the level $0X_3$.

Changes in Net Economic Benefits.   Measures of consumer's and producer's surplus obtained from market data are useful for assessing changes in net social economic benefits following alterations in the conditions of supply or demand. In figure 3.7, a fixed quantity $0X_1$ of good X is assumed to be supplied to the market at a total cost of $0P_1AX_1$. With a vertical supply curve at point X_1, the equilibrium market price is $0P_1$. In this case, net benefits equal the sum of areas I, II, and III and take the form of consumer's surplus. If the quantity were equal to $0X_2$, a reduction of net benefits equal to area P_2BAP_1 would occur.

Figure 3.7 can also be used to show what happens when a good is offered to the market at a fixed price and the price is changed. Assume initially that good X is sold at a fixed price of $0P_1$. The supply curve is a horizontal line at point P_1. The quantity purchased is $0X_1$, and net social benefits are measured as the area of the region DAP_1. Net social benefits in this instance consist entirely of consumer's surplus. When the price is raised to $0P_2$, the quantity demanded

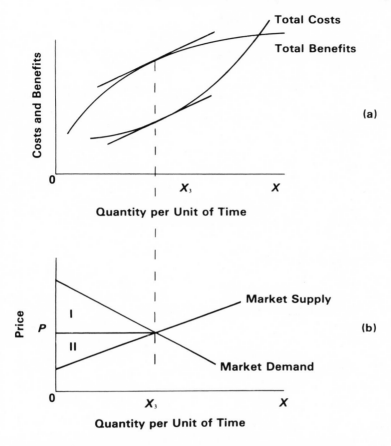

Figure 3.6 Optimal level of production and consumption of good _X_.

falls to $0X_2$. Consumer's surplus is reduced to the area of region I. The decline in net social benefits is a loss of consumer's surplus equal to the sum of areas II and III.

Figure 3.8 shows how a change in net benefits is measured when, as an example, an improvement in production technology occurs. The initial supply curve is S_1, giving an equilibrium price of $0P_1$ and quantity sold of $0X_1$. Net benefits comprise the area ABC, consisting of consumer's surplus (area BCP_1) and producer's surplus (area ACP_1). The improvement in technology is assumed to lower the marginal costs of production, and the supply curve shifts downward to S_2 so that $0X_2$ is bought at a price of $0P_2$. In the new situation, net benefits equal the area BDE. The change in net benefits is measured by the area $ACDE$, comprising an increase in consumer's surplus (area FCD) and an increase in producer's surplus (area $AFDE$).

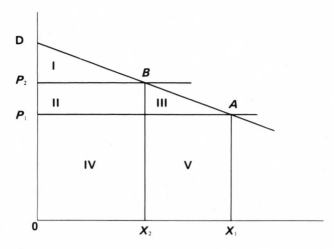

Figure 3.7 Changes in net benefits.

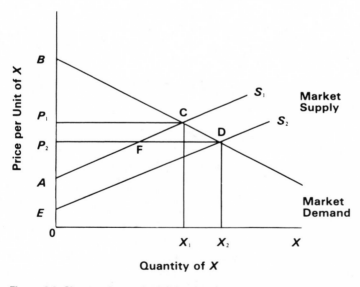

Figure 3.8 Changes in net benefits with new technology.

Compensated Demand—Compensating Variation. Some economic theorists have questioned the use of a Marshallian demand curve to measure changes in individual utility. It is generally agreed that around an actual price-quantity point on a Marshallian curve, the price will correctly reflect a marginal change in utility. For a large variation in price or quantity consumed, however, the area under the Marshallian demand curve will not, in general, accurately measure the utility effect. In such situations, compensating adjustments of the demand curves are required. This topic is discussed in the appendix to this chapter.

Sources of Social Economic Welfare.

Consumer Goods and Services.   Utility is derived from the consumption of final goods and services supplied by producing agents in the economy. Examples are clothing, food, housing, and health services. Assessment of the economic value of such goods and services can be made in terms of market demand curves.

Producer Goods and Services.   Utility is indirectly obtained from producer goods, such as cement and steel, that enter into production processes. The economic benefits of these goods are reflected in the willingness to pay for the products that are ultimately derived from them.

Other Welfare Considerations.   A society may have goals other than economic efficiency. One is the rectification of adverse income distribution effects. If an undesirable distribution of income exists or is created, maximization of net social monetary benefits will not necessarily be a valid criterion of optimality. Various analytical approaches, discussed by Helmers (1979), can be applied to this problem. Little and Mirrlees (1974) suggest that specific weights should be attached to benefits received by different groups and that net-weighted monetary benefits should be maximized. Benefits accruing to poor people might be given greater weight than benefits accruing to those with high income and wealth. Value judgments clearly are needed. Economists can advise objectively on the magnitude and incidence of monetary effects.

Decision makers may determine a society's objectives directly without attempting to assess individual values. As an economic philosophy, this approach has both ethical and practical limitations. On economic welfare grounds, it is not likely to lead to efficient or desirable solutions, as explained by Little (1950). Economic plans are likely to be more successful if they reflect individual preferences. Even if planning authorities make final decisions, the process will be greatly facilitated by information on what the various groups and interests in a community want.

Other social goals may concern such things as the development of cultural values, the promotion of healthy life styles, or improving the safety of working conditions. If conflict arises between such goals and economic efficiency, there is no special reason why the economic efficiency criterion should predominate. Value judgments are again required. The economic analyst can indicate the trade-offs between economic and other goals, quantifying the relevant costs if economic efficiency must be compromised for other social purposes.

Centrally Determined Outputs and Prices.   In countries that rely heavily on centrally planned resource allocation, individual consumers have only limited power in determining social economic objectives. The way in which plans are drawn up and implemented can vary considerably in practice, depending on the nature of objectives pursued and on the specific institutional arrangements established by a particular country. Generally, some system of pricing is adopted. It would be impossible for any centralized planning body to determine precisely the details of all resource allocation requirements; therefore, some degree of decentralized management or decision making will, in reality, usually be found. Prices can still play an important role in relating decentralized production decisions to the overall plan by guiding the use of resources for lower priority outputs and by facilitating the distribution of commodities to consumers.

It is highly unlikely that maximum economic efficiency would be achieved if central planners attempted to control all outputs and all prices. An economic plan usually focuses on the attainment of prescribed output levels for commodities such as steel, food, or electricity, which are judged to be of prime importance for social economic welfare. Prices might also be fixed for some factors of production or consumer products. Economic equilibrium is reached by allowing remaining prices and outputs to adjust freely. If the resultant pattern is what the central planners intended to achieve, then prevailing prices could be regarded as optimal and accepted as a basis for valuation in benefit-cost analysis. In principle, benefit-cost analysis techniques can be applied just as successfully in such a setting as in an economic environment based exclusively on the market mechanism. Should inefficiencies arise, however, actual prices will not represent socially optimal planning prices. Commodity shortages or the emergence of black markets are sure signs that the plan might not be working properly. Revision of the plan can then be expected. Pearson and Pryor (1978) contend that in developing countries, where new projects and investment programs are frequently instigated by government, market prices will tend to be very poor indicators of economic scarcity. Corrections must be made to derive correct shadow prices. This topic is too involved to be discussed here. Guidance manuals on appropriate procedures have been published by the OECD (Little and Mirrlees 1968, 1974), the United Nations (Dasgupta et al. 1972), and the World Bank (Squire and van der Tak 1975).

INVESTMENT PLANNING AND DECISIONS

Levels of Investment Planning

Benefit-cost analysis evolved as a method of making economically efficient investments in the public sector, and this is probably still its most important area of application. It can also be used to estimate the net social benefits of private investments and to guide the formulation of public policies that require a commitment of resources within the private sector. Programs for air quality management are a good example. The approach introduces to public decision making the same criterion of economic efficiency that would be used in a perfectly operating market system, assuming a favorable distribution of income.

Decisions about public investments are usually made at several different levels. As discussed in Chapter 2, these can be classified as follows:

1. The formulation of a specific project—for example, a dam and reservoir, an irrigation development, a highway, or a timber plantation;
2. The preparation of a program of self-contained projects within a given sector or region—for example, the highway transport sector, or a regional development program, such as the Damodar Valley regional program in India; and
3. The preparation of a national development plan and program composed of a number of individual sector and regional programs.

The criteria for choosing methods of allocating resources take different forms, depending on the specific context and other relevant circumstances, such as the existence of budgetary constraints. Our analysis will focus on the project level and will be concerned with developing criteria for deciding whether or not to undertake a specific project or, where multiple alternatives within a project exist, how investment should take place so as to maximize social economic welfare. Project alternatives may be mutually exclusive— that is, selection of one alternative would automatically preclude implementation of all of the others. In other situations, a project may involve several production activities, and the optimal scale of operations for each activity must be determined.

Project Costs and Benefits

Project Costs.   Because in practice resources are usually committed at the project level, the costs of public investment proposals can be most conveniently discussed in connection with project appraisals. The true measure of the economic cost of using a resource for any particular purpose is its *opportunity cost,* that is, its value in its next best economic use. In this respect, economic costs can differ quite significantly from financial costs. Correct shadow prices for resource inputs should reflect the scarcity of resources relative to all social economic goals. For a variety of reasons, public decision-making institutions may not be aware of economically efficient shadow prices. In public investment decisions, the problem can, in principle, be overcome through the application of economic valuation techniques. Within the private sector, where decisions are based on private financial costs rather than social economic costs, various forms of government intervention are often required to modify resource allocation decisions.

Opportunity costs arise at the time when resources are actually used. Thus, in economic terms the capital costs of a project are incurred when construction takes place. Interest paid on funds borrowed by an investing agency is a financial cost to the investing agency; however, it does not represent the economic cost of capital inputs because it is simply a transfer payment from the agency to the lender. Depreciation allowances also are financial costs that do not, in general, correspond with economic cost. They are purely an accounting concept. The economic capital costs comprise the costs of labor, materials, machinery, and other inputs valued at correct shadow prices needed for capital construction.

Another important category of costs consists of project operating, maintenance, and replacement costs. Estimates of these should correspond to the time of resource commitment. Correct shadow prices should be used to value inputs.

Costs can also be in the form of externalities. Environmental quality damage is an important example. A full analysis of environmental quality effects is given later in this chapter.

Project Benefits. Benefits should also be measured at their time of accrual. It is common to refer to the economic benefits for which the project was designed as direct benefits—for example, the value of electric energy from a hydroelectric power scheme. External benefits can arise. If flood prevention is an additional effect of a new hydro scheme, extra economic benefits will be created, such as the value of averting damages to crops, livestock, and property.

Secondary benefits may also arise, but are often difficult to estimate. For example, wages earned by workers employed in a new project are frequently claimed as a secondary benefit. This neglects the possibility that such workers might have obtained similar wages elsewhere in the economy. If some of the workers had no other employment prospects and would have remained unemployed in the absence of the project, their wages could be included as a benefit. It is preferable, however, to reflect such employment effects through use of shadow wage rates in computing labor costs.

Further secondary benefits may flow from income multiplier effects. The true economic efficiency benefits of this type comprise the differential in income generated by the project as compared with some other use of the resources embodied in the project. Secondary benefits may also be purely regional and can be quite important in assessing the regional impacts of investments. The information could play a crucial role in public decisions if emphasis is placed on regional distributional effects as well as on those of economic efficiency.

Finally, benefits may arise from environmental quality improvements created by the project. Apart from flood control, a hydro scheme may produce a large artificial lake, which may be used for boating, fishing, and swimming, or as a source of aesthetic appreciation.

Time Streams of Benefits and Costs. Each investment alternative typically involves streams of costs and benefits over time, as shown in simplified form in figure 3.9. The benefit stream is B_t and the cost stream C_t. The net-benefit stream NB_t is obtained by taking the difference between B_t and C_t. Net benefits are frequently negative in the initial stages of a project, because this

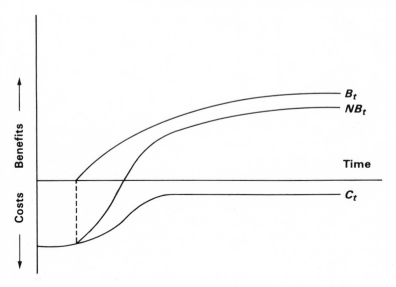

Figure 3.9 Project costs and benefits over time.

is when most of the capital construction usually takes place. Further, until capital installations are complete, there is often no output from the project and hence no benefits.

Investment Criteria

Factors Affecting Investment Decisions. What criteria can be used to compare investment alternatives when different time streams of net benefits are involved? The answer depends largely on the specific objectives and value judgments of the relevant decision-making authority. Constraints on available funding, the size of projects, and reinvestment opportunities for project benefits are also important considerations. Decisions may be made on the basis of what Mishan (1976) describes as crude investment criteria or in accordance with criteria that are more soundly embedded in economic theory of intertemporal resource allocation. Some of these concepts will now be discussed in greater detail.

Crude Financial Criteria. Several crude investment criteria have been used in business decisions in the past. These include the cutoff period approach, the minimal payback period, and the average rate of return approach. Because these approaches are not soundly grounded in economic theory, they are not discussed further here.

The Social Discount Rate. Costs and benefits at different points in time may, according to economic theory, be compared by means of a social discount rate. This reduces future net benefits to a smaller value at the present time. Specifically, the present value PV of a net benefit NB_t at time t is calculated as

$$PV = \sum_{t=0}^{n} \frac{NB_t}{(1 + r)^t} , \tag{3-1}$$

where r is the rate of discount.

Three explanations can be offered to legitimize the practice of discounting in making investment decisions (Page 1977). First, economists have observed that individuals value future consumption less than that in the present. A dollar's worth of consumption in thirty years' time usually will be valued much less than a dollar's worth today. Individuals thus discount future benefits in favor of the present. The rate at which they do this, measured by the discount rate, is known as the *pure-rate-of-time preference*. Because social preferences comprise a summation of the preferences of individuals, the existence of private discount rates justifies the assumption of a social discount rate.

A second explanation lies in the theory of capital productivity. A dollar's worth of net benefits or resources at the present time, put to productive use until time t in the future, should yield compound benefits. If the discount rate measures the rate of productivity growth, then future net benefits will become

$$NB_t = PV (1 + r)^t. \tag{3-2}$$

These results show the similarity between the role of the discount rate in public investment decisions and the private market rate of interest whereby individuals are compensated with interest payments, inducing them to forego current consumption in order to provide the resources for private capital formation. This explanation is the basis for the opportunity-cost-of-capital approach to discounting.

The third justification for a social discount rate is as an instrument of government policy, which guides investment within the economic system. The magnitude of the discount rate vis-à-vis private market interest rates will, for example, be an important determinant of the level of public investment relative to investment in the private sector. Further, once budget allocations to investing authorities have been made, choice of the discount rate can have a major influence on priorities for specific projects. A high discount rate will favor projects with immediate net benefits, whereas a low discount rate will encourage selection of projects with long-term net benefits. When used as an instrument of allocation, no discount rate can be regarded as the "optimal" or "correct" rate because it is only a convenient way of incorporating value judgments about the time rate of resource use in investment decisions. The literature on this topic is by no means consistent, especially for projects creating long-term ecological effects or those involving the exploitation of exhaustible resources.

Table 3.1. Present Value of $100 in Future Years at Various Discount Rates

Time (year)	Discount rate (%)			
	2	5	8	10
0	$100.00	$100.00	$100.00	$100.00
10	83.33	62.50	45.45	38.50
20	66.67	37.03	21.28	14.92
40	45.45	14.08	4.61	2.22
60	30.30	5.35	0.99	0.33
100	13.70	0.76	0.05	0.01

Time Horizons.   The choice of an appropriate time horizon can play an important role in the calculation of the net benefits of projects. Traditionally, economists have tended to rely on engineering specifications of project life when choosing a time horizon. The most distant horizons thus would be found in development schemes, such as land reclamation projects or hydroelectric power schemes. Closer planning horizons would be chosen for capital development schemes with a shorter physical life.

Beyond a certain point in time, all consequences of an investment project will be ignored if the usual practice of discounting is followed because the present value of far-off costs and benefits will approach zero. Table 3.1 shows the present value of a fixed amount ($100) for different discount rates and planning horizon years. It can be seen that after about sixty years, subsequent effects can be ignored unless a very low discount rate is used.

The Net Present Value Criterion.   The net present value criterion is widely relied upon as a guide to economic efficiency and can be used in the formulation and appraisal of new development projects and programs and environmental improvement policies. When applied to project formulation, however, maximization of net present value is legitimate only in the rather uncommon situation in which the investing agency is not subject to capital funding constraints (Helmers 1979). In determining the optimal scale of a project, the allocation of resources among noncompeting projects or sectors, or the best of a set of mutually exclusive investment alternatives, the net present value criterion requires that the present value of expected net benefits accruing over the life of the project or program be maximized. The criterion can be stated as

$$\text{maximize } NPV = \sum_{t=0}^{n} \frac{(B_t - C_t)}{(1 + r)^t} , \qquad (3\text{--}3)$$

where *NPV* is net present value, B_t and C_t are benefits and costs at time *t*, *r* is the rate of discount, and *n* is the planning horizon. An alternative expression is

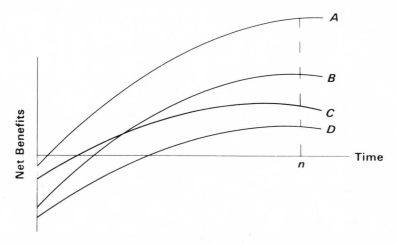

Figure 3.10 Net-benefit streams for four investment alternatives.

$$\text{maximize } NPV = \sum_{t=0}^{n} \frac{NB_t}{(1 + r)^t} , \qquad (3–4)$$

where the separate cost and benefit streams are replaced by a single time stream of net benefits.

Whether the discount rate is or is not significant in ranking investment alternatives depends essentially on the comparative time streams of net benefits for the different alternatives (Mishan 1976). An example is given in figure 3.10.

The net-benefit stream for alternative A at all times lies above the streams for alternatives B, C, and D. Thus, A is said to be a dominant investment and is clearly superior to B, C, and D at any discount rate. Similarly, D is clearly inferior to alternatives A, B, and C. It is impossible, however, to rank B and C unless the discount rate is specified because their net-benefit time profiles intersect. The significance of the discount rate can be seen with the aid of figure 3.11, which measures net present value on the vertical axis and rates of discount on the horizontal. The net present value of all four alternatives diminishes as higher discount rates are employed. Alternative A still is superior to B and C, and alternative D still is inferior to them. At low discount rates, however, C is preferred to B, and at high discount rates B is better than C. At discount rate r_e, alternatives B and C are equally preferable. This diagram shows that sensitivity analysis of the discount rate in various investment alternatives can often reveal whether the discount rate is a crucial factor in a decision and, if so, where critical ranges of values for the discount rate might lie.

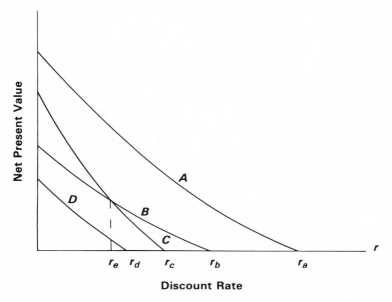

Figure 3.11 Net present value as a function of discount rate.

The Internal Rate of Return.   As shown in figure 3.11, the present value of the net-benefit streams for investment alternatives A, B, C, and D is reduced to zero at discount rates r_a, r_b, r_c, and r_d, respectively. The rate of discount that equates the net present value of each alternative to zero corresponds to the internal rate of return of the investment. The internal rate of return of any project can be determined by solving for i in either of the two equations below:

$$\sum_{t=0}^{n} \frac{NB_t}{(1 + i)^t} = 0, \tag{3--5}$$

or

$$\sum_{t=0}^{n} \frac{B_t}{(1 + i)^t} = \sum_{t=0}^{n} \frac{C_t}{(1 + i)^t} \tag{3--6}$$

The first equation is expressed in terms of discounted net benefits. The second equation identifies the internal rate of return as that rate of discount i that equates total discounted project costs with total discounted project benefits.

The internal rate of return has frequently been used, especially by funding agencies, as a criterion for ranking public investment alternatives because of its apparent connection with the profitability of financial investments. It has been argued that in deciding whether or not to invest public funds in a particular project, only if the internal rate of return exceeds the prescribed discount rate should the project be undertaken. Similarly, where multiple alternatives are being considered, highest priority should be given to the alternative with the largest internal rate of return.

Unfortunately, following this approach will not always lead to selection of the alternative with the highest net present value. First, solving for i in the above equations is equivalent to solving for the roots of a polynomial of degree n, yielding up to n different values for the internal rate of return. The formula itself cannot specify which of these roots is the correct one. Second, evaluating alternatives on the basis of the internal rate of return precludes a decision-making authority from adopting a preferred discount rate, which in turn affects the calculation of net present value. As can be seen in figure 3.11, alternative B would be superior to C according to the internal rate of return criterion (since r_b is greater than r_c), yet the net present value of the B time stream exceeds that of C only for discount rates greater than r_e. If a discount rate lower than r_e were preferred, the net present value of C would be greater than that of B. Finally, the internal rate of return provides no information about the relative size of projects and, hence, none about the absolute magnitude of net present values for different investment alternatives.

Optimal Investments under Funding Constraints.   In certain situations, as previously discussed, capital funding may not be a constraint on development projects, so investment can proceed up to the point where net benefits are maximized. Physical limitations on investment productivity determine the optimal project scale and the need for funds. Such a situation is illustrated in figure 3.12. Provision of good X reaches an optimal level at X_1, where net benefits are maximized. At this level, marginal benefits and marginal costs are equal; thus, the marginal benefit-cost ratio is unity. The reason unlimited investment does not take place is that diminishing marginal physical returns set in as the project scale increases. The investing agency might be an electricity authority empowered to borrow funds on capital markets to construct a hydroelectric generating station. Once the dam reaches a certain size, further increments of electricity become increasingly difficult to obtain. In addition, the marginal costs of capital construction and plant operation may rise rapidly as the scale of the project is increased.

Constraints on funding C_1 can result in an economically inferior scale of operation, as at X_2. At this level, net benefits are clearly less than at X_1.

Quite commonly a public agency is responsible for a development program and must determine the best levels of investment in all projects, since the agency itself is working within a fixed budget determined by a higher public authority (Steiner 1969). If total monetary outlays are constrained, net benefits for the entire program of projects will be maximized when the marginal benefit-cost ratios for specific investment alternatives are equalized. When

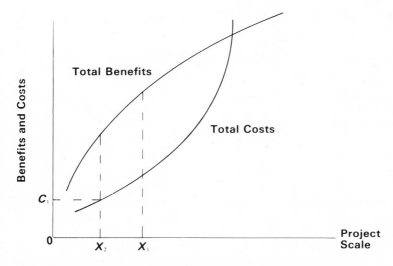

Figure 3.12 Project scale with and without funding constraints.

the restriction applies only to current capital funding, investments should be made up to the point at which the marginal ratio of net present value per unit of capital is the same in all projects. Because of rationing of capital within the agency, a shadow price for allocation of capital must be used that exceeds its nominal price (Sugden and Williams 1978, Helmers 1979). More complicated decisions are required when constraints on capital and on operation and maintenance are imposed at all points in time. Decisions about the postponement of investments frequently need to be made. A full treatment of optimal dynamic investment decision making that deals with many of these problems can be found in Marglin (1963).

EXTENSION OF BENEFIT-COST ANALYSIS TO ENVIRONMENTAL QUALITY

Economic-Environment Interactions and Government Policy

The natural environment—air, water, land, biota—provides goods and services that directly or indirectly generate economic benefits. Environmental services can occur as consumer goods and services, such as the amenity value of a pristine river or lake, and/or as producer goods and services—for example, the capacity of the atmosphere or bodies of water to assimilate pollutants from an industrial plant (fig. 3.13).

The concept of the common-property resource, which derives from the so-called tragedy of the commons (Hardin 1973), has been used to explain why

Economic System

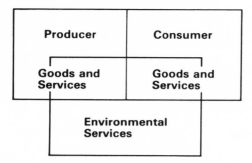

Figure 3.13 Sources of economic welfare, including environmental services.

economic activity can lead to damage to the environment. Numerous owners have equal rights to use common-property resources, such as the oceans, air, fisheries, groundwater aquifers, and oil and gas fields. Rights are not lost through nonuse, but neither is there a restriction—in quantity or time—on each user's level of activity (Ciriacy-Wantrup and Bishop 1975). With no control over the joint activities of the users, overexploitation of the resource can occur. Users independently seek to optimize their own economic positions on the assumption that if they do not make maximum use of the resource, others will. An extensive literature on the theory of common-property resources has accumulated over the past quarter century (Hardin and Baden 1977), specifically for fisheries (Gordon 1954) and for groundwater and oil and gas fields (May et al. 1979).

From an economic viewpoint, abuse of common-property resources occurs because there is no self-equilibrating mechanism to curtail exploitation rates. Many of these resources are "free," so real scarcities (threats to long-term sustainable yields or services) are not reflected in costs to the user. Incorporating the true social costs of natural resource exploitation in development planning is one way of ensuring that economically efficient resource allocation decisions will be made.

Effects on the Environment as Economic Externalities.   The theory of externalities offers an alternative explanation of the causes of damage to the environment. As shown in the preceding section, the need for explicit management in order to prevent or repair damage to the environment arises because individuals, groups, and development agencies in society do not take full account of the stress they place on the environment. The coal-mining enterprise is not concerned primarily with acid runoff. Its job is to produce coal. The electric utility is not concerned primarily with air pollution. Its job is to produce electric energy. Farmers are more concerned with this year's crop than with the ill effects of soil erosion several years in the future. A similar type of abuse can arise with other ecological resources, such as fisheries. Fisherman have open access to ocean fish stocks and seek to maximize their catches without regard to the effects of their actions on the size of the stock and, hence, on the fishing opportunities of others. Overfishing can occur.

All of the above impacts can be described as "external effects." An external effect arises when the utility or production function of one person is dependent upon the activities of other persons. Externalities can be good or bad. Externalities affecting environmental quality arise when the dependence is a physical one and the connection is made through a natural system. Air pollution is a familiar example. A less obvious externality is the biological concentration of industrial pollutants in food chains, which can damage human health.

In economic terms, externalities affecting environmental quality arise when the social costs and benefits of effects on the environment are not taken into consideration by the person or group that creates the effects. Managers of a paper mill, left to their own devices, might minimize costs by dumping wastes into a river instead of disposing of them in an environmentally sound manner. Individuals who fail to use their time and resources to dispose of their refuse properly impose cleanup costs on society.

Sometimes ignorance is the explanation for such externalities. Thirty years ago, farmers probably were unaware of the risks associated with the use of pesticides. At other times, people might have full knowledge of the damage they cause, but for institutional reasons they are not held responsible for their actions. This is a common failure of an uncontrolled or imperfect market system. Similar failures have also occurred in centrally planned economies (Goldman 1977). Fundamentally, such failures can be attributed to institutional inflexibilities that have prevented environmental quality objectives from being absorbed into economic development decisions, and to the divergence between social and private benefits and costs.

Damages discussed so far relate to the off-site effects of economic activities. Damage can also be an on-site effect; for example, when soil erosion leads to decreases in agricultural or grazing productivity. The long-term significance of such effects is often ignored by private landowners and managers, who may have restricted planning horizons and high discount rates. Divergences between private and social planning horizons and discount rates may arise as a kind of intertemporal externality. Similarly, this is a failure of an uncontrolled market system. Such failures also occur in centrally planned economies (Goldman 1977).

The Role of Government.   Because sustained economic and social development requires the maintenance of adequate levels of ambient environmental quality, it is the responsibility of government to take an active role in managing environmental quality. External damage effects must be "internalized" in economic decision making. The deterioration of environmental quality creates real costs and undermines long-term development objectives, but programs for managing environmental quality may also be costly in terms of the scarce resources they use. No country can afford complete protection in all areas. Benefit-cost analysis is a tool to help determine how far the maintenance and enhancement of environmental quality should proceed.

Benefit-cost analysis can assist in the protection and management of environmental quality in several ways. At the individual project level, it can help to prevent projects from being undertaken that might lead to reduced levels of social economic welfare because of damage to the environment. It can also guide the design of desirable projects by indicating economically efficient modifications that prevent excessive damages from occurring. Similar applications of benefit-cost analysis can be made at the sectoral, regional, or national levels, where many projects or economic activities must be considered in economic development planning. Another important application is in the formulation and implementation of policies for managing environmental quality—policies that can generate costs and benefits for existing and proposed economic activities in both the public and private sectors. Programs for managing air quality are a good example. Finally, the approach can be incorporated in the management of natural resources when management goals are specified in terms of net social economic benefits.

Estimation of Damages to the Environment

Utility, Disutility, and Effects on the Environment. As previously shown, many environmental goods and services are available ''free'' to society. The demands for environmental quality are usually implicit. Although individuals may not be able to describe directly the utility derived from the consumption of environmental goods and services, they will have positive demands for them. The benefits derived from environmental goods and services should be included in a benefit-cost analysis.

Individuals can experience negative utility or disutility as well as utility. An important source of disutility is any bad characteristic of the environment, especially damage arising from economic activity. Air, water, and noise pollution are examples. Just as with environmental ''goods,'' individuals may not be able to indicate directly the effect that environmental ''bads'' might have on their welfare. In conducting a benefit-cost analysis, disutility caused by environmental bads can be represented as a monetary cost.

Costs and benefits also arise from changes in utility and disutility. If the benefits enjoyed from the use of the environment as a ''free'' resource (e.g., as a source of fish or firewood) are reduced because of damage created by economic activity, the decrease in utility can be interpreted as an external cost of the economic activity. Conversely, a reduction in disutility arising from the prevention of damage through protection of the environment can be classified as a benefit. Thus, costs can be defined as *benefits foregone* and benefits as *costs avoided*. The correct classification depends on the context in which the various effects on environmental quality are being assessed.

Techniques of valuing the costs and benefits of environmental quality are discussed later in this chapter.

Damage Functions.   Economic activities have many different impacts on the environment. Those that generate disutility impose costs on society. Economists contend that multiple effects on the environment can be amalgamated into a single measure of damage if the physical impacts are weighted by implicit or explicit monetary values and aggregated to obtain an estimate of the total social cost incurred. Thus, the set of environmental damages accompanying a specific development project or program can be translated into a point estimate of damage cost. As the scale or design of projects is altered, so will physical damages to the environment. Each new set of effects leads to a new point estimate of damage cost. In principle, continuous variation in the level of economic activity leads to a continuum of costs, forming a monetary damage cost function.

A theoretical cost curve for environmental damage caused by emissions of sulfur oxides associated with a regional development program is shown in figure 3.14. Damage to the physical environment is assumed to increase with higher emission rates, leading to higher levels of damage cost. The damage cost curve thus slopes upward to the right.

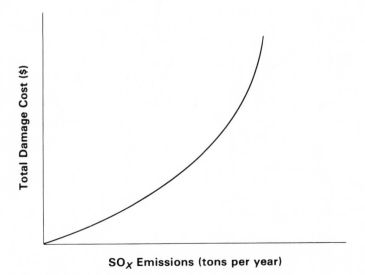

Figure 3.14 Hypothetical damage cost curve for SO_x.

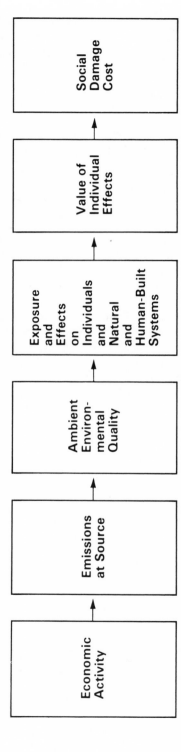

Figure 3.15 Estimation of social damage cost.

Derivation of Damage Cost Functions.   In practice, a complex chain of analysis is required to derive an environmental damage cost function. Figure 3.15 shows the steps involved in obtaining a point estimate of the damage cost caused by the discharge of residuals (unwanted gases, liquid effluents, or solids) into the ambient environment from a particular economic activity. This example deals with emissions of air pollutants. Engineering data are needed to determine emissions at source. Monitoring must be carried out at receptor points to ascertain ambient concentrations of residuals and to establish accurately the links between discharges and receptor concentrations at receptor points. Chemical or biological reactions, such as the creation of photochemical smog, and background concentrations of pollutants can greatly complicate this task. Receptors may be humans, animals, plants, and structures or materials. Assessing the physical effects of ambient pollution on individuals requires detailed information on human activity patterns to determine degrees of exposure, as well as medical information on dose-response relationships. Other disutilities may be involved, such as feelings of repugnance caused by foul-smelling air, or diminished enjoyment of natural surroundings due to the damage to vegetation that is associated with air and water pollution. Monetary estimates must be made that reflect the disutility effects for all individuals affected. Finally, value judgments about comparative utility levels of different individuals must be made, and individual values must be aggregated to obtain a single figure for the level of social costs incurred.

This estimation process is difficult enough for an existing situation where the various effects can at least be observed. To derive the complete damage function, hypothetical variations in all the relevant variables need to be considered. Mathematical functions, or even sophisticated systems-analysis models, must replace the arrows in figure 3.15, which connect successive stages of the estimation process. More detailed discussion of economic activity and natural-systems models will follow in Chapters 4 and 5.

Incorporating Environmental Costs and Benefits in Project Design and Appraisal

Economic development proposals often have adverse impacts on environmental quality. The problem is explicitly to incorporate measures to reduce adverse environmental effects on ambient environmental quality—both on-site and off-site—in the original formulation of the development project. Such measures usually require, at least initially, the use of additional resources. These environmental protection costs plus any damage costs from the remaining adverse environmental effects plus normal production costs represent total project costs. Total project benefits consist of the benefits of project outputs plus any benefits from improvements in ambient environmental quality arising from the project. In economic terms, a development project is desirable only if total project benefits, including those arising from environmental improvement, exceed total project costs, including environmental protection costs and the costs of any remaining damage to the environment. Environmental impacts can be reduced through changes in project design and other preventive measures. Limited benefit-cost analyses can help determine the optimal level of environmental protection for the project. Such analyses can also convert projects with negative overall net benefits to economically desirable ones by promoting economically efficient handling of environmental effects. Any project with negative overall net benefits that cannot be appropriately modified, however, should not be undertaken on economic grounds.

To show how cost and benefit valuation of effects on environmental quality and natural systems enters the project planning and analysis process, it is useful to look at a schematic representation such as figure 3.16. The water-resource project presented here (a large dam constructed for flood control, irrigation, and electric energy generation) has a set of resource inputs and outputs. A narrow benefit-cost analysis would consider only those factors outlined with double lines: the resource inputs (and their valuation) and the direct project outputs (and their valuation). Even within these areas, costs and benefits occur that are not always directly measurable, such as the shadow prices of capital and labor (those prices that measure the true social economic cost of these resources) or the benefits from the project, such as recreation and tourism, that are difficult to quantify.

By extending the benefit-cost analysis, as indicated by the single-line boxes, the whole array of effects on the natural system, the receptors, and the economy are incorporated. The extent to which these effects have been incorporated in benefit-cost analyses in the past varies. Some analyses are quite sophisticated and attempt to measure both direct and indirect costs or benefits; other analyses are very narrow and only consider direct, easily quantified inputs and outputs.

Projects can be classified according to the way in which they interact with the environment. At times, natural systems are replaced by systems of human origin, such as agricultural and silvicultural activities. At other times, the physical environment is modified, as in mining projects, road construction, and hydroelectric projects. Industrial projects, such as factory or power-plant construction, and housing developments can have important effects on environmental quality, including physical changes to the environment and damages arising from residuals discharges. These distinctions, however, cannot be rigid. New irrigation and agricultural projects, for example, can lead to increased pesticide and fertilizer runoff and to contamination of local water supplies. On the other hand, some industries, such as electronics manufacturing, are very clean and produce minimal air and water pollution. In each specific example, a comprehensive examination of the entire system, as outlined in figure 3.16, identifies the interactions involved and indicates the direct and indirect effects.

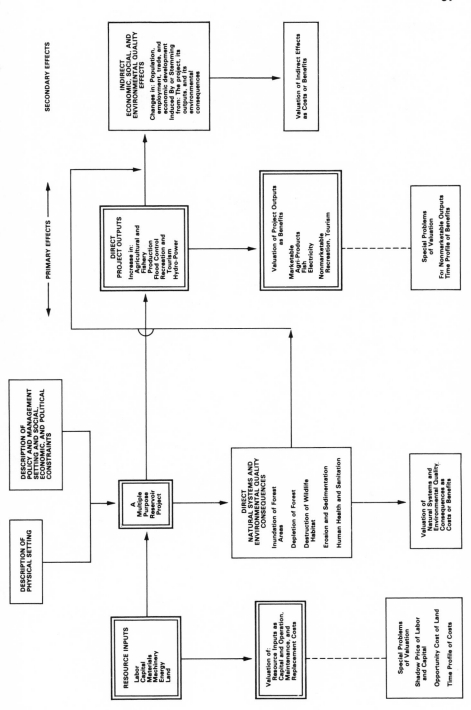

Figure 3.16 A comprehensive examination of benefits and costs of a typical development project.

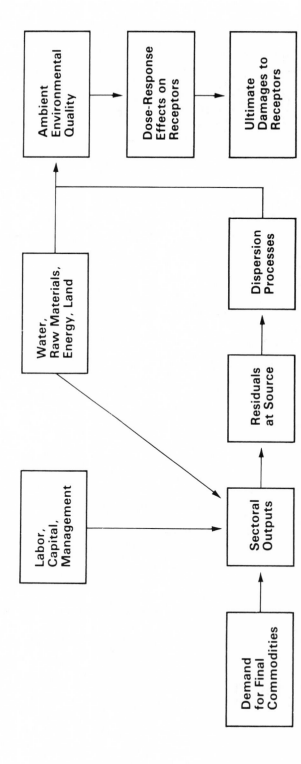

Figure 3.17 Economic-environmental quality input-output model.

Multiple-Activity Development Programs

The preceding discussion has shown that valuation of effects on natural systems can be carried out only after the physical effects of economic activity have been identified. One of the difficulties in assessing environmental quality is the correct selection of the boundaries of analysis. Many effects on environmental quality occur in a regional rather than a site-specific context. Others may have national or even international significance.

When benefit-cost analysis is used to assess the effects of an individual project on ambient environmental quality, some of the effects could be considered relatively minor and, hence, could be given little weight in the evaluation process. In seeking optimal trade-offs between economic gain and ambient environmental quality, a small degree of degradation in environmental quality is often an acceptable part of a development decision. If many such projects take place simultaneously in a specific region, however, the combined effects may lead to serious deterioration in regional environmental quality. A series of uncoordinated benefit-cost analyses might fail to capture the system-wide impacts of a number of project proposals.

The need for a comprehensive framework for assessment often arises for regional or national program formulation. Large-scale industrial or natural-resource development programs frequently contain production activities that encompass a broad spectrum of industries.

Direct and indirect environmental effects in a multiple-activity context are shown diagrammatically in figure 3.17. Final demands for economic commodities "drive" the extended system. Assessment of effects is handled best by means of a general-equilibrium framework; that is, a regional or national information system that takes all major economic activities into consideration when analyzing the interface between economic and environmental quality factors. Some aggregation of activities into industries or sectors is often needed, yet the analysis usually becomes fairly complex and requires mathematical modeling techniques, assisted by electronic computers. General-equilibrium economic models can be integrated with natural-systems models to produce national or regional economic-environmental quality models. Input-output analysis and mathematical-programming models are the most widely used techniques for comprehensive analysis of economic and environmental systems (Chapter 8). Valuation of costs and benefits, however, is still required under these mathematical approaches when used for development planning and environmental management. General-equilibrium modeling and benefit-cost analysis thus are complementary techniques in planning exercises involving many activities.

Environmental Protection Policies and Programs

Benefit-cost analyses based on environmental damage functions have frequently been applied to the management of air and water quality. The concepts that follow are applicable to the management of residuals discharges or ambient environment quality where economic activities already exist, or in situations where controls are needed with the introduction of new development projects or programs.

The theory developed here extends the previous discussion of environmental damage functions and uses emissions of air pollutants as an example. The approach is relevant to individual economic activities or to a regional (or even national) economic system. In figure 3.18(a), the total social economic costs of emissions from a given economic activity appear on the vertical axis and emission levels on the horizontal. A particular level of emissions $0G$ is as-

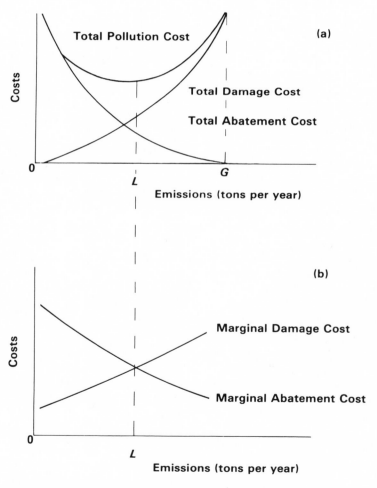

Figure 3.18 The optimal level of emissions.

sumed to occur. The damage cost curve is similar to the one shown in figure 3.14 and rises from left to right. The emissions abatement cost curve rises from right to left; that is, levels of emissions can be reduced, but only at increasing total cost.

Vertical addition of the two curves yields a U-shaped total cost curve for emissions. An economic optimum is reached where total cost is minimized. As seen in figure 3.18(b), this point represents the equality of the marginal abatement and marginal damage costs and shows the optimal level of emissions $0L$ that society is prepared to tolerate.

Emissions must, of course, be translated into their effects upon ambient environmental quality and receptors in order to establish the optimal level of emissions. In practice, tolerance levels are usually determined in terms of ambient concentrations of pollutants, from which an appropriate pattern of emissions controls must be derived. The optimal level of emissions depends on the degree of damage to the environment and the opportunity cost of using scarce resources to reduce emissions instead of using them for other forms of production.

In an alternative approach, shown in figure 3.19(a), the vertical axis measures costs and benefits and the horizontal axis indicates the level of pollution abatement (quantity of pollutants removed) measured from left to right. Total abatement costs are assumed to rise with higher levels of abatement. The total benefit curve represents the value of damages prevented and would be derived from an environmental damage cost function. From an economic viewpoint, an optimal policy is one that maximizes the net benefits of abatement. Net benefits are maximized when the marginal social costs and benefits of abatement are equal. The corresponding marginal curves and the optimal intersection point $0P$ are shown in figure 3.19(b).

Various policy instruments—or implementation incentives—are available to bring about a desired level of emissions or effluent control. In a multiple-activity situation—for example, an airshed or river basin with many residuals—a system of charges on emissions or effluents can, in theory, be used (OECD 1980a). If the charge is set at a level corresponding to the intersection point of the regional marginal abatement and marginal damage cost curves, resources will be used in an economically efficient manner to bring about the optimal level of regional emissions or effluent control. Each discharger will carry out abatement up to the point at which his marginal discharge reduction costs are equal to the charge.

A more common approach, in practice, is implementation of environmental standards, which may be specified in terms of permissible discharge rates for emissions and effluents or in terms of ambient environmental quality. Benefit-cost analysis can assist in determining an optimal set of discharge standards or an optimal set of ambient environmental quality standards. An economically efficient solution is reached when the net social benefits of a system of standards are maximized. Further discussion of this topic appears later in this chapter.

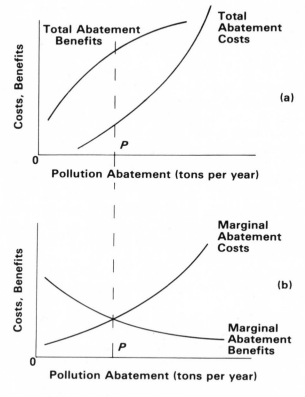

Figure 3.19 Optimal level of pollution abatement.

Application of Benefit-Cost Analysis to Natural Resources

Classification of Resources.   Benefit-cost analysis can be applied to the management of natural resource systems, but its appropriateness depends largely on the dynamic properties of the resource under consideration. According to Pearce (1976), benefit-cost analysis is not well suited to an assessment of situations involving complex ecosystem behavior, cumulative impacts, and diffuse spatial effects. Management objectives for natural systems frequently require the explicit use of dynamic optimization or simulation models (Clark 1976; Patten 1976; Hall and Day 1977; Holling 1978). Detailed discussion of such models is beyond the scope of this report. Costs and benefits of management actions at different points in time, however, still need to be quantified; thus, benefit-cost analysis can be viewed as a complementary technique.

In analyzing the rate of resource use, it is usual to distinguish between renewable and nonrenewable resources. The conventional economic approach to the time rate of use of both types of resources is to maximize the net present value from the consumption stream of final output produced from resource inputs. The formal models of optimal resource use for nonrenewable resources, however, are quite different from those for renewables.

Nonrenewable Resources. The economics literature does not directly tackle the problem of the ultimate exhaustion of minerals and fuels because it concentrates on a relatively short time-horizon and relies optimistically on technological change to provide substitutes. Under the conventional approach, the basic problem of resource use is to find an extraction rate that maximizes the present value of net benefits to society during the period of availability of that resource, in the expectation that technical and economic changes will encourage transition to substitutes when the resource has been exhausted. Assumptions concerning future technological change are critical in such analyses (Herfindahl and Kneese 1974; Baumol and Oates 1974; Pearce 1975).

In general, most of the resources-use optimization models fail to consider the environment itself as a depletable resource (Smith and Krutilla 1979). There is a need for incorporating environmental elements such as residuals management, including recycling and resource recovery, into resource depletion models.

Renewable Resources. The time rate of renewable-resource use is significant in fisheries, forestry, grazing, and agriculture (Scott 1955). The usual conservationist position is that a renewable resource should be managed on a maximum sustained yield basis. In forestry and fisheries this has often been interpreted by biologists as maximizing annual physical output over a perpetual time-horizon (May et al. 1979).

Clark (1976) has applied optimal control theory to determine economically desirable harvest rates for renewable resources such as fisheries and forests. Optimal control theory determines what should be done at each point in time given the inverse proportionality between consumption and resource stocks (Dorfman 1969). With renewable resources, the growth or replenishment rate of the natural resource must be taken into account.

The economic approach to optimal management of renewable resources requires maximization of the present value of net benefits obtainable from production of the resource. Such a management policy often leads to a steady state situation with a sustainable physical yield. With high discount rates and low biological growth rates, however, an economically optimal policy may lead to depletion of the resource (Page 1977).

Uncertainty and Irreversibilities

Considerable controversy has arisen over the economic concept of discounting, especially in situations in which long-term effects on the environment are uncertain or irreversible. Even if substantial damage costs occurring in the distant future were known with complete certainty, use of a discount rate could lead to almost total disregard for such consequences and could favor development plans that generate more immediate economic benefits. With typical discount rates (table 3.1), most effects will tend to be ignored after a period of about sixty years. Rigid application of benefit-cost analysis as the only criterion for decisions could ultimately lead to significant and irreversible damage to natural systems.

As an answer to this problem, low discount rates have been suggested whereby long-term damages to the environment are given greater present weight in development decisions. General use of low discount rates, however, may lead to higher rates of investment and create even greater damage in the future, as pointed out by Fisher and Krutilla (1975). An alternative approach (Krutilla and Fisher 1975) is to value appropriately the services of irreplaceable environmental assets, so that long-run damage costs rise rapidly if such resources are threatened by economic development. Ciriacy-Wantrup (1952) and Bishop (1978) argue that a "safe minimum standard" determined by experts should be incorporated in the analysis to prevent irreversible damage to critical resources. Holling (1978) has advocated development strategies that create information feedback on environmental impacts and maintain flexible choice throughout time.

ECONOMIC VALUATION TECHNIQUES

Benefit Valuation

The techniques discussed briefly here and in greater detail in Chapter 6 concern the valuation of benefits of improvements to natural systems and ambient environmental quality (or the obverse, valuation of damages associated with degradation of such systems). The techniques are based largely on consumer or producer willingness to pay for an improvement (or willingness to accept compensation for a deterioration) in natural systems and ambient environmental quality.

Productive Resources.   The benefits to productive resources of preserving or improving environmental quality can often be valued directly through market information. Changes in environmental quality can result in shifts of the supply curves for the products of activities such as agriculture, forestry, fisheries, and sometimes manufacturing. The effects on net social benefits can be measured by comparing consumer's and producer's surplus before and after environmental change (Freeman 1979). This class of effects, which relates marketed goods and services affected by environmental change to national income, is the most powerful illustration of why developing countries pursuing sustained development must consider measures for protecting the environment.

Benefits can be measured as the increased market value of crops, fish, and other products attributable to improved environmental quality. If the estimates take the form of benefits foregone (costs) as a result of the damage created by development projects or programs, changes in benefits can be quantified in terms of the market value of reductions in output—for example, a decline in agricultural yield, decreased production from forests, reductions in fishery catches, and lowered output of electricity from hydroelectric schemes caused by premature siltation of reservoirs. Also, market values can frequently be obtained for damages to structures, such as buildings and bridges, and for materials—for example, paint and rubber. The acceptance of monetary compensation by producers for damages inflicted on them through the environment is a further measure of benefits foregone for productive resources.

Human beings can also be viewed as a productive resource. When the damages are to human health, the valuation problem is more difficult, but several methods are available, including estimating economic losses due to the decline in workers' productivity because of poor health and premature death.

Other measures of willingness to pay for environmental improvement to productive resources may be obtained indirectly, still in market prices, in the form of producer expenditures for the prevention of environmental damage—for example, the costs incurred for water input treatment processes in a vegetable canning plant. The cost of replacing productive assets damaged by effects on the environment is another measure that can be used.

Willingness of Consumers to Pay for Environmental Services. Valuations of environmental quality by consumers as well as by producers can be measured in monetary terms on the basis of compensation payments for damages to property or persons or for other negative effects on the environment. Market values similarly can provide estimates from the cost side, where preventive expenditures and replacement costs incurred by individuals serve as indirect measures of the demand for better environmental quality.

Demands for environmental services for consumer purposes (for example, for some types of recreation activities or to satisfy aesthetic needs) are usually implicit. Actual prices are generally not paid, and values have to be determined by indirect methods. Valuation techniques are frequently based on the theory of pure public goods, which uses the concept of "willingness to pay" to measure consumer benefits (Samuelson 1954).

Consider an individual with an implicit demand for recreation (figure 3.20). The vertical axis measures the implicit marginal valuation, expressed in monetary units, of recreation days spent in a natural environment. The horizontal axis measures the number of recreation days. If the individual actually were charged to use the natural resources for recreation, a Marshallian demand curve *DD* could be derived from the willingness-to-pay behavior. If the resource were made available to the individual at no cost, the benefits of the recreation (total willingness to pay) would be represented by

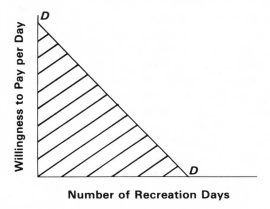

Number of Recreation Days

Figure 3.20 Individual demand curve for recreation in a natural environment.

the area of the shaded region in the diagram. This area consists entirely of consumer's surplus.

Pure public goods are provided by government for collective consumption in the interest of social welfare. Provision of a pure public good has welfare implications for all members of society because it is assumed that it is physically impossible or prohibitively expensive to exclude consumption by any individual. A bell tower that chimes the time of day is a good example of a pure public good. It would be impracticable to exclude individuals from listening for the time.

Environmental quality services—natural amenities, clean air, and clean water—can frequently be classified as pure public goods. Because it is not possible or worthwhile to force all individuals who enjoy the benefits of improved environmental quality to pay for them—the so-called free-rider problem—implicit demands are taken to be indicators of individuals' willingness to pay and must be assessed by indirect valuation techniques. Because the total social benefits of consuming environmental services are a reflection of the number of individuals who enjoy the benefits, the individual demand curves for environmental quality must be added vertically to obtain the implicit market or social demand curve. In figure 3.21 the implicit demand curves for an environmental amenity for three individuals appear as *A*, *B*, and *C*. The social demand curve is shown as *D*, representing the vertical addition of curves *A*, *B*, and *C*. The total social benefit (willingness to pay) of the amenity is measured by the area under curve *D*, that is, the overall consumers' surplus.

Appropriateness of Willingness to Pay as a Measure of Environmental Benefits. Although the willingness-to-pay concept is useful in assessing the economic benefits of marketed goods and services, it is not altogether clear that it can be transferred to the valuation of environmental quality benefits.

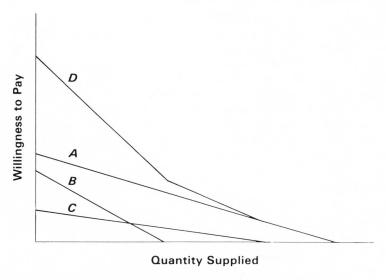

Quantity Supplied

Figure 3.21 Demand for environmental amenity as a public good.

The approach can be questioned on both theoretical and empirical grounds. As pointed out by Mooney (1978), a willingness-to-pay approach to the valuation of environmental quality implies that individuals are the best persons to make judgments about environmental quality, that they believe they are the best persons to do so, that they can make the best decisions about the effects of environmental quality on their own welfare, and that they want to make such decisions. In practice, some or all of these conditions may not be fulfilled. Information about marketed goods and services is usually readily available to consumers. Effects of changes in environmental quality on individual welfare (health, for example) are less well known by the general public. In many countries, individuals are content to hand over the responsibilities of managing environmental quality to government agencies that are expected to make informed judgments in the interests of social welfare.

The assumption that the distribution of income is acceptable leads to other complications. Valuations based on willingness to pay are actually based on both willingness and ability to pay. Both the distribution of money income and the incidence of environmental quality effects can influence welfare levels of specific individuals or groups within the community. Only the very rich, for example, might be capable of indicating strong preferences for certain types of environmental services. The poor may have no ability to pay for environmental measures that could lead to significant gains in welfare. Environmental improvement programs leading to better community health might never be instituted if they were dependent on consumer willingness to pay. In such cases, it seems perfectly rational for decision makers, especially with the aid of technical experts, to determine appropriate environmental quality goals. Such a philosophy underlies the common practice of establishing standards for ambient environmental quality. Individual values may not be properly known, but decision makers can nevertheless consider themselves on safe ground by assuming that improvements in health and the prevention of serious damages would represent a high priority for most individuals, even if incomes were low. Indeed, incomes might be low because of a degraded physical environment. The cycle of ill health, low productivity, and inability to raise income and living standards is a common occurrence in countries at a low level of development.

Valuation of Costs

Estimation of the resource costs of development plans has already been discussed under Project Costs. What needs to be examined here are methods of measuring the costs of measures for protecting environmental-quality—for example, the incremental costs of environmental safeguards in project design and the resource costs incurred in programs for improving environment quality. Such costs may be incurred in the private or public sectors. Further discussion of cost valuation techniques appears in Chapter 7.

At the project or activity level, it is often difficult to separate the costs of environmental protection measures from normal project costs. This frequently occurs with combustion processes, such as coal-fired boilers for electric power stations, blast furnaces for steel production, and internal combustion engines for transportation equipment. Designs that raise combustion efficiency often lead simultaneously to reduction in discharges of some air pollutants. External costs also can be generated by measures for protecting environmental quality. At the plant or activity level, most environmental control technologies or practices have secondary effects on the environment. Attempts to prevent air pollution, for instance, may lead to water pollution, as can occur when flue-gas desulfurization scrubbers are fitted to electric power stations to control sulfur oxide emissions. Further energy inputs required to operate scrubbers can result in other secondary discharges. Chemical sludges from the scrubber are often stored in settling ponds, with a risk of contaminating surface waters or underground water tables, leading to new environmental damage costs. Other examples can be found in alternative environmental management practices in the natural resources area. Secondary effects on the environment may be especially significant in national and regional programs aimed at improving environmental quality. Damage costs in such cases are analyzed best by means of general-equilibrium frameworks (Chapter 8).

Cost-Effectiveness Analysis

In some situations, it may be too difficult to value the benefits of improving environmental quality in economic terms. Policy making must then be based on cost-effectiveness rather than on full benefit-cost analysis. In cost-effectiveness analysis, environmental quality targets such as aesthetic properties, ecosystem functions, ambient concentrations of pollutants, or levels of community health are fixed, and an economically efficient solution is found by minimizing the costs of attaining the targets. Environmental objectives can frequently be met by a variety of measures, and systematic analysis of costs will indicate the optimal approach.

In many situations, the credibility of economic information as an input to making decisions about environmental quality may be considerably enhanced if a cost-effectiveness, rather than a full benefit-cost, approach is taken. Environmental health is one area in which this applies. Methods of placing economic values on the health benefits of improving environmental quality are often viewed with suspicion by decision makers. More notice might be paid to physical and psychological effects determined by medical experts. Instead of attempting to translate these effects into monetary terms, a more realistic approach might be to derive a set of environmental quality standards based on scientific opinion and to focus attention on the least-cost way of reaching the standards.

Emissions Standards for Activities.   Emissions standards for activities frequently are established and implemented in conjunction with cost analysis. Where the benefits of abatement cannot be easily specified in monetary terms, arbitrary levels of control can be introduced. Figure 3.22 illustrates the principle; emission control costs for a given activity are shown on the vertical axis and the degree of abatement on the horizontal axis. A weak emissions standard might be $0W$, and a stringent standard $0S$. The sensitivity of abatement costs to changes in standards is a valuable guide to environmental quality managers in trading off physical pollution control benefits against economic costs. If the total abatement cost curve is fairly flat, the incremental costs of moving from weak to stringent standards are small. The opposite applies if the curve slopes steeply. In practice, the cost curve is usually a series of points describing alternative control technologies. The incremental costs incurred in

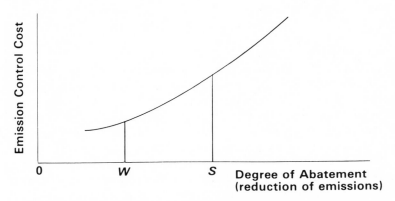

Figure 3.22 Cost of emission controls as a function of degree of abatement.

moving from one point to another often clearly indicate a sensible cutoff level for abatement activity.

Emissions Standards in a Regional Context.   As was shown in figures 3.18 and 3.19, a full benefit-cost analysis is required to derive an optimal set of emissions standards for regional ambient environmental quality management. In the absence of accurate data on the benefit side, policy makers, guided by health authorities, scientists, and other experts, frequently decide upon an arbitrary set of standards. Cost-effectiveness analysis can help ensure that standards are met and implemented without wasting scarce resources. It can be shown, for example, that to reduce regional emissions by a given amount, the marginal costs of discharge reduction for all polluters in the region should be equal (OECD 1980*a*). In theory, this can be attained by imposing a uniform emissions charge. Cost-effective implementation schemes designed to meet prescribed ambient environmental quality standards need to be tailored to specific economic, technical, and environmental circumstances.

The OECD defines charges that are high enough to induce polluters to modify their behavior as *incentive charges.* Even if new residuals disposal techniques cannot be induced, charges on effluents can still be used as redistributing devices to achieve improvement in ambient environmental quality. Funds collected from polluters can be allocated to public investments designed to treat discharges from the government sector or from households. Other uses of such funds include subsidizing of antipollution activities by industries or by households (e.g., on noise insulation products or on electric heaters to replace open fireplaces), financing systems for monitoring the environment, and paying the administrative costs of regulating environmental quality.

Where the links between emissions and ambient concentrations of pollutants are poorly known and a cost-effectiveness approach is adopted, charges and emissions standards can be operated in an iterative manner to achieve desired standards for ambient environmental quality. Arbitrary charges or restrictions on emissions can be imposed and the reactions observed. Adjustments can be made until acceptable standards of ambient quality are reached. The costs of acquiring information under this approach are mainly the adjustment costs of polluters. Serious under- or overinvestment in antipollution activities could occur. If environmental management authorities gain a reputation for inconsistency because of vacillating policies, further cooperation from private industry may be difficult to achieve. In some countries, regulatory bodies have attempted to overcome these problems by starting at a low level of charges, gradually raising them over time, and informing industry of planned levels of charges. Direct regulations, furthermore, have been used in conjunction with charges. A fuller analysis of the economics of environmental quality policy instruments can be found in James, Jansen, and Opschoor (1978), OECD (1980*b*), and Bower et al. (1981).

Classification of Valuation Techniques

Economic valuation techniques for assessing effects on environmental quality can be classified in a number of different ways. The approach used here and illustrated in table 3.2 is to classify the techniques in decreasing order of reliance upon market data, beginning with valuation of costs and benefits using actual market prices of outputs and ending with survey-oriented and other hypothetical valuation methods.

Within the market-oriented category are listed first methods of valuing environmental quality benefits using actual market prices. Such prices, of course, must be converted where necessary to appropriate shadow prices. These market-based techniques—value of output and loss of earnings—are discussed in Chapter 6. The second subcategory under market-oriented approaches is valuation of costs using actual market prices. These approaches—preventive expenditures, cost-effectiveness, replacement cost, and the shadow project concept—are taken up in Chapter 7. The third subcategory is concerned with valuations based on surrogate markets—where market prices for environmental services, project outputs, and external effects are not readily available. These approaches comprise marketed goods and services as environmental surrogates, property value, other land value approaches, travel costs, wage differentials, acceptance of compensation, and Krutilla's opportunity-cost approach to natural-resource decisions with irreversible consequences. These techniques are dealt with in Chapter 6.

Survey and other hypothetical valuation methods appear in the last group of techniques. These are subdivided into direct questioning of willingness to pay and indirect estimation of willingness to pay via direct questioning on choices of commodities. These techniques are also discussed in Chapter 6.

GENERAL CONCLUSIONS

The main advantage offered by benefit-cost analysis—regardless of the institutional context in which it is applied—is that it forces decision makers to consider all of the effects of an investment or management program. Effects on environmental quality, including those that might be indirect, intangible, or difficult to measure, should be taken into account.

Valuation of effects on ambient environmental quality can differ among countries, as do the political processes from which economic values are derived. Western economists place greatest emphasis on individual values but recognize that in some areas of decision making government responsibility will be required. Decisions involving environmental quality comprise an important area in which the need for government involvement is explicitly recognized.

Regardless of the political climate, all economic decisions will lead to costs

Table 3.2. Classification of Cost and Benefit Valuation Techniques for Assessing Effects on Environmental Quality

Valuation technique	Examples of application	
	Producer goods and services	Consumer goods and services
Market oriented		
1. Benefit valuation using actual market prices of productive goods and services		
(a) Changes in value of output	Loss of value of agricultural crops caused by seepage of toxic chemicals	
(b) Loss of earnings	Value of productive services lost through increased illness and death caused by air pollution	
2. Cost valuation using actual market prices of environmental protection inputs		
(a) Preventive expenditures	Cost of environmental safeguards in project design	Cost of noise insulation; cost of intake water treatment
(b) Replacement cost	Cost of replacing structures damaged by acid rain	Cost of additional painting of houses damaged by air pollution
(c) Shadow project	Cost of restoring commercial fresh-water fisheries damaged by discharges	Costs of supplying alternative sport fishing and recreational facilities destroyed by development project
(d) Cost-effectiveness analysis	Costs of alternative means of disposing of waste-water from a geothermal energy project	

3. Benefit valuation using surrogate markets

(a) Marketed goods as environmental surrogates — Cost of sewage treatment processes as proxy for water purification by ecosystems

(b) Property value approach — Changes in residential property value from air pollution; Changes in commercial property value as a result of water pollution

(c) Other land value approaches — Prices paid by government for land reserved for national parks

(d) Travel cost — Valuation of recreational benefits of a public park; Price paid for visits to private parks and entertainment as proxy for value of visits to wilderness area

(e) Wage differential approach — Estimation of willingness of workers to trade off wages for improved environmental quality

(f) Acceptance of compensation — Compensation for damage to crops; Compensation for adverse health effects, e.g., Minamata disease

Survey Oriented
(hypothetical valuation)

1. Direct questioning of willingness to pay

(a) Bidding games — Estimate of willingness to pay for access to an urban park

2. Direct questioning of choices of quantities

(a) Costless choice method — Hypothetical applications to air pollution and benefits. Implicitly or explicitly, therefore, benefit-cost evaluations will be made and scarce resources will be allocated. Benefit-cost analysis provides useful information for this allocation process. In the final assessment, differences of opinion about the appropriateness of benefit-cost analysis as a development planning tool may be attributed to divergences in sociopolitical values or to variations in the degree of rigor with which the method is actually applied.

In many Western countries, the general framework of benefit-cost analysis is now in common use in planning and policy making in the areas of public investment, natural resources, and environmental quality. The technique is especially suitable for water-resource development programs for the purposes of irrigation, reducing flood damage, and generating hydroelectric energy. The cost-effectiveness approach is valuable in the management of air and water quality. In the field of natural resources, particularly agriculture, fishing, and forestry, benefit-cost analysis also has many applications.

Benefit-cost analysis does have limitations, and its adaptation for use in developing countries is still being explored.

APPENDIX

Compensated Demand—Compensating Variation

The integral of the Marshallian demand function or the area under the demand curve at times will not measure precisely individual economic welfare. This can be illustrated by referring to an individual with a demand for good X. The Marshallian demand curve for good X is shown as DD in figure A3.1.

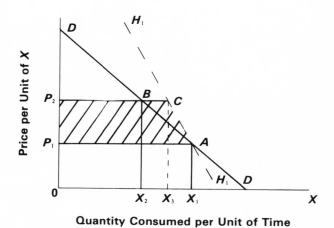

Figure A3.1 Compensating variation measured by Hicks-compensated demand curve.

Suppose, as at point A, the individual has been paying a price of $0P_1$ for good X and consuming $0X_1$ units. If the price were raised to $0P_2$, demand for good X would fall to $0X_2$ units and the individual would move to point B on the demand curve. The loss of consumer's surplus measured by the Marshallian demand curve would be the area of the region P_2BAP_1. In addition to the substitution effect, which decreases the consumption of good X, the higher price also represents a loss of real income to the individual, forcing a reduction in consumption of other commodities as well. To keep the individual at the same utility level as at point A, extra money income termed "compensating variation" would need to be provided. Some of this extra income could be spent on good X, leading to a final equilibrium at point C where, at the new price $0P_2$, the individual would demand $0X_3$ units.

By similar reasoning, further points like C can be plotted for higher prices. A new demand curve H_1H_1 passing through the original point A will be obtained; it is known as a "Hicksian," or income-compensated, demand curve. This curve shows the price-quantity combinations for good X required to keep the individual at a constant level of utility. At prices below $0P_1$, income would have to be confiscated from the individual because increases in real income or welfare could otherwise occur. Compensating variation can be measured as the area under the Hicksian demand curve. When price is raised from $0P_1$ to $0P_2$, compensating variation will equal the area of the region P_2CAP_1. This measure is a theoretical ideal sought by economists when trying to derive an estimate of the money transfer needed to keep an individual at an original welfare level, following a change in the price of a good or in the quantity consumed. The same concept can be applied to a physical deterioration in environmental quality. To assess the monetary value of a decline in air quality caused by pollution, for example, a Hicksian demand curve for clean air might, in theory, be specified and monetary damage assessed in terms of compensating variation.

Compensated Demand—Equivalent Variation

A second type of Hicks-compensated demand curve is often discussed in the theory of welfare measurement. This curve can be described by continuing with the demand for good X. Consider once again the price increase for good X shown in figure A3.1. The higher price $0P_2$ puts the individual on a lower utility or welfare level at point B. The equivalent loss of income, given the original price $0P_1$, that would lead to the same utility level as at B is known as the "equivalent variation." Since A represents a higher utility level than B, less income is required to keep the individual at B than at A. A lower amount of good X is needed at price $0P_1$ to yield the welfare equivalent of point B. This amount is shown as $0X_4$ in figure A3.2. Point E lies on the Hicksian demand curve H_2H_2 passing through point B. Other points on H_2H_2 show the amounts of good X that would keep the individual at the same level of welfare as at B. The equivalent variation of any price change can be measured as the

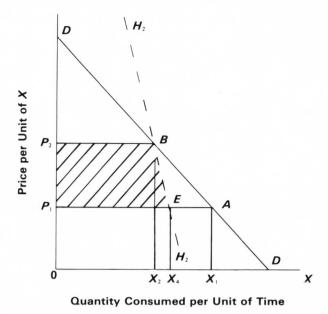

Quantity Consumed per Unit of Time

Figure A3.2 Equivalent variation measured by Hicks-compensated demand curve.

area under the Hicksian demand curve. In figure A3.2, the equivalent variation of the price rise from $0P_1$ to $0P_2$ is the area of the region P_2BEP_1.

The difference between compensating variation and equivalent variation is that the former measures money transfers needed to keep the individual at the same utility level as in an initial situation, whereas the latter measures the monetary equivalent of a change in welfare from one situation to another.

Comparison of Marshallian and Hicksian Demand Curves

The preceding analysis is based on the assumption that the individual has a positive income elasticity of demand for good X. The higher the income elasticity and the larger the ratio of consumer's surplus to income, the greater will be the divergence of Hicksian and Marshallian demand curves. From inspection of figures A3.1 and A3.2, a comparative table can be drawn up, as in table A3.1, showing the relationship of compensating variation and equivalent variation to Marshallian consumer's surplus for price increases and decreases.

The income elasticity of demand and the ratio of consumer's surplus to income have to be very high before there is a significant difference between Marshallian and Hicksian estimates. In most practical cases the distinction can be ignored. It is virtually impossible, furthermore, to derive either of the Hicksian functions empirically. Typically, the only data available are those giving rise to the Marshallian demand curve. With a zero income elasticity of

Table A3.1. Comparison of Compensating Variation and Equivalent Variation with Marshallian Consumer's Surplus

	Compensating variation	Equivalent variation
Price increase	Exceeds consumer surplus	Is less than consumer surplus
Price decrease	Is less than consumer surplus	Exceeds consumer surplus

demand, the curves DD, H_1H_1, and H_2H_2 in figures A3.1 and A3.2 will coincide, and all three measures will be equal. If it is suspected that income elasticity or the magnitude of consumer's surplus is large enough to produce an inaccurate estimate, table A3.1 will at least indicate the direction of bias. For further discussion of this problem, more advanced references are recommended (Mäler 1974, Freeman 1979).

REFERENCES

Baumol, W. J. *Economic Theory and Operations Analysis*. 3rd ed. Englewood Cliffs, N.J.: Prentice-Hall, 1972.

Baumol, W. J., and W. E. Oates. *The Theory of Environmental Policy*. Englewood Cliffs, N.J.: Prentice-Hall, 1974.

Bishop, R. "Endangered Species and Uncertainty: The Economics of a Safe Minimum Standard." *American Journal of Agricultural Economics* 60 (1978): 10–18.

Bower, B. T.; R. Barre; J. Kuhner; and C. S. Russell. *Incentives in Water Quality Management: France and the Ruhr Area*. Washington, D.C.: Resources for the Future, 1981.

Ciriacy-Wantrup, S. V. *Resource Conservation Economics and Policies*. Berkeley and Los Angeles: University of California Press, 1952.

Ciriacy-Wantrup, S. V., and R. Bishop. "Common Property as a Concept in Natural Resources Policy." *Natural Resources Journal* 15 (1975): 713–737.

Clark, C. *Mathematical Bioeconomics*. New York: Wiley-Interscience, 1976.

Cooper, C. M. *Economic Evaluation and the Environment*. London: Hodder and Stoughton for the United Nations Environment Programme (UNEP), 1981.

Dasgupta, P.; A. Sen; and S. Marglin. *Guidelines for Project Evaluation*. New York: United Nations Industrial Development Organization, 1972.

Dorfman, R. "An Economic Interpretation of Optimal Control Theory." *American Economic Review* 59 (1969): 817–831.

Fisher, A. C., and J. V. Krutilla. "Resource Conservation, Environmental Preservation and the Rate of Discount." *Quarterly Journal of Economics* 89 (1975): 358–370.

Freeman, A. M. III. *The Benefits of Environmental Improvement: Theory and Practice*. Baltimore: Johns Hopkins University Press, 1979.

Goldman, M. "The Convergence of Environmental Disruption." In *Economics of the Environment*, ed. R. Dorfman and N. Dorfman. New York: Norton, 1977.

Gordon, H. S. "The Economic Theory of a Common Property Resource: The Fishery." *Journal of Political Economy* 62 (1954): 124–142.

Hall, C. A. S., and J. W. Day. *Ecosystem Modeling in Theory and Practice*. New York: Wiley-Interscience, 1977.

Hardin, G. "The Tragedy of the Commons." In *Toward a Steady-State Economy*, ed. H. E. Daly. San Francisco: Freeman, 1973.

Hardin, G., and J. Baden, eds. *Managing the Commons*. San Francisco: Freeman, 1977.

Helmers, F. L. C. H. *Project Planning and Income Distribution*. The Hague: Martinus Nijhoff, 1979.

Herfindahl, O. C., and A. V. Kneese. *Economic Theory of Natural Resources*. Columbus, Ohio: Merrill, 1974.

Holling, C. S. ed. *Adaptive Environmental Assessment and Management*. New York: Wiley, 1978.

James, D. E.; H.M.A. Jansen; and J. B. Opschoor. *Economic Approaches to Environmental Problems*. Amsterdam: Elsevier, 1978.

Krutilla, J. V., and A. C. Fisher. *The Economics of Natural Environments*. Baltimore: Johns Hopkins University Press, 1975.

Lange, O., and F. Taylor. *On the Economic Theory of Socialism*. Minneapolis: University of Minnesota Press, 1938.

Lerner, A. P. *The Economics of Control: Principles of Welfare Economics*. New York: Macmillan, 1944.

Little, I.M.D. *A Critique of Welfare Economics*. Oxford: Clarendon Press, 1950.

Little, I.M.D., and J. A. Mirrlees. *Manual of Industrial Project Analysis*. Paris: OECD, 1968.

———. *Project Appraisal and Planning for Developing Countries*. New York: Basic Books, 1974.

Mäler, K. G. *Environmental Economics*. Baltimore: Johns Hopkins University Press, 1974.

Marglin, S. A. *Approaches to Dynamic Investment Planning*. Amsterdam: North Holland, 1963.

May, R.; J. Beddington; C. Clar; S. Holt; and R. Laws. "Management of Multispecies Fisheries." *Science* 205, 4403 (20 July 1979): 267–277.

Mishan, E. J. *Cost-Benefit Analysis*. New York: Praeger, 1976.

Mooney, G. H. "Human Life and Suffering." In *The Valuation of Social Cost*, ed. D. W. Pearce. London: Allen and Unwin, 1978.

OECD. *Pollution Charges in Practice*. Paris, 1980a.

———. *Water Management in Industrialized River Basins*. Paris, 1980b.

Page, T. *Conservation and Economic Efficiency*. Baltimore: Johns Hopkins University Press, 1977.

Patten, B. C. *Systems Analysis and Simulation in Ecology*. New York: Academic Press, 1976.

Pearce, D. W. "The Limits of Cost-Benefit Analysis as a Guide to Environmental Policy." *Kyklos* 29 (1976): 97–112.

Pearce, D. W., ed. *Economics of Natural Resource Depletion*. New York: Wiley, 1975.

———. *The Valuation of Social Cost*. London: Allen and Unwin, 1978.

Pearson, C., and A. Pryor. *Environment: North and South*. New York: Wiley-Interscience, 1978.

Samuelson, P. "The Pure Theory of Public Expenditure." *Review of Economics and Statistics* 36, 4 (1954): 387–389.

Scott, A. *Natural Resources: The Economics of Conservation*. Toronto: University of Toronto Press, 1955.

Smith, K., and J. V. Krutilla. "Resource and Environmental Constraints to Growth." *American Journal of Agricultural Economics* 61, 3 (1979): 395–408.

Squire, L., and H. van der Tak. *Economic Analysis of Projects*. Baltimore: Johns Hopkins University Press, 1975.

Steiner, P. O. *Public Expenditure Budgeting*. Washington, D.C.: Brookings Institution, 1969.

Sugden, R., and A. Williams. *The Principles of Practical Cost-Benefit Analysis*. New York: Oxford University Press, 1978.

van de Graaf, J. *Theoretical Welfare Economics*. Cambridge: At the University Press, 1957.

4

Analyzing Activities

The preceding chapters have emphasized the importance of understanding the relationship between human activities, including economic activities, and the generation of residuals and other effects on the environment that may affect ambient environmental quality and receptors, thus imposing economic costs on the society. These links are depicted in figure 1.1 in Chapter 1 and in figure 3.14 in Chapter 3. This chapter is concerned with understanding and analyzing the activity step in the process. Only a general presentation of activity analysis is given here. For detailed discussions, the reader should consult the extensive literature on the subject, including Bower (1975), Russell (1973), Russell and Vaughn (1976), and Basta, Lounsbury, and Bower (1978). Key definitions and concepts begin the chapter, are followed by some approaches to analyzing activities, and then are succeeded by examples of such analyses, including one for an industrial activity—an integrated pulp and paper mill—one for an agricultural activity, and one for a forest management activity.

KEY DEFINITIONS AND CONCEPTS

Nonproduct Outputs and Residuals

Human activities such as manufacturing, agriculture, mining, forestry, transportation, and household maintenance produce both desired products or services and unwanted materials and energy, because no production or use activity transforms all of the inputs to the activity into desired outputs. The flows of unwanted materials and energy from the activity are termed *nonproduct outputs*. If a nonproduct output has no value in existing markets or has a value less than the costs of collecting, processing, and transporting it for input into the same or another activity, the nonproduct output is called a *residual*. The word *residual* therefore is defined in economic terms.

Residual is a neutral term used instead of such words as *waste, pollutant,* or *contaminant* because a residual may or may not fit the dictionary definitions of any of these. For example, not all discharges of unwanted materials and energy into the environment have adverse impacts on ambient environmental quality.

Whether or not a nonproduct output is a residual depends on the relative costs of alternative outputs that could be used instead of the nonproduct output. This, in turn, varies with time in a given society, depending on changes in relative prices. Changing technology, changes in the relative scarcity of raw materials, and governmental actions are the primary factors that affect relative prices.

Figure 4.1 illustrates the definition of a residual by depicting a hypothetical industrial plant with two production processes. Two points merit emphasis. First, even if constraints on the discharge of residuals into the environment are absent, some of the nonproduct outputs may still be recovered and reused in the same production process or in other production or use activities at the same site or elsewhere. Those nonproduct outputs that are recovered economically and reused are by definition not residuals. Second, the discharge of a residual does not occur until the residual enters the environment across the boundary of the activity site. The residuals may or may not be modified before their discharge into the environment or before their transport from the plant site in a sewer line or by truck.

Interrelationships among Residuals

Nonproduct outputs and residuals exist as materials or energy. Material residuals occur in three forms: liquid, gaseous, and solid. Energy residuals occur as heat, noise, light, vibrations, and certain forms of radioactivity.

One form of material residual can be transformed into one or more other forms, or into different types of the same form. A liquid residual may be converted into other residuals—another type of liquid, a gas, and a solid—to be disposed of in a body of water, in the atmosphere, and on land, respectively; or a solid residual may be transformed into liquid, gaseous, and other solid residuals. Modifying a residual into other forms requires inputs of material and energy, of which portions may become residuals in turn. Modification of residuals is undertaken because of the assumption that the discharge of the modified residuals will have fewer adverse effects on environmental quality than the discharge of the original residual.

Thus, sewage modified in a sewage treatment plant becomes a semisolid residual sludge plus various types of liquid and gaseous residuals. If the sludge is incinerated, gaseous residuals, such as particulates, are generated. If the sludge is placed in a landfill, seepage of residuals into groundwater sources or into surface water may occur, and so on. Finally, because virtually all residuals modification requires inputs of energy, additional gaseous, liq-

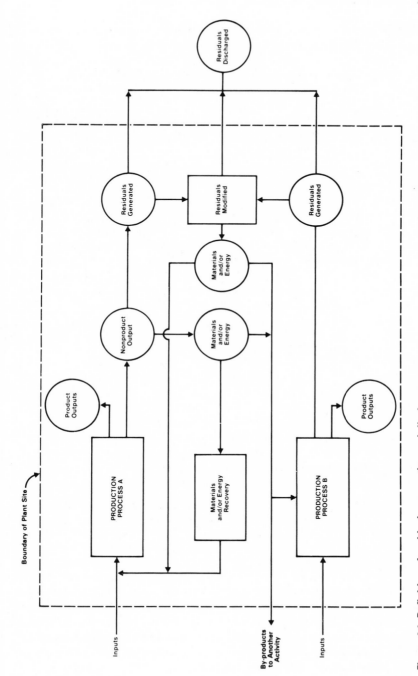

Figure 4.1 Definition of residuals generation and discharge.

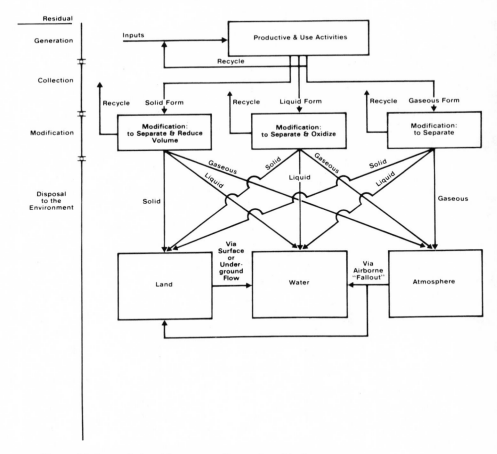

Figure 4.2 Interrelationships among forms of residuals.

uid, and solid residuals are generated from the combustion of fuel to produce the needed energy. Figure 4.2 illustrates the interrelationships among the three forms of material residuals.

Activities that Generate Residuals

An *activity*, as the term is used in this chapter, is a decision unit involving a set of one or more unit processes.* This is illustrated in figure 4.3, which shows unit processes in a vegetable cannery. An industrial plant, a farm, a mining operation, an office building, a household, a management unit of a national forest—each is an activity. Each generates one or more types of gaseous, liquid, solid, and energy residuals.

*The term *unit process* is used here to include both unit processes and unit operations as employed in chemical engineering (Ayres 1972).

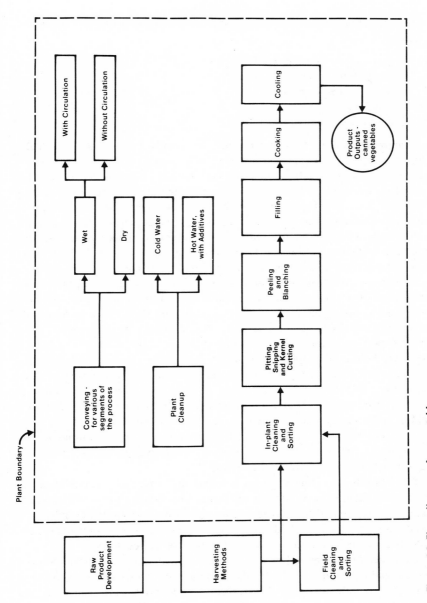

Figure 4.3 Flow diagram of a vegetable cannery.

Activities that generate residuals can be characterized by various attributes, including

1. Geographical locus of residuals generation
2. Time pattern of residuals generation
3. Links with decision units
4. Status, and
5. Importance of on-site effects.

Geographical Locus of Generation.   Activities, as sources of residuals, can be categorized as (1) concentrated, or "point," sources; (2) areal, or dispersed, sources; and (3) line sources, both mobile and stationary. An integrated steel mill, a hospital, and an office building are examples of concentrated activities. However, the steel mill, an integrated pulp and paper mill, a petroleum refinery, or a metallurgical plant each represents a set of unit processes occupying a site that may be several square kilometers in size, and each will have multiple stacks for discharging gaseous residuals and may well have several outlets for discharging liquid residuals.

In addition, most manufacturing activities involve many interprocess and interoperation transport systems, typically using flumes, pipes, or conveyor belts and requiring pumps, valves, junctions, and flow dividers. Residuals generation and discharge may occur in relation to both the unit processes and the transport operations. Gas leaks from valves and the solids blown from a conveyor belt are examples of the latter.

The term *source,* as applied to concentrated sources, is often used ambiguously to refer to different phenomena. A petroleum refinery as a whole is often referred to as a "source" of residuals discharges; however, "devices" within the refinery—such as valves and pumps—also are referred to as "sources," as is each discharge stack in the refinery. Thus, multiple *origins* of residuals generation often exist in an activity, as well as multiple *locations* of residuals discharges from an activity.

Activities that generate dispersed residuals are those that generate residuals over some defined area, such as an agricultural field, a forest management area, or a residential subdivision in a city. In the last case, the individual residences are not identified separately as residuals generators; rather, residuals generated from the entire subdivision are aggregated.

Activities that generate line residuals are classified in two subcategories—mobile and stationary. Activities that generate residuals while in motion are generating mobile line residuals as a result of one or both of the following: the unit processes involved and the interaction between the activity and the environment—for example, the dust stirred up by a motor vehicle on an unpaved road. Motor vehicles, trains, airplanes, boats, barge tows—all are individual generators of residuals. Such a generator, in moving along its path, represents a variable or mobile generator of residuals. A stationary line generator of residuals is represented by an unpaved road or trail that generates particulate matter when the wind blows.

Time Pattern of Generation.   Residuals generation by activities can be classified as *continuous,* such as a plant that operates on a twenty-four-hour, seven-day-a-week basis, or *discontinuous,* such as a plant with only one or two shifts or a seasonal activity—for example, a beach resort or a ski lodge. If the interval of time between periods of residuals generation is always the same, the time pattern is characterized as *discontinuous-regular,* as in an activity with a one-week production cycle of five days of production and two days of downtime. Otherwise, the time pattern is *discontinuous-irregular.* Residuals can be generated at either constant or variable levels for each of these time patterns.

Links with Decision Units.   Although defining an activity as a set of unit processes is straightforward, defining the boundary of the decision unit and the extent to which activities are linked is less clear. In any given situation, at least two levels may exist at which decisions are made that affect residuals generation and discharge. For example, a chemical plant producing several hundred products on a given site is likely to be organized into separate departments, each one with a high degree of flexibility as to choice of factor inputs that will affect residuals generation and discharge. Simultaneously, other decisions are made at the plant level that also affect residuals generation and discharge.

Several contexts can be identified that are comparable to the department-plant link. These include:

1.   An industrial park in which a single authority has responsibility through a contract for water-supply and liquid residuals handling and disposal—up to and from the boundaries of each plant—for all activities within the park;
2.   A national, state, or provincial forest that is divided into subareas for management purposes—for example, ''working circles'';
3.   A collective farm that includes separate but related cropping, livestock, and processing operations; and
4.   An irrigation project composed of a number of separate, independent farm units, but for which an institution, such as an irrigation district, has responsibility for development, transport, and distribution of irrigation water and for collection and disposal of drainage water.

In all of these situations, *on-site* can be defined as either the lowest level decision unit or the highest. For the latter, on-site would include the interactivity effects. Any analysis would still have to include consideration of factors and alternatives within each subunit.

Two other types of links, both of them sequential, are important. One type is a set of activities separated spatially to produce a single output—a product or service. An example is the sequence coal mining-coal preparation-coal transport-coal combustion to produce electric energy. Another example is that shown in figure 4.3: A raw product for canning is produced on a farm; presorting and cleaning take place on the farm, at a location central to a number of farms, or at the cannery; and the raw or presorted raw product is transported to the cannery.

The second type of link is a set of activities separated spatially for residuals handling, modification, and disposal. For example, a municipal sewage treatment plant generates sludge in the process of modifying liquid residuals that flow into the plant. Some moisture may be removed from the sludge by vacuum filters. The semisolid sludge may be dried further (with the resultant liquid being discharged) and then incinerated, or the sludge may be incinerated directly. Incinerated particulates may be generated, and these would have to be collected and disposed of as solids in a landfill. Alternatively, the sludge as generated might be pumped directly to drying beds or conveyed in tank trucks for disposal on agricultural land. Another alternative would be to dry the sludge sufficiently for disposal as a soil conditioner, with the water removed being pumped to and sprayed on irrigated pastures.

Status.   Status refers to whether the activity being analyzed is in existence or is only a proposal. The range of measures possible for modifying residuals generation and discharge is normally larger for a new plant than for an existing plant. Status also refers to the nature of the technology involved. The technology in a multiprocess, multiline plant often involves equipment of widely varying ages. Synchronization of equipment technology rarely exists for more than a few years after a plant is constructed.

Importance of On-site Effects.   Activities that generate residuals can be classified by the importance of the on-site effects of the activity. In general, on-site effects related to concentrated and line activities are unimportant and can be ignored. On the other hand, on-site effects of areal or dispersed activities—for example, agricultural, forest management, or grazing—are almost always significant and must be considered.

ANALYZING ACTIVITIES

Within the context of an environmental planning and decision-making process, as outlined in Chapter 2, an analysis would be made of each major residuals-generating activity or group of activities—manufacturing plant, block of residences, municipal incinerator, forest management project, or transport system. Such an analysis, which can be simple or complex, depending on the specific situation, would

1.   Indicate alternative combinations of factor inputs to produce outputs of products and services with specified characteristics;
2.   Delineate for each combination of factor inputs the types, quantities, and time patterns of residuals generated per unit of activity—for example, per ton of steel produced, or kilowatt hour of electric energy generated—and the associated on-site effects, as on agricultural or forest lands;

3. Identify the various physical measures available for reducing the on-site effects and the discharge of residuals from the activity into the environment;
4. Estimate the costs of these various physical measures, both in terms of the economic cost and the cost to the activity; and
5. Identify possible implementation incentive systems that would induce a given activity to reduce the discharges of specified residuals.

Collective residuals handling, modification, and disposal facilities—incinerators, resource recovery plants, and landfills—are themselves generators and dischargers of residuals and therefore must also be included as possible activities to be analyzed in any given context.

Approaches for Analyzing Activities

The approach to be used in analyzing activities in a given context depends on (1) the importance of the activity's effect on natural resources and environmental quality, (2) the data available, and (3) the other analytical resources available, such as time, personnel, computer facilities, and money.

Two approaches exist for analyzing activities: the so-called "black-box" approach and the engineering-economic-process model approach. Both require that some parameter be selected to indicate the activity level—tons of steel output produced, number of employees, vehicle kilometers traveled, or tons of wheat produced. Employee statistics usually are readily available for such an activity and are frequently used to indicate present and projected activity levels. For industrial, agricultural, and forest management activities, the use of physical units of input or output is desirable because they are related directly to residuals generation. Coefficients for residuals generation may then be expressed in the relevant unit for each activity. For example: mixed solid residuals generated by an industrial activity are expressed in kilograms per metric ton of product output; five-day biochemical oxygen demand (BOD_5) generated in residences is expressed in grams per day per inhabitant; hydrocarbons generated by automobiles are expressed in grams per vehicle kilometer traveled; and soil lost from a field of maize is expressed as inches of topsoil per ton of maize produced per hectare.

Black-Box Approach. In this approach, no attempt is made to delineate and analyze individual unit processes in an activity. A black-box model of a given activity represents a set of fixed coefficients for residuals generation per unit of output associated with some fixed set of inputs and with an assumed combination of production process and product output. The set of coefficients relates to some unspecified set of factor input prices, production or use technology, product characteristics, and government policies. Possible physical measures for modifying the residuals generated are limited to additions of unit processes—"end-of-pipe" treatment—and occasionally to changes in inputs of raw material, such as a change in the sulfur content of a fuel or in the type of pesticide applied. No analysis is made of possible alternative combinations of production processes, materials or energy recovery, by-product production, or changed product characteristics.

In the black-box approach, the coefficients are obtained either by adopting or modifying coefficients found in the literature or by deriving coefficients from specific data obtained on the activity—for example, by measurements at individual operations in the plant (Basta et al. 1978).

Engineering-Economic-Process Model Approach.   The engineering-economic-process model approach has two subcategories: One is characterized by an incremental search for a cost-effective solution; the second is a mathematical-programming approach. Both subcategories begin with the same data, which include information about materials and energy balances for each unit process under various combinations of alternative raw material inputs, alternative technologies of production, and alternative product characteristics. Each also takes account of alternative combinations of physical measures for modifying residuals, of materials or energy recovery, and of by-product production, including the costs of these alternative combinations of physical measures. The cost-effective search method then calculates the cost-effectiveness of each physical measure—for example, cost per unit of discharge reduction—and then incrementally combines physical measures until the desired degree of reduction in discharges and in on-site effects is achieved at least cost. The mathematical-programming approach sets up the analysis more formally, with an objective function to be maximized or minimized. Usually, the objective is to minimize the costs of producing a specified set of outputs and to achieve a specified level of reduction in discharges. Linear programming is the principal mathematical-programming approach used.

An example of a cost-effective search is described later, using the case of an integrated pulp and paper mill. Two excellent examples of the mathematical-programming approach are in Russell (1973) and Russell and Vaughan (1976).

Selecting Activities and Activity Categories for Analysis.   Two types of situations exist for the analysis of activities. One has a well-specified focus, such as a petroleum refinery or an irrigation project at a specific location.

The second situation, such as a metropolitan area, has a large number of discrete activities that generate and discharge residuals. Assuming that it is not possible to analyze each activity in detail, the problem then becomes one of delineating activity categories for the purpose of analysis. Most individual activities would be aggregated into a relatively few categories for analysis. Single large residuals generators, such as individual power plants, however, would be considered sufficiently important to be analyzed as separate activities.

Several important factors must be considered when delineating activity categories: (1) the relative importance and magnitude of residuals generated by each activity and the resulting effect on ambient environmental quality; (2) significant differences in residuals generation among activities; and (3) the availability of data and other analytical resources needed to specify different categories of residuals.

A good illustration of how activity categories are derived for a regional study is contained in an environmental-quality management study of the Ljubljana area of Yugoslavia, as reported in Basta, Lounsbury, and Bower (1978). The study area encompassed about 900 square kilometers, with a population of about 260,000 and a work force of about 105,000. The economic base was varied, with mixed industrial and commercial activities and tourism.

Seven major activity categories were delineated in the study: industrial, commercial, residential, institutional, transportation, power plant, and collective residuals handling and modification activities such as municipal incinerators and sewage treatment plants. No agricultural activity category was included because the contribution of agriculture to total residuals generation appeared to be relatively small.

Based on additional analyses of data, these major categories were subdivided into thirty subcategories (table 4.1). For example, using the Yugoslavian standard industrial classification, *industrial activities* were primarily subdivided by production processes, by product mixes, and to a limited extent by the types of raw materials used. These three variables plus prices of factor

Table 4.1. Activity Categories and Subcategories Used in Analysis for Environmental Quality Management in Ljubljana Area of Yugoslavia

Industrial activities	Institutional activities
Metal processing	Government
Electrical products	Research
Chemical	Hospitals
Building materials	Cultural institutions[a]
Pulp and paper	University facilities
Paper products	Schools other than university
Textile	
Food products	Transportation activities
Graphics	Vehicular travel[b]
All other	Services[c]
Residential activities	Power plant activities
Multi-flat	Moste plant
Single-flat	Siska plant
Commercial activities	Collective residuals handling
Restaurants	and modification activities
Hotels and motels	Municipal solid residuals
Retail stores	collection agency
Offices	Municipal sewerage agency
Wholesale stores and warehouses	Salvaging operations

[a]Refers to cinemas, playhouses, art galleries, museums, etc.
[b]Vehicular travel is further subdivided into seven road types in urban and nonurban areas.
[c]Refers to service stations, garages, repair shops.
Source: Basta, Lounsbury, and Bower (1978).

inputs are the major factors affecting residuals generation in industrial activities. *Residential activities* were subdivided into two categories, based on
the differences in space-heating technology and types of fuels, plumbing,
building designs, internal space per dwelling unit, ownership, and socioeconomic status. These factors cause substantial differences in both the
residuals generation per dwelling unit and per capita and in the alternative
physical measures available for reducing generation and discharge.

Implementation Incentive Systems.   Activity analysis as discussed in this
chapter is a part of the plan formulation step (no. 3) of the planning process
depicted in figure 2.2 in Chapter 2. In this step, it is not enough to find only
the least-cost set of physical measures that will reduce by a desired amount the
adverse effects of an activity on environmental quality. It is also necessary
that these measures actually be constructed and operated by the various relevant activities so that the desired reductions in adverse effects are achieved—
in a word, implementation.

Thus integral parts of activity analysis are (1) specifying sets of implementation incentives to be applied to particular activities so that discharges of
particular residuals are reduced (e.g., suspended sediment, SO_2), and (2)
imputing the likely response of the activity to the set of implementation
incentives. The basic elements of the implementation system are (1) directives
and other incentives; (2) inspection, measurement, and monitoring; and (3)
sanctions. Implementation incentives can be applied at many points in the
activity process—at the points of resource inputs, in the production process,
and at residuals discharge points. The incentives must always be related to
specific residuals, physical measures, and activities and must be tied to a
particular institutional arrangement, such as a local, provincial, or national
agency or set of agencies.

To predict the probable response of an activity to an incentive system, one
must estimate the costs to be borne by the activity. Sometimes these costs are
affected by direct and indirect subsidies, such as grants and tax concessions,
and by artificial prices of raw materials. To the extent that an activity behaves
to minimize its costs, its probable response to a given implementation incentive system can be imputed from the estimated costs. Although other, non-
economic factors may affect such responses, using the cost-to-the-activity
factor will usually give the best estimate of behavior in the absence of any
other information.

For a detailed discussion of implementation incentives, see Bower et al.
(1981).

SOME EXAMPLES OF ACTIVITY ANALYSIS

In this section, examples are given to show how three types of activities can
be analyzed: for *concentrated* activities, an integrated pulp and paper mill is
used; for *dispersed* activities, examples of agricultural and forest management

are used; and for *linked* activities, the example is a coal-electric system. In all of these activities, the residuals generated and discharged are a function of a large number of physical, economic, financial, and administrative factors—internal and external to the activity—that operate directly or indirectly to affect generation and discharge. Some of these factors are discussed in the following sections.

Analyzing Concentrated Activities

A manufacturing activity acts on one or more raw materials through physical, chemical, and biological transformations by using capital equipment and human and nonhuman energy inputs to produce one or more desired outputs. No production activity can be designed to convert inputs completely into desired outputs, however; some nonproduct outputs are inevitable. These consist of (1) nonproduct materials formed in production; (2) raw materials, such as catalysts, that are not transformed in production; and (3) unused or undesired energy outputs. Often it is economically necessary to recover and reuse substantial portions of the nonproduct materials and energy outputs.

The extent of materials recovery is a function of the relative costs of recovered materials versus new materials. The costs of materials recovery are a function of the technology of both the production activity and materials recovery. Trade-offs are possible between the designs of the production and the materials recovery systems. In effect, the plant optimizes the combination of the set of unit production processes plus the materials recovery system in the absence of outside constraints on residuals discharges. When constraints are imposed on residuals discharges, the total system of production process, materials and energy recovery, and residuals management measures is optimized. Thus, materials and energy recovery and by-product production are undertaken to the level at which the net annual cost of modifying nonproduct materials is minimized (fig. 4.4).

In analyzing a concentrated activity, the first step is to identify the unit processes that produce the desired outputs. Second, an analysis of materials and energy balances for each of the unit processes must be carried out, with explicit consideration of the cross-flows and recycling flows among the unit processes. This analysis will provide information about the quantity of material and energy residuals generated for a specific factor set, each set containing input prices, raw material qualities, production technologies, product mixes, product output characteristics, materials and energy recovery technologies, by-products produced, and constraints on residuals discharges.

Third, alternative sets of physical measures to reduce residuals generation and discharge from the unit processes must be analyzed. Then the cost of each alternative must be estimated and should include any additional costs of necessary changes in technology for a unit process, or from loss in output. The analysis should identify the alternative that minimizes costs to the activity of meeting the constraints on residuals discharge.

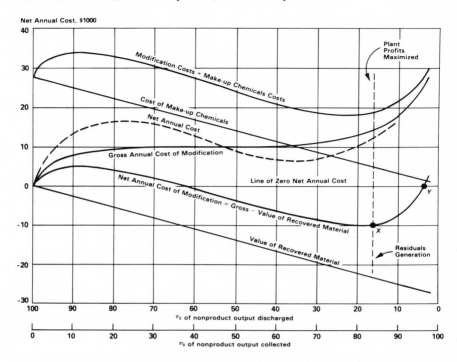

Figure 4.4 Hypothetical cost curve for modification of nonproduct material that can be used in-plant. (*Source:* Löf, Hearon, and Bower, 1973.)

An Integrated Pulp and Paper Mill.   The types and quantities of residuals generated when producing a specific type of paper are functions of the raw materials employed, the pulping process used, the extent of bleaching, and the characteristics desired in the paper product. All of these factors are interrelated; for example, the desired brightness of the paper product determines the amount of bleaching required for a given raw material and pulping process. Similarly, the desired strength of the paper limits the combinations of type of raw material and pulping process that can be used.

As an example, consider a 500-tons-per-day, integrated mill producing jumbo rolls of tissue paper. Table 4.2 shows the residuals generated when producing one ton of tissue paper from various combinations of raw material, pulping, bleaching, and product brightness. Not shown are by-products and the normally innocuous nonproduct outputs, water, carbon dioxide, and nitrogen. Included are the residuals generated during the burning of purchased fuel to generate steam and electric energy used in the production process.

The effects of the major variables are readily apparent; for example, pulping process—Ti 3 (magnefite) vs. Ti 4 (kraft); brightness—Ti 31 (GEB 25) vs. Ti 4 (GEB 80); and type of raw material—TI 34 (wastepaper) vs. Ti 31 (softwood). For these comparisons, respectively, the magnefite process generates no reduced sulfur compounds and less than half the particulates, but almost 2½ times the SO_2, compared with the sulfate process. Reducing the product brightness and, hence, the extent of bleaching needed from 80 to 25 GEB (the brightness of unbleached kraft) cuts SO_2 in half, dissolved solids by more than 85%, and BOD_5 by almost 80%. Using No. 1 Mixed wastepaper as the raw material, instead of softwood logs and kraft pulping, results in an SO_2 increase of almost 50%, no reduced sulfur compounds, essentially no particulates, some increase in dissolved solids, and many times more suspended inorganic solids. For other types of wastepaper, the quantities would be different.

Table 4.2. Residuals Generated in the Production of 1 Ton of Tissue Paper in a 500-Tons-per-Day Mill (lb./ton)

Residual	Production combination no. and pulp mix (brightness 80–82 GEB)		Production combination no. and pulp mix (brightness 25 GEB)	
	Ti 3 (100% Mg/CEH)	Ti 4 (100% K/CEHD)	Ti 31 (100% K/O)	Ti 34 (100% WPM/F)
Cl_2	1.1	1.2	0	0
ClO_2	0	0.6	0	0
SO_2	48.7/15.0	5.6/20.0	5.1/7.0	0/17.0
RS	0	25.5	23.2	0
Part.	27.7/0.8	57.5/1.0	52.4/0.3	0/0.8
DIS	108	263	22	21
DOS	190	244	41	63
SS-O	109	113	107	92
SS-I	4.1	4.5	4.1	202
BOD_5	92	147	31	36
So-I	77.9	82.0	73.7	13.8
So-O	63.1	0	0	12.8

Abbreviations		Residuals-Gaseous	
Ti	= tissue paper	Cl_2	= chlorine
Mg	= magnefite (sulfite) pulping	ClO_2	= chlorine dioxide
K	= kraft (sulfate) pulping	SO_2	= sulfur dioxide
WPM	= wastepaper, No. 1 Mixed (raw material)	RS	= hydrogen sulfide and organic sulfides
CEH, CEHD, etc.	= kraft or magnefite bleaching sequences, where C = chlorination; E = caustic extractions; H = hypochlorite bleaching; and D = chlorine dioxide bleaching	Part.	= particulates
		Residuals-Liquid	
		DIS	= dissolved inorganic solids
		DOS	= dissolved organic solids
		SS-I	= suspended inorganic solids
0	= no bleaching	SS-O	= suspended organic solids
F	= wastepaper processing—defibering	BOD_5	= 5-day biochemical oxygen demand
		Residuals-Solid	
GEB	= General Electric brightness	So-I	= inorganic solids
		So-O	= organic solids

Source: Adapted from Bower (1975).

The data in table 4.2 are based on materials, energy, and heat balances for each of the steps in the production processes involved and represent the sums of all of the individual residuals generated, after accounting for economic degrees of recirculation of water and heat and recovery of materials. These data represent the results of the first two steps in analyzing the concentrated activities specified above.

Suppose government agencies require that residuals discharges from the mill into both the air and the adjacent body of water be reduced. One could use the engineering-economic-process model and cost-effective increment approach discussed earlier to analyze alternative ways to reduce discharges. This would require analysis of the alternative physical measures, including their costs, associated with each residual of interest and each of the production process streams containing that residual. This is illustrated for particulate generation in an integrated kraft mill producing 500 tons per day of bleached tissue paper, labeled as Ti 4, in table 4.2.

Table 4.3 shows the six significant sources of particulate generation for the integrated kraft paper mill. Most of the particulates normally recovered from the lime kiln stack and recovery furnace stack are assumed to be recycled to the chemical system; thus, the quantity shown in the table is in excess of the economically recoverable amount.

Using the recovery furnace stack as an example, figure 4.5 shows the net annual cost for various levels of modification of the particulates formed in the flue gases from the recovery furnace. The points shown above the curve represent alternative measures for the same level of particulate modification, but with higher costs. Up to the level designated by X, particulate modification represents economic materials recovery—that is, measures that would be undertaken in the absence of effluent controls because of the value of the recovered chemicals. For higher levels of modification, increased costs are only partially offset by benefits from the value of recovered materials, and the net-cost curve rises sharply. In this example, the technology involves end-of-

Table 4.3. Main Sources of Particulate Generation in an Integrated Kraft Paper Mill

Source	Particulates generated (lb./ton of paper)
Recovery furnace stack	5.0
Lime kiln stack	11.7
Combination bark-fuel boiler stack	27.6
Slaker vent	0.7[a]
Smelt dissolving tank vent	1.2
Fuel-fired boiler stack	1.0
Total	47.2

[a] Estimated.
Source: Löf, Hearon, and Bower (1973).

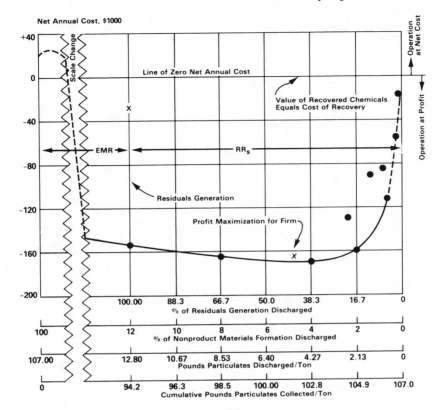

Figure 4.5 Net annual cost of particulate modification from a recovery furnace: integrated Kraft mill producing 500 tons per day of tissue paper. (*Source:* Löf, Hearon, and Bower, 1973.)

pipe measures, such as electrostatic precipitators and wet scrubbers. Similar relationships were developed for each of the particulate streams indicated in table 4.3. These were combined in cost-effective increments to develop the least-cost system for various degrees of particulate modification (table 4.4).

Similar analyses were made for the various types of liquid residual streams listed in table 4.2. Two important differences between the gaseous and liquid residuals are (1) that few alternatives for modifying liquid residuals yield any monetary returns to the activity, and (2) unlike the case of gaseous residuals, the least-cost measures for modifying liquid residuals often involve combining various streams of the same residual for simultaneous modification.

Often, residuals management analysis is focused on the cost implications of achieving different degrees of discharge reduction for all relevant residuals for the entire plant. To illustrate this approach to the analysis, three sets of increasingly stringent discharge standards for the five principal residuals are

Table 4.4. Net Annual Cost of Particulate Modification in an Integrated Kraft Paper Mill Producing 500 Tons per Day of Bleached Tissue Paper

	No modification		Low modification		Medium modification		High modification	
	Particulates (lb./ton)	Annual net costs ($)	Particulates (lb./ton)	Annual net costs ($)	Particulates (lb./ton)	Annual net costs ($)	Particulates (lb./ton)	Annual net costs ($)
Particulate discharge	47.2		30		8		4	
Particulate removal								
Bark boiler stack	0	0	17.2	8,940	25.9	14,300	26.0	19,500
Lime kiln stack	0	0	0	0	10.3	17,000	11.6	32,900
Recovery furnace stack	0	0	0	0	2.5	5,000	3.9	32,400
Lime slaker vent	0	0	0	0	0.5	750	0.6	2,390
Smelt tank vent	0	0	0	0	0	0	1.0	10,560
Fuel boiler stack	0	0	0	0	0	0	0	0
Total removal	0	0	17.2	8,940	39.2	37,050	43.2	97,750
Cost of solids disposal		0		3,150		4,540		4,560
Cost of liquid residual disposal		0		0		0		0
Total net annual cost of particulate control		0		12,090		41,590		102,310

Notes:
1. Costs are in 1970 dollars and are based on estimates of operating labor, maintenance labor and supplies, power and material requirements, and a 12.5 percent annual charge on estimated capital investment, and are credited with chemical recoveries at typical market prices. Operation 350 days per year was assumed.
2. The gas streams to be treated and the extent of particulate removal from a stream were selected so as to obtain the lowest cost of removing the required quantity of particulates, regardless of particulate composition.
3. Cost of solids disposal includes only the solids resulting from removal of particulates not recycled to the process, and excludes disposal costs for other solid residuals. It is based on a nominal $2 per ton hauling and landfill cost.
4. None of the particulate removal processes used results in generation of a liquid residual.
Source: Löf, Hearon, and Bower (1973).

presented in table 4.5. These standards are expressed in terms of the discharges permitted per ton of output, a format that ignores the size of a plant and, hence, implicitly ignores the assimilative capacity of the ambient environment. This analysis approach represents a commonly adopted one, however.

The residuals management costs to meet levels I, II, and III of table 4.5 are shown in table 4.6 for both bleached and unbleached tissue paper, in terms of dollars per ton. These levels correspond to the low, medium, and high residuals modification levels shown for particulates in table 4.4. The much higher costs of modification of liquid residuals than for gaseous residuals for production of bleached tissue paper reflect the substantial value of materials recovered from gaseous residuals streams; comparable alternatives do not exist for the liquid residuals streams. Also, the effect of changing one product specification—from bleached to unbleached tissue paper—is very significant; total residuals management costs for unbleached tissue paper are only about 15, 24, and 21%, respectively, of those for bleached tissue paper at levels I, II, and III.

The outputs of the analysis are (1) costs for different degrees of discharge reduction from the mill for each residual and (2) the quantities of all residuals discharged for each level of discharge. These quantities become the inputs to the models for analyzing effects on natural systems and receptors, which are discussed in Chapter 5.

The Difficulties of Analyzing Concentrated Activities. Analyzing concentrated activities is not as straightforward as the preceding discussion might imply. Major difficulties exist, especially concerning the availability of data and their interpretation.

First, data typically are available for only some of the relevant residuals because few plants regularly measure all of the major residuals. Furthermore, most of the data published deal with residuals discharges that are the result of

Table 4.5. Specification of Increasingly Stringent Residuals Discharge Standards in an Integrated Kraft Paper Mill Producing 500 Tons per Day of Tissue Paper (lb./ton)

Residual	Level 0	Discharge standards (per ton of output)		
		I	II	III
SO_2	No control[a]	50	35	20
Particulates	No control	30	8	4
Reduced sulfur compounds	No control	10	2	0.5
Suspended solids	No control	50	20	10
BOD_5	No control	60	35	20

Note: Standards apply to total mill operation (i.e., from all sources).
[a]No restrictions on discharges; reflects basic production costs.
Source: Löf, Hearon, and Bower (1973).

Table 4.6. **Net Residuals Management Costs per Ton of Output, Integrated Kraft Paper Mill Producing 500 Tons per Day of Tissue Paper**

Production combination	Level of discharge standards		
	I	II	III
Ti 4: Bleached tissue paper	$/ton		
Gaseous residuals modification	0.16	0.59	1.66
Liquid residuals modification	3.07	4.09	6.76
Solid residuals disposal	0.38	0.38	0.38
Total	3.61	5.06	8.80
Ti 31: Unbleached tissue paper			
Gaseous residuals modification	0.12	0.46	0.83
Liquid residuals modification	0.10	0.40	0.72
Solid residuals disposal	0.33	0.33	0.33
Total	0.55	1.19	1.88

Notes:
1. Costs are in 1970 dollars and are based on estimates of operating labor, maintenance labor and supplies, power and material requirements, and a 12.5 percent annual charge on estimated capital investment, and are credited with chemical recoveries at typical market prices. Operation 350 days per year was assumed.
2. The costs of any secondary solid residuals generated in liquid and gaseous residuals modification (sludge) are included in the liquid and gaseous residuals modification costs.
Source: Löf, Hearon, and Bower (1973).

partial modification of the residuals originally generated by the production process. Such data may preclude any analysis of the effects on residuals generation of the variables discussed earlier in this section. Even when data on residuals generation are available, they are rarely related to the causal variables; instead, they are given in terms of rates per overall production—such as pounds of BOD_5 per ton of paper produced in total by the integrated paper mill, or pounds of BOD_5 per barrel of crude petroleum input to a petroleum refinery—rather than as rates per unit processes.

Second, an adequate industry study requires the calculation of almost all materials, electric energy, and heat balances for the production processes involved. Such balances are rarely available, even in unpublished form. This means that such calculations will have to be made from very sketchy data. Nonetheless, determining all of the residuals associated with producing a given product requires computing the amount of energy generated within the plant, as well as the amounts of materials and energy used in modifying residuals in response to outside constraints on effluents.

Third, suitable data on capital and operating costs of factor inputs, process units, and residuals modification measures are often lacking. For example, depending on the bookkeeping practice, wood products residues obtained from another company mill for use as input in paper production at the home mill may be priced at the going market price for such material, at zero cost, or at some intermediate price. Also, many costs are site specific, or are significantly affected by such factors as topography, access to water, energy or fuel costs, and availability of raw materials. For example, for a single company producing the same product by the same process in two different paper mills, the ratio of raw wood costs of the two mills can be as much as two to one. Usually, economies of scale and, often, discontinuous cost relationships exist.

A fourth difficulty is the short-run variability in residuals generation. Such variations are rarely reflected in published data on residuals generation and discharge. A given production process—such as the manufacture of paper—normally is designed to produce a range of types of outputs (i.e., grades of paper), with one particular grade likely to be dominant in proportion to total output. Maximum production efficiency is achieved when producing this grade. But once production has begun, several variables, such as the quality of incoming logs and chips, the sharpness of the saws in the wood preparation operation, and the demand for different product outputs, affect residuals generation from day to day and from season to season. Pressure for increased daily output can result in using certain components of the production process, such as digesters, beyond design capacity, with consequent increases in rates of residuals generation. Variations of almost two to one in rates of generation of BOD residuals have been recorded within a single month for a given linerboard mill. In addition, there may be variations because of startups, breakdowns, or accidental spills.

Fifth, decisions at the activity level take place in a dynamic context, with frequent changes in factor prices, technology, product mix, product specifications, and social tastes. Such changes must be taken into account to avoid large inaccuracies in estimates of residuals generation and discharge.

Finally, until relatively recently, use of the environment for the disposal of residuals was free. Consequently, a rational plant manager would use as much of that costless factor input as possible in producing the good or service. Because the assimilative capacity of the relevant environment is essentially fixed, however, the environmental resource will become more scarce in the future as population and economic activity increase. The price for the use of that resource will increase just as for any increasingly scarce resource. This is true no matter how the price is reflected, whether in input constraints, in product restrictions, or by effluent standards or charges.

Analyzing Dispersed Activities: Agricultural Activities

Dispersed activities are those that take place over extensive areas and that generate and discharge residuals from these areas, such as soil surfaces, rather than from stacks or pipes. Conceptually, however, the approach to analyzing a dispersed activity is the same as that for analyzing a concentrated activity.

Background.   Agricultural activities include all those that directly produce food and fiber; accordingly, operations that do not take place on the farm, such as packaging or processing of agricultural products before they go to markets, are excluded from the definition.

Three types of agricultural production activities can be delineated: crop production, animal raising (including dairy farming), and combined operations. Crop production activities can be subdivided further as irrigated and nonirrigated cropping. Animal raising can be subdivided into range, range-feedlot combinations, range-irrigated hay, and pasture-feedlot combinations. Factor inputs—including natural inputs such as land, precipitation, and sunlight—are transformed through production processes into desired product outputs and nonproduct outputs, and into changes in the land itself; for example, changes in soil characteristics. Usually, the nonproduct outputs are discharged directly into the environment as residuals. Figure 4.6 depicts these processes.

In agricultural activities other than shifting agriculture, the same area of land is used again and again as an input to agricultural production processes. Thus, the condition of the land after its use in one production process over a given time period affects the amount of land and other factor inputs, such as fertilizers and pesticides, that will be used in subsequent production. For example, when land has been overgrazed, the number of animals per unit area must be decreased if forage production per unit area is to be maintained. When land is used for crops, the extent to which nitrogen, phosphorus, and moisture have been depleted determines the amount of fertilizer and water inputs required for the next cropping operation.

A number of important factors are involved in agricultural production. A specified level of product output (e.g., kilograms of wheat per hectare) can be produced by many possible combinations of factors, including natural inputs, other factor inputs, and unit processes. Natural inputs differ from region to region and can be varied, more or less, within a region by undertaking operations at different times of year. Each combination of factor inputs, unit processes, and product outputs produces an accompanying set of nonproduct and residuals outputs and effects on the land used.

Factors Affecting Residuals Generation and Discharge.

Production of Nonirrigated Crops.   The time patterns of generation and discharge of residuals from the production of nonirrigated crops are functions of many variables: precipitation distributions and wind velocities and directions; soil type; slope; exposure; crop type and rotation pattern; plowing and tillage methods, including disposition of residues, and technology; methods of pest and disease management; types, frequency, and methods of fertilizer application; and the on-site physical measures installed to reduce discharges (e.g., terraces, grassed waterways, and debris basins). Because the frequency and duration of precipitation and wind are basically indeterminate (stochastic) phenomena, the time patterns of generation and discharge of liquid and gaseous residuals are likely to be predominantly stochastic.

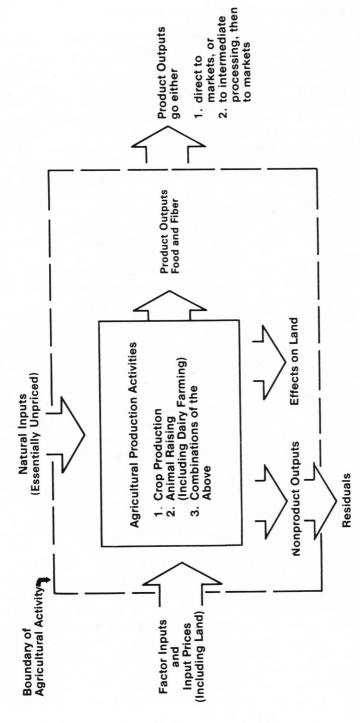

Figure 4.6 Generalized diagram of agricultural activities.

Production of Irrigated Crops. The time patterns of generation and discharge of residuals from the production of irrigated crops are functions of the same variables as those affecting the production of nonirrigated crops, plus several other factors: method, frequency, and magnitude of irrigation; leaching requirement; quality of irrigation water; method of drainage; and extent of on-site treatment of drainage water. The leaching requirement is the amount of water that must be leached through the root zone in order to maintain a salt balance in this zone that does not reduce crop yield. The time, location, and magnitude of residuals discharges during the irrigation season can be approximated from the amount, timing, and location of water applications to the land. Residuals discharges from irrigated cropland are composed of the same constituents present in residuals discharges from nonirrigated cropland. The liquid residual of greatest concern from irrigated cropland, however, is total dissolved solids, loosely referred to as *salinity*. Effluents from irrigation operations are returned to surface waters, often to be reused for irrigation downstream. Each successive irrigation operation contributes an additional increment of salt to the return flow, with a consequent increase in concentration of total dissolved solids in surface waters and a decrease in their suitability for further irrigation use.

Production of Nonirrigated and Irrigated Crops. Several factors common to the production of both nonirrigated and irrigated crops are significant in the generation of residuals. These are (1) fertilizer practices, (2) pesticide practices, and (3) trade-offs among factor inputs.

Fertilizer practices relate to the types, methods, amounts, and timing of fertilizer applications to crop-producing land. Fertilizers are used to supplement the nutrients available in the soil to improve crop yields and quality. Nutrients—predominantly nitrogen (N), phosphorus (P), and potassium (K) compounds—in runoff from agricultural lands can have significant effects on ambient water quality, particularly in eutrophication. When nutrients from cropland enter receiving waters, they are either attached to suspended soil particles in runoff (e.g., rock phosphate) or are in solution in runoff (e.g., organic nitrogen). The amount of nutrient residuals discharged in runoff is directly related to the amount of nutrients not absorbed by crops and, thus, available for transport by the runoff. Consequently, the amount of nutrient residuals is dependent to a large degree on the fertilizer practices used.

Fertilizers applied to cropland can also affect air quality in two ways. First, in the process of application, fertilizers can enter the air as suspended particles, or they may return to the air from fields that have been overfertilized. Second, some chemical compounds, such as ammonia, can enter the air as a result of volatilization. This is especially true when animal manures are used.

Pesticide residuals generally enter receiving waters and the atmosphere by the same pathways as fertilizers. The type of pesticide, however, is a particularly important factor that influences the extent of adverse environmental effects of discharges. Pesticides with low toxicity and persistence tend not to build up through food chains, in contrast to those with strong toxicity and persistence. Some nonpersistent pesticides, however, such as organophosphates, can have acute effects on some nontarget species. Pesticides also vary in their solubility and the extent to which they attach to soil particles. Consequently, different pesticides used on the same agricultural area will have different potentials for residuals discharges.

Trade-offs among Factor Inputs. A given output from a crop production activity can be produced by many different combinations of factor inputs. Each combination is likely to have different effects on natural systems as well as different demands for water, fuel, and electric energy. Therefore, information on the types of trade-offs among possible inputs is important to the analyst.

One example of a trade-off is a shift in the proportion of tillage to herbicide inputs. Conventional tillage, with four to eight cultivations per year for a given crop, can be combined with a relatively low use of herbicides. (Cultivation and herbicides are the two principal ways to reduce weed growth.) As the frequency of cultivation is reduced, the magnitude of gross soil erosion substantially decreases, at the same time reducing both on-site and off-site effects from soil loss and suspended sediment, respectively. But to limit weed growth as the amount of cultivation is decreased, the amount of herbicide applied must be increased. Although soil erosion now has been reduced, the discharge of herbicides into the environment has been increased.

Labor inputs also can be substituted for other inputs in crop production to decrease adverse on-site and off-site effects. For example, using more labor to apply water, fertilizer, and pesticides can achieve more efficient applications, resulting in less need for these inputs and reduced residuals generation and discharge.

Analyzing Dispersed Activities: Forest Management

Forest management involves a time pattern and a mix of management inputs to produce an output mix of goods and services from a given forest area. The spectrum of tasks ranges from research and planting and fertilizing to harvesting and slash disposal. The planning task is to determine the optimal mix of outputs from the area as a whole as well as from each of the subareas, which differ in their resources, production potentials, and responses to management practices. The planning time horizon is likely to be a function of rotation cycles of the principal wood species, which are in turn a function of economic factors as well as factors affecting physical growth.

Typical outputs from a forest management area are wood products, outdoor recreation, water resources, wildlife, forage for livestock, minerals, and residuals (fig. 4.7). The way in which the wood is produced—for example, logging, road design and construction, harvesting methods, and slash disposal—generally affects all other outputs. Any output can be produced by

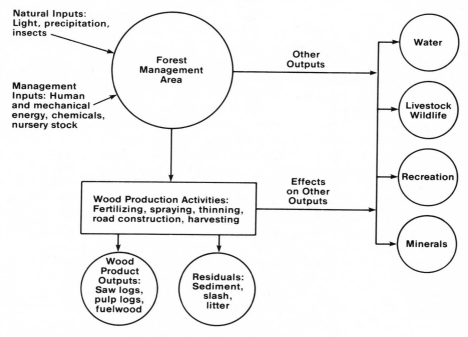

Figure 4.7 Typical outputs from a forest management area.

several different combinations of inputs, and each combination has different implications for on-site and off-site effects.

In developing a management plan for a management unit (working circle) or for an entire forest, various mixes of outputs are selected, and the alternative management practices needed to produce this level of each output are specified. One such set of management practices with their associated outputs, arranged by management category, is shown in table 4.7.

Because of these multiple outputs and because of the interactions among them in the forest area, functional relationships must be developed (1) between management practices and each specific output, such as between the practice of thinning and pruning and wood growth, or between predator control and effects on wildlife; (2) between management practices and residuals generation and discharge; (3) among management practices, outputs, and the resulting state of the forest area; and (4) between different outputs, such as trade-offs between timber production and recreation use, water yield, and hunting, respectively, and stock and wildlife grazing.

An example of the relationship between timber output and recreation use is shown in figure 4.8. As the intensity of recreation use increases, the annual timber harvest and its value will probably decrease (fig. 4.8, a and b), although the total value of the combined outputs will probably increase up to

Table 4.7. Outputs Produced on a Forest Management Project Area by Management Category with a Given Set of Management Practices

Management categories and outputs	Output units	Current status	Outputs expected to change to—	Amount of change
Watershed management: Stream flow	Inches per year	3.4	7.4	+4
Timber management: Timber growth	Cubic feet per acre per year	33.5	18.3[a] / 24.8[b]	−15.2[a] / −8.7[b]
Forest management—pathology: Mistletoe incidence	Percentage of total trees	8.3	4.1	−4.2
Range management: Herbage production	Pounds per acre per year	160	380	+220
Wildlife management: Mast-producing trees	Number per acre residual	3.8	3.4	−0.4
Percentage of area stocked	5 trees per acre, at a 25 square-foot basal area level	7.0	6.2	−0.8
Recreation management: Stocking of trees 18 inches dbh and larger	Percentage of area with 10 or more trees per acre	47	16	−31
Cost of management change: Budget cost	Dollars: With a sawtimber market / With an additional pulpwood market	0 / 0	10,761 / 5,530	+10,761 / +5,530
Value of timber harvested: Immediate harvest returns	Dollars: With a sawtimber market / With an additional pulpwood market	0 / 0	2,957 / 3,646	+2,957 / +3,646

[a] Immediately.
[b] In five years.
Source: Smith (1961).

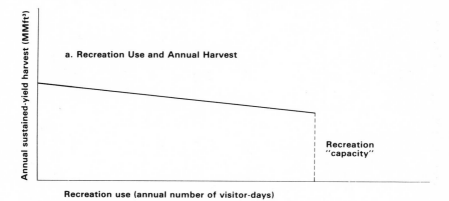

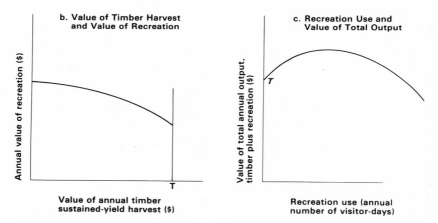

Figure 4.8 Relationship between timber output and recreation use. (*Sources:* 4.8a, Teeguarden and Werner, 1968; 4.8b and c, Amidon and Gould, 1962.)

some level of recreation use (fig. 4.8c) (Teeguarden and Werner 1968, Amidon and Gould 1962).

Another example is the relationship between timber production and hunting. The return on investment in high-yield forestry is dependent on the control of game and of hunters. Game populations affect forest regeneration rates; hunters affect fire hazard and regeneration rates. Effective forest management requires that the range of possible management activities be delineated. These would include revegetation measures, changes in the mix of vegetation by introducing new plant species, thinning and pruning, construction of facilities, maintenance of trails to reduce erosion, forest-user education programs, and various systems for rationing forest use. Associated with each management technique are its costs to the management agency and its impacts—on-site effects on the natural system, effects on users, and off-site effects.

Liquid residuals from forest management activities come primarily from runoff due to precipitation. Residuals in the runoff include sediments, pesticides, and nutrients. Solid residuals may also be generated as a result of mass wasting initiated by logging.

Factors Affecting Residuals Generation and Discharge from Forest Management Activities. As with agricultural activities, many factors affect the time pattern, type, and magnitude of a given residual generated by and discharged from forest management activities. These factors, which also affect the types and magnitudes of products and services produced, include soil type; elevation; exposure; parent material; precipitation and wind; vegetative cover; extent of disease, pest, and rodent control; extent of fertilization; design, construction, and maintenance of roads and trails, including siting and drainage; degree of cutting (e.g., selective cutting or clear cutting); technology of harvesting; method of slash control; proportion of trees removed from forest; and extent of replanting. As examples, the on-site and off-site effects of two of these factors, degree of cutting and harvesting method and technology, are discussed below.

Degree of Cutting. The intensity of cutting in any given area may affect water yield and is likely to affect the availability of forage and browse. In turn, water yield is a function of the method of cutting, exposure, elevation, location in relation to stream bottoms or side slopes, and time. Water yield is time-dependent because of forest growth characteristics. Figures 4.9 and 4.10 show the effect of degree of cutting on water yield in two actual cases of temperate forests.

Harvesting: Road Construction and Harvesting Practices. Accessibility of the site is essential for the harvesting of trees. Both the design of the transport network and the logging practices themselves can substantially affect the amount of erosion from the forest land. The road network should be designed and constructed with reference to topography, soils, and parent material, but often is not. Systematic planning of road patterns can often reduce by 25 to 30% the area of road surface needed per kilometer of watershed and can also reduce the average gradient of roads with consequent savings in construction and maintenance costs.

Similarly, harvesting methods are a major factor in soil erosion and consequent residuals generation. Figure 4.11 shows the percentage of different levels of soil disturbance for each of four types of logging methods. For example, only about 57% of high-lead logged areas were undisturbed, compared with 78% of balloon-logged areas. Likewise, only 16% of the area was slightly disturbed from balloon logging compared with 21 to 26% for tractor,

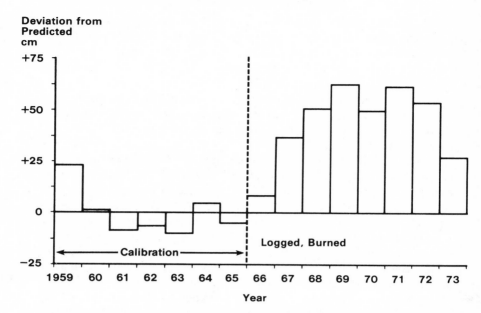

Figure 4.9 Increases in annual water yield after 82% clear-cut logging in Needle Branch Watershed, Alsea watershed study, western Oregon, United States. (*Source:* Harr, 1976.)

high-lead, and skyline logging. And only a small percentage of the total logged area was compacted under balloon logging, in contrast to about 25% with tractor logging (Dyrness 1972).

The proportion of soil exposed after the logging operations is another indicator of impact. The study cited in the previous paragraph reported that these proportions were 14% for high-lead, 12% for skyline, and 6% for balloon logging. Because much surface erosion occurs in areas of bare soil, balloon logging reduces the likelihood of large-scale erosion.

The erodibility of a forest soil is a function of rock type, vegetative cover type, elevation, aspect or exposure, and slope. For example, an analysis of 208 soil samples in terms of these five variables showed that granodioritic soils at high-elevation forest sites are potentially 2 to 2½ times more erodible than the same soils on similar sites at low elevations (Willin 1965). Above 6,500 feet, soil-forming processes produce soils that are potentially extremely erodible. Under such conditions, even minor disturbances of the soil can result in a large amount of erosion.

Two mechanisms primarily are involved in the generation of residuals in forest management activities: surface soil erosion and mass soil erosion. On steep forest lands, the latter mechanism generates more material for subsequent transport beyond the boundary of the area than does surface erosion.

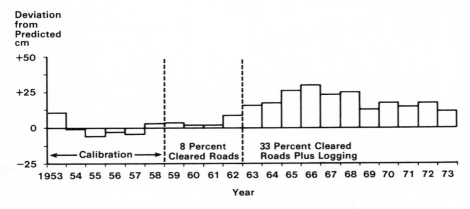

Figure 4.10 Increases in annual water yield after road-building and patch-cut logging in watershed 3, H. J. Andrews Experimental Forest, western Oregon, United States. (*Source:* Harr, 1976.)

Mass soil erosion is a normal geomorphologic process—a function of slope, climate, soil type, and parent material. Such erosion occurs when the integral strength of a soil is exceeded. Roads often undercut upslope soils, may alter the natural drainage, and expose previously buried material to weathering. This may change the strength of the slope. As a result, landslides, at least on steep lands, are associated with roads.

For example, during a two-year period, 72% of the landslides in the H. J. Andrews Experimental Forest, in western Oregon, United States, were associated with roads, even though the roads accounted for only 1.8% of the area of the forest (Dyrness 1967). Also, a single road slide in a watershed in the same region produced 40% of the total sediment load for the year.

Harvesting of trees from an area also can have major impacts on erosion, because a significant part of the strength of a soil mass comes from the anchoring effect of tree roots. As the roots gradually decay after a tree is cut, the susceptibility of the soil to landslides increases.

Summary of a Forest Management Project.   For illustrative purposes, assume that the primary objective of a forest management project is wood production. The possible alternative management practices for wood production are shown in table 4.8. From these alternative practices, two forest management programs—one *intensive* and the other *extensive*—are selected for analysis. The time streams of returns and costs for the two programs are shown for the fifty-year management period in table 4.9. For the extensive forest management program, it is assumed that current trends in management practices will continue throughout the planning period. With extensive management, there would be (1) a slow increase in fire protection and a corresponding reduction in fire losses, (2) a slow decrease in the extent of grazing

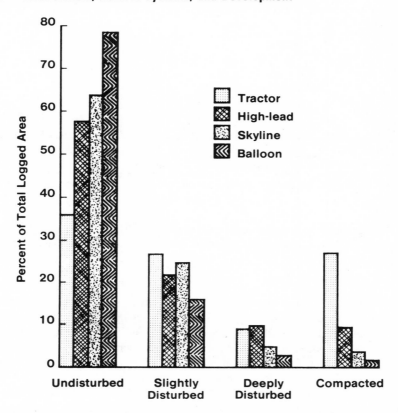

Figure 4.11 Soil surface conditions following tractor, high-lead, skyline, and balloon logging in the western Cascades, Oregon, United States. (*Source*: Dyrness, 1972.)

on forest lands, (3) a slow recovery by natural regeneration and growth of the cutover areas, (4) minimal thinning and culling of forests, and (5) no restocking. The annual costs of extensive management would average about $100,000 throughout the period. The annual harvest would increase slightly from 46 million board feet (MMBF) in the first decade to 50 MMBF in the last decade of the fifty-year management period.

With intensive forest management, the following would occur: expanded scope and intensity of fire protection; culling and thinning of the forest as necessary to encourage the most productive age distribution of trees; restocking where necessary; and elimination of grazing, except where it may be compatible with wood production. As a result, the harvest would increase to 70 MMBF in the last decade of the fifty-year period. Costs would be substantially higher, however, so the net returns would be less than for the extensive management alternative.

Table 4.8. Possible Forest Management Practices in Relation to Wood Production

Silvicultural practices

Degree of thinning	Pruning	Fire protection	Replanting or reseeding	Erosion control
None	None	Extensive	None (natural regeneration)	None
Light	Once	Intensive	Low density	Slopes of logging roads limited
Heavy	Optimum (e.g., to achieve desired length of clean log)		Medium density	Slopes of logging roads limited and drainage installed
			High density	

Harvesting practices

Logging method	Cutting pattern	Slash disposal
A-frame truck	Selective	None
Dozer and skidder	Patch	Pile
Highline	Strip	Pile and control burn
Alpine	Clear cut	
Grapple yarding		
Balloon/helicopter		

Intensity of practice

—Increasing intensity→

—Increasing intensity→

Table 4.9. Time Streams of Returns and Costs for Two Forest Management Programs in the Meramec Basin, Missouri, United States

	Intensive management					Extensive management				
Years	Annual harvest (MMBF)	Stumpage value ($/MBF)	Value of output (10³$)	Forest management costs (10³$)	Annual net returns (10³$)	Annual harvest (MMBF)	Stumpage value ($/MBF)	Value of output (10³$)	Forest management costs (10³$)	Annual net returns (10³$)
1–10	37	25	925	2,200	−1,275	46	25	1,150	900	250
11–20	43	25	1,075	2,600	−1,525	47	25	1,175	900	275
21–30	29	50	1,450	1,750	−300	48	50	2,400	900	1,500
31–40	43	75	3,225	2,600	+625	49	75	3,675	900	2,775
41–50	70	100	7,000	4,200[a]	+2,800	50	100	5,000	900	4,100

Note: MMBF = million board feet; MBF = thousand board feet.
Source: Smith (1961).
[a] Estimated for the 70 MMBF harvest level by Richard C. Smith. Costs in other decades are assumed to be directly proportional to the magnitude of the annual harvest.

Having defined the production costs and the associated net returns, the next steps are (1) to estimate the on-site and off-site effects of each set of practices, as described in Chapter 5; (2) to value those effects as described in Chapters 6 and 7; (3) to incorporate those values with the production costs to determine overall project costs and benefits; and (4) to specify possible modifications in management practices to reduce on-site and off-site effects in order to find the combination of management practices, product output, and values of on-site and off-site effects that maximizes net returns.

Analyzing Linked Activities

The quality of the raw material inputs to an activity has a significant effect on the quantities of residuals generated by an activity that produces a product and, hence, on off-site environmental quality. One way to account for this effect is to expand the boundaries of analysis to include the prior activities that determine the quality of the raw material input. This backward link allows the analyst to consider many more alternatives for reducing adverse effects on natural systems and on environmental quality. A coal-electric energy system is used to illustrate the analysis of spatially separate but linked activities.

Instead of restricting the analysis to the power plant activity, as has traditionally been done, all activities from mining the coal through delivering the energy at the load-centers are included. The four principal elements of this system, as shown in figure 4.12, are coal mining, coal preparation, coal or energy transport, and energy generation through coal combustion. Coal preparation generally takes place at or very near the mine. Occasionally, an additional coal preparation step may be included at the power plant. Always there will be coal storage at the power plant.

The analysis takes the following form: With estimated energy demand at the load-center as given, determine the minimum-cost system of coal mining, processing, transport, and combustion; electric energy transport; and residuals handling activities that will meet specified environmental quality standards for all three media—air, water, land—throughout the system.

Trade-offs are possible among raw coal quality, degree of coal preparation, transport of coal or energy, and combustion and residuals handling technology at the mine, preparation plant, and power plant. For example, the objective may be to reduce the ambient concentration of sulfur dioxide in the specified region. Given this objective, several combinations of alternatives among the many elements of the system can be utilized, such as high- or low-sulfur coal, different levels of coal preparation, various methods of coal or energy transport, and various measures for removal of sulfur dioxide in the stack of the power plant. Thus, at least a partial alternative to the removal of residuals present in the stack gas is to increase the degree of coal preparation to remove sulfur and ash. The coal preparation process itself, however, produces residuals that must be handled in a satisfactory fashion. Furthermore,

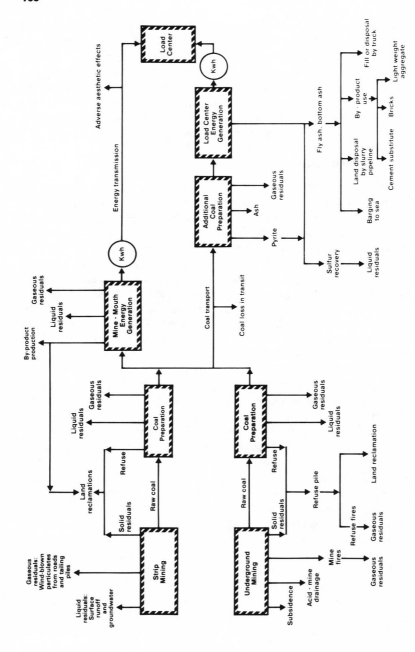

Figure 4.12 Linked activity analysis of coal-electric energy system. (*Source:* Adapted from Bower, 1975.)

because preparation of coal inevitably involves some loss of heat value in each ton of raw coal, additional coal will have to be mined to provide the equivalent heat input to the power plant. This additional coal will cause additional problems for residuals management. Nevertheless, by expanding the scope of the system being analyzed, the possibility of finding a more cost-effective set of measures for handling residuals is likely to be increased.

Figure 4.12 also shows the various residuals streams generated from each element of the system. The principal residuals generated in the coal-electric energy system are

1. Acid mine drainage from underground mining;
2. Overburden from strip mining;
3. Suspended solids in the wash water of the coal preparation plant;
4. Particulates from air-flow cleaners and thermal driers at coal preparation plants;
5. Particulates in power plant gaseous emissions;
6. Sulfur oxides in power plant gaseous emissions;
7. Oxides of nitrogen in power plant gaseous emissions; and
8. Water-borne heat from the power plant.

Blowdown from the water circuit of a recirculating wet-cooling tower can also be a major problem because of high concentrations of dissolved solids. Additional energy is also required throughout the system for residuals collection, handling, and disposal. Examples include energy for irrigation to reclaim strip-mined land; coal preparation at the power plant; electrostatic precipitators or wet scrubbers to reduce particulate and SO_2 discharges at the power plant; cooling towers to reduce heat discharges at the power plant; and ultimate disposal of various sludges and solid residuals from coal preparation at the power plant.

A number of strategies exist for reducing discharges of residuals to the three environmental media. Some of these are shown in table 4.10, along with their impacts on each of the elements of the coal-electric energy system and on the related residuals streams. The interrelationships among the residuals and the strategies are also delineated. For example, increasing the degree of coal preparation to remove some portion of the ash and sulfur from the power-plant fuel reduces the residuals generated by combustion but increases the residuals generated in coal mining (because more hydrocarbons are discarded, thereby requiring more coal to be mined for the same energy output). Modifying power-plant flue gas and using cooling towers to reduce thermal discharges into waterways are both energy-intensive measures. They require more coal to produce an equivalent net energy output and, hence, generate more residuals in coal mining and preparation.

A strategy for reducing the discharge of one residual may add to the costs of handling another residual or may generate additional residuals that cause other environmental quality problems. For example, removing sulfur in power-

Table 4.10. Impacts of Strategies for Improving Ambient Environmental Quality in the Utilization of Coal to Produce Electric Energy

Impacts	Strategy									
	1	2	3	4	5	6	7	8	9	10
Impacts on system										
Quantity of coal mined	0[a]	0	0	0	−[a]	+[a]	−	+	0	+
Quantity of raw mine drainage	−	0	0	0	−	+	−	+	0	+
Quantity of refuse at mine	0	+	+	+	−	+	−	+	0	+
Quantity of coal transported	0	0	0	0	−	−	−	+	0	+
Quantity of solid residuals at power plant	0	0	0	0	−	−	−	+	0	+
Impacts on residuals										
Useful land	+	0	0	0	+	−	+	−	0	−
Acid and iron effluent	0	−	0	0	−	+	−	+	0	+
Suspended solids discharged from preparation plant	0	0	−	0	−	+	−	+	0	+
Particulate discharged from preparation plant	0	0	0	−	−	+	−	+	0	+
Particulate and sulfur oxides discharged from power plant	0	0	0	0	−	−	−	−	0	+
Heat discharged from power plant to water courses	0	0	0	0	−	0	0	+	0	−
Suspended solids discharged from power plant to water courses	0	0	0	0	−	−	−	+	−	+
Solid residuals from power plant	0	0	0	0	−	−	−	+	+	+

Strategies:
1. Grade and replant land
2. Treat acid mine drainage
3. Treat wastewater from preparation plant
4. Collect particulates from preparation plant
5. Increase generator efficiency
6. Use more coal preparation
7. Use higher quality raw coal
8. Treat power plant flue gas
9. Treat suspended solids from power plant
10. Use cooling towers

[a] 0 = no change; − = less; + = more. All + changes represent negative impacts except for land; that is, increasing quantity of coal mined increases amount of acid and iron effluent, a negative impact.
Source: Bower (1975).

plant flue gas increases the resistivity of the fly ash, thereby making electrostatic precipitation less efficient. The use of cooling towers to reduce thermal discharges into water courses involves a transfer of the residual heat from a liquid discharge to a gaseous discharge. This emission from a cooling tower may cause undesirable environmental effects, such as local fogging and icing, cloud formation, and increased precipitation. Various alternatives are in turn available for modifying these secondary effects, such as superheating the plume or using finned heat exchangers. These further modifications add to the costs of residuals modification.

Table 4.11. Residuals Management Costs and Residuals Discharges for Three Levels of Environmental Quality (Coal-Electric Energy System)

	Case 1: Mine-mouth plant,[a] high-impurity seam, area-strip mine			Case II: Load-center plant,[b] low-impurity seam, deep mine		
Environmental quality design level	I	II	III	I	II	III
Price of power (mills/kwh):						
At busbar	6.00	7.05	8.57	6.94	7.92	9.37
At load-center substation	7.64	9.00	11.78	7.17	8.20	9.98
Residuals flow to environment (annual basis, except for transmission)						
Acres of disturbed land/acres of reclaimed land	[^{980}/0]	[^{1040}/1040]	[^{1250}/1250]	rs	rs	rs
Gross increase in mine drainage:						
Million gallons	rs	rs	rs	110	80	90
Tons of sulfuric acid	rs	rs	rs	360	180	0
Preparation plant water (1 to 8% solids), million gallons	0	0	0	0	0	0
Preparation plant refuse, tons	0	1,600,000	2,600,000	0	0	300,000
Preparation plant air-borne dust, tons	0	4,400	900	0	0	700
Power-plant stack emissions, tons:						
Particulates	140,000	900	100	25,000	700	100
Sulfur oxides (sulfur content)	200,000	29,000	15,000	28,000	7,500	3,500
Nitrogen oxides (nitrogen content)	10,000	8,000	2,000	10,000	8,000	2,000
Power-plant solid waste, tons	1,000,000	950,000	800,000	300,000	450,000	300,000
Thermal discharge to watercourse, billion BTU	6,000	0	0	6,000	0	0
Water consumption (extra evaporation), million gallons	7,500	5,000	0	7,500	5,000	0
Transmission-line towers:						
Lattice type	4,000	2,500	0	120	0	0
Tubular poles	0	2,000	4,000	0	150	0
Underground circuit-miles/ total circuit-miles	[^{0}/800]	[^{0}/880]	[^{80}/800]	[^{0}/25]	[^{0}/25]	[^{25}/25]

Notes: Residuals management costs are based on 1968 prices; 8% rate of return on power plant investment, 10% on coal mining/preparation investment. Power plant consists of two 800-MW units; other elements of system are sized to provide the requisite input to the power plant. The term rs indicates not relevant.

[a] Four-year construction period, with annual outlays of 10%, 40%, 40%, and 10%; half of draft and flue gas equipment replaced after 15 years; insurance and local taxes at 1% of plant investment; 30-day supply of coal; heat rates 9,010, 9,300, 9,690 BTU/net kw, for Levels I, II, and III, respectively, reflecting the increased energy required for residuals modification.

[b] Five-year construction period, with annual outlays of 5%, 20%, 50%, 20%, and 5%; half of draft and flue-gas equipment replaced after 15 years; insurance and local taxes at 3% of plant investment; 60-day supply of coal; heat rates 8,850, 9,175, 9,565 BTU/net kw, for Levels I, II, and III, respectively.

Source: Bower (1975).

Each of the two coal-electric energy generation systems—mine-mouth and load center—shown in figure 4.12 was analyzed in relation to three sets of increasingly stringent environmental quality standards, comparable to the analysis of the pulp and paper mill described earlier. The three levels are characterized as follows: Level I approximates the relatively low standards in force in the United States in the early 1960s, which required little or no modification of nonproduct outputs except what would normally be done in the absence of effluent controls—that is, economic materials recovery; Level II approximates the U.S. discharge reduction standards of 1972–1973; and Level III reflects a still larger reduction in discharges. The analysis uses the engineering-economic-process model and the cost-effective increment approach because the systems have many nonlinearities in cost relationships and a number of joint cost problems. The analysis is applied to three alternative levels of land reclamation for strip-mined land; five alternative levels of coal preparation; three alternative levels of reduction of particulate discharges at the coal preparation plant; and three alternative levels of reduction of discharges of particulates, SO_2, and heat at the power plant. The cost-effective increment approach determined the least-cost overall system to meet the environmental quality standards at all locations of the system. The results of the analysis, in terms of residuals management costs, price of energy at the load-center, and residual discharges, are shown in table 4.11.

CONCLUDING COMMENT

The analysis of activities is an integral and critical component of project and program formulation and evaluation. It provides the basis for estimating basic production costs and residuals generated and discharged that provide the inputs to analysis of effects on natural systems and receptors. The economic costs of these effects are combined with project and program costs to provide a complete benefit-cost valuation of a development project along with its natural-systems and environmental quality effects. The analysis of activities must yield outputs of data on residuals discharges that are consistent with the inputs needed for the models to be used to analyze the effects of such discharges on natural systems and receptors.

REFERENCES

Amidon, E. A., and E. M. Gould, Jr. *The Possible Impact of Recreation Development on Timber Production in Three California National Forests.* Technical Paper 68. Pacific Southwest Forest and Range Experiment Station. Berkeley, Calif.: U.S. Forest Service, 1962.

Ayres, R. U. "A Materials-Process-Product Model." In *Environmental Quality Analysis: Theory and Method in the Social Sciences,* ed. A. V. Kneese and B. T. Bower. Baltimore: Johns Hopkins University Press, 1972.

Basta, D. J.; J. L.Lounsbury; and B. T. Bower. *Analysis for Residuals-Environmental Quality Management: A Case Study of the Ljubljana Area of Yugoslavia.* RFF Research Paper R-11. Washington, D.C.: Resources for the Future, 1978.

Bower, B. T. "Studies of Residuals Management in Industry." In *Economic Analysis of Environmental Problems,* ed. E. S. Mills. New York: National Bureau of Economic Research, 1975.

Bower, B. T.; R. Barre; J. Kuhner, and C. S. Russell. *Incentives in Water Quality Management: France and the Ruhr Area.* RFF Research Paper R-24. Washington, D.C.: Resources for the Future, 1981.

Dyrness, C. T. *Mass Soil Movement in the H. J. Andrews Experimental Forest.* Research Paper 42. Pacific Northwest Forest and Range Experiment Station. Portland, Oreg.: U.S. Forest Service, 1967.

———. *Soil Surface Conditions Following Balloon Logging.* Research Note 182. Pacific Northwest Forest and Range Experiment Station. Portland, Oreg.: U.S. Forest Service, 1972.

Harr, R. D. *Forest Practices and Stream Flow in Western Oregon.* Technical Report 49. Pacific Northwest Forest and Range Experiment Station. Portland, Oreg.: U.S. Forest Service, 1976.

Löf, G. O. G.; W. M. Hearon; and B. T. Bower. "Residuals Management in Pulp and Paper Manufacture." *Forest Products and the Environment.* AICHE Symposium Series 69, 133 (December 1973): 141–149.

Russell, C. S. *Residuals Management in Industry: A Case Study of Petroleum Refining.* Baltimore: Johns Hopkins University Press, 1973.

Russell, C. S., and W. J. Vaughan. *Steel Production: Processes, Products and Residuals.* Baltimore: Johns Hopkins University Press, 1976.

Smith, R. C. *Forestry in the Meramec Basin.* Meramec Basin Research Project. St. Louis: Washington University, 1961 (unpublished report).

Teeguarden, D. E., and K. R. Werner. "Integrating Forest-Oriented Recreation with Timber Growing: A Case Study of Economic Factors." *California Agriculture* (October 1968): 10–13.

Willin, D. W. "Surface Soil Texture and Potential Erodibility Characteristics of Some Southern Nevada Forest Sites." *Proceedings of the Soil Science Society of America* 29, 2 (1965): 213–218.

5

Analyzing Effects on Natural Systems and Receptors

As indicated in Chapters 1 and 3, two essential analytical steps precede the valuation step described in Chapters 6, 7, and 8. The first is the formulation of project, program, and sector plans, including the analysis of the various activities contained in the plans, as described in Chapter 4. The second is the identification and quantification of (1) the effects of each plan on the relevant natural systems, on-site and off-site—for example, the effects on ambient environmental quality,* and (2) the physical, chemical, and biological effects of the changes in environmental quality on receptors—humans, animals, vegetation, buildings, and materials other than buildings. Environmental quality is measured by such indicators as the concentration of dissolved oxygen (DO) in a stream, the biomass of fish per cubic meter of water in an estuary, and the concentration of sulfur dioxide (SO_2) in the atmosphere over an urban area.

Thus, the analysis of natural systems and receptors, which is the focus of this chapter,† provides the link between the analysis of activities and the economic valuation of their effects on natural systems and environmental quality (fig. 5.1). Two points merit emphasis. In this linked system, the outputs of the analysis of activities become the inputs to the analysis of effects on natural systems and receptors. For each activity, the problem is to ascertain quantitatively what happens to the relevant natural systems under the impetus of sets of management inputs and technological options.

For planning purposes, it is important to distinguish between on-site and off-site effects (fig. 5.2). In this example of a forest management activity, harvesting usually leads to significant changes over time in the state of the forest ecosystem, as measured by such indicators as depth of topsoil and infiltration capacity. These changes in turn affect the productivity of the on-site forest ecosystem. Simultaneously, residuals transported beyond the

*Subsequently referred to throughout this chapter as *environmental quality*.
†Portions of this chapter draw on Basta and Bower (1982).

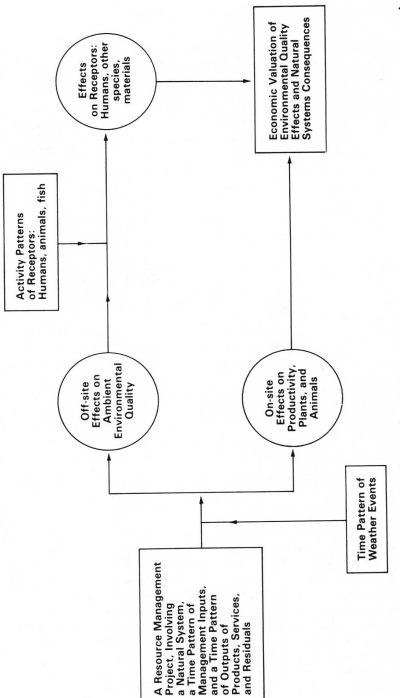

Figure 5.1 The links among activities, effects, and economic valuation.

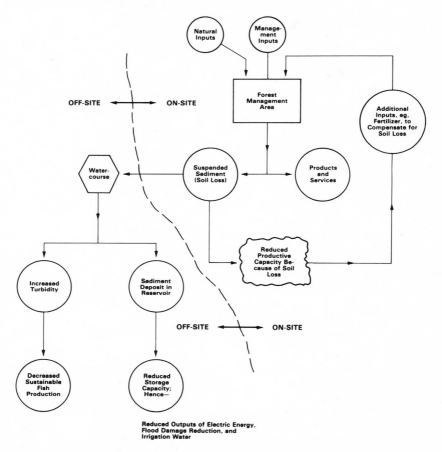

Figure 5.2 On-site and off-site effects on natural systems of a forest management activity.

boundaries of the area of the activity usually affect the environmental quality off-site. A typology of projects and their effects is shown in table 5.1.

Estimating effects on receptors usually involves three steps prior to the monetary evaluation of the effects. These are (1) estimating the time and spatial patterns of changes in environmental quality; (2) estimating the exposure of receptors to these changes; and (3) estimating the physical, chemical, and biological effects of the exposure. Sometimes there is a fourth step, one which involves the *perception* by humans of changes in environmental quality and the effects of those changes.

Distinguishing between effects on environmental quality and effects on receptors is not always simple. The difference is basically an operational one

Table 5.1. Typology of Projects Having Effects on Natural Systems and Receptors

Project category number	Description
I	The project involves management of a natural system (e.g., a forest area, a groundwater aquifer, a grazing area) to produce the desired outputs.
II	The project has no significant natural system on the project site, but it affects natural systems and receptors off-site (e.g., a surface coal mine with off-site air and water quality effects).
III	The project eliminates a natural system and replaces it with an alternative, human-built system (e.g., a water storage reservoir), which inundates the natural system and replaces it with a "lake." Such a project may also have significant off-site consequences (e.g., deposition upstream from the reservoir and degradation and aggradation downstream from the reservoir).
IV	The project modifies or replaces the on-site ecosystem with a more or less artificial system on the site through alteration of the existing natural system (e.g., plantation forests, monoculture, construction of artificial reefs to enhance shellfish/finfish production, offshore aquaculture of seaweed).

that depends on whether the analysis of receptors is done separately or as a part of the analysis of environmental quality.

Receptors can be classified in various ways. One useful typology distinguishes between stationary and mobile receptors (table 5.2). The greater the mobility of a receptor, the more difficult it is to estimate exposure to environmental quality and, hence, to estimate effects. The typology also shows that various activities—for example, industrial, agricultural, or residential—not only generate and discharge residuals that affect environmental quality, but also are affected by changes in environmental quality.

Table 5.2. Typology of Receptors

Receptors	Stationary	Mobile within fixed habitat	Mobile
Resident fish species		X	
Migratory fish species			X
Resident animal species		X	
Migratory animal species			X
Natural vegetation	X		
Materials in structures	X		
Materials in vehicles			X
Agricultural and forestry activities	X		
Industrial and commercial activities	X		
All other activities	X		
Residences	X		
Humans			X

SOME PROBLEMS IN ANALYZING EFFECTS

In analyzing effects on natural systems and on receptors, some difficult problems arise because of the complex characteristics of residuals generation and discharge and the effects of such discharges on receptors. Five of these characteristics are briefly discussed here.

First, discharges of material and energy residuals into the three environmental media—air, land, and water—are of many different types. They range from sudden discharges of residuals as a result of equipment breakdowns, spills, and transportation accidents to relatively constant discharges that occur over considerable periods of time, such as a leak from a crude petroleum pipeline, drainage through tile drains from an irrigated area, or discharge of wastewater through an outfall from an industrial operation.

Second, a wide range exists for both the *time rate of change* in environmental quality and for the *geographical area of influence* of residuals discharges on environmental quality. An example of a short-run time scale is an acid spill into a stream so turbulent that the acid is mixed in after only a few hours. An example of a long-run effect is an oil spill into a groundwater aquifer of low permeability, in this case, dispersion throughout the aquifer may take several decades (table 5.3). Geographical extent may range from the localized effect of a minor spill into a small tributary stream to a global effect involving long-distance transport of DDT in the atmosphere. Continental, hemispheric, and global effects typically are long-run phenomena.

Third, there is a wide range in the time rates of effects on receptors from changes in environmental quality. For example, long latency periods may occur for particular effects on humans, such as the serious effects on human respiratory systems from a long-term exposure to poor air quality. Also, accumulations of chlorinated hydrocarbons in certain species of birds can eventually affect reproduction.

Fourth, a large element of randomness exists in the levels of environmental quality over time. This is because of variations in the time pattern of residuals discharges and in environmental (e.g., hydrologic and meterologic) conditions and, hence, in the assimilative capacity of the environment. Both types of variability must be accounted for in any assessment of effects on natural systems.

Fifth, residuals discharged from human activities are not the only factors affecting the quality of the environment. Many constituents of residuals are also generated in and discharged to natural systems as the result of natural processes. Examples of these constituents, termed *nature's outputs*, are listed in table 5.4. In any given context, the analyst must be careful to separate the background effects arising from natural processes from the effects resulting from the given project or program.

Table 5.3. Examples of Different Time Rates of Response of Natural Systems to Residuals Discharges

Action	Response mechanism	Final state of system	Time from action to final state
Spill or leak of oil or chemical substance	Flow through porous media	Eventual contamination of aquifer	Several decades
Pumping from groundwater aquifer with hydraulic connection to ocean	Gradual encroachment of seawater	Salination of aquifer	Several decades
Construction of major dam	Degradation immediately downstream from dam, aggradation in reaches further downstream	Channel modification with more flooding in some locations, more phreatophyte growth	1–3 decades
Time pattern of pesticide application	Uptake by and accumulation in particular bird species	Demise of bird species in region because of reproduction failure	1 decade
Discharge of sewage effluent into lake	Increased production of algae	Accelerated eutrophication	Few years
Tussock moth control program with pesticides	Modification of moth population, other insect or bird populations, increased wood growth per acre	Reduction in nontarget species	1–3 years
Spill of acid into well-mixed estuary	Mixing by turbulence and tidal action	Increase in acidity	Few days

Table 5.4. Examples of Nature's Outputs of Constituents Affecting Environmental Quality

Constituent	Natural process	Environmental medium
Particulates	Wind erosion	Air, water
	Weathering	Air, water
	Volcanic action	Air, water
	Forest and brush fires	Air, water
Hydrogen sulfide	Biological decay: oxidation of SO_2 and $SO_4 =$ aerosol in air	Air, water
	Volcanic action: oxidation of SO_2 and $SO_4 =$ aerosol in air	Air, land, and water
Nitrogen oxides	Biological decay: oxidation of NO to NO_2 in air	Air, land, and water
Carbon monoxide	Photochemical oxidation of terpenes emitted due to forest and brush fires, biological decay, and plant emanations yields CO	Air, land, and water
Hydrocarbons	Biological decay of organic materials	Land, water
Methane	Seepage of natural gas	Land
Terpenes	Photochemical reaction of terpenes from plant emanation forms aerosols	Air, land
Petroleum	Natural seepages	Land, water
Dissolved solids	Deposition and concentration of salts due to evaporation, e.g., sea spray, salt springs, saline soils	Air, water, land
Heavy metals	Biological action or changes in chemical oxidation state of heavy metal-rich sediments, e.g., geological weathering and erosion	Land

TYPES OF MODELS FOR ANALYZING EFFECTS

The term *model* is defined as a predictive relationship between some dependent variable of interest—for example, the concentration of dissolved oxygen in a stream, or the decrease in productivity of a forest or agricultural ecosystem—and one or more independent variables. Models can be simple or complex; whatever the degree of complexity, however, models are used to determine the effects of specific residuals discharges on natural systems and receptors.

In the discussion to follow, models are classified in three ways: (1) by degree of mathematical rigor; (2) by types of natural systems or environmental media to which the model is applied; and (3) by kinds of phenomena being analyzed—that is, effects on natural systems, on receptors, or on both.

Classification According to Mathematical Rigor

Four types of models are discussed, in the order of increasing degree of mathematical rigor.

The first type is an *empirical, qualitative* model based on field observations with few, if any, actual field measurements. This model simply indicates the *direction* of effects. For example, an analyst observes that mass wasting of soil occurs in a forest area after clear-cutting on north-facing slopes of greater than 10% with granodiorite parent material. The model then states that if clear-cutting is done under this set of conditions, subsequent mass wasting is likely.

Another example is a qualitative geomorphological model that indicates degradation and aggradation in a stream as a result of the construction of a reservoir, as illustrated in figure 5.3. This model simply indicates the general nature of the results and provides no information on either the extent of degradation and aggradation over time or the change in the profile of the streambed over time.

The second type of model, which yields *quantitative* estimates, has two subtypes. The first is a *simple, two-variable, empirical correlation* model. For example, for a given season, an analyst measures (1) soil loss from a maize field with a given soil type on a given slope and (2) precipitation. Soil loss under maize cultivation on that combination of soil type and slope, as a first approximation, is assumed to be a linear function of precipitation.

The second subtype is a *simple materials* or *mass-balance* model. For example, as a first approximation, the airshed over a metropolitan area is defined as the volume represented by the area times the height to the mixing layer of the atmosphere. Discharges of total suspended particulates into the airshed are assumed to be mixed homogeneously. The model then defines the mean concentration of total suspended particulates in the metropolitan area as simply the total mass of discharge, in kilograms, divided by the total volume of the airshed, in cubic meters.

The third type is characterized as a *multi-variate regression* model, in which a number of independent variables affecting the variable of interest have been identified and measured, and one of a number of possible forms of multiple regression equations has been selected as most accurately representing the phenomenon in relation to the available data. Thus,

$$\text{gross soil erosion by rainfall} = f(x_1, x_2, x_3, \ldots, x_n),$$

where x_1 is rainfall intensity, x_2 is the soil erodibility factor, and $x_3, \ldots, x_n$ are other independent variables.

The fourth type is an *analytical* model based on some fundamental principles, such as the laws of conservation of mass and energy. Examples are plume dispersion models in air quality management, which indicate the concentration of a material downwind of a stack from which the material was discharged, and various ambient water quality models.

Regardless of the degree of mathematical rigor and of the form of the relationship between the dependent and independent variables, validation of

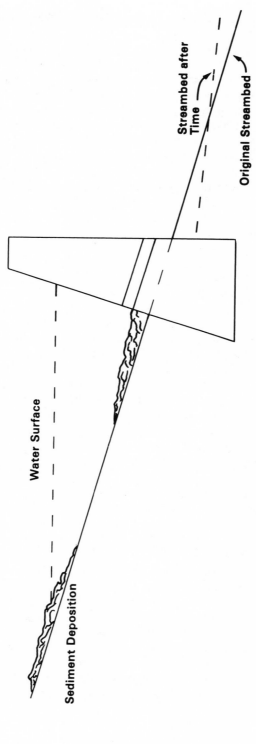

Figure 5.3 Effects of dam and reservoir on streambed profile.

any model requires collection of field data to determine coefficients and to enable testing of the assumed relationships.

Classification According to Natural Systems and Environmental Media

Natural-systems models also can be classified into six types, according to the system and environmental media being analyzed:

1. Surface water: rivers, lakes, estuaries, and coastal waters
2. Subsurface water: confined and unconfined aquifers
3. Atmospheric
4. Residuals generated on and discharged from land surfaces (e.g., soil erosion)
5. Terrestrial ecosystems
6. Geomorphic; for example, degradation and aggradation in streams, and mass wasting.

Models of the first three subtypes produce estimates of the temporal and spatial patterns of environmental quality as a result of the discharge of residuals from human activities into natural systems. Models of the fourth subtype produce estimates of residuals generated from land surfaces as a result of the combination of human activities on the land surface and natural agents such as precipitation and wind. Two examples of this subtype are the discharge of particulates from cropland to the atmosphere because of wind action; and the discharge into surface waters of organic material, heavy metals, and suspended solids resulting from precipitation on, and the flow of water over, the land surface. Models of the fifth subtype produce estimates of the state of the natural system itself as a result both of processes at work within the system and of forces imposed on it from outside the system. For example, this model would yield estimates of the effects on soil structure and its constituents of a combination of crops, pests, pesticides, cultivation practices, and weather. Models of the sixth subtype produce estimates, for example, of upstream and downstream changes in a streambed profile as a result of the construction of a dam and reservoir.

Any one of these categories can be subdivided further. For example, surface water models can be subdivided into (1) physical models (e.g., sediment transport); (2) physical/chemical models (e.g., salinity, Streeter-Phelps dissolved oxygen); (3) physical/biological models (e.g., coliform); and (4) physical/chemical/biological models (e.g., aquatic ecosystem models). Atmospheric models can be subdivided as to types of residuals being analyzed (e.g., oxides of sulfur, total suspended particulates, carbon monoxide) and by geographic scope (e.g., regional, long-range interregional transport).

Classification According to Effects Being Estimated

A classification of natural-systems models as to the nature of the effects being analyzed is less straightforward than the previous classifications but is useful for analyses. At least five subtypes can be identified:

1. Effects on natural systems in terms of environmental quality—for example, an atmospheric dispersion model for residuals discharged into the atmosphere, or an oil spill model to estimate dispersion of oil (Smith, Slack,and Davis 1978);
2. Effects on receptors—for example, ambient air quality-human health, ambient air quality-crop damage, or ambient water quality-crop yield in irrigated agriculture;
3. Joint environmental quality and receptor effects—for example, an aquatic ecosystem model yielding estimates of both ambient water-quality indicators and biomass of fish species;
4. On-site effects—for example, vegetation succession with forest management practices, with uncontrolled grazing, and in the rehabilitation of strip-mined land; and
5. Combined effects on environmental quality and receptors, plus economic evaluation of such effects—for example, a complex forest management model such as that found in Holling (1978).

Examples of the first three subtypes are provided in a later section of this chapter.

APPROACHES TO ESTIMATING EFFECTS

Five types of processes are at work in natural systems: chemical, biochemical, physical, physicochemical, and ecological. These processes affect the movement of materials and energy and their transformation into other related forms in natural systems, thereby altering environmental quality in both time and space. Chemical processes involve the reaction of two or more components to form one or more different compounds; for example, the transformation of SO_2 into SO_3 and eventually into H_2SO_4 in the atmosphere. In biochemical processes, the transformation is the result of chemical-biological interaction, such as the bacterial decomposition of organic material in a body of water where the reaction takes place within a biological organism. Examples of purely physical processes are the movement of particulate matter in the atmosphere by wind currents and the downstream transport of suspended solids not subject to decomposition. Physicochemical processes involve the chemistry and physics of molecules as they interact with their surroundings; for example, the adsorption of organic molecules on solid sediment particles in a stream. Ecological processes involve interactions among different species of organisms in the food chain and organism processes such as respiration, growth, consumption by prey, and mortality.

Most modeling of natural systems involves one of two approaches, or a combination of them. These approaches are based on statistics or on the conservation of mass and energy. Models based on statistics do not explicitly simulate the processes at work in a natural system; they simply provide estimates of the values of the output variables, given the values of the independent variables.

In contrast, models based on the conservation of mass and energy explicitly attempt to simulate the processes that transport and transform materials and energy in a natural system. Such models typically divide a natural system into a number of segments, and then simulate the material and energy flows into each segment, the transformations that take place within each, and the resulting flows from each segment into adjacent ones.

Both models of natural systems—statistical or conservation of mass and energy—have three important characteristics: (1) temporal variation, (2) averaging time, and (3) spatial dimensionality. The first characteristic refers to the way in which values of variables in a model change from one time period to the next. The second refers to the time unit over which values of the variables in the model are averaged. The third refers to the number of physical dimensions—one, two, or three—incorporated in the model and to the number of segments into which the natural system is divided.

Temporal variation has two facets: the number of time periods analyzed and the pattern of variation, if any, in values of input variables from one time period to the next. Analysis of one or more time periods in isolation from others is termed *steady-state* analysis. When a number of successive time periods are involved, in which the outputs of the analysis of the first period become the inputs to the analysis of the second period, a *nonsteady-state* analysis is required.

Between a steady-state model—in which no variables change for the given time period—and a pure nonsteady-state model—in which all variables change from one period to the next—there are models termed *quasi-nonsteady state,* in which some but not all variables change from one period to the next.

Averaging time must be specified for all models. This is the unit of time for which the values of the variables—environmental conditions, residuals discharges, and environmental quality indicators—are estimated. For example, dissolved oxygen concentration in a lake can be estimated as an annual, seasonal, monthly, or weekly average. The appropriate averaging time depends on the management questions to be answered and on the models used. For example, when episodic air quality conditions are being investigated in an urban area, averaging times can be as short as one hour. In such cases, a nonsteady state air quality model would be used to analyze, hour by hour, a total period of several days, long enough to cover the episode. This produces estimated average hourly values of ambient air quality indicators throughout the episode.

In spatial dimensions, any natural system is in reality three-dimensional. Simplifying assumptions are often made, however, to permit analysis of fewer than three dimensions. The more spatial dimensions explicitly considered in a model, the more complex it is and the greater are its data and computational requirements. Depending on the natural system to be analyzed and the context, a model that considers transport and transformation of residuals in only one or two dimensions may be adequate.

Specifying spatial segments of a model involves selecting the number and sizes of the linear, areal, or volumetric elements into which the natural system is to be divided for the analysis. For example, the surface of an urban area 400 kilometers square can be segmented into 400 one-kilometer-square rectangles, or alternatively, into 100 four-kilometer-square rectangles for the purpose of estimating gaseous residuals discharges and the resulting air quality.

Statistical Approach

The statistical approach has long been used to analyze natural systems. Various statistical methods have been applied to a broad range of problems and in varied contexts. The approach involves determining a statistically significant relationship between a dependent variable and a number of independent variables. The dependent variable is some indicator of environmental quality and the independent variables are the residuals discharge variables, climatic variables, and other variables reflecting characteristics of the natural system being analyzed, such as soil depth, slope, and elevation.

Conceptually, the approach is simple. First, for a natural system, independent variables affecting the dependent variable are identified from knowledge of the relevant physical, chemical, and biological phenomena. Second, one or more structural forms of the relationships between the independent variables and the dependent variables are assumed. Third, a set of data with values for each of the variables is obtained. Observations can be taken over time, in which case they are termed time-series data, or can represent a sample of individuals, groups of individuals, geographical areas, or even objects, in which case they are termed cross-sectional data.

The statistical approach views the natural system as a "black box" (fig. 5.4). The inputs to the box are the independent variables; the outputs are the dependent variables. The internal workings of the black box remain unknown and unspecified. The black-box approach implies that in some instances, several dependent variables can be functions of the *same* independent variables. For example, BOD_5 and DO concentrations in a given reach of stream are functions of the same variables.

Regression analysis is the most common method used in developing a

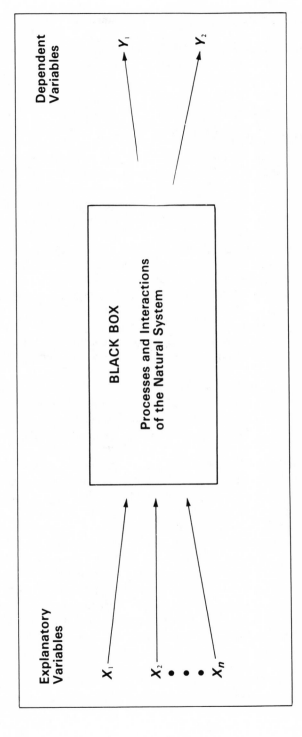

Figure 5.4 The "black box" concept in the statistical approach to analyzing natural systems. (*Source:* Basta and Bower, 1982.)

statistical model. Common structural forms of a hypothesized relationship are linear, semilog, and log-log. For example:

$$Y = A + B_1X_1 + B_2X_2 + \ldots + B_nX_n + E; \tag{5-1}$$

$$\log Y = A + B_1X_1 + B_2X_2 + \ldots + B_nX_n + E; \text{ and} \tag{5-2}$$

$$\log Y = A + B_1\log X_1 + B_2\log X_2 + \ldots + B_n\log X_n + E. \tag{5-3}$$

Y represents the dependent variable; $X_1 \ldots X_n$, the independent variables; E, a random disturbance term; A, the constant; and $B_1 \ldots B_n$, the coefficients to be estimated. Statistically significant coefficients indicate the relative degrees to which the various independent variables explain variations in the value of the dependent variable. Statistical significance is usually defined in terms of a probability level. For example, if a coefficient is significant at the 95% level, then the inference is that only a 5% chance exists that the coefficient could be of such magnitude solely by chance.

Statistical methods are also used to develop inputs for the conservation-of-mass-and-energy approach to analyzing natural systems. For example, many of the environmental conditions and residuals discharge variables are stochastic; hence, using as inputs the statistically determined probability distributions of their values is appropriate. Examples are the estimation of diffusivity coefficients for some receiving-water models and wind field coefficients in some air-quality models.

A natural-systems model based on the statistical approach cannot be transferred intact from the region for which it was developed to other regions when it contains coefficients empirically derived for a particular area. These coefficients are functions of the geologic, hydrologic, hydraulic, and meteorologic conditions and the spatial pattern of residuals discharges in the area. A statistically significant relationship found in a given area, however, would suggest both relevant variables and a structural form to try in another area, for the same dependent variables. Examples include the results of regression analysis applied to eutrophication in lakes and the Universal Soil Loss Equation for estimating gross soil erosion from agricultural areas.

The statistical approach to analyzing natural systems has the problems of all statistical analysis—that is, specification and multicollinearity. When time-series data are used, autocorrelation may be a problem. The most important limitation, however, is that the statistical relationship developed from a given set of data for some natural system reflects the particular spatial arrangement of activities and natural-systems processes that existed when the data were collected. For any markedly different spatial pattern or natural-systems processes, new data would have to be obtained and a new statistical relationship developed. As a result of these problems and limitations, the statistical approach to analyzing natural systems has been used primarily when, first, only a crude analysis is required, or second, no model based on the conservation-of-mass-and-energy approach is available or can be developed, either because of scarce resources or because of the complexity of the natural system to be analyzed.

Conservation-of-Mass-and-Energy Approach

The conservation-of-mass-and-energy approach, in one form or another, is the one used in most of the models developed for analyzing natural systems, including most of the models that are operational.* In their most elementary form, the fundamental principles of conservation of mass and energy assert that mass and energy can neither be created nor destroyed, although they can be altered in form. Because all residuals are in the form of either material (mass) or energy flows, these principles allow one to develop a set of equations for keeping account of the flow of mass and energy in a natural system. These *mass-balance* and *energy-balance equations* indicate that for any size volume in space—in air, water, or soil—the increase or decrease of mass or energy over any given time interval must be accounted for by either or both (1) inputs to or outputs from the volume and (2) transformations in the form of mass or energy within the volume. Mass and energy cannot simply disappear. Analyzing a natural system according to these principles entails dividing the system into volume segments and tracing the movement over time of material and energy flows from segment to segment, using mass- and energy-balance equations.

Before mass and energy balances can be made for a natural system, both the segments to which the balance equations will be applied and the averaging time over which the balances will be made must be specified. Both spatial dimensionality and averaging time can vary widely. For example, an entire reservoir or the atmosphere above an entire metropolitan area can be defined as a single space (e.g., as a lumped system). A lumped system can be analyzed in one, two, or three dimensions. At the other end of the scale, a natural system may be divided into a large number of one-dimensional, two-dimensional, or three-dimensional spaces. Figure 5.5 provides some examples of how various natural systems can be sectioned for writing mass/energy-balance equations. By writing balance equations for each of the segments and then manipulating the equations simultaneously, the flows of material and energy residuals can be traced in one, two, or three dimensions, as deemed necessary.

In terms of time, one may wish to predict changes in environmental quality indicators over a twenty-year period at one-year intervals, over a period of a few years at monthly intervals, or over a period of several days at hourly

---

*An operational model is defined as one that has been verified in at least one field application and for which documentation is available.

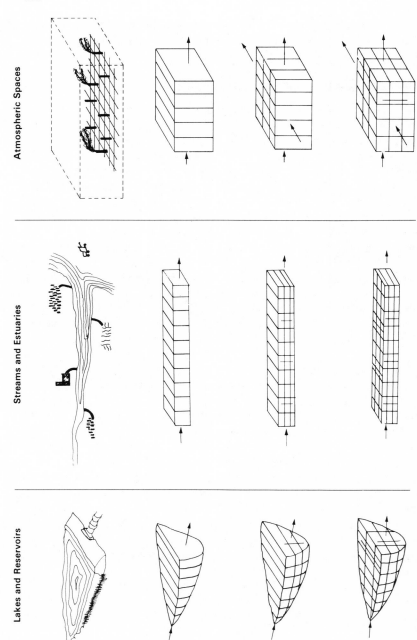

Atmospheric Spaces

Streams and Estuaries

Lakes and Reservoirs

Figure 5.5 Illustrations of sectioning natural systems for writing mass- and energy-balance equations. (*Source:* Basta and Bower, 1982.)

intervals. By writing mass and energy equations for each successive time interval, the flow of mass and energy can be traced over time in any given segment, or for the entire system being analyzed.

Because balance equations are written about gross changes of mass and energy within a given space and about inputs and outputs across the boundaries of that space, the equations provide no information about the spatial distribution of mass or energy *within* the space. Also, no conclusions can be drawn about the distributions of mass and energy from any time interval less than the interval over which the equations are written.

CHOOSING A MODEL OR SET OF MODELS

In any environmental planning context, regardless of the level of economic development of the country, the effects on natural systems and receptors will have to be estimated. The analysis may take the form of an extremely simple calculation or of a sophisticated, numerically integrated, multicompartment, conservation-of-mass-and-energy ecological model. Usually, several factors will determine the scope and type of analysis to be undertaken. These include the questions to be answered, the residuals of concern, the availability of relevant analytical resources, and the relative importance and characteristics of the activities generating residuals. Therefore, setting up the analysis of natural systems requires careful consideration of other segments of the environmental planning and analysis process, including the activity analysis segment discussed in Chapter 4.

Assuming that a preliminary analysis of these considerations has been made, the next step is to specify in detail the level of complexity necessary to generate the required information about each part of the natural system to be analyzed. Levels of complexity are defined in terms of the time intervals of analysis, spatial aggregations, and aggregations of constituents and species to be explicitly considered. This specification process defines the characteristics that are used to identify the appropriate model or set of models to be used.

The next step is to determine whether or not the analysis at the selected level of complexity is feasible within the available analytical resources—that is, the data, personnel, time for the analysis, and computer facilities and "software." Assessing the available data is a critical task in this step and requires the detailed enumeration of (1) available data that can be used without modification; (2) available data that must be modified before use, the details of the required modifications, and the analytical resources required to execute the modifications; and (3) additional data that would have to be obtained and the resources required to obtain them. If the data ready for use are insufficient or cannot be modified, and additional data cannot be obtained within the time available, then the level of complexity specified is infeasible.

Checking the feasibility of a particular level of analysis may be aided by

Table 5.5. Characteristics of Models for Estimating Effects on Natural Systems

Characteristic	Description
Time properties	Description of how temporal variations in flow and transport of residuals are represented in a model, both conceptually and computationally. Information includes (1) time variability: steady state, quasi-nonsteady state, and nonsteady state; and (2) time units of application: input and output values and computational time step.
Space properties	Identification of capability of model to represent spatial variations of residuals concentrations. Information includes (1) model dimensionality: one-dimensional, horizontal or vertical plane; or multidimensional, longitudinal and vertical plane; (2) spatial aggregation: size and number of segments, layers, and volumes possible; and (3) typical areal units of application.
Physical properties	Identification of the physical processes considered that account for the transport of residuals. Information includes (1) the principal hydraulic and meteorologic driving forces—i.e., tidal action, wind currents, and stream currents; and (2) the individual physical processes involved: advection, diffusion, dilution, convection, heat budget-temperature, wind, and Coriolis acceleration forces.
Chemical processes	Description of the chemical transformations and interactions considered that result in changes in concentration over time. Information includes (1) basic chemical processes: thermochemical equilibrium and coupled or noncoupled chemical reactions; and (2) ambient quality indicators represented: conservative and nonconservative substances.
Ecological processes	Identification of basic biological processes that affect interactions between environmental quality indicators and constituents, and among the various organisms represented in a model. Included are (1) biochemical processes—i.e., photosynthesis and respiration-biological decay; and (2) trophic dynamics—i.e., trophic levels, population growth dynamics, mortality, and predator-prey interactions.
Mathematical properties	Description of the theoretical basis for the mathematical representation in, and the methods of solution applied to, a model. Information includes (1) theoretical aspects: deterministic, stochastic, and combinations; and (2) various methods of solution: statistical, i.e., regression methods, and other mathematical techniques, i.e., analytically integrated or numerically integrated.
Computational status	Identification of status of model in relation to manipulation on digital computers. Information includes (1) whether model is coded or uncoded; (2) computer language used, e.g., FORTRAN; and (3) the various computer and accessory equipment required (hand calculator, analogue computer, or digital computer, including needed storage capacity, compilers, and magnetic tapes or disks for storage).

Input data requirements	Description of the various data required to set up, run, calibrate, and verify a model. Generalized historical data bases and site-specific data may be required, depending on the extent of prior applications.
Ease of application	Description of expected difficulties in obtaining, modifying, and applying a model. Information includes (1) the availability of model and supporting documentation from various sources; and (2) identification of anticipated areas of difficulty in model application.
Output and output format	Identification of model output with respect to the types of information produced, spatial and temporal distributions possible, and the format in which the output is presented.
Links to other models	Description of links between a model and other types of models used in environmental quality analysis and the forms of such links. Information provided includes links to other natural-systems models, damage-benefit models, and models of activities and the ways in which the links are structured.
Personnel needs	Identification of types, number, and desired levels of experience of personnel required to apply a model. Requirements for additional model development and/or major internal modification may differ significantly from those for model application. Information includes (1) position descriptions (engineer, programmer, systems analyst, ecologist, others); (2) need for specialized training or capabilities; and (3) the related experience of interdisciplinary team members.
Costs	Specification of all costs involved in applying a model, from initial acquisition of the model through analysis of model output. Model costs are a combination of (1) labor-hour expense required to complete certain tasks (including data collection), and (2) expense of obtaining a model itself and available user's manuals and documentation reports; and they are divided under the categories of model acquisition, data preparation, actual computation expense, computer accessory costs, and output analysis. Complete cost information is not available for most natural-systems models.
Model accuracy and sensitivity	Description of the overall capability of a model to represent accurately a natural system and its essential processes. Information includes (1) the representativeness in relation to the "real" system, especially the extent of the description and simplifying assumptions; (2) numerical accuracy—stability and dispersion (in numerically integrated models); and (3) sensitivity to input errors or rate coefficients, both known and estimated values.
Other comments	Description of miscellaneous facts concerning a model, its history of development and modification, and informative observations as to its utility in environmental quality analysis. Information includes (1) model limitations and restrictions; (2) special features and options; and (3) model originators or producers of current derivations (if modification of existing model).

Source: Basta and Bower (1982).

two procedures. The first involves specifying characteristics for describing models to analyze natural systems (table 5.5). These were selected as the most important attributes for deciding on the applicability of a model to a given context. The fifteen characteristics listed are applicable to all models classified according to environmental media.

The second procedure is the use of a systematic method of selecting a model, as illustrated by the flow diagram in figure 5.6 developed by Basta and Bower (1982) for regional environmental quality management. Four evaluative criteria were suggested: (1) accuracy of estimation, (2) capability of estimating environmental quality responses to various physical measures, (3) commonalities that a feasible model has with prior natural systems analyses in the given area or region, and (4) contributions the model would make to long-term analyses in the region.

As for accuracy of estimation, one model would be preferred over another if the anticipated range of error in the first were smaller than the range in the second, but only up to the point where (1) the errors fall within acceptable limits and (2) the models are capable of distinguishing among significantly different environmental quality responses. If both conditions are satisfied, however, the models are equally acceptable, and the choice between them must be made on other grounds.

The capability of a model to estimate changes in environmental quality that are *responses* to the application of various physical measures is an appropriate criterion because models are not equally sensitive to the possible physical measures that might be adopted. In most analytic contexts, models that yield estimates of environmental quality responses to a broad range of physical measures would be preferred over those with less flexibility.

Commonalities that a model may have with prior models used in a region is an important factor. The extent to which a model incorporates prior knowledge and experience in a region affects the credibility of the model's estimates among resident professionals, on whom decision makers rely for technical judgments. This is true regardless of how accurate the estimates may actually be. Consequently, a model that has processes and variables in common with previously accepted analyses usually will be preferred over one that hypothesizes relationships and involves variables that have not been tested in the region.

A model should also be evaluated in terms of the contributions it might make to the analysis of long-term development issues in the region. One such contribution might be the development of additional technical expertise within a region; another, the ability to use a model for an additional purpose—for example, the use of a runoff model to assess strategies for flood damage reduction. In a context in which spatial and temporal patterns of activities are changing rapidly over time, a model that is easily adapted to new locations of discharges and to a wide range of environmental conditions generally would be preferred to one that is not.

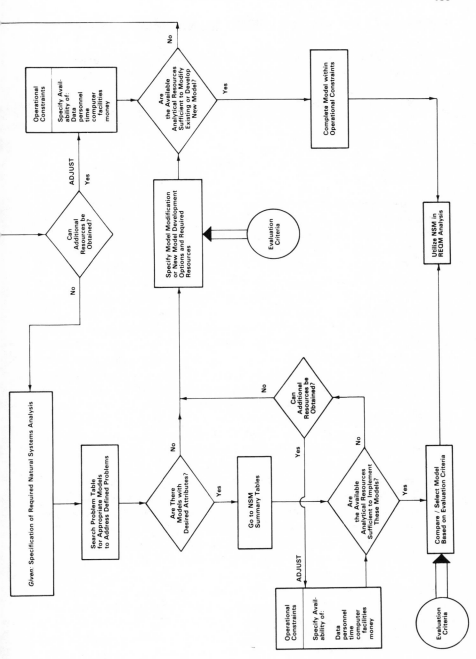

Figure 5.6 Flow chart of procedure for selecting a model for estimating effects on natural systems. (*Source:* **Basta and Bower, 1982.**)

EXAMPLES OF ESTIMATING EFFECTS ON NATURAL SYSTEMS

This section provides some examples that illustrate the approaches for estimating effects of activities on natural systems. The statistical approach is illustrated with examples of agricultural and forest management activities. The conservation-of-mass-and-energy approach is illustrated with examples of multiple discharges into the atmosphere and into a body of water from one or more activities in a region.

Effects of Agricultural Activities on Natural Systems: An Example of the Statistical Approach

Processes Involved in Soil Erosion. Figure 5.7 indicates the sequence of analysis necessary to estimate effects of agricultural activities on natural systems. The analysis of both on-site and off-site effects begins with estimating gross soil erosion, both water- and wind-induced. With water-induced erosion, runoff begins when precipitation exceeds the infiltration capacity of the soil. Once runoff begins, the velocities and directions of the water moving over the land surface and in conveyance systems are functions of the intensity and duration of the precipitation and the physical characteristics and geometry of the land surface and of conveyance systems. Characteristics include slope, composition of strata, configuration of conveyances (e.g., depth, side slopes, length of channels and ditches, and surface roughness), and barriers to flow.

Runoff picks up residuals either by dissolving material that has accumulated on the land surface or by physically suspending the material and carrying it along. Material that tends to remain suspended and seldom comes in contact with the streambed is termed *washload*. The term *sediment* usually is used to refer to solid materials that are moved by water. This combination of materials and process is referred to as the *sediment transport process.*

What constitutes sediment is poorly defined. Many different residuals may be present in any so-called sediment load, either as solid particles or attached to solid particles. Methods that can accurately analyze the total sediment transport process are not yet available. The factors that influence the process are known, however; namely, the size, shape, specific gravity, and concentration of the particles; temperature, viscosity, and density; velocity of flow, distribution of velocity, and turbulence, roughness of the surface; and shape of the channel.

The characteristics of, or the constituents associated with, the sediment from erosion are primarily the result of adsorption-desorption processes. *Adsorption* is the adhesion of a substance to the surface of a solid or liquid. Adsorption is an important process in relation to effects from agricultural activities because many residuals—for example, nitrogen, phosphorus, various pesticides, and heavy metals—attach themselves to particles of sediment and are in turn transported with the particles in runoff. The quantities of

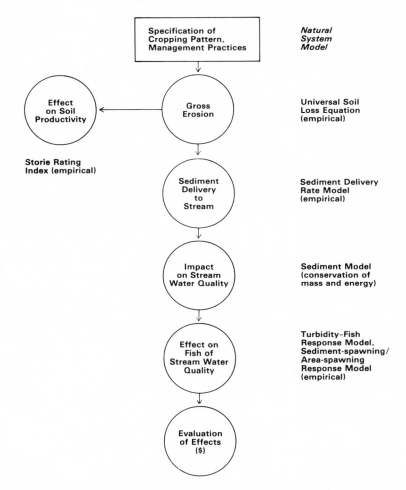

Figure 5.7 Sequence of analysis for estimating on-site and off-site effects of agricultural activities.

residuals that become attached to particles are functions of the concentration of residuals in the runoff stream and of temperature. *Desorption* is the adsorption process in reverse; that is, it is what occurs when the residuals are detached from the particles of sediment.

Two additional factors that affect the quantity and characteristics of the sediment eroded from agricultural areas are solids accumulation and the first-flush effect. Solids accumulation refers to materials deposited on land surfaces through dry or wet fallout from the atmosphere. Some of these materials may have been transported hundreds of miles. Solids accumulation is an important process because it affects the quantities and qualities of residuals available for pickup by runoff. The first-flush effect refers to the high concentration of residuals, especially solids, that often occurs in the early stages of a runoff event. Material that has accumulated on the land surface and on vegetation during dry weather conditions, and material that has been deposited in channels, are the primary sources of the first-flush effect.

Estimating Gross Soil Erosion.   Given the situation depicted in figure 5.8, two procedures exist for estimating the quantities of residuals discharged from a land area into a body of water. First, for each of the subwatersheds that are tributary to the conveyance channel, the quantities of residuals reaching the conveyance channel are estimated by a statistical model. Then, the residuals in the conveyance channel are routed to discharge point D at the river using a conservation-of-mass-and-energy model. Second, the quantities of residuals entering the river at point D from the entire watershed are estimated by a statistical model.

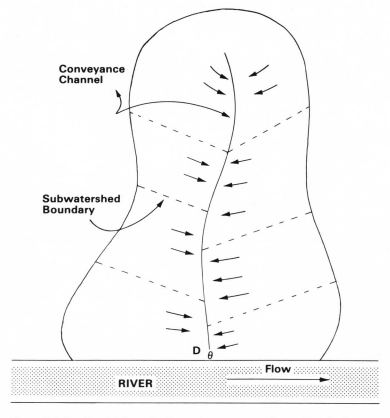

Figure 5.8 Representation of soil erosion movement in a watershed.

The approach to developing a statistical model for estimating gross erosion from a given land area involves assuming a functional relationship between water quality—in this case, suspended sediment or soil loss—and the relevant variables, based on knowledge of the physical processes involved. Values for each of the relevant variables are developed for different sets of conditions, from empirical measurement on experimental plots or from actual field conditions. The most well-known and widely used statistical model of this type is the Universal Soil Loss Equation, used to estimate gross sheet and rill erosion from a land surface. This equation is

$$GE = R \times K \times LS \times C \times P, \qquad (5\text{--}4)$$

where GE is the gross erosion or soil loss from rainstorms, tons per acre per year; R is the rainfall factor per time period; K is the soil erodibility factor; LS is the slope-length, slope-gradient factor; C is the cropping management factor or cover index factor; and P is the erosion control practices factor.

The rainfall factor reflects the fact that in the eastern United States, soil erosion has been found to be directly proportional to the product of the kinetic energy of a storm and the maximum thirty-minute intensity of the storm. This product is characterized as the erosion index because it is intended to account for the energy from the impact of raindrops required to loosen soil particles. To estimate mean annual soil loss from a given land area, the rainfall factor R equals the total number of erosion index units associated with the mean distribution of rainfall events in a year. The soil loss from any other distribution of rainfall events in a year, of course, can also be estimated. Suggested annual values of the erosion index for use in various parts of the United States have been developed and are available in maps and charts, such as those contained in Stewart et al. (1975).

The values of the other factors in equation 5–4, K, LS, C, and P, likewise have been developed from experimental and field data. The data typically are displayed in tables and graphs, such as those contained in Soil Conservation Society of America (1979) and U.S. Environmental Protection Agency (1973) for K, U.S. Soil Conservation Service (1975) for C, and True (1974) for P. Empirical formulae such as the following have also been developed to calculate LS values (U.S. Soil Conservation Service 1975):

$$LS = \left(\frac{\lambda}{72.6}\right)^m \left(\frac{430x^2 + 30x + 0.43}{6.57415}\right), \qquad (5\text{--}5)$$

where λ is the field slope length in feet; m is 0.5 if slope is 5% or greater, 0.4 if slope is 4%, and 0.3 if slope is 3% or less; and x is the sine of the slope angle.

The Universal Soil Loss Equation was developed primarily to estimate soil loss from agricultural cropland in temperate climates. Many modified forms of the equation have been developed, however, for making estimates of sediment in runoff for land uses other than agricultural cropland. Numerous references describing every aspect of applying the equation are available; for example, Wischmeier and Smith (1965), U.S. Environmental Protection Agency (1973), and McElroy et al. (1976). The equation is not directly applicable, however, to estimating soil erosion from snowmelt or from the application of irrigation water. Other limitations of the equation are discussed in El-Swaify, Dangler, and Armstrong (1979).

An analogous empirical equation has been developed in the United States for estimating gross erosion of agricultural lands by wind. This formula, known as the Chepil equation, is

$$GE = I \times K \times C \times L \times V, \tag{5–6}$$

where GE is the gross erosion, tons per acre per year; I is the soil erodibility index; K is the field roughness; C is the climate factor; L is a function of the field width; and V is the equivalent vegetative cover (Chepil 1946; Wilson 1975; Simmons and Dotzenko 1974).

Soil erodibility is primarily a function of size of the soil particles, organic matter content, and moisture content. Estimates of the five variables have been made, by region, based on empirical data from experimental plots and actual cultivated fields.

Estimating On-site Effects of Soil Erosion.   Gross erosion may affect soil productivity and, hence, agricultural crop or forage yields in different ways, depending on soil type and soil depth. By affecting vegetation, there can also be negative effects on wildlife habitat. Basically, no formal analytical models exist by which the effects on yield can be estimated. Two approaches have been adopted. One reflects an implicit statistical method that involves simply compiling simultaneous field data on soil loss and yield loss, with or without compensating inputs such as additional fertilizer. The other approach is an implicit statistical one involving a rigorous soil-rating system, such as the Storie Soil Rating Index (Storie 1954). This index associates soil productivity with certain variables, such as soil depth and structure. Thus, as soil depth is reduced by erosion, the rating on that variable decreases and the overall productivity rating decreases. Similarly, as soil structure is changed—for example, organic matter in the A horizon is depleted as a result of erosion—the rating on that variable and the overall productivity rating both decrease.

The simple correlation approach is reflected in the measurements of topsoil depth and crop yield (table 5.6). Unfortunately, no data are provided in the table on other factors that affect yield—precipitation, fertilizers or pesticides applied, and cultivation practices. It is assumed that all of these factors were held constant and only topsoil depth was varied. For some soils the change in productivity is more abrupt than shown in the table, particularly for soils with shallow A horizons.

More rigorous analysis of the effects of soil loss on yield is reflected in the work of Harmon, Knutson, and Rosenberry (no date) and Scrivner and Neill

Table 5.6. Relationship between Corn Yield and Topsoil Depth

	Corn yield (bushels per acre)		
Topsoil depth (inches)	Range	Average	Decrease in average yield from 12″ topsoil depth
0–2	25–56	36	38
2–4	28–69	47	27
4–6	39–83	56	18
6–8	49–97	65	9
8–10	50–102	69	5
10–12	50–125	74	—

Source: Pimental et al. (1976).

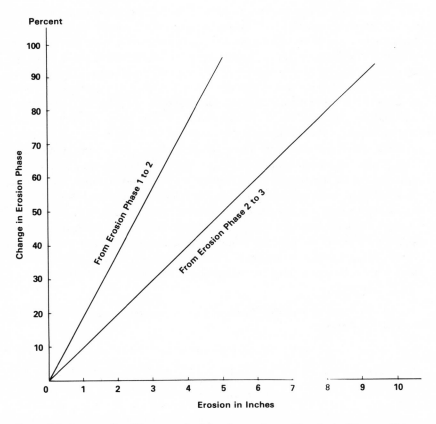

Figure 5.9 Amount of soil loss required for change in erosion phase. (*Source:* Harmon et al., no date.)

(1978). In the former, soils in the Southern Iowa Rivers Basin were identified as being in one of three erosion phases. Levels of crop yields were associated with soils in each erosion phase and were associated with the concomitant inputs of fertilizer, machine energy, and management practices necessary to achieve those yields. Finally, the amounts of soil loss for each soil type necessary to shift the soil from erosion phase 1 to erosion phase 2 and from erosion phase 2 to erosion phase 3 were estimated. Figure 5.9 shows the amount of soil loss required for a change in erosion phase. Table 5.7 shows the increases in fertilizer needs per acre, by crop, as soil loss increases. Even with the added fertilizer, crop yields generally decrease (table 5.8). This is because nutrient replenishment alone is often insufficient to restore soil productivity. The data on changes in crop yields and on increased factor inputs to production represent inputs to the evaluation step.

In the Scrivner and Neill work, the approach taken was to convert soil losses—computed with the Universal Soil Loss Equation—into yield reductions based on a soil productivity index. This index consists of aggregating productivity components for 4-inch soil layers to depths of 20 inches. The productivity of each layer for each crop is hypothesized to be dependent on sufficient supplies of plant-depletable water and on aeration, basic fertility, and density. The relative importance of each soil layer is based on the predicted fraction of water that is extracted from the layer for plant growth. Soil loss affects several of the indicated variables and, hence, overall productivity.

Estimating Off-site Effects of Soil Erosion. The gross erosion from an agricultural area is not necessarily the amount of sediment that actually enters a body of water. In fact, rarely would this be the case. To estimate how much of the gross soil eroded actually reaches a body of water, gross erosion must be multiplied by the *sediment delivery ratio.* This ratio equals the sediment measured at a specified location in a watershed divided by the gross soil eroded. Because the sediment delivery ratio is a function of a number of variables—slope, drainage pattern, elevation, vegetation, intensity of precipitation, volume of runoff per unit time, duration of storm events, and degree of channelization—no analytical model exists for estimating the ratio. Thus, it must be determined by measurement for each area of interest.

Table 5.7. Increases in Fertilizer Needs as Soil Is Depleted, Southern Iowa Rivers Basin, United States

Change in erosion phase	Corn			Soybeans		Oats			Meadow	
	N	P_2O_5	K_2O	P_2O_5	K_2O	N	P_2O_5	K_2O	P_2O_5	K_2O
				—pounds per acre—						
1 to 2	10	2	6	1	5	5	2	6	2	10
2 to 3	30	1	7	1	7	15	1	7	1	12

Source: Harmon, Knutson, and Rosenberry (no date).

Table 5.8. Reduction in Yields as Soil Is Depleted, Southern Iowa Rivers Basin, United States

Change in erosion phase	Reduced yield per acre			
	Corn	Soybeans	Oats	Hay
	——————bushels——————			tons
1 to 2	16	5	9	0.6
2 to 3	7	3	4	0.5

Source: Harmon, Knutson, and Rosenberry (no date).

Estimating Discharge of Residuals Other than Sediment.   As discussed in Chapter 4, suspended sediment is only one of the residuals generated by, and discharged from, agricultural activities. Nutrients, particularly nitrogen (N) and phosphorus (P), pesticides, and salts (measured as total dissolved solids, TDS) are other major residuals associated with agricultural activities. Such residuals are discharged in two ways. They are (1) attached to soil particles eroded from an agricultural area and transported in runoff, or (2) dissolved in either or both surface and groundwater runoff from the area. In general, more phosphates are discharged attached to soil particles and more nitrogen compounds are discharged in dissolved form. More or less of a pesticide will be discharged through one or the other pathway, depending on its form when applied (Loehr et al. 1979).

Because a significant portion of residuals discharge from agricultural activities is by attachment to soil particles, the most common approach for estimating gross discharges of these residuals is to relate the discharge to gross soil erosion; for example, as described in Hartman, Wanielista, and Baragona (1977). An example is the following equation (McElroy et al. 1976) for estimating nitrogen in runoff from agricultural cropland:

$$NT_E = 20 \times M \times A \times (NT)_s \times r_N , \tag{5-7}$$

where NT_E is the total nitrogen load from soil erosion, pounds per year; M is the average annual soil erosion estimated by equation 5–4, tons per acre per year; $(NT)_s$ is the total nitrogen concentration in soil, grams per 100 grams; A is the land surface area, acres; and r_N is the nitrogen enrichment ratio—that is, the nitrogen content of the eroded soil divided by $(NT)_s$. The coefficient, 20, was determined empirically from a number of observations; the values of $(NT)_s$ and r_N are measured for each case. To estimate how much of the estimated nitrogen load actually enters a body of water, a sediment delivery ratio would have to be applied to the total nitrogen load as estimated by equation 5–7.

In an analogous procedure, various empirical equations have been developed to estimate the concentration of nitrate-nitrogen in water leached through an agricultural area. An example is

$$C_{NO_3} - N = 4.42 \times N_f \times (P_i) \times (L_p/100) \, , \tag{5-8}$$

where $C_{NO_3} - N$ is the concentration of nitrate-nitrogen in the leaching water, milligrams per liter; N_f is the nitrogen fixed, pounds per year; P_i is the rainfall, inches per year; and L_p is the water leached beyond the root zone, inches per inches of rainfall.

All of these empirical methods start with an assumption about the quantity of a given material actually available from the agricultural crop or range land subjected to the transport process. This assumption is itself based on a set of assumptions about the effectiveness of fertilizer and pesticide application. For example, some portion of a pesticide applied by spray—from airplane or from a ground machine—will never reach the target plants because of drift. Another portion will become unavailable for runoff because of volatilization. Finally, depending on the time between application and the first rainfall or irrigation that produces runoff, there may be degradation of the pesticide into other forms.

Another important residual that can have adverse off-site effects is total dissolved solids (TDS). This residual is primarily generated in and discharged from irrigated agricultural operations. Off-site effects are most commonly determined by a salt-balance model, which relates the quantities of TDS discharged into a stream from each successive irrigated area to streamflow at each point. Generally, a range of possible streamflow conditions is investigated.

Total dissolved solids discharged from an irrigated area are a function of irrigation method, irrigation efficiency, quality of irrigation water, soil type, crop type, drainage system, if any, and leaching requirement—that is, the amount of water that must be leached through the root zone in order to maintain a salt balance in the root zone that does not reduce crop yield. Thus, before the salt-balance approach can be applied off-site, it must be applied on-site to estimate the TDS loading from the given irrigated area into the relevant body of surface or groundwater.

Effects of Forest Management Activities on Natural Systems: An Example of the Statistical Approach

Because both agricultural and forest management activities involve the manipulation of natural systems, many of the on-site and off-site effects derive from the same phenomena and can be analyzed with similar models. The processes related to soil erosion, described in the previous section, are relevant to both types of activities.

The most common type of model used to estimate gross erosion from forest management activities is statistical. Most commonly used are regression models based on empirical measurements. The estimates of gross erosion are then multiplied by sediment delivery ratios to yield estimates of sediment delivered to bodies of water. As for agricultural activities, most estimates of discharges into bodies of water of other residuals from forest management activities, such as pesticides and nutrients, are based on empirical relationships between those residuals and gross soil erosion. Off-site effects are then estimated using the various types of receiving-water models discussed in the section on agricultural activities. Empirical drift models are used to estimate pesticides that are transported in air beyond the area of application.

Assuming that the magnitudes of erosion from different subareas of the forest management area have been estimated by a residuals generation and runoff model, the on-site effects of soil losses can be assessed in terms of loss of site productivity. Soil loss affects productivity principally by reducing available nitrogen and decreasing moisture retention capacity. A study by Klock (1976) in the U.S. Pacific Northwest exemplifies the approach. Klock estimated on-site and off-site effects in both physical and monetary terms. A succinct description of the study is included here because it illustrates a rigorous and relevant analytical procedure.

The area used for the analysis consisted primarily of ponderosa pine habitat at the lower elevations and Douglas fir habitat at the higher elevations. Given the distributions of site classes and habitat types, an average production per acre was estimated based on 1975/76 management practices and a rotation of

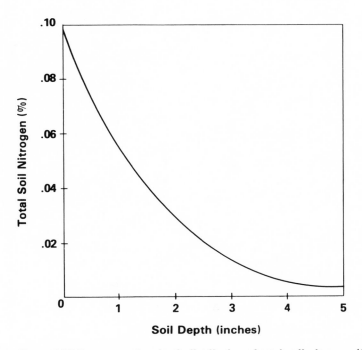

Figure 5.10 Representative depth distribution of total soil nitrogen. (*Source:* Klock, 1976.)

120 years. Productivity is related to soil nitrogen content, which in turn is related to soil depth (fig. 5.10). Based on these productivity estimates, the road construction and logging practices in the area, and frequency of natural precipitation events obtained from the historical record, the relation between cumulative soil loss and productivity loss was developed (fig. 5.11). This relationship represents the physical on-site effects as determined by the forest management study.

In the study, off-site effects were estimated from sedimentation in a downstream reservoir. This step involved (1) estimating sediment delivered to the river from gross soil loss; (2) estimating the transport and deposition, if any, of the sediment in the river reach to the downstream reservoir; and (3) estimating the ultimate destination of the sediment transported to the upstream end of the reservoir—for example, how much was deposited in the reservoir area and where, and how much passed through the reservoir via the outlet gates.

Given the estimates of on-site and off-site physical effects, the next step in the study was to evaluate the economic damages represented by these effects. Although this valuation step is relevant to Chapter 7, it is included here in the interest of continuity.

The monetary loss associated with on-site soil loss was estimated by cal-

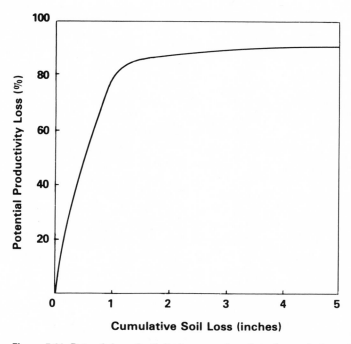

Figure 5.11 Potential productivity loss as a function of cumulative soil loss. (*Source:* Klock, 1976.)

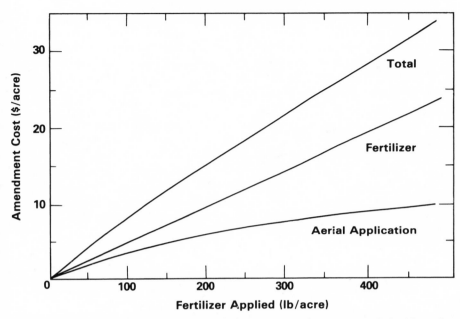

Note: Fertilizer costs were calculated at $100 per ton and aerial application costs were obtained from a fertilization program conducted by helicopter, as described in Perkins et al. (1970).

Figure 5.12 Amendment application cost for the study area. (*Source:* Klock, 1976.)

culating (1) the representative distribution of total soil nitrogen in the study area, and (2) the quantity of ammonium-phosphate-sulphate fertilizer needed to maintain the original level of available nitrogen in the soil. The costs of adding the fertilizer are shown in figure 5.12. Combining (1) and (2) yields the relationship between cumulative soil loss and on-site monetary losses (fig. 5.13). (In fact, the fertilizer cost may not be a good estimate of the economic costs of on-site soil loss. The true measure of such cost is the loss of productivity. The fertilizer cost could be greater than the economic value of the loss of productivity; alternatively, fertilizer could be a less than perfect substitute for the lost topsoil. However, in this example, fertilizer cost is assumed to be an adequate estimate of the economic value of lost productivity.)

Off-site damage estimates were based on the estimated costs of removing the sediment that had been deposited in the reservoir by transporting it from the study area. Unit costs for sediment removal were derived from various reservoir sediment removal projects.

Soil productivity losses plus downstream sedimentation damages were added to direct production costs to yield a total estimated cost per 1,000 board feet of merchantable lumber output at the mill. Table 5.9 lists total costs for six yarding systems and conditions.

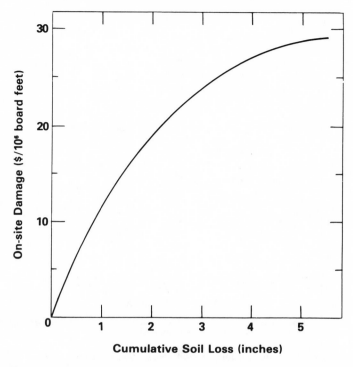

Figure 5.13 On-site damage due to cumulative soil loss. (*Source:* Klock, 1976.)

Table 5.9. Estimated Total Costs per 1,000 Board Feet of Merchantable Lumber for Six Yarding Systems

Yarding system, conditions	Estimated soil erosion	Direct cost[a]	Productivity losses	Sedimentation damages	Total costs
	Inches		Dollars/1,000 board feet		
Tractor, slopes 0–30%	0.20	34.85	3.30	12.50	50.65
Tractor, slopes 30–50%	0.80	34.85	10.60	50.00	95.45
Tractor, over snow, slopes 0–40%	0.08	38.60	1.50	5.00	45.10
Cable skidding	1.50	35.00	17.00	93.80	145.80
Skyline (Wyssen)	0.04	52.73	0.80	2.52	56.05
Helicopter	0.04	74.98	0.80	2.52	78.30

[a] Cost figures are for timber delivered at the mill for each yarding method used in the study area and were provided by Pack-River Lumber Company, Peshastin, Washington, United States.
Source: Klock (1976).

Valuation of the off-site effects of forest management by calculating the costs of removing sediment from the reservoir is only one method of valuation in such a context. A more appropriate method would be to estimate the losses associated with the reduction of fish life in the stream channel upstream from the reservoir and the losses in outputs from the reservoir as a result of sedimentation there. For example, sedimentation in the reservoir will reduce reservoir capacity, which in turn may decrease the quantity of hydroelectric energy, irrigation water, and flood damage protection provided by the reservoir, particularly if the reservoir is designed to store water from runoff over several years.

Table 5.9 illustrates how the on-site and off-site effects on natural systems can be incorporated directly into the project analysis. That is, the productivity losses and the sedimentation damages are added to the direct production costs to determine total costs of the project. These can be compared with the benefits expressed in terms of the value of the merchantable lumber produced.

Effects of Multiple Discharges on an Atmospheric System: An Example of the Conservation-of-Mass-and-Energy Approach

Ambient air quality in an atmospheric system at any time is the result of both natural and human factors (fig. 5.14). Natural factors include sunlight, wind, precipitation, vegetation, topography including the presence of bodies of water, cloud cover, and temperature gradient. Human factors include the spatial pattern and topography of structures, the types of activities, and the time patterns of generation and discharge of gaseous residuals from the activities. Various air quality models have been developed that take some of these factors into account in different degrees of detail.

Once discharged into the atmosphere, residuals are transported and transformed depending on existing meteorologic conditions and on the specific residuals discharged. The problems stemming from these combinations include acid rain; transport of fugitive dust; pesticide volatilization; transport of radioactivity; transport and deposition of toxic materials; transport and deposition of nutrients; transport of aeroallergens; formation and transport of sulfates; transport of conventional residuals such as sulphur dioxide (SO_2), total suspended particulates (TSP), carbon monoxide (CO), hydrocarbons (HC), and nitrogen dioxide (NO_2); and the formation and transportation of photochemical smog. Depending on the residuals discharged and the meteorologic conditions, residuals concentrations may have adverse effects on humans, plants, animals, fish, inanimate objects, and various types of nonbiological productive activities.

Unfortunately, current knowledge of most of these problems is only rudimentary and provides a meager basis for developing air quality models that are relevant and operational. Hence, the scope of the combinations of re-

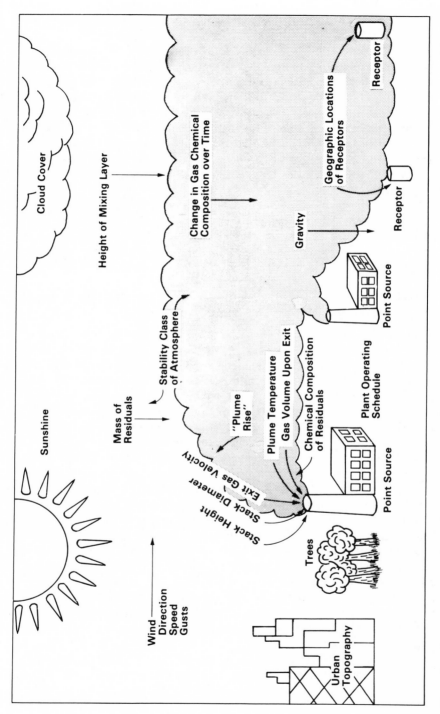

Figure 5.14 Some factors affecting ambient air quality. (*Source:* Kron et al., 1978.)

siduals discharges and meteorologic conditions that can be analyzed with the existing operational models is limited. Of the problems identified above, existing operational models generally deal only with combinations of them related to conventional residuals and photochemical smog.

Ambient concentrations of SO_2 and TSP are probably the two most widely used indicators of ambient air quality. Both are generated in the combustion of fossil fuels—coal, and oil, for example—and in various production processes—manufacture of steel, manufacture of pulp and paper, and petroleum refining. Particulates also are generated by a variety of other sources, such as wind erosion of agricultural lands and salt spray in coastal areas. The nature of the source is important because not all air quality models can analyze the effects of all types of sources on ambient air quality. Sources can be grouped in the following way:

1. *Stationary point source,* such as factory, with one or many discharge points within the source;
2. *Stationary area source* involving either
    a. an aggregate of individual discharge points, such as a neighborhood with a number of individual residences that are not individually identified, or
    b. an agricultural or silvicultural area from which particulates may be generated by wind, or from which pesticides may volatilize from the surface of plants and trees after spraying; and
3. *Line source,* which can be either
    a. mobile, such as moving vehicle, or
    b. stationary, such as a dirt road from which airborne particulates are generated as a result of wind action.

For purposes of analysis, receptor points are defined as the points in a region at which estimates of ambient concentrations are desired. Important characteristics of receptor points are their number, height, and spatial location. Receptor characteristics must be specified because air quality models vary in their capabilities for producing estimates of concentrations at specified receptor locations.

Most operational air quality models can be applied where the terrain is smooth or gently rolling and open, or where urban areas are situated on smooth terrain.

Air quality models are usually defined as either *long-term* or *short-term.* Long-term refers to air quality models capable of estimating annual average concentrations; short-term is associated with models that can estimate concentrations for averaging periods ranging from 24 hours to 8 hours, 3 hours, and 1 hour. Such short-term models often are of the nonsteady-state type because in such models meteorologic and residuals discharge conditions are varied for each averaging period, and the estimates of concentrations for the previous period are inputs as initial conditions for the following period. On the other hand, models that estimate annual or seasonal average concentrations are usually of the steady-state type. In this type of model, the meteorologic and residuals discharge conditions can also be varied for each averaging period analyzed; however, estimates of concentrations from the previous period are not used as initial conditions for the following period.

Short-term models typically are applied to problems related to episodic conditions and, therefore, are run for an analysis period of about seven consecutive days. If an averaging time of one hour is used, ambient concentrations would be estimated for 158 successive time periods. In contrast, a long-term model using annual averages could be run for only a few annual periods.

Air quality models currently in use have been classified into four geographic scales: (1) up to 5 kilometers (km); (2) from 5 km to about 50 km; (3) from 50 km to 200 km; and (4) greater than 200 km. Models that analyze the transport of residuals on a scale greater than 200 km are called long-range transport models; these have been developed only recently in response to an increased understanding of the importance of long-range transport of gaseous residuals.

A typical situation involving several point sources of discharges of gaseous residuals was shown in figure 5.14. To estimate ambient concentrations in such a situation, a Gaussian continuous plume model would be used. The following assumptions must be made in applying a model of this type:

1. The concentration of a residual in the discharge plume downwind from a source is distributed normally in each dimension—that is, the x, y, and z directions;
2. The rate of discharge from the source is uniform and continuous;
3. The mean wind speed affecting the plume is in the x-direction;
4. The plume is reflected totally at the earth's surface—that is, no deposition on or reaction with the surface takes place;
5. Diffusion in the x-direction can be neglected; and
6. Steady-state conditions prevail.

To assume that diffusion in the x-direction can be neglected, either the discharge must be continuous or the duration of discharge must be equal to or greater than the time of travel from the source to the location of interest. Based on the above assumptions, the resulting model is

$$C = \frac{Q}{2\pi\sigma_y\sigma_z U}\left[e^{-\frac{1}{2}\left(\frac{y}{\sigma_y}\right)^2} \right]$$

$$\left[e^{-\frac{1}{2}\left(\frac{z-H}{\sigma_z}\right)^2} + e^{-\frac{1}{2}\left(\frac{z+H}{\sigma_z}\right)^2} \right] \tag{5-9}$$

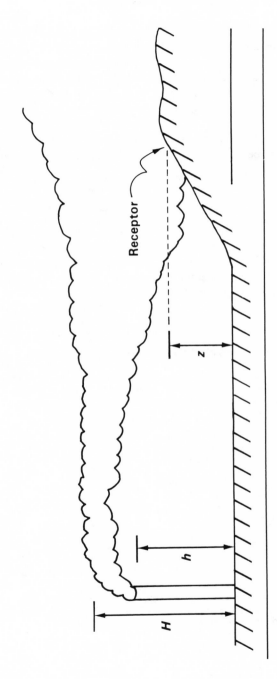

H = effective stack height; h = stack height; z = receptor height; $H - h$ = plume rise.

Figure 5.15 Relationship among stack height, effective stack height, and receptor height: point source discharge of gaseous residuals. (*Source:* Basta and Bower, 1982.)

where C is the concentration, units per cubic meters; Q is the discharge rate, units per second; H is the effective stack height, meters; σ_y is $2k_y t$, horizontal plume diffusion parameter, meters; σ_z is $2k_z t$, vertical plume diffusion parameter, meters; U is wind speed, meters per second; z is receptor height, meters; and y is receptor crosswind distance from plume, meters. Figure 5.15 shows the relationship among stack height, effective stack height, and receptor height.

For some applications, equation 5–9 can be simplified. For example, if concentrations were to be calculated only at ground level, z would equal zero, the term $e^{-\frac{1}{2}\left(\frac{z-H}{\sigma_z}\right)^2}$ in the equation would become zero, and the term $e^{-\frac{1}{2}\left(\frac{z+H}{\sigma_z}\right)^2}$ would become $e^{-\frac{1}{2}\left(\frac{H}{\sigma_z}\right)^2}$. In addition, if the discharge were at ground level and there were no plume rise, effective stack height H would also become zero and the equation would be further simplified.

Table 5.10 summarizes the characteristics of a Gaussian-type model used for estimating ground-level concentrations of sulfur dioxide and particulates from multiple sources in an urban, industrialized region.

Table 5.10. Summary of Characteristics of a Gaussian-plume Atmospheric Dispersion Model

Inputs of residuals (annual average tons/day):	Target outputs (ground-level, annual average ambient concentrations—μm/m³):
Sulfur dioxide	Sulfur dioxide
Particulate matter	Suspended particulates

Model characteristics: deterministic, steady-state
Input requirements:
  1. Sources
      (a) x–y coordinates of each stack
      (b) discharge rates for each source
      (c) physical stack height
      (d) stack diameter
      (e) stack exit temperature
      (f) stack exit velocity
  2. Receptors
      x–y coordinates of each receptor location
  3. Atmosphere
      (a) annual joint probability distribution for wind speed (6 classes), wind direction (16 directions), and atmospheric stability (5 classes), using 1970 data for Philadelphia; the result is 480 discrete meteorological situations
      (b) mean temperature: 68° F (20° C)
      (c) mean annual pressure: 1,017 millibars (30.03 inches of mercury)
      (d) mean maximum afternoon atmospheric mixing depth: 1,000 meters

Source: Adapted from Spofford, Russell, and Kelly (1976).

SOME PROBLEMS IN ESTIMATING EFFECTS ON NATURAL SYSTEMS

Regardless of the type of natural-systems model, a number of common problems complicate its adoption, operation, and utility. Raising these underscores the difficulty of selecting, modifying, and developing appropriate models for any given analysis. This section briefly describes five problems. The order of discussion does not imply order of importance.

Complexity of Natural-Systems Models

A critical problem in any analysis is determining how complex a model to use. Four facets of model complexity can be identified. These are the relationship between model complexity and (1) model accuracy, (2) model cost, (3) the amount of information generated toward answering the questions being addressed, and (4) the degree to which observed data are available for model calibration and verification.

Model complexity is defined as a function of the number of variables explicitly included in the model structure and the accuracy of the estimates of the values relating to each of those variables. Presumably, the accuracy with which a model predicts the values of indicators of effects increases as model complexity increases. But in actuality, as complexity increases, the rate of increase in accuracy diminishes and the rate of increase in cost of modeling rises (fig. 5.16). In fact, accuracy may actually decrease if the model becomes so complex that it is unstable.

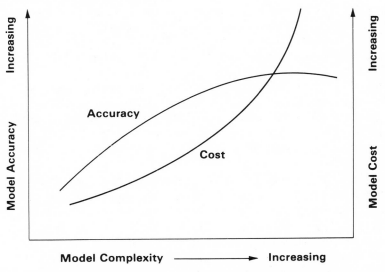

Figure 5.16 Relationships among model complexity, model accuracy, and model cost.

Increasing model complexity usually increases the amount of information produced. For example, a Streeter-Phelps model only yields estimates of dissolved oxygen (DO) and five-day biochemical oxygen demand (BOD_5) concentrations, whereas an aquatic ecosystem model might yield not only DO and BOD_5 concentrations, but also algal concentration, biomass of fish, and turbidity. A model can become so complex, however, that the information generated becomes difficult to interpret.

The complexity of a natural-systems model to be used in a given situation depends also on the accuracy of the model relative to the accuracy of the available residuals discharge data and to the accuracy of the valuation estimates of effects on natural systems and receptors.

Finally, if empirical data to calibrate and verify a model are limited, there is little point in developing a complex model. In such cases, no way exists to determine whether a complex model would predict effects on natural systems better than a simple model.

Calibration and Verification

Calibration and verification are sequential but separate steps required before a model can be used to estimate the effects on natural systems of (1) production activities and residuals discharges and (2) applying physical measures for reducing residuals discharges. For *calibration*, a set of observed data is used to adjust the model's structure and internal coefficients so that the values of the indicators of effects estimated by the model are within acceptable limits in relation to the observed values. If the differences between the estimated and the observed values are greater than the limits established for calibrating the model, the model is considered unacceptable and must be analyzed for possible causes of error. Three primary sources of error are inaccurate input data, inaccurate internal coefficients, and inadequate model structure.

After adjustments are made, the model is run again, and the new estimates of effects are compared to the observed values. The process is repeated until either estimated values fall within the specified limits of accuracy and the model therefore is acceptable, or all known errors have been eliminated and the estimated values are still not acceptable, and therefore the model must be abandoned.

For *verification*, a set of observed data different from the set used in calibration is compared with estimated values generated by the model. If the differences between the estimated and the observed values fall within specified limits, then the model is said to be verified and is ready for use. If differences between the estimated and the observed values are greater than the limits specified, the model would not be used. The sources of possible discrepancies must be identified. In some situations, the cause will be errors in the new data; in others, the model may have to be recalibrated, perhaps modified, and then reverified; in still others, the model may have to be abandoned.

A major problem affecting calibration and verification of models is the lack of adequate data, particularly independent sets of data. Seldom are sufficient data available to satisfy the needs of both calibration and verification. This places severe limits on the availability of suitable models, because a model that has not been calibrated and verified should never be used in final analyses.

A second major problem is the specification of acceptable limits of accuracy for a model. In general, most operational models are relatively inaccurate if conventional notions of accuracy are applied. For example, in applications of Gaussian air quality models to metropolitan regions for estimating seasonal averages of air quality indicators, acceptable accuracy is considered achieved when estimated values are within a factor of one or two of the observed values. In a model that estimates values for more than one indicator, different accuracy limits can be specified for different indicators. The limits of accuracy should be set relative to the accuracies of other segments of the analysis, the questions being asked, and the levels of accuracy attainable with the models.

Background Concentrations of Residuals

Background concentrations of residuals are ambient concentrations that result from sources for which no explicit estimates of discharges from individual sources are made and for which no explicit physical measures to reduce discharges are considered in the analysis. These sources include (1) natural sources within the region; (2) human activities within the region that are so small in scale that the discharge from each individual activity is insignificant, but when added to other similar discharges may become significant; and (3) sources outside the region—that is, cross-boundary transfers of residuals. The third source can consist of any one or a combination of single major sources, natural sources, and many small-scale sources. In any given analysis, all of these sources may be incorporated in the background concentrations, and no measures to reduce discharges from these sources would be included.

These background concentrations obviously are important because they represent the upper bound of air quality improvement that is attainable by adoption of physical measures within the region. If residuals discharges from all targeted human activities in a region were reduced to zero, the ambient air quality would reflect only background concentrations. In some situations, the *intra*regional natural sources and *extra*regional sources may be large enough that the desired level of ambient air quality *within* the region could not be achieved even with zero discharges from targeted activities within the region.

Links between Models of Natural Systems and the Analysis of Activities

The links between models of natural systems and the analysis of activities are another critical aspect of the analysis of natural systems. The analysis of activities provides residuals discharge data as inputs to models of natural systems; hence, the accuracy of the outputs from the natural-systems model depends on the accuracy of the input data generated in the analysis of activities.

Frequently, the natural-systems model being used requires residuals discharge data that are more detailed than the data that can be provided by the analysis of activities. For example, an air quality model used to analyze an episodic condition—that is, three or four days of extremely poor air quality—typically will use an averaging time of one hour. Almost always, however, it is impossible to estimate daily—not to mention hourly—variations in residuals discharges for (1) even the most important activities in a region, (2) natural sources in a region, and (3) sources outside of the region. In such situations, residuals discharges are usually assumed to be constant over the selected time period, and an estimated average hourly discharge rate is used as input to the model. The effect on the accuracy of the output will vary depending on the type of model, the types of activities in the region, the importance of background sources, the importance of sources outside the region, the nature of the problem, and meteorologic and hydrologic conditions.

Interpreting Results of Applying Models

The accuracy of the outputs of most natural-systems models is at best only one order of magnitude. This is partially attributable to the low accuracy of input data. But in fact, regardless of the accuracy of the input data, models are only abstractions of reality, and this in itself leads to difficulties in interpreting the results of applying them. Thus, the chemical, biochemical, physical, physicochemical, and ecological processes at work in nature are stochastic phenomena. But almost all operational models consider these processes and the associated relationships to be nonstochastic. Also, most relationships among variables in natural systems are *nonlinear,* but are formulated as *linear* relationships for computational convenience in many models. In addition, not all of the relevant variables in natural systems can be incorporated in a model. Finally, the calibration and verification of a model are always done for some range of conditions for which data are available, and the relevant set of conditions estimated for some point in time in the future may lie far outside that range; hence, the model would no longer be valid.

Given these factors, one way to enhance the interpretation of results in applying models is to investigate the sensitivity of model outputs to changes in values of input variables and in the structure of the model itself. This is commonly referred to as *sensitivity analysis,* which is the investigation of changes in values of indicators of effects on natural systems that result from changes in values of independent variables and in the assumed relationship among the variables. An independent variable has more or less relative importance depending on the effect it has on the dependent variable. The variable that causes the largest change in the dependent variable for a unit change in its own value is, by definition, the most important.

Sensitivity analysis can be a difficult analytical task, but nevertheless is an important tool for evaluating results. At the very least, it is important to identify the most important variables that affect estimates of effects, because low accuracy in these variables will yield low accuracy in the estimation of effects. Sensitivity analysis can often indicate where more data collection and respecification of relationships in the model can improve accuracy and, hence, overall results.

APPROACHES FOR ESTIMATING EFFECTS ON RECEPTORS

In common with estimating effects on natural systems, two approaches are used to estimate effects on receptors: statistical, and conservation of mass and energy. The statistical approach has two categories: the first is a rudimentary or implicit statistical approach that involves either or both laboratory and field measurements, which are then used to impute simple graphical relationships. The second category is regression analysis, as previously described and illustrated in this chapter.

The conservation-of-mass-and-energy approach also has two categories, each of which involves an engineering-economic model that uses mass and energy balances for each process or operation. In one category, however, the analysis is carried out as a judgmental search for possible alternatives. In the second category, the analysis uses some form of mathematical programming.

Statistical Approach: Rudimentary

The rudimentary statistical approach is illustrated by the problems of estimating the effects of discharges of suspended sediment on resident fish species; of photochemical oxidants on vegetation; and of discharges of total dissolved solids on irrigated crops and a vegetable cannery. As previously discussed, the time pattern of sediment entering a stream, as estimated from gross soil erosion and the sediment delivery ratio, becomes the input to a receiving-water model. For example, a particular receiving-water model translates the sediment load into (1) stream turbidity and (2) fine sediment in a salmon spawning bed. Then, field measurements are made to develop empirical relationships that translate these variables into effects on fish (figs. 5.17–18). The estimated effects on fish species become the inputs to the valuation step.

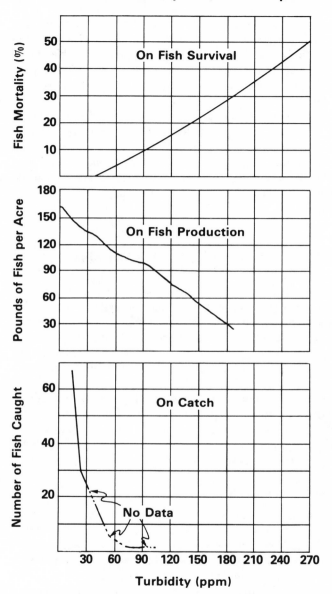

Figure 5.17 Effects of turbidity on the survival, production, and catch of fish. (*Source:* U.S. Department of Agriculture, 1969.)

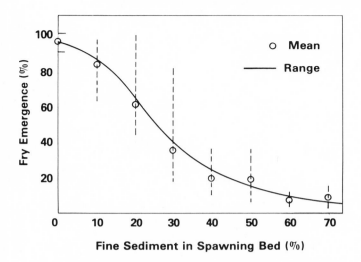

Figure 5.18 Relationship between fine sediment in salmon spawning bed and emergence of fry. (*Source:* U.S. Department of Agriculture, 1969.)

The effects of photochemical oxidants—resulting from discharges of certain gaseous residuals in the presence of sunlight—on vegetation are functions of ambient concentration and the duration of the concentration. One outward manifestation may be discoloration of leaves, but the crucial biological effect is the reduction in crop yield or annual tree growth (fig. 5.19). Such a relationship would be developed for a particular crop or tree species in a particular location based on laboratory experiments and field observations and measurements. Similarly, the quality of irrigation water is an important factor in productivity of irrigated agriculture. Different crops have different degrees of tolerance to concentrations of total dissolved solids. For any given crop and given amount of irrigation water applied, as the concentrations increase, yield generally decreases. Possible responses to the problem include applying additional water to leach the salts through the soil or changing crops.

Increased concentrations of total dissolved solids in intake water can have adverse effects on industrial activities as well as on agricultural activities. For example, in canning green beans, at some concentration of total dissolved solids the quality of the product begins to decrease (fig. 5.20). Beyond a certain level, product quality has decreased so much that the output is no longer acceptable. The circles on the figure represent empirical measurements that would be made to develop the indicated relationship.

Statistical Approach: Regression Analysis

A common application of regression analysis is to estimate effects of air quality on human health. Assuming that the discharges of gaseous residuals

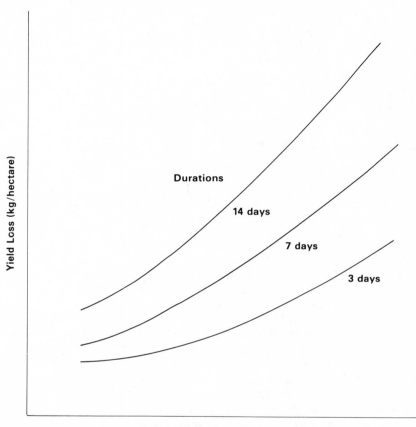

Figure 5.19 Relationship between oxidant concentration and crop yield loss.

into the atmosphere can be translated with reasonable accuracy into the resulting time and spatial patterns of ambient concentrations for each residual, the next problem is to estimate the exposure of individuals to air quality conditions. The actual exposure of individuals is a function of their activity patterns—the time spent in the home, at work, in transit to and from work, in recreation, and in other nonwork, nonrecreational activities.

The World Health Organization (WHO) has estimated that most people spend approximately 85% of their time indoors. This indicates that outdoor exposures to ambient air quality must constitute but a small portion of total exposures for humans. Indoor concentrations of certain gaseous residuals typically exceed outdoor concentrations. Thus, for most of the individuals in the WHO study, the average total exposures were closer to the levels in the home than to those at other sites. Table 5.11, based on one set of measure-

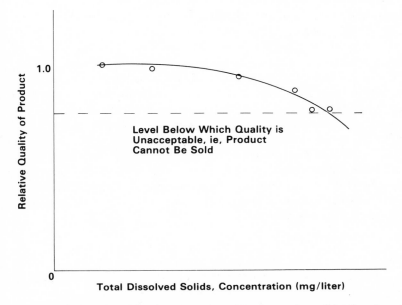

Figure 5.20 Relationship between quality of intake water and quality of product in canning of green beans.

ments, shows that the ratio of indoor to outdoor concentrations exceeds 1.0 for CO, respirable particulates, and NO_2. Because humans spend a large portion of their time indoors, outdoor air quality concentrations cannot be relied upon to estimate total exposure.

Once the cumulative exposure and the time pattern of exposure are estimated for individuals or groups of individuals, the next step is to estimate the effects of the exposure; that is, the dose-response relationship. Effects on health are usefully defined in terms of (1) premature death, (2) progressive

Table 5.11. Ratio of Indoor to Outdoor Concentrations of Selected Air Quality Indicators

Air quality indicator	Ratio of indoor to outdoor concentrations
Carbon monoxide (CO)	greater than 1
Respirable particulates	greater than 1
Nitrogen dioxide (NO_2)	greater than 1
Total suspended particulates (TSP)	approximately 1
Sulfur dioxide (SO_2)	less than 1
Ozone (O_3)	less than 1

Note: Simultaneous measurements were obtained in U.S. cities in Massachusetts, Tennessee, Ohio, Missouri, Wisconsin, and Kansas.
Source: U.S. General Accounting Office (1979).

deterioration of the human system, and (3) temporary discomforts. Acute mortality effects generally occur for individuals who are already in poor physical condition. Progressive deterioration occurs with bronchitis or cancer and can eventually lead to death. The death may or may not be a result of the chronic disease, however; that is, some other disease, such as pneumonia, may well be the proximate cause of death. In contrast, temporary discomfort, such as eye irritation, allows the system to return essentially to normal after exposure ceases because there is no deterioration in the capacity of the human system to operate as a result of the temporary exposure.

The dose-response function for a given segment of the population is an estimate of the relationship between levels of one or more residuals to which the population segment has been exposed and the effects. Regression analysis has been used to estimate dose-response relationships for both acute and chronic effects. The basic formulation is

$$M_j = f(AQI_i, BI_j, OEI_k), \tag{5-10}$$

where M_j is the disease-specific mortality for an age group; AQI_i is a set of air quality indicators i, such as concentrations of sulfur dioxide and respirable particulates; BI_j is a set of behavioral indicators for group j, such as nutritional level, smoking habits, and exercise habits; and OEI_k is a set of other environmental indicators, k, such as concentration of various chemicals in drinking water, total annual quantities of various chemicals in food intake, and temperature and humidity. Various equations have been specified and various sets of cross-sectional and time-series data have been used to derive dose-response effects.

Estimating the effects of substances on humans is extremely complicated. Even when concentrations are high enough to produce acute effects, isolating the cause is not straightforward. Exposure to a given substance occurs through a variety of pathways, including the skin, the digestive system, and the respiratory system (fig. 5.21). Depending on the pathway and the chemical nature of the substance, a variety of systems within the body may be affected before expulsion or excretion occurs. Causality is difficult to establish when exposure is at low levels, and the effect may take place over a number of years, at different locations, and in combination with other stressors. Finally, susceptibility differs substantially among individuals.

The concept of a dose-response relationship implies causality; but as an analytical approach, multiple regression does not imply causality. The air quality data are either assumed to be representative of geographic areas, or the points at which they are measured are assumed to represent the average exposure of all individuals in the population of any given geographic area. At the same time, morbidity and mortality data pertain to specific individuals. All of the data used are either general purpose information or statistics collected for a purpose other than to establish dose-response relationships. The results of the many regression analyses done in the United States to relate air

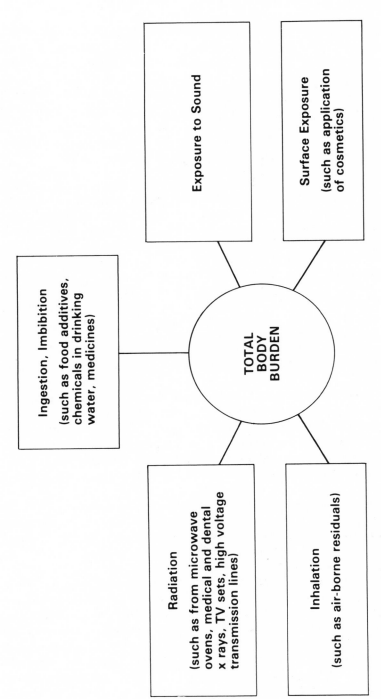

Figure 5.21 Modes of effects on humans.

quality to disease-specific mortality are not very consistent and are, at best, suggestive and not conclusive. Even more uncertainty exists about the use of regression analyses to relate air quality to disease-specific or general morbidity.

Some of the problems and results of developing dose-response relationships are discussed in Lave and Seskin (1977), Crocker et al. (1979), and Mendelsohn and Orcutt (1979).

Conservation-of-Mass-and-Energy Approach

Activities such as pulp mills, power plants, vegetable canneries, instrument manufacturers, and municipal water plants require inputs from, as well as make discharges to, the environmental media. The inputs are in the forms of intakes of water and air. To the extent that the quality of the intake water and air is degraded by discharges from neighboring activities, adverse effects occur at the plants using the intake water or air.

For example, a power plant upstream from a paper mill discharges heat into a stream from its cooling operation, thereby increasing the temperature of the stream, particularly in the summer and fall. The increase in water temperature decreases the efficiency of water withdrawn from the stream to provide cooling services to the paper mill. The losses arising from this decrease in efficiency can be reflected by the equipment that must be installed or procedures that must be followed—and the costs thereof—to compensate for the decrease.

Increased concentrations of suspended sediment at intakes of municipal and industrial water users may require additional water treatment facilities, or increased operating expenditures, to produce the desired quality of water for drinking, manufacturing, and other uses. Therefore, a relationship between concentration of suspended sediment and extent of water intake treatment and, hence, cost must be developed for each user withdrawing water from the river.

An instrument-manufacturing plant requires air that is virtually 100% free of particulates for the final assembly of the instruments. As the concentration of particulates in the ambient air increases, additional filtering equipment must be installed, or operating expenditures must be increased, to obtain the quality of air required.

In such typical situations, the effects on receptors are estimated (1) by developing materials and energy balances of alternative combinations of production process units, materials and energy recovery units, and treatment process trains; and (2) by selecting the combination that minimizes total production costs relative to the intake environmental conditions, using either the judgmental search or mathematical-programming approach. Judgmental search takes advantage of the experience of the plant or resident engineers who normally have considerable knowledge of alternatives that are likely to work. In such situations, it is not necessary to analyze many combinations or to put the analysis into a programming format. Where many options are available, however, and many different combinations of input conditions are to be analyzed, mathematical-programming formulations can be useful (Russell 1973).

CONCLUDING COMMENTS

In conclusion, five points require emphasis. First, in activities that involve the management of natural systems in producing goods and services, the fundamental question during the analysis for the planning decision is, What combination of management inputs and attributes of the natural systems will yield the best mix of outputs of products and services? In each situation, the analyst must try to ascertain quantitatively what happens to the relevant natural systems with alternative sets of possible management inputs. This requires models of the relevant natural systems, no matter how meager the data for such models may be.

Second, effects on natural systems and receptors are always dynamic. Acute short-run effects, long-run cumulative effects, and irreversibilities may exist. The effects of human activities are superimposed on the variability inherent in natural systems. Although much of the analysis necessarily will be of steady-state conditions because of the many limitations faced by the analyst, explicit recognition of the longer-run setting is nevertheless essential.

Third, when assessing natural systems in a natural-resources management context, it is essential to consider the effects of alternative production processes—for example, forest management, range management, agricultural operations, irrigation systems, and reservoir design and operation. Thus, the analysis of effects must be an explicit part of the project and program design, not an afterthought embodied in a separate environmental impact statement after the project and program variables have been fixed. Often, the effects on natural systems will be such that the on-site project benefits estimated without regard to these effects will not be achieved.

Fourth, the illustrations of the relationships between management inputs and alternative production processes and effects described in this chapter are taken from United States experience and data. The results for a temperate forest are not likely to be directly applicable to a tropical forest. But the general approach is applicable, and the examples illustrate the types of relationships that need to be developed for any given context. We recognized that for most developing countries, programs for collecting and analyzing the empirical data essential for developing such relationships and making such estimates of effects on natural systems are extremely limited. Although such relationships developed for the U.S. situation are suggestive, for developing countries, of variables that are probably relevant and directions that effects are likely to take, new structural relationships and associated coefficients must be developed for any given situation.

Finally, the accuracy of the estimates of effects on natural systems is subject to wide variations. For example, the variability may be ±25% for certain water quality indicators in a particular reach of stream, in a lake, or in a small estuary, and may be ±100% or more for air quality indicators involving transport of gaseous residuals over long distances (1,000–3,000 kilometers). Even so, the accuracy of the estimates of effects may be substantially better than the accuracy of the estimates of the economic values associated with effects, provided that the estimates of discharges into the environmental media are reasonably accurate (±25–50%). Therefore, an important part of the analyst's task is to look at the linked set of analyses that must be made in any context in which the output of one analysis becomes the input to the next. The level of sophistication of analysis at any one step should be no greater than necessary in relation to the accuracies of the analyses in the other steps.

REFERENCES

Basta, D. J., and B. T. Bower, eds. *Analyzing Natural Systems: Analysis for Regional Residuals Environmental Quality Management.* Washington, D.C.: Resources for the Future, 1982.

Chepil, W. S. "Dynamics of Wind Erosion." *Soil Science* 60 (1946): 305–20, 397–411, 475–80.

Crocker, T. D.; W. D. Schulze; B. D. Shaul; and A. V. Kneese. *Methods Development for Assessing Air Pollution Control Benefits.* Experiments in the Economics of Air Pollution Epidemiology. vol. 1. Washington, D.C.: Environmental Protection Agency, 1979.

El-Swaify, S. A.; E. W. Dangler; and C. A. Armstrong. *Soil Erosion by Water in the Tropics: A State of the Art.* Final Report to the U.S. Agency for International Development. Honolulu: Department of Agronomy and Soil Science, University of Hawaii, 1979.

Harmon, L.; R. Knutson; and P. Rosenberry. *Soil Depletion Study Reference Report, Southern Iowa Rivers Basin.* Des Moines, Iowa: U.S. Soil Conservation Service, n.d.

Hartman, J. P.; M. P. Wanielista; and G. T. Baragona. "Prediction of Soil Loss in Nonpoint-Source Pollution Studies." In *Soil Erosion: Prediction and Control: Proceedings of a National Conference on Soil Erosion. May 24–26, 1976.* Ankeny, Iowa: Soil Conservation Society of America, 1977.

Holling, C. S., ed. *Adaptive Environmental Assessment and Management.* New York: Wiley, 1978.

Klock, G. O. *Estimating Two Indirect Logging Costs Caused by Accelerated Erosion.* General Technical Report PNW-44. Pacific Northwest Forest and Range Experiment Station. Portland, Oreg.: U.S. Forest Service, 1976.

Kron, N. F.; A. S. Kohen; and L. M. Mele. *Emission Density Zoning Guidebook.* Publication No. 450/3–78–048. Research Triangle Park, N.C.: Environmental Protection Agency, 1978.

Lave, L. B., and E. P. Seskin. *Air Pollution and Human Health.* Baltimore: Johns Hopkins University Press, 1977.

Loehr, R. C.; D. A. Haith; M. F. Walter; and C. S. Martin. *Best Management Practices for Agriculture and Silviculture.* Ann Arbor, Mich.: Ann Arbor Science Publishers, 1979.

McElroy, A. D.; S. Y. Chiu; J. W. Nebgen; A. Aleti; and F. W. Bennett. *Loading Functions for Assessment of Water Pollution from Nonpoint Sources.* Report No. EPA-600/2–76–151. Washington, D.C.: Environmental Protection Agency, 1976.

Mendelsohn, R., and G. Orcutt. "Empirical Analysis of Air Pollution Dose-Response Curves." *Journal of Environmental Economics and Management* 6 (1979): 85–106.

Pimental, D.; E. C. Terhune; R. D. Hudson; S. Rocherau; R. Samis; E. Smith; D. Denman; D. Reifschneider; and M. Shepard. "Land Degradation: Effects on Food and Energy Resources." *Science* 194 (8 October 1976): 149–155.

Russell, C. S. *Residuals Management in Industry: A Case Study of Petroleum Refining.* Baltimore: Johns Hopkins University Press, 1973.

Scrivner, C. L., and L. Neill. *A Proposed System for Evaluating Productivity of Missouri Soils.* Columbia, Mo.: Department of Agronomy, University of Missouri, 1978.

Simmons, S. R., and A. D. Dotzenko. "Proposed Indices for Estimating the Inherent Wind Erodibility of Soils." *Journal of Soil and Water Conservation* 25, 5 (1974): 275–76.

Smith, R. A.; R. Slack; and R. K. Davis. *An Oilspill Risk Analysis for the North Atlantic Outer Continental Shelf Lease Area.* Open-File Report 76–620. Reston, Va.: U.S. Geological Survey, 1978.

Soil Conservation Society of America. *Effects of Tillage and Crop Residue Removal on Erosion, Runoff, and Plant Nutrients.* Ankeny, Iowa, 1979.

Spofford, W. O., Jr., C. S. Russell, and R. A. Kelly. *Environmental Quality Management: An Application to the Lower Delaware River Valley.* Research Paper R-1. Washington, D. C.: Resources for the Future, 1976.

Stewart, B. W.; D. A. Woolhiser; W. H. Wischmeier; J. H. Caro; and M. H. Frere. *Control of Water Pollution from Cropland.* vol. 1. A Manual for Guideline Development. Prepared by Agricultural Research Service. Washington, D.C.: Environmental Protection Agency, November 1975.

Storie, R. E. *Revision of the Soil-Rating Chart.* Berkeley, Calif.: College of Agriculture, Experiment Station, University of California, 1954.

True, H. A. *Erosion, Sedimentation and Rural Runoff: A Gross Assessment Process.* Athens, Ga.: Surveillance and Analysis Division, Environmental Protection Agency, July 1974.

U.S. Department of Agriculture. *Douglas-Fir Supply Study.* Pacific Northwest Forest and Range Experiment Station. Portland, Oreg.: U.S. Forest Service, 1969.

U.S. Environmental Protection Agency. *Methods for Identifying and Evaluating the Nature and Extent of Non-point Sources of Pollutants.* Pub. No. EPA-430/9–73–014. Washington, D.C., October 1973.

U.S. General Accounting Office. *Air Quality Monitoring: A Report to the Congress.* Washington, D.C., 1979.

U.S. Soil Conservation Service. *Procedure for Computing Sheet and Rill Erosion on Project Areas.* Technical Release No. 51. Washington, D.C., January 1975.

Wilson, L. "Application of the Wind Erosion Equation in Air Pollution Surveys." *Journal of Soil and Water Conservation* 30, 5 (1975): 215–19.

Wischmeier, W. H., and D. D. Smith. *Predicting Rainfall-Erosion Losses from Cropland East of the Rocky Mountains.* Agriculture Handbook 282. Washington, D.C.: Department of Agriculture, 1965.

6

Environmental Quality Valuation from the Benefit Side

VALUING BENEFITS—A BRIEF SUMMARY

This chapter presents a variety of techniques for placing a value on the benefits (or costs) of changes in environmental quality. These techniques are symmetrical to the extent that they value benefits from the uses of environmental goods that would become costs if these uses were lost. Chapter 7, on the other hand, presents a number of techniques that value the environment by measuring the costs of preventing or offsetting an undesired environmental change.

The primary feature of the techniques described in this chapter is the use of actual market prices whenever possible. The techniques have been divided into three broad categories: (1) those based directly on market values or productivity, (2) those using market values of substitute (surrogate) or complementary goods, and (3) those approaches using survey techniques. A fourth approach, based on litigation and compensation, is mentioned but not discussed in detail.

Market value or productivity approaches are a basic benefit-cost analysis technique. When environmental goods or services are involved, it may be difficult to determine the appropriate market prices. A soil conservation project in Nepal is used to illustrate the productivity approach and the ways of valuing outputs under both the existing system and a new management scheme. Market prices are used to value products that are marketed both directly and indirectly.

The *human capital,* or *foregone earnings, approach* uses market prices and wage rates to value the potential contribution of an individual to society. No benefits are measured in this approach, but a minimum value is established for a life or for illness or incapacity. Although one may object to its ethical basis, the technique does provide some measure of these values. These values are then used in making decisions about the benefits and costs of changes that might affect worker safety, sickness, and death.

When market data are sparse, the *opportunity-cost, or foregone income, method* may be suitable. This approach uses market data to calculate not the value of benefits but rather the cost of preserving these benefits. What economic benefits must be given up when a resource is not developed or exploited is the question posed. In a situation where irreversible changes in environmental quality are likely, this may be a useful first approach to placing some minimum value on the environmental benefits involved. A more sophisticated version of this approach incorporates the fact that the value of environmental goods and services, such as public parks, open rivers, or wilderness areas, may increase faster than the value of capital goods.

Surrogate market price approaches are a second way to value environmental changes. With these the prices of substitute or complementary goods are used to value an unpriced environmental good or service.

Sometimes, the value of environmental amenities, such as clean air, or of different levels of these amenities becomes a factor in the price of marketable assets. An analysis of the price differentials of such assets (e.g., houses or land) may help one determine an implicit price for the environmental amenity. The *property value approach* is based on this principle and has been used to value changes in the level of air pollution. Major limitations of the approach stem from problems of data accuracy and acquisition. Other land value approaches are also presented. These have been used to value the benefits of preserving wetlands and the nonproductivity-related benefits from improved range management. In each case market prices of land have been used to value environmental benefits—either environmental goods or services or aesthetic factors.

The *wage differential approach* is very similar to the property value approach. It uses information about wages for similar jobs in different locations to value implicitly the different environmental quality dimensions of the locations. The approach is based on the theory that higher wages would be paid for jobs in polluted areas or with greater risk to life and health.

The last major surrogate market technique is the *travel-cost approach*. It is widely used for valuing recreational facilities and relies on the premise that the time and money spent traveling to a free or low-cost recreation site indicate the consumer's true valuation of that site. Therefore, it can be used to estimate the true economic value (including consumer's surplus) of an existing recreation site, even if no admission charge is levied.

Survey techniques are the basis for the last category of approaches. These approaches use surveys and games to help determine people's preferences and thereby place values on environmental goods and services. Bidding games can bring out either a person's willingness to pay or willingness to accept compensation for some environmental change. Budget allocation and trade-off games yield similar information.

A second group of survey techniques relies on direct questioning about choices of quantities to *infer* an individual's willingness to pay or accept compensation. The *costless choice technique* is one of these approaches. A more sophisticated method is the *priority evaluator technique,* which is based on the theory that people will maximize their utility under budgetary constraints.

Delphi techniques rely on the informed opinions of a group of experts and are commonly used in many complex planning and decision-making situations. For economic valuation the technique depends heavily on the knowledge and background of experts and on the skill with which the technique is applied.

MARKET VALUE OR PRODUCTIVITY APPROACHES

Theoretical Basis

The techniques included in this group are straightforward benefit-cost analysis methods. The emphasis, however, is on the economic valuation of environmental quality effects on natural or human-built systems. The effects on these systems are reflected in the productivity of the systems (including both the physical and human components) and in the products that derive from them and enter into market transactions. Examples of such effects on natural systems are found in fisheries, forests, and agriculture; effects on human-built systems include those on buildings, materials, and products in the producer and household sectors.

Environmental quality is viewed here as a factor of production. Changes in environmental quality lead to changes in productivity and production costs, which lead in turn to changes in prices and levels of output, which can be observed and measured. For example:

1. A reduction in soil erosion may stabilize or even increase upland rice paddy yields (fig. 6.1). Comparison of the situation with and without the soil conservation scheme shows the productivity benefits arising from soil conservation. These gains in productivity can be measured as the shaded area in figure 6.1; gross economic benefits can be computed as the extra yield in rice multiplied by its market price.
2. Improvement in the quality of irrigation water (such as by reducing salinity) may improve crop productivity. The resulting increase in output multiplied by the price of output can be taken as the benefit of the improvement in water quality.
3. Air pollution from a chemical plant may adversely affect agricultural productivity around the plant. Again, the economic value of the lost agricultural output is a measure of the benefit that could be obtained if the pollution were reduced.
4. Air pollution can cause damage to materials through corrosion. The damage can be repaired by treatment, painting, or replacement of the

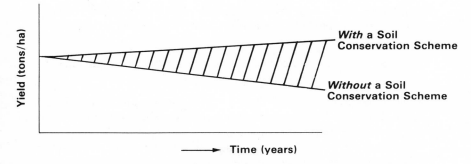

Figure 6.1 Benefits of a soil conservation program in terms of increased yields.

materials. The monetary value of these repairs can be measured; in some circumstances these repair costs can be used to represent the value of the benefits from eliminating the air pollution.

5. Air pollution can adversely affect the productivity of the human labor force through increases in illnesses and deaths. Improvement in the level of ambient air quality may lead to increases in productivity through a reduction in morbidity and mortality rates. The economic value of these increases in productivity represents one possible measure of the benefits from air pollution control. The reduced costs associated with reductions in morbidity and mortality are another benefit.

In all of these examples, the change in ambient environmental quality, E, will lead to a change in productivity. Sometimes the change affects the production function and, hence, the supply of the marketable good, Q, from given resources. At other times, it will lead to a loss of output or to earnings foregone. Because the effects can be expressed in terms of changes in the quantity of a marketable good, the value of these changes—using market prices—can be taken as a measure of the benefit or loss from the change in E.

Before market prices can be used to value outputs, assumptions must be made about the shape of the relevant demand and supply curves. Two situations can be distinguished; these are discussed in terms of an agricultural example.

No Change in Factor Prices. If the increase in output Q is small relative to the total market for Q, and the increase of inputs is small relative to the market for variable factors, it can be assumed that product and variable factor prices will remain constant after the change in Q. In that case, projected output change in Q (estimated from production-function work, farm-practice studies, or expert advice) can be multiplied by market prices to obtain the economic value of the change. The following are different ways of doing this:

1. One can calculate a gross margin, gm, for each unit of output: for one unit of Q, q, the gross margin is $(q \times P) - (q \times \text{variable costs})$. Then

multiply all the changes in output: $Q \times gm$. If increased output is the only benefit from the program, then the net benefits of the whole program will be

$$Q \times gm - \text{Cost of the Scheme (i.e., Fixed + Operation + Maintenance and Replacement).}$$

In some programs, such as those for soil conservation, care should be taken that the projected output change, Q, represents the true with and without situation over time, as depicted in figure 6.1.

2.   Alternatively, one can use total farm budgets (total revenue less total cost) for the with and without situation.

3.   A third alternative is to estimate changes in land values per hectare (ha) as a result of changes in productivity. This assumes that land values are based solely on physical productivity, and not on other factors as well.

Although these examples refer to agriculture, changes in the level of profits can also be used for industrial examples, as when increased water quality reduces the cost function for an industry.

Changed Factor Prices.   If the increase in output Q affects the output and factor prices, information is needed about both demand and supply curves. If some information about the price elasticity of demand for the good is available and if we can assume that the demand curve is linear, then the price effect, P, as a result of changes in the production of the good, Q, can be calculated, and the gross benefit of the extra output can be approximated as equal to

$$Q \times \frac{(P \text{ before} + P \text{ after})}{2}.$$

A further problem is that market prices do not always represent competitive equilibrium prices. This may occur because of market imperfections (such as monopolies), indirect taxes, support prices, and other subsidies. The analyst should correct for such imperfections—for example, by adding subsidies back into prices, by taking taxes out of prices, or by calculating completely new prices. In some countries, domestic prices are not acceptable for benefit-cost analysis, and shadow prices based on border prices must be used (Squire and Van der Tak 1975).

Regardless of whether factor or product prices change or not, all of these approaches rely on physical measurement of natural or human systems. Observable market prices are employed to value the changes in productivity, operation, maintenance and replacement costs, human health, or whatever was affected by a change in environmental quality.

Three groups of examples are considered. The first deals with *changes in productivity and the value of outputs;* the second deals with *loss of earnings;* and the third deals with the *opportunity costs* of different actions. In each of these examples the changes in actual production, or the capability for production, of a factor are measured and valued as a way of determining the cost or benefit of the change in environmental quality. These methods must demonstrate that changes in environmental quality have affected the productivity of the system and that these changes in productivity can be quantified and valued.

Change in Productivity Approaches.   Many development plans are designed to affect a natural system and either increase the physical productivity of the system or prevent its deterioration over time. These plans are found in developed and developing countries. Examples include watershed management schemes, erosion prevention programs, and reforestation programs. In these programs the costs of implementation are easily determined—the funds necessary for labor, capital investment, operation, and maintenance and replacement. The benefits, however, are frequently much harder to quantify. The benefits can be either the value of increased production or the value of damages prevented; they may combine both aspects.

The following case study is a detailed examination of how analysis of such a project can be approached. The essential components are identification of the inputs, outputs, and residuals generated; the quantification of these flows; and the valuing of these flows. Often, fairly imaginative approaches are necessary in placing values on some of the flows. This is especially true where markets are imperfectly developed. The economic analysis is of the present value of net benefits of alternative management plans in a with and without situation.

A Case Study: Soil Conservation in Nepal

This study involves a soil conservation land management program in a small watershed in Nepal, as reported by Fleming (1981). Only a summary of the report is given here. Emphasis is placed on the economic analysis of the watershed management program, and especially on the use of market prices and proxy values to estimate the benefits of the program.

Site Description.   The watershed, a hilly, upland region, has an area of 113 square kilometers (km²) and drains into one of Nepal's most important lakes, Phewa Tal, as shown in figure 6.2. The principal economic activities in the area are subsistence agriculture and animal husbandry (cattle and buffalo). The animals produce manure and milk and are used as draught animals. The forests supply fuelwood and timber. Tourism also supplies some income to the area. Of the 10,000 hectares in the watershed, half are terraced for annual crops. About 30% of the total area is still forested, with the remainder divided between grazing land and scrub forest.

Resource Management Problems.   The principal resource management problems involve water supply, water quality, soil erosion, sedimentation, and overgrazing. A serious water shortage exists in some areas. Phewa Lake

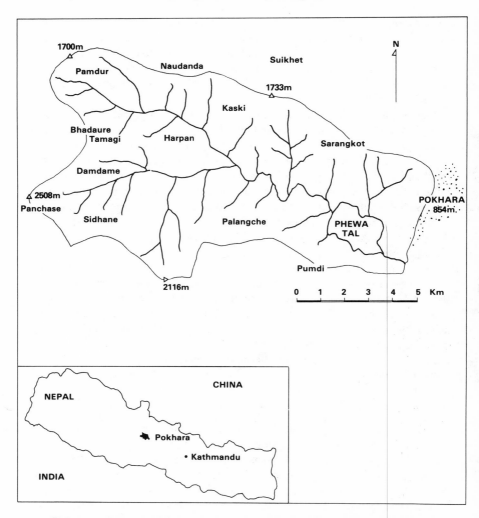

Figure 6.2 Location and orientation of the Phewa Tal watershed, Gandaki Zone, Nepal. (*Source:* Fleming, 1981.)

is becoming eutrophied with algal blooms, which reduce the recreational and fishing value of the lake. Soil erosion is widespread; and rates vary with different types of land use (table 6.1).

Sedimentation in Phewa Lake is increasing, with sediment delivery estimated at 87,000 tons per year. The increasing sediment deposits will reduce the life of the existing hydroelectric power development.

Severe overgrazing of the grazing land (12% of the total area) is a major problem. Current production of green fodder from this land is approximately

Table 6.1. Annual Erosion Rates by Land-Use Categories, Phewa Tal Watershed, Nepal

Land type	Acreage (ha)	Activity or product	Erosion rate (tons/ha/yr)
Terrace land	5,410	Agriculture, cropping	10
Scrub land	1,0702	Grazing, fuelwood	15
Grazing land	1,264	Grazing	35
Natural forests	2,935	Grazing, fuelwood, timber	8

Source: Adapted from Fleming (1981).

1,200 kilograms (kg) per ha per year. Experiments have shown that this production rate can be increased fivefold by managing the grazing land as pasture.

The Resource Management Program. A resource management program was developed on the basis of the local political units *(panchayats),* of which there are seven in the Phewa Tal watershed. For this study, however, the discussion will be at the watershed level alone, and the data for the seven *panchayats* will be aggregated.

The management program has three objectives:

1. To supply forest and agricultural products up to the long-term carrying capacity of the watershed;
2. To manage the forest and agricultural resources on a sustained-yield basis to meet the basic needs of the people affected;
3. To carry out a conservation program that holds, within defined tolerable limits, the losses of soil and nutrients through erosion and that reduces the sedimentation rate in Phewa Lake to maintain the hydroelectric energy, fisheries, and irrigation benefits.

Fleming assumes that the one-half of the watershed land that is privately owned and terraced will remain in terraces. Land-use changes will therefore only be possible on the remaining one-half, which is government-owned forest, scrub, and grazing land.

Projected Land Use with Present Growth Rates with No Management Intervention. If present population growth rates of 1.95% per year continue in the future, all forest land is likely to be converted to scrub or grazing land within twenty years (table 6.2).

This projection is based on the following assumptions:

1. Agricultural productivity does not increase and, hence, the area of terrace land will increase with population growth at a rate of 1.95% per year;
2. Animal populations will increase at the same rate as the human population and, therefore, land devoted to grazing will increase at the rate of 1.95% per year;

Table 6.2. Projected Land Uses with No Management Intervention, Five-Year Intervals, 1978–98 (ha)

Land	1978	1983	1988	1993	1998
Terrace	5,238	5,770	6,354	6,999	7,707
Grazing	1,180	1,300	1,431	1,576	1,736
Pasture	71	71	71	71	71
Scrub	924	1,018	1,121	1,234	565
Forest	2,666	1,921	1,102	200	0

Source: Adapted from Fleming (1981).

3. Scrub land will also increase at the rate of 1.95% per year; and
4. Forest land area will decrease to supply the demand for the other land uses.

Proposed Management Program. To provide needed forest and agricultural products on a continuing basis, the forest, scrub, grazing, and terrace lands must be managed. Two management alternatives are presented to policymakers. The first assumes that a separate agricultural program will increase productivity on cultivated terrace land over the next twenty years at a rate equal to or greater than the rate of population increase. In this alternative, the area of terrace land would remain at 5,238 ha, or one-half of the watershed, and no grazing, pasture, scrub, or forest land would be converted to terraces. This is the "with project" option.

The second management alternative assumes that no agricultural program would be implemented, and that terrace, grazing, and scrub land will all increase at the rate of 1.95% per year. In this "without project" option, all forest land will be gone by 1998 (table 6.2). The analysis covers the period 1978 to 1998.

The data for the managed alternative are presented in table 6.3. Other features of this plan are a water-supply plan, gully control, fencing, and forest and pasture protection.

Establishment and protection of pasture land, along with gully control procedures, are estimated to reduce the soil erosion rate of 35 tons/ha/year for grazing lands to 15 tons/ha/year. Soil losses from all land-use types would then be within the estimated tolerable limits of 15 tons/ha/year. With this decrease in erosion, sedimentation in Phewa Lake would be reduced by an estimated 15%, which, according to hydrological information, would lead to an increase in the life of the lake from 350 to about 400 years.

Benefit-Cost Analysis of the Program. The proposed management plan will both reduce erosion and increase the productivity of the different land uses found within the watershed. The costs of the conservation program will not be given, but are included in the final economic analysis. The problem here is to value the benefits from the existing and improved land-use types within the watershed after the management program is implemented.

Table 6.3. Projected Land Uses with Proposed Management Program, Five-Year Intervals, 1978–1998 (ha)

	1978	1983	1988	1993	1998
Terrace	5,238	5,238	5,238	5,238	5,238
Grazing land (unmanaged)	1,180	229	0	0	0
Pasture land (managed)	71	1,022	1,251	1,251	1,251
Scrub (unmanaged)	924	341	341	341	341
Government forest (unmanaged)	2,666	1,743	1,243	743	363
Government forest (managed)		873	784	1,000	1,380
Plantation forest (managed)		633	1,222	1,506	1,506

Note: This plan assumes the existence of a separate agricultural management plan that eliminates future conversion of forest and pasture land to terraces.
Source: Adapted from Fleming (1981).

The proposed management of the grazing lands consists of upgrading these lands to pasture lands by providing fences and new grass species. The resulting increase in grass yield will support more cows per hectare, which will increase milk and dung production. Forest management and scrub land afforestation will lead to a greater output of fuelwood and leaves, which can be used in turn as fodder. Reduced sedimentation will decrease the eutrophication rate of the lake, increase the life of the hydroelectric power plant and the lake fishery, and increase the number of tourists. An improved domestic water supply will create health benefits. The preservation of a balanced resource base will maintain the above benefits indefinitely.

The benefit-cost analysis is performed by estimating the economic value of the products of the different land-use types shown in tables 6.2 and 6.3 under the two situations, with and without the management program. In the following sections, the procedures for placing values on different kinds of output will be described based on the data provided by Fleming (1981).

Grazing Land. A grazing animal produces fertilizer (dung) and milk. Average fertilizer production of a grazing animal is 30 kg per year of readily available nitrogen (N) and 4 kg per year of readily available phosphorus (P). This fertilizer is collected and used on the terraced fields for crop production or burned as fuel. One-half of this production is lost through partial collection, incomplete composting, or runoff.* Hence, using average 1978 market prices (Rs6/kg for N and Rs18/kg for P), the value of collected fertilizer per grazing animal is Rs126, computed as follows (Rs1 = US$0.125):

$$(15 \text{ kg N} \times \text{Rs6/kg} = \text{Rs90}) + (2 \text{ kg P} \times \text{Rs18/kg} = \text{Rs36}).$$

---

*Technically, part of this "lost" production is captured by the grazing land itself and increases its productivity. This amount is ignored here.

An average animal consumes 14,000 kg per year of grass and agricultural by-products. Hence, 14,000 kg of grass produce N worth Rs90 and P worth Rs36. A hectare of unmanaged grazing land produces 1,200 kg per year of grass. Therefore, the fertilizer value per hectare of grazing land is

Rs126 × 1,200/14,000 = Rs11/ha/year (US$1.38).

Average annual milk production per grazing animal is 60 liters per 1,000 kg of grass fodder. The 1978 price of milk is taken as Rs1/liter. Therefore, the annual milk value per hectare is

60 × 1,200/1,000 × Rs1 = Rs72 (US$9.00).

Market prices were used to establish the fertilizer and milk values per hectare of grazing land. In both cases, care needs to be taken to determine that these prices reflect true opportunity costs or marginal willingness to pay. If input prices are subsidized, the subsidy needs to be added to the price. If milk prices are controlled by the government, alternative prices, which more accurately reflect marginal willingness to pay, need to be obtained.

Pasture Land. The fodder production of established pasture land is taken to be approximately five times that of grazing land, or 6,000 kg of grass per year, resulting in annual values of Rs55 per ha for fertilizer and Rs360 per ha for milk.

Scrub Land. Scrub land comes from degraded forest lands. Such land produces 500 kg of grass, 1,500 kg of fodder leaves, and 4 m³ of wood per ha annually. The values for 500 kg of grass are Rs5 per ha for fertilizer and Rs30 per ha for milk. An animal can consume 7,100 kg per year of tree foliage in place of 14,000 kg per year of grass. Using the same unit value for N and P as above, the fertilizer production values per animal consuming 7,100 kg of tree leaves per year are Rs90 for N and Rs36 for P. One hectare of scrub produces 1,500 kg per year of fodder leaves; accordingly, the annual fertilizer value per hectare is

(Rs90 + Rs36) (1,500/7,100) = Rs27 (US$3.38).

In calculating the value of milk production from fodder leaves, the nutritive value of leaf foliage is taken as twice that of grass, or 120 liters per 1,000 kg of leaf foliage. On this basis, the annual value of milk production from leaf foliage per hectare is computed as

1,500/1,000 × 120 × Rs1 = Rs180 (US$22.50).

Fuelwood. Both scrub land and forest land produce fuelwood. Three ways are presented to estimate the value of fuelwood.

1. *Direct approach* (market value). A small proportion of the fuelwood produced is sold in local markets at Rs13 for a bundle weighing 37.3 kg. Assuming an average density of wood of 500 kg per m³, fuelwood would

be worth Rs174 per m³. Because the markets for fuelwood are small and isolated, the market price may not be representative of the average value of fuelwood.

2. *Indirect approach* (substitute method). Fuelwood can also be valued in an indirect way in terms of the resources it would replace (e.g., the productive value of the cattle dung that is burned when wood is not available). The assumptions are as follows:

   a) 1 m³ of wood equals 0.6 tons of dried cattle dung, which equals 2.4 tons of fresh manure;

   b) an average family (5.5 members, 3 livestock units) uses 6 tons of fresh manure per year on a cultivated area of 0.75 ha; and

   c) the expected increase in maize yields is assumed to be 15%; this gives an opportunity cost of Rs40 per ton for fresh manure.

   On the basis of these assumptions, the value of fuelwood is Rs 96 per m³ (Rs 40 × 2.4).

3. *Indirect approach* (opportunity-cost method). A third method of valuing fuelwood uses an opportunity-cost approach based on the value of the time spent by families collecting fuelwood in the forest. In this method, it is assumed that 30 kg of fuelwood are collected per day, and that an average of 132 work-days effort are spent each year by a family in fuelwood collection, and that the 30 kg of fuelwood are equivalent to 20 kg of dry wood, with a volume of 0.04 m³. Therefore, each family gathers 5.28 m³ of fuelwood per year. At an opportunity cost of Rs5 per day, the estimated value is

$$Rs5 \times 132/5.28 = Rs125/m^3 \ (US\$15.63).$$

In this case, no distinction was made between the opportunity-cost value of women, children, unemployed men, and working men when calculating the work-days per year required for wood gathering; all work-days are valued at the average daily wage.

These three approaches provide three different estimates of the value of fuelwood. Only one is based on the direct market value. Since this is a very small and imperfect market, other indirect estimates were made. The results are as follows:

Method	Value (Rs/m³)
Market value	174
Substitute	96
Opportunity cost	125

To be conservative, the lowest value was chosen. On this basis, one obtains an annual fuelwood value per hectare of scrub land of

Rs96/m^3 × 4m^3 = Rs384.

Unmanaged Forest.   This land is open to grazing, cutting for firewood, and harvesting of leaves for fodder. Annual fodder production from this land is estimated at 3,000 kg per ha of leaf fodder. This amount has an annual fertilizer value of Rs53 (Rs126/7,100 kg × 3,000 kg/ha) and an annual milk value per hectare of Rs360 (Rs120/1,000 kg × 3,000 kg/ha). In addition, fuelwood is produced at an annual rate of 12m^3 per ha, with a value of Rs96/m^3 × 12m^3 = Rs1,152(US$144).

Managed Forest.   The application of sustained-yield (not plantation) management to the unmanaged forest would result in an increase in annual fuelwood productivity from 10–15m^3 per ha to 25–30m^3 per ha. For the entire watershed, Fleming assumes that yields will be 20m^3 per ha per year after a waiting period of six years, with an annual per hectare value of Rs 96/m^3 × 20m^3 = Rs1,920(US$240).

It is also assumed that the productivity of fodder leaves will increase proportionally with wood productivity, from the unmanaged level of 3,000 kg per ha per year to a level of 5,000 kg per ha per year. When used as fodder, these leaves will have a fertilizer value of Rs89 per ha per year, and a milk production value of Rs600 per ha per year.

Plantation Forests.   These are scrub and other lands that are converted to forests through afforestation. After five years, the plantations will have estimated yields of 5 m^3 per ha per year of fuelwood plus 1,250 kg of fodder leaves. After ten years, the estimated yields will be 10 m^3 per ha per year of fuelwood plus 2,500 kg of fodder leaves. The values of the fuelwood, fertilizer, and milk produced are as follows:

	Annual value (Rs/ha)	
Product	5–10 years	After 10 years
Fuelwood	480	960
Fertilizer	22	44
Milk	150	300

Hydroelectric Power Benefits.   As stated earlier, the reduction in the annual sediment load to the lake will increase the useful life of Phewa Lake from approximately 350 to 400 years. Because this anticipated benefit is so long-term compared to the 50–100 year planning horizon for the Phewa Lake hydroelectric power project, these benefits have not been calculated. Had these benefits been relevant within the time horizon of the analysis, the additional electricity generated would have been valued at the market price of electricity and incorporated into the benefit-cost analysis.

Market prices for electricity are not always available. Alternative ways of obtaining value estimates include willingness-to-pay surveys and estimating the cost of the least costly alternative source of electricity production. These techniques will be discussed later in this chapter.

Tourism and Recreation.   The current income from tourism is small, but it could increase significantly in the future. Eutrophication of the lake would adversely affect tourism. Therefore, a benefit of the management plan would be the associated increase in the number of tourists when eutrophication is controlled. No data were available to calculate these benefits. A technique discussed later in this chapter, the travel-cost approach, might have been used in this case had tourist visitation data been available.

Fisheries.   No data were available on the fishery industry. Should eutrophication and siltation reduce the fish catch over time, the management program could be expected to slow or even reverse this trend. The value of the fishery could be determined in several ways similar to those used to value fuelwood; that is, the market value of the fish catch, the value of substitutes for the fish, and opportunity cost of catching the fish.

Summary of the Benefit-Cost Analysis.   The benefits of the management program are calculated by comparing the value of the agricultural and forest products from the unmanaged land (the no-management alternative shown in table 6.2) with the value of the same products under the proposed management program shown in table 6.3. These values are calculated by multiplying the number of hectares of each type of land by the computed benefits (table 6.4). The results are summarized in table 6.5. The values are presented for each year of the twenty-year management program with a discount rate of 10%. The present value of the benefits of the program is equal to approximately $Rs22 \times 10^6$ ($54 \times 10^6 - 32 \times 10^6$). The present value of the cost of the management program is about $Rs12 \times 10^6$. (Detailed calculations of these costs are not presented here.) Accordingly, the net present value (NPV) of the management program over twenty years, using a discount rate of 10%, is $Rs10 \times 10^6$.

The Human Capital, or Foregone Earnings, Approach

Changes in environmental quality can have significant effects on human health. The monetary damages associated with health effects consist of three major components: foregone earnings through premature death, sickness, or absenteeism; increased medical expenses; and psychic costs. Information about the monetary value of lives saved or about illnesses prevented is desirable for efficient resource allocation among competing uses, such as allocation of resources for air quality management programs versus other investment opportunities.

Many people oppose this kind of quantification on the grounds that it dehumanizes life, which is considered to have "infinite" value. In practice, however, society implicitly places values on human life and illnesses in day-to-day safety, health, and environmental quality decisions (Hyman 1981).

Table 6.4. Estimated Annual Benefits per Hectare with Proposed Management Program in the Phewa Tal Watershed (Rs/ha/yr) (Rs1 = US$.125)

Land use	Grass		Fodder leaves		Fuelwood	Total
	Fertilizer	Milk	Fertilizer	Milk		
Grazing	11	72				83
Pasture	55	360				415
Scrub	5	30	27	180	384	626
Forest, unmanaged			53	360	1,152	1,565
Forest, managed, after 6 years [a]			89	600	1,920	2,609
Plantation forest, 5 to 10 years			22	150	480	652
Plantation forest, after 10 years			44	300	960	1,304

[a] Although these forests have some outputs during the transition period to age six years, the report gives no information about the value of these outputs.

Source: Adapted from Fleming (1981).

Table 6.5. Total Direct Benefits, Phewa Tal Watershed, with and without the Proposed Management Program, Rs 1,000 (Rs 1,000 = US$125)

Year	With no management (present situation)		With management program	
	Annual value	Present value (10% discount rate)	Annual value	Present value (10% discount rate)
1978	4,878	4,878	4,878	4,878
1979	4,668	4,244	5,117	4,652
1980	4,454	3,681	5,356	4,426
1981	4,234	3,181	5,595	4,204
1982	4,009	2,738	5,834	3,985
1983	3,781	2,348	6,075	3,772
1984	3,548	2,109	5,964	3,367
1985	3,313	1,700	5,853	3,004
1986	3,072	1,433	5,742	2,679
1987	2,826	1,199	5,631	2,388
1988	2,575	993	5,520	2,128
1989	2,318	812	5,710	2,001
1990	2,059	656	5,900	1,880
1991	1,791	519	6,090	1,764
1992	1,522	401	6,280	1,654
1993	1,246	298	6,468	1,548
1994	963	210	6,548	1,425
1995	851	168	6,628	1,311
1996	745	134	6,708	1,206
1997	637	104	6,788	1,110
1998	527	78	6,865	1,020
Total		31,884		54,402

Source: Adapted from Fleming (1981).

Economists have proposed several methods for valuing human lives; of these, the human capital approach is one of the most highly developed.

Theoretical Concepts. In the case of premature illness or death, social costs are incurred by the partial or total loss of the individual's services to society. The value of the life or working time lost is usually equated with the value of an individual's labor, assuming the validity of the theory of marginal productivity of labor. The value of an individual's labor is the individual's projected future earnings, discounted to the present, with age, sex, and education taken into account. According to Mishan (1972), this can be stated as

$$L_1 = \sum_{t=T}^{\infty} Yt \, P_T^t \, (1 + r)^{-(t-T)} \tag{6-1}$$

where Yt is the expected gross earnings of or, alternatively, value added by the person during the t-th year exclusive of any yields from his ownership of nonhuman capital; P_T^t is the probability in the current, or T-th, year of the person being alive during the t-th year; and r is the social rate of discount expected to rule during the t-th year.

Some economists have made auxiliary calculations to take account of the suffering of the victims, the loss of their utility due to death, and the bereavement of their families (Kneese 1966, Ridker 1967). The human capital approach, therefore, is simply based on viewing the human being as a unit of capital. This immediately raises the question of how to value children, homemakers, and retired and handicapped people. Ridker (1967) assigned a value of zero to an unemployed person or to those who are not paid a direct wage. In the case of homemakers, it could be argued that rational family decisions require that the value of noncommercial home activities exceeds their opportunity cost and, therefore, that the average wage of workers can be a proxy for the salary of homemakers (Hyman 1981). The fact that a zero economic value is assigned to the truly nonproductive members of the population, those people who are totally disabled by illness or handicap, raises serious ethical questions.

Example. In the following example, material is taken from several studies to demonstrate

1. The calculation of the value of human life in terms of foregone earnings;
2. The steps required in calculating medical expenses arising from air pollution; and
3. How knowledge of an air pollution damage function and the value of human life allows the calculation of the net benefits of a reduction in air pollution.

Ridker's study (1967) was one of the first applications of the human capital approach. His calculations of the cost of premature death and the cost of medical expenses are shown below.

Cost of Premature Death. Ridker used the total-output approach to calculate foregone earnings, with the following formula:

$$V_x = \sum_{n=x}^{\infty} \frac{(P_x^n)_1 \cdot (P_x^n)_2 \cdot (P_x^n)_3 \cdot Y_n}{(1 + r)^{n-x}} \tag{6-2}$$

where V_x is the present value of the future earnings of an individual of age x; $(P_x^n)_1$ is the probability that an individual of age x will be alive at age n; $(P_x^n)_2$ is the probability that an individual of age x living to age n will be in the labor force at age n; $(P_x^n)_3$ is the probability that an individual age x living and in the labor force at age n will be employed at age n; Y_n is the earnings at age n; and r is the discount rate.

Using the above formula, Ridker calculated the cost of different diseases related to air pollution. The cost for each disease is classified by age groups and sex. In table 6.6, an example is given of earnings lost for males dying from chronic bronchitis. Total losses are shown as US\$16,126,000 at a 5% discount rate and US\$12,285,532 at a 10% discount rate. A similar table was

Table 6.6. Present Value of Earnings Lost for Males Dying from Chronic Bronchitis, United States, 1958

Age	Number of deaths	Present value of earnings per individual using discount rates of		Total loss from premature death using discount rates of	
		0.05	0.10	0.05	0.10
10–14	7	$47,624	$17,826	$333,368	$124,782
15–19	4	49,800	28,635	199,200	112,140
20–24	3	69,676	37,690	209,028	113,070
25–29	6	73,143	43,098	438,858	258,588
30–34	7	70,523	43,982	493,661	307,873
35–39	11	64,038	41,834	704,418	460,174
40–44	23	55,638	38,129	1,279,674	876,967
45–49	30	45,836	33,077	1,375,080	992,310
50–54	84	35,001	26,690	2,940,084	2,241,960
55–59	150	23,419	18,920	3,512,850	2,838,000
60–64	269	11,685	9,917	3,143,265	2,667,673
65–69	314	4,056	3,559	1,273,584	1,117,526
70–74	268	692	951	185,456	174,468
Total losses	1,176			$16,126,000	$12,285,532
Average losses per individual				$13,713	$10,447

Source: Adapted from Ridker (1967).

calculated for females, with estimated total losses of US$1,526,423 at a 5% discount rate and US$1,052,550 at a 10% discount rate. For males and females combined, the estimated total loss from premature death, assuming a 10% discount rate, is US$13,338,082. One-half of this loss, or about US$6,600,000, was assumed to be air pollution-related.

Cost of Treatment. Ridker calculated the cost of treatment for four major diseases: cancer of the respiratory system, chronic bronchitis, asthma, and pneumonia. For example, for chronic bronchitis, the Ridker procedure works as follows (Mäler and Wyzga 1976):

1. Estimated number of chronic bronchitis patients, age eleven or older, in the United States in fiscal year 1958 was 416,500 with at least one bed-disability day and 468,000 without any bed-disability days.

2. The portion of chronic bronchitis deaths due to air pollution was estimated using a study by Lave and Seskin (1970) of adjusted bronchitis death rates in the United States, which indicated that bronchitis deaths would be reduced by 50% if urban air pollution concentrations were reduced to rural levels.

3. The estimate of total number of chronic bronchitis nonfatal illnesses due to air pollution was based on the assumption that the proportion of chron-

ic bronchitis morbidity due to air pollution is the same as the proportion of bronchitis mortality due to air pollution. Using this assumption, the estimated number of chronic bronchitis patients with bed-disability days suffered because of air pollution is $0.5 \times 416,500 = 208,250$, and the estimated number of chronic bronchitis patients without bed-disability days suffered because of air pollution is $0.5 \times 468,000 = 234,000$.

4. Treatment costs were estimated by assuming that the cost of treating patients with bed-disability days was the same as the cost of hospital inpatients suffering from chronic bronchitis. The average cost of this treatment was \$169 for each chronic bronchitis inpatient, of which \$41 was for an attending physician's services. The latter amount was assumed to be the average cost of treating the chronic bronchitis patient with no-bed-disability days. The total medical treatment costs for pollution-caused chronic bronchitis in the United States in 1958 are then estimated to be

$$US\$169 \times 208,250 + US\$41 \times 234,000 = US\$44,788,250.$$

Absenteeism. The direct annual loss of output caused by absenteeism arising from air pollution can be calculated by multiplying estimates of days lost during the year due to sickness by the average daily earnings of the people suffering from the particular disease. For any particular disease, an estimate must be made of the proportion of the cases of the disease that can be attributed to air pollution. To obtain overall annual monetary damages, the number of days lost by different working groups (men, women, and home-makers) because of air pollution is multiplied by the average daily wage rate for each group.

Air Pollution and the Cost of Disease. Knowledge of the average cost to society from death and illness is only one part of the valuation process. The next step is to obtain damage functions that link levels of ambient air pollution to health damage. Ridker (1967) was unable to derive such functions. Others have claimed more success; for example, Lave and Seskin (1977) and Schwing and McDonald (1976). The results of the latter study were used in a benefit-cost analysis of automotive emission reductions (Schwing et al. 1980). Some of these results are used here to demonstrate the procedure for placing monetary values on the benefits of air pollution control.

To go from changes in levels of air pollution to monetary benefits to society, it is first necessary to obtain some age-specific associations that indicate for each age group the number of deaths associated with current average pollution levels. These associations, obtained by Schwing and McDonald (1976), are presented in the second and third columns of table 6.7. The HC/CO/TEL measure is an index of carbon monoxide and tetraethyllead levels.

To translate the benefits from air pollution control into dollar values, estimates of the economic value of life are used. These figures on foregone

Table 6.7. Health Benefits for White Males in the United States from Total Abatement of Air Pollutants

	Change in mortality due to reduction of pollution from mean to zero (deaths per 100,000 white males)		Cost per death ($)	Abatement benefits per 100,000 white males (1968 dollars)		
	Nitrogen compounds	HC/CO/TEL		Nitrogen compounds	HC/CO/TEL	Total
Under 25	1.62	0.44	75,000	122,000	33,100	155,100
25–44	0.37	0.12	121,000	44,700	14,500	59,200
45–64	0.42	0.14	78,000	32,900	11,000	43,900
65 and over	7.69	0.00	41,000	316,000	—	316,000
Total health benefits				515,600	58,600	574,200
Savings of costs of morbidity and treatment				309,300	20,800	330,100
Benefits due to restoring foregone earnings				206,300	37,800	244,100

Source: Adapted from Schwing et al. (1980).

earnings and the direct and indirect expenses associated with illness and premature death, by age group, come from Rice (1966).* The reduced number of deaths is multiplied by the economic cost per death to give dollar benefits per 100,000 white males.† To derive benefits for the total U.S. population, it is necessary to determine the total number of persons exposed and the impact on persons other than white males.

The total number of persons exposed to air pollution in the United States in 1968 was estimated at 133 million, and the adjustment factor used to translate from effects on white males to effects on the total population exposed was 1.055. Total health benefits are presented in table 6.8. As seen in this example, the health benefits from reduced illness and treatment exceed those from preventing premature death (restoring foregone earnings).

The costs of air pollution reduction have not been included here. They are substantial and will have to be compared to the estimated benefits in formulating policy.

Conclusion.   The human capital, or foregone earnings, approach is a valuation methodology that pays only lip service to the concept of consumers' preferences, since there is no necessary relationship between the results obtained and the values based on individual willingness to pay. According to Freeman (1979), the human capital approach cannot be accepted as an approximation of willingness to pay for use in benefit measurement. Although

---

*These figures by Rice have been updated by Cooper and Rice (1976). Freeman (1979) presents some of these updated results in a table on page 170.

†The figures from Rice (1966) were adjusted to 1968 dollars.

Table 6.8. Total Health Benefits in the United States Due to Total Abatement of Air Pollutants (in Millions of 1968 Dollars)

	Nitrogen compounds	HC/CO/TEL	Total
Total health benefits	720	82	802
Savings of costs of morbidity and treatment	431	29	460
Benefits due to restoring foregone earnings	289	53	342

Note: Figures were obtained by multiplying the benefit figures in table 6.7 by

$$\frac{1.33 \times 10^8 \times 1.055}{10^5} = 1.4 \times 10^3.$$

Source: Adapted from Schwing et al. (1980).

by definition individuals could pay no more than the present value of their earnings streams (plus presently held assets) to avoid certain death, their valuations of their lives based on willingness to pay for small improvements in life expectation could be several times their discounted expected earnings streams. The human capital approach is therefore derived from an alternative value judgment; namely, that one is worth what one does and that society ought to be prepared to pay this as a *minimum* to save a life (Pearce 1978).

If one is worth what one does, then the question arises of which exact measure to use—gross or net output. Netting out a person's consumption expenditures leaves a measure of the individual's worth as a producing asset to the rest of society. But this would mean that the death of any person whose consumption is greater than his or her production (e.g., retired, ill, or disabled people) would confer a net benefit on society. This may be satisfactory on the basis of pure economic measurement, but it is clearly not satisfactory on ethical grounds for the simple reason that no weight is given to the feelings of those concerned (Mishan 1972).

Another criticism of the human capital approach is that it ignores the probabilistic element in the calculation. According to Needleman (1976), "Government measures aimed at reducing deaths are intended, not to save the lives of certain named individuals, but to reduce the risks for each group of people dying within a particular period. The benefits to be valued, then, are reductions in risk, not lives saved."

In conclusion, the human capital approach suffers from many ethical, theoretical, and practical shortcomings. The method requires much data and can be applied only after a satisfactory relationship has been established between environmental pollution and damage to life and health. Since the appearance of Schelling's influential paper (1968), almost all economists writing on the topic of valuation of human life and suffering have rejected the human capital approach in favor of the view that changes in risk, not lives saved, is the appropriate statistic to be valued. Most economists hold that the valuation of the risk by the group at risk can be measured by how much they are willing to pay to avoid it, or by the compensation they are prepared to accept to incur it.

An extensive literature has appeared on this topic (Mishan 1972, Jones-Lee 1976, Mooney 1977, Needleman 1980). Proposed alternative approaches to valuing life are sophisticated, difficult to implement, and as yet not proven in practice. This, then, leaves a void in the attempt to value human life, health, and suffering. According to Pearce (1978), if the social welfare function is based solely on the gross national product, the human capital approach is applicable. The approach is relatively easy to apply and is the one most commonly encountered. Although it ignores the question of consumer sovereignty, if the appropriate decision makers choose to use the approach to provide minimum estimates of values of human life, and *if they state the ethic on which it rests,* then the approach is defensible.

Opportunity-Cost Approach

Many different techniques can be placed under the heading of opportunity cost. The concept underlying this approach is that the opportunity cost of unpriced uses (e.g., preserving land for a national park instead of cutting the trees for timber) can be estimated from the foregone income from other uses, such as agriculture or forestry.

Note that this approach measures what has to be given up for the sake of preservation; it does not measure the benefits of land preserved for unpriced uses. To estimate such benefits, other techniques such as the travel-cost, property value, or land value methods should be used. Such techniques attempt to measure a society's willingness to pay for maintenance of the land in its natural state. In situations where these techniques cannot be used, however, analysis with the opportunity-cost approach is often a feasible alternative.

Theory of Alternative Uses of Natural Systems.   Some alternative uses of natural systems are incompatible with the system's continuity and have irreversible consequences. A development project may change an area so much that the original natural system is destroyed and cannot be reestablished. In such cases, the opportunity cost of the project is the present value of the net benefits accruing from the natural system as a preserved resource for an indefinite time span in the future. These benefits may be difficult to measure. Conversely, the opportunity cost of preservation is the present value of development benefits foregone. This is the approach most commonly used. Since the two alternatives (preservation and development) are mutually exclusive, the economically efficient use of the resource is the one that maximizes the present value of net benefits. One or the other alternative must be chosen.

Most analyses of this sort calculate the opportunity cost of preservation and then let decision makers decide if preservation of the natural resource is worth at least this amount. If the benefits of preservation rather than only the costs of not developing the resource are included, questions arise about the future relative values of environmental services. Decisions still have to be made about whether to develop or to preserve a natural environment, but these decisions are complicated by both theoretical and ethical factors. With preservation, it is tempting to assume that benefits might approach infinity, for a natural environment could be enjoyed by future generations. Ethical problems arise from the intertemporal externality involved; that is, the economic benefits of developing a resource in the present are largely gained by the current generation at the possible expense of future generations who might have wished to preserve the resource. Placing a low discount rate on future preservation benefits may not be sufficient to overcome this difficulty, especially because future preferences are unknown.

Krutilla and Fisher (1975) tackled this problem in a different way. Because natural environments are in fixed supply, whereas economic goods are reproducible, the relative values of environmental services and economic goods change over time (fig. 6.3). Environmental services appear on the vertical axis and ordinary economic goods on the horizontal axis. At a particular point in time, feasible trade-offs between the environment and economic goods can be represented by the curve QQ_1. A consumption optimum arises at point X where a community preference curve $I_1 I_1$ is tangential to the curve QQ_1. The

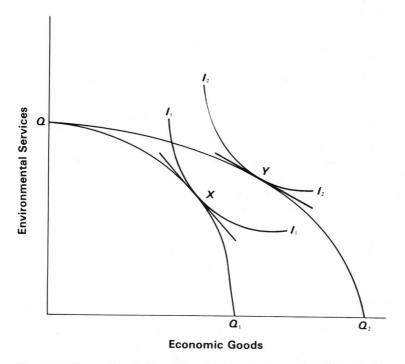

Figure 6.3 Changes in relative values of economic goods and environmental services over time.

slope of the tangent at X indicates the relative values of environmental services and economic goods.

In time, production potential for economic goods increases and the trade-off curve moves outward to QQ_2. The maximum feasible supply of environmental services, however, is the same as before. A new consumption optimum arises at Y with the preference curve $I_2 I_2$. The tangent at Y has a flatter slope than that at X, indicating that the value per unit of environmental services has risen relative to the price of economic goods.

The same argument can be demonstrated in a partial-equilibrium analysis of development and preservation alternatives. In figure 6.4(a), a supply curve S_t and demand curve D_t at time t, lead to an equilibrium market price P_t for an economic good. The figure shows three such sets of curves with equilibrium market prices P_1, P_2, and P_3. It is assumed that because of technological improvement the long-term trend in price is downward, and total annual benefits decline. In a mathematical formulation, the general trend for development benefits takes the form Ke^{-vt}, where K is an initial level of benefits, e is the base of natural logarithms, v is the rate of change of benefits, and t is time.

Supply and demand curves for a natural environment appear in figure 6.4(b). The supply curve S is inelastic, but the demand curve D_t shifts upward and outward over time, raising the value per unit of environmental services. In the figure four demand curves are illustrated, D_1 to D_4. These shifts can be attributed to changes in population, preferences, income, and technology. Evidence suggests that the demand for environmental amenities is highly income-elastic. This relationship can also be expressed mathematically. In this case annual benefits from preservation increase over time, taking the form Le^{gt}, where g is now a positive growth rate and L is an initial level of benefits.

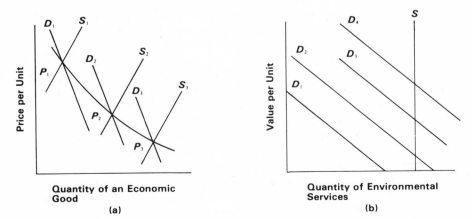

Figure 6.4 Supply and demand for economic goods and environmental services over time.

Despite the different rates of change of benefits from the two alternatives, total benefits depend on the absolute levels of the demand curves. This can be readily established for ordinary economic goods because prices and quantities bought are observable market phenomena. With environmental services, however, only imputed prices can be used. Because of the difficulties of valuing natural environments, the opportunity-cost approach can be used to ask whether a natural environment is worth preserving.

Examples

1. In New Zealand the opportunity cost, or foregone income, approach was used by environmental groups to persuade the government to save some indigenous forests. The conflict in this case was between clear-cutting or selective logging and complete preservation. Because benefits from preservation of these types of forests are difficult to estimate, the group concentrated its efforts on calculating the income foregone when not using the indigenous forests for timber and pulpwood. Their calculations showed that the net present value of income foregone was very small. The decision makers then had to decide whether or not this income foregone would impose a significant cost on society. The data did provide better information for decision making and effective public participation.

2. A second New Zealand example deals with a conflict between raising the level of a scenic lake for further hydroelectric power development and preserving the lake for tourism, wildlife, and aesthetic values. A complete benefit-cost analysis was performed on the development alternatives, incorporating the value of hydroelectric power and the loss of recreation and fishing values. Some of the main attributes of the lake, however, are its scenic beauty and wildlife, the values of which are difficult to quantify.

The net present values of the development alternatives were in the range of NZ\$20–\$25 million (1973 prices). On a per capita basis, this amounted to about a NZ\$8.00 lump-sum payment or a NZ\$0.60 yearly payment. Were the scenic, ecological, and wildlife values worth such an income sacrifice? The New Zealand government considered that they were and decided not to raise the level of the lake.

The opportunity-cost criterion was probably not the only input in this decision-making process (the intense public outcry was a factor too), but the approach did provide important information about the trade-offs involved.

3. In Western Australia, a conflict of land uses between forestry development and preservation was analyzed in a similar fashion. The net present value of a woodchip project (requiring the cutting of all 420,000 hectares of a forest) was estimated to be \$A8,293,000. The preservation of 100,000 ha for natural-systems purposes would reduce the yield of chips and, thus, the net present value by about 8% to \$A7,708,000 (Commonwealth of Australia 1975).

4. The proposed damming of Hells Canyon in the United States for hydroelectric power generation would have irrevocably altered a unique wilderness

area. A conventional benefit-cost analysis was performed on the hydroelectric project to determine the present value of net benefits. Net benefits were taken as the difference between the costs of supplying electricity from the project and the next cheapest alternative—in this case, a nuclear plant of equivalent size. The benefits from reducing flood damage were also included in the analysis.

The opportunity cost of preserving Hells Canyon thus was the difference between the cost of hydroelectric power and the next cheapest power source. Krutilla (1969) and Krutilla and Fisher (1975) examined the assumptions made for hydroelectric versus nuclear power and analyzed the sensitivity of the results to changes in the average rate of technological progress in nuclear energy and to different discount rates. In this case, the decision was made not to build the dam; it was decided that the opportunity cost of preservation—the additional expense of generating power from nuclear rather than hydro sources—was worth it.

Conclusion.   The opportunity-cost approach is a very useful technique when net social benefits of certain uses cannot be directly estimated. Indeed, social opportunity cost is the net social benefit of the best foregone use and so is an integral part of a full benefit-cost analysis (Hitchens, Thampapillai, and Sinden 1978). The method is relatively quick and straightforward and provides valuable information for decision makers and the public.

SURROGATE MARKET APPROACHES

In the previous section, techniques were examined that monetized environmental benefits by using the direct market value of goods or services affected by changes in environmental quality. In this section, surrogate markets are used to value these goods and services. As stated earlier, the distinction between market and surrogate market approaches is used here as a matter of convenience. The techniques to be discussed in this section use market values indirectly. These techniques are (1) marketed goods and services as environmental surrogates, (2) property values, (3) other land values, (4) wage differentials, and (5) travel costs.

Each technique has its particular advantages and disadvantages, as well as its requirements for data and resources. The task of the analyst is to determine which of the techniques or which combinations thereof are relevant and useful to the particular situation at hand.

Marketed Goods and Services as Environmental Surrogates

Sometimes, situations may be encountered where an environmental service is a perfect substitute for a private marketable good. For example, private swimming pools may be regarded as substitutes for clean lakes or streams, or private parks may be considered substitutes for national parks. If such substitutions are made, then the benefit of an increase in the supply of an environmental good, such as national parks, may be deduced from observing the reduction in the purchase of the private good. Because the two goods are substitutes, the welfare level of the users does not change.

With pure substitutes, the problem is to specify the situation carefully and identify the exact changes in expenditures on private goods and the causes of the changes. Even though private parks can be identified as substitutes for national parks, to measure the impact of a change in the supply of national parks on expenditures on private parks may create an insurmountable problem in identification. For these reasons, this approach will not be discussed any further. Instead, we refer the reader to the market value or alternative cost approaches for more practical techniques when dealing with substitutes or partial substitutes.

Property Value Approach

The property value approach belongs to a much broader group of techniques called land value approaches. The use of land values to estimate the benefits of government programs, such as flood plain protection, is a well-established approach, and most benefit-cost practitioners are familiar with it. In the case study of soil conservation in Nepal, which illustrates market value approaches, imputed land prices based on their productive value were used to estimate the benefits of the program.

This section, however, considers a specific application of the approach by using land or property values to determine people's willingness to pay for an environmental good; that is, the use of observed market values to estimate indirectly a demand curve for a particular environmental good. With such a demand curve in hand, one can calculate the benefits or losses from changes in the quality or supply of that environmental good.

The value of a fixed asset, such as land, a house, or other capital facility, equals the discounted present value of the future net-benefit stream associated with the use of that asset. Thus, the flow of utility from all characteristics of the fixed asset is aggregated in the price of property. The characteristics of a property from which consumers derive utility affect the demand for property, while the opportunity costs of providing property with such characteristics influence the supply of property. A change in the price of a property therefore can result from a change either in any one of the property's characteristics or in the opportunity cost of providing alternative property with equivalent characteristics, or both.

Ambient environmental quality is a spatial phenomenon, and the basic assumption of the property value approach is that changes in ambient environmental quality affect the future benefit stream of a property, with the result that, with other factors remaining constant, the sale price of the property changes. Thus, a negative effect on the value of property could be expected in polluted areas. For this actually to occur in the marketplace, a sufficient number of buyers must agree on the reduced desirability of a location and must act accordingly.

Approaches that analyze the relationship between certain environmental quality characteristics and prices of private goods are variously termed "property value," "land value," or "hedonic price" techniques. According to Rosen (1974), hedonic prices are defined as the implicit prices of the characteristics of a property (e.g., size, location, quality, and neighborhood characteristics of a housing unit) and are revealed to economic agents from observed prices of differentiated properties and the specific amounts of characteristics associated with them. An extensive literature appeared on this approach in the 1970s. Much of this literature concentrated on the use of residential property values as the basis for estimating the benefits of improvements in air quality.

Theoretical Basis.   The aim of the property value approach is to enable analysts to place values on the benefits of improvements in environmental quality. For expository purposes, air pollution will be used, but the method can be applied to the valuation of other environmental quality or aesthetic factors as well. The use of this technique is based on the assumption that an individual's willingness to pay is appropriate for defining and measuring the benefits of improvements in air quality.

Housing is a product class differentiated by certain characteristics. These characteristics include the type of construction, the number of rooms, and the size and location of the property. An urban area will contain a variety of housing types differentiated by location, size, and other characteristics, and, if air quality varies across the urban area, by different levels of air quality. To apply the property value aproach, two assumptions have to be made: (1) that the entire urban area can be treated as a single market for housing (i.e., individuals must have information about all alternatives and must be free to choose a housing location anywhere in the urban market); and (2) that the housing market is in or near equilibrium (i.e., that all buyers have made their utility-maximizing residential choices, given the existing stock of housing and its characteristics) (Freeman 1979a).

Given these assumptions, the price of a house can be taken to be a function of its structural, neighborhood, and environmental quality characteristics. If P is the price of housing, this function can be written as

$$P_i = f(S_i, N_i, Q_i), \tag{6-3}$$

where S_i represents various characteristics for the i-th housing unit such as size, number of rooms, age, and type of construction; N_i represents a set of neighborhood characteristics for the i-th house including quality of local schools, accessibility to parks, stores, or workplace, and crime rates; and Q_i is the level of air quality at the i-th site (Freeman 1979b).

This function is the hedonic, or property value, function. If observations on prices and characteristics are available, this function can be estimated by multivariate analysis. For example, if the function is linear, we get

$$P_i = \alpha_0 + \alpha_1 C_{1i} + \alpha_2 C_{2i} + \ldots + \alpha_n Q_i, \qquad (6\text{–}4)$$

where the C's are different individual characteristics of the house, the neighborhood, or the location, and Q is air quality in the vicinity of house i.

The implicit price of any property characteristic can be found by differentiating the property-price equation with respect to the characteristic. In equation 6–5, if a_n is an estimate of α_n, then:

$$\partial P/\partial Q = a_n, \qquad (6\text{–}5)$$

where a_n measures the marginal willingness to pay for an extra unit improvement of air quality Q.

If the hedonic price function is linear in the characteristic (as in equation 6–4), then the implicit price for any characteristic is constant for unit changes in the characteristic, such as air quality. The incremental benefits ΔV of an air pollution abatement program that improves air quality from Q_1 to Q_2 can then be calculated by multiplying the implicit price a_n times the air quality improvement and summed over all sites, or,

$$\Delta V = \sum_{i=1}^{s} a_{n_i}(Q_2 - Q_1). \qquad (6\text{–}6)$$

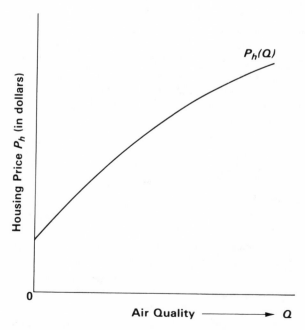

Figure 6.5 The rent function for air quality for urban housing.

If equation 6–3 is nonlinear, however, then the implicit price of an additional unit of a characteristic such as air quality depends on the quantity of the characteristic being purchased.

To show the second case graphically, consider only the implicit price of air quality Q. Figure 6.5 shows the partial relationship between P and Q as estimated from equation 6–3, that is, holding all other characteristics constant.* Interpretation of this curve is as follows: If the household is assumed to be a price taker in the property market, it can be viewed as facing an array of alternative property value-air quality combinations. The household maximizes its utility by moving along the array from site to site in the direction of increasing Q until that point where its marginal willingness to pay for an additional unit of Q just equals the additional cost or marginal purchase price of Q. Figure 6.6 shows the implicit marginal purchase price of Q, $R(Q) = \partial P/\partial Q$, the first derivative of $P(Q)$.†

Figure 6.6 also shows the inverse demand or marginal willingness-to-pay functions for two households, i and j, and the equilibrium positions for these two households at points A and B, respectively. For each individual, the quantity of Q purchased is known by observation, and its implicit price is known from equation 6–8. The points A and B can therefore be interpreted as the utility-maximizing equilibria for the two households resulting from the intersection of their inverse demand or marginal willingness-to-pay functions $D_i(Q)$ and $D_j(Q)$ and the locus of opportunities to purchase Q, as defined by $R(Q)$.

Having come this far, can these curves (or estimated equations) be used to evaluate changes in air quality? The answer is "yes" for marginal changes and "no" for nonmarginal changes, unless one is willing to make certain assumptions. To explain this further, in figure 6.6 we saw that $R(Q)$ is a locus of equilibrium points and not a marginal benefit function for air quality. (Those are the functions such as $D_i(Q)$ that are not known).

Because we lack full knowledge of each individual's marginal benefit function, to approximate benefits either we must fall back on some assumption about the shape of the functions through the known points, or further analytical work must be done to determine their shape. We will consider both alternatives.

---

*If equation 6–3 is linear (see equation 6–4), then the curve in figure 6.5 would be a straight line with a positive slope and the curve in figure 6.6 would be a horizontal line indicating a constant marginal willingness to pay.

†The actual form of the house price equation will depend on the form of the underlying utility function. If the utility function is linear, then the equation will be like equation 6–4. If we have a multiplicative utility function we get a log-linear regression equation:

$$\log P = \alpha_1 \log C_1 + \alpha_2 \log C_2 + \ldots + \alpha_n \log Q. \tag{6–7}$$

In this case, the implicit price for air quality will be

$$\partial P/\partial Q = \alpha_n P/Q. \tag{6–8}$$

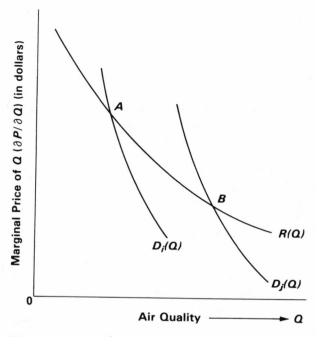

Figure 6.6 Household demand curves for air quality for urban housing.

Assumptions about the Shape of the $D_i(Q)s$. Freeman (1974) has presented three methods, as follows:

1. Assume that the marginal benefit for each individual household is constant; that is, the marginal benefit (or willingness-to-pay) function is a horizontal line through the known points on $R(Q)$ in figure 6.7. Then an improvement in air quality ΔQ from D to C gives a benefit of $ABCD$. The aggregate benefit is obtained by summing over all individuals; that is,

$$\sum_{i=1}^{n} \partial P_i/\partial Q_i \quad \Delta Q$$

Figure 6.7 also shows by how much benefits are overestimated if the marginal willingness-to-pay function is not linear but equals $D_i(Q)$.

2. Assume that each household's marginal willingness-to-pay curve decreases linearly from its observed point (A) to zero, where Q equals Q_{max} or air pollution is zero. If we know this, we can approximate the benefit by areas of triangles.

3. Assume that all households have identical incomes and utility functions. Then, the curve $R(Q)$ is itself the inverse demand function. Recall that the marginal implicit price curve is a locus of points on the households'

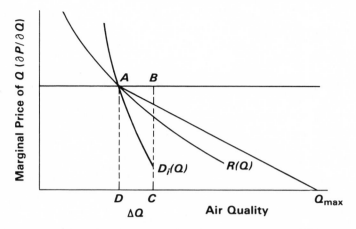

Figure 6.7 Household demand curve for air quality assuming constant marginal benefits for all households.

marginal willingness-to-pay curves. With identical incomes and utility functions, all these points fall on the same marginal willingness-to-pay curve. And, in that case, the benefits from an improvement in air quality can be calculated as the integral under the curve $R(Q)$ in figure 6.7.

What can be said about these assumptions? According to Freeman (1979b), they are "plausible" assumptions. Plausibility will depend very much on the problem that is being analyzed and on the circumstances. Anyone using this approach should be aware of the need to appraise the reasonableness of the assumptions and the amount of over- or underestimation of benefits that can result therefrom.

If none of the special assumptions mentioned above apply, then a second stage in the analysis is required. Here, the information about implicit prices and the data pertaining to environmental quality levels are combined in an effort to identify the inverse demand functions. The hypothesis is that the household's demand price or willingness to pay for Q is a function of the household's socioeconomic level, income, and other variables that influence preferences. Each household's observed $\partial P_i/\partial Q_i$ is taken to be a measure of $D_i(Q)$. The form of the actual regression function will depend on the assumption one makes about the slope of the housing supply function.

Attempts to Estimate the Actual Slope of the $D_i(Q)s$.   According to Freeman (1979b), there are again three possibilities:

1. If the supply of houses with given bundles of characteristics is perfectly elastic at the observed prices, then the implicit price function of a characteristic can be taken as exogenous to individuals. A regression of observed levels of the characteristic against the observed implicit prices,

income, and other socioeconomic characteristics of individuals should identify the demand function. Or, estimate

$$Q_i = Q_i \left(\partial P / \partial Q_i, C_i, \ldots \right). \tag{6–9}$$

2. If the available quantity of each type of housing is fixed, individuals can be viewed as bidding for fixed quantities of housing types with desired bundles of characteristics. A regression of each individual's implicit price against the quantity of the characteristic actually taken, incomes, and other variables should identify an inverse demand function. In this case, estimate

$$D_i(Q) = D_i(Q_i, C_i, \ldots), \tag{6–10}$$

where $\partial P / \partial Q_i$ is taken as an observation on D_i.

3. If quantities of characteristics demanded and supplied are both functions of prices, a simultaneous equation approach must be used.

Summary. This long discussion of the theoretical concepts underlying the property value approach was necessary to avoid leaving the impression that the property value technique consists simply of fitting a regression equation relating house prices to air quality levels.

The property value technique consists of two steps, which will be illustrated in the following section. First, one must calculate a house rent function. From this function, hedonic or implicit prices for air quality and other house or neighborhood characteristics can be obtained. These implicit prices can then be used to estimate the value of marginal changes in air quality. Since most air quality changes are not marginal, however, more information is needed about the actual shape of the inverse demand function for air quality. Hence, to evaluate nonmarginal changes in air quality, either one must make assumptions about the willingness-to-pay function (assumptions which are rather unrealistic), or the function must be estimated using regression techniques.

In the second estimation step, the problem of identification occurs. Whenever one has observations on quantities and prices, which are the results of the interaction of demand and supply, in order to identify the demand function the supply curve must be fixed. To achieve this, two alternatives that would allow identification of the inverse demand function are described in the following example. If neither of these two alternatives is applicable, then simultaneous equation models would have to be used.

In the literature, all three alternatives for identifying the inverse demand function have often been applied without much argument or explanation as to why the particular alternative was chosen. Freeman (1979c) wrote that in principle, the answer is "yes" to the question "Can this demand function be identified with the information at hand?" Others have claimed, however, that because of some of the questionable assumptions inherent in the approach, the whole technique is based on very shaky foundations (Pearce 1978).

The Property Value Technique: An Example. This example is taken from the work of Harrison and Rubinfeld (1978a,b). The purpose is to demonstrate the practical steps involved in the property value technique. Alternative approaches will also be mentioned. Only a brief summary of the highlights of the paper is presented. Estimated equations are reproduced, but there is no discussion of the significance of the statistical estimates.

The first step in the analysis is to estimate a hedonic housing-value equation with air pollution as one housing attribute. To this end, the authors utilized data from census tracts in the Boston Standard Metropolitan Statistical Area (SMSA) in 1970.*

The dependent variable in the housing equation is the median value of the owner-occupied homes in the census tract.[†] The independent variables in the equation include two structural variables, eight neighborhood variables, two accessibility variables, and one air pollution variable. The pollution variable is the concentration of nitrogen oxides, NO_x, expressed in the equation by *(NOX)*.

With the relevant variables chosen,[‡] the next decision relates to the functional form of the hedonic housing-value equation.[§] Both linear and semilog functions are compared, with the latter giving a better fit. The *NOX* variable is included in a nonlinear form as NOX^P, where P is an unknown parameter.

---

*The most commonly used source of United States data in property value–air pollution studies is the U.S. Census of Population and Housing. The census asks each owner to estimate the value of his or her property. The census also gathers data on structural characteristics as well as socioeconomic data on occupants. These data are aggregated by census tracts and reported as means or medians. The use of this type of data presents several problems. Freeman (1979b) provides a detailed discussion of these problems. An alternative source of data is individual observation. The individual observations are usually records of house sales. These data have the advantage of being actual market prices of individual units. Such data are not generally available, however, for all urban areas or even for large segments of a single urban area.

[†]Some researchers prefer to use pure land rent (site value) instead of the price of housing (Freeman 1979b).

[‡]The most important issue in estimating air pollutant coefficients involves a proper specification of the determinants of housing prices. Misspecification can lead to biases in the estimated air pollutant coefficients. If an important variable influencing housing prices is left out of the regression, and if the omitted variable is related to an air pollutant variable, the air pollutant coefficient will be a biased estimate of the true coefficient; part of the omitted variable's influence on housing price is incorrectly attributed to the pollutant variable.

[§]Three functional forms normally are used for such regressions; the linear, semilog, and log-log forms. They are represented by the following equations:

$$\text{Linear } P = \alpha_0 + \alpha_1 C_1 + \ldots + \alpha_n Q; \tag{6-11}$$

$$\text{Semilog log } P = \alpha_0 + \alpha_1 C_1 + \ldots + \alpha_n Q; \tag{6-12}$$

$$\text{Log-log log } P = \alpha_0 + \alpha_1 \log C_1 + \ldots + \alpha_n \log Q. \tag{6-13}$$

Harrison and Rubinfeld believed that determining the proper exponent for *NOX* is important because different exponents imply different patterns of the influence of air pollution on housing values and, thus, different patterns of the assumed willingness to pay for air quality improvements.

The statistical fit of the equation is best when *P* is set equal to 2.0.

The basic equation estimated has to be corrected for heteroscedasticity. Several nonpollution variables were tried, but the equation finally adopted is of the following form:

Variable	*Coefficient*	*Explanation of Letter Variable*
Dependent:		
Log *MV*		Median value of owner-occupied housing, dollars
Independent:		
Constant	9.66	
RM²	0.0057	Average number of rooms
AGE	1.26×10^{-4}	Proportion of owner units built prior to 1940
Log (*DIS*)	−0.20	Weighted distance to five employment centers in the Boston region
Log (*RAD*)	0.017	Index of accessibility to radial highways
TAX	-3.53×10^{-4}	Full value property-tax rate
PTRATID	−0.030	Pupil-teacher ratio by town school district
$(B - 0.63)^2$	0.43	Black proportion of population
Log (*STAT*)	−0.38	Proportion of population that is lower status
CRIM	−0.014	Crime rate
ZN	2.82×10^{-4}	Proportion of residential land zoned for lots greater than 25,000 ft²
INDUS	-2.22×10^{-4}	Proportion of nonretail business acres
CHAS	0.090	River dummy. Amenities of riverside location
NOX²	−0.0058	Nitrogen oxide concentration, parts per hundred million (pphm)

The variable of most interest, *NOX,* has a negative sign and proves to be highly significant. Assessing the quantitative importance of the *NOX* coefficient (−0.0064)* requires some calculation because, with the nonlinear speci-

---

*The value of −0.0064 was the coefficient before the equation was adjusted for heteroscedasticity. After adjustment, the coefficient was −0.0058. This would slightly lower the estimate of change in house value.

fication, the change in housing value resulting from a 1 pphm change in *NOX* concentration depends on the level of *NOX* and on the level of the other explanatory variables. When *NOX* and the other variables take on their mean values, the change in the median housing values from 1 pphm change in *NOX* is $1,613.

The second step involves the estimation of the willingness-to-pay equations. Harrison and Rubinfeld assume that the amount of air pollution is perfectly inelastic at each location. They calculate the derivative of the housing-value equation with respect to *NOX* and in this way obtain information about the amount that households would be willing to pay for small reductions in air pollution levels in their census tracts. These values of willingness to pay for marginal improvements are now regressed on the level of air pollution and other variables.

Five different formulations were tried for this regression. The results are as follows:

$$W = -1040 + 209\ NOX + 12.1\ INC, \tag{6-14}$$

$$W = -581 + 189\ NOX + 12.4\ INC - 119.8\ PDU, \tag{6-15}$$

$$\mathrm{Log}W = 1.08 + 0.87\ \mathrm{log}NOX + 1.00\ \mathrm{log}INC, \tag{6-16}$$

$$\mathrm{Log}W = 1.05 + 0.78\ \mathrm{log}NOX + 1.01\ \mathrm{log}INC - 0.24\ \mathrm{log}PDU, \tag{6-17}$$

$$\mathrm{Log}W = 2.20 + 0.97\ \mathrm{log}NOX + 0.80\ \mathrm{log}INC - 0.03\ (Y_1)\ \mathrm{log}NOX - 0.07\ (Y_2)\ \mathrm{log}NOX, \tag{6-18}$$

where W is marginal willingness to pay ($); *NOX* is nitrogen oxides concentration (pphm); *INC* is household income in (100) dollars; *PDU* is persons per dwelling unit; Y_1 is 1 when $95 < INC < 130$, 0 otherwise; Y_2 is 1 when $INC \geq 130$, 0 otherwise.

The relationship between marginal willingness to pay, *NOX* level, and household income implied by these results is shown in figure 6.8 for equation 6–16. The three curves illustrate the marginal willingness to pay as a function of *NOX* level for three income levels: low ($8,500 per year), medium ($11,500 per year), and high ($15,000 per year). The positive slope for all curves implies that households perceive damage from air pollution to be greater at higher pollution levels. Thus, the willingness to pay for reductions is greater as pollution levels increase. The graphs also show that the willingness to pay for a marginal improvement in *NOX* concentration is greater for households in the higher income groups.

The straight line at $2,052 illustrates the willingness-to-pay curve implicit in a simple linear housing equation in which households are assumed to place the same dollar value on a unit improvement in *NOX* regardless of the existing level of air pollution and of their income.

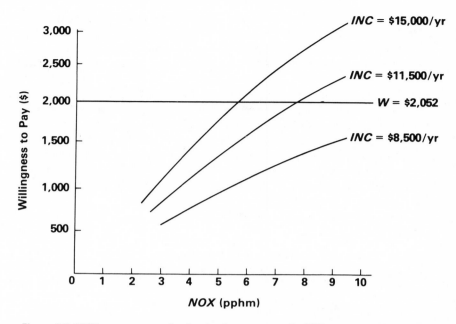

Figure 6.8 Willingness to pay for 1 pphm improvement in *NOX* concentration, by *NOX* level for households at three income levels (log-log version). (*Source:* Harrison and Rubinfeld, 1978*a,b*.)

Application.   The estimated equations were used to calculate the benefits of reductions in *NOX* levels from automobile emission controls. The projected change in air quality from 1970 to 1990 is based on the different emission characteristics of automobiles in those two years. The number of households and the level of nonauto emissions are assumed to be the same in the two years.

The results presented in table 6.9 are average annual benefits per household. Calculating average benefit figures ignores variations in average benefits enjoyed by subgroups of the population that are classified by income, race, and other variables.

Problems and Shortcomings of the Technique.   Great care is required in applying the property value technique to environmental quality problems and in interpreting the results obtained. In a report of this type, it is impossible to discuss in detail all aspects of the technique. In the first part of this section, the major assumptions and approaches were discussed. Any analyst intending to use the technique, however, should read further before doing so.

First, a careful study should be made of the realism of the underlying assumptions. Mäler (1977) criticized the following assumptions embedded in the approach:

Table 6.9. Average Annual Benefits per Household in the Boston SMSA from Reductions in Nitrogen Oxide (*NOX*) Levels Due to Automobile Emission Controls Based on Different Housing-Value Equations

Housing-value equation	Assuming that willingness-to-pay, *W*, is	
	$W = f(NOX, INC)$ (log-log version)	W = Constant
Linear		$118.00
Semilog ($P = 1$)	$101.26	105.26
Semilog ($P = 2$)	83.00	92.03
Semilog ($P = 3$)	59.17	78.32

Note: The formula used to calculate annual benefits per household in 1990 for the linear specification is

$$AB = \frac{\sum\limits_{i=1}^{N}(HH_i)(\Delta NOX_i)(a_P)}{10\sum\limits_{i=1}^{N}(HH_i)}, \tag{6–19}$$

where AB is average annual benefits per household; HH is number of households in census tract i; ΔNOX is improvement in NOX concentration in tract i in 1990 compared to 1970; a_P is coefficient of NOX from linear housing-value equation; N is number of census tracts in sample; and 10 is 10% discount rate.

For the nonlinear equation, the average benefit is calculated as above, except that average benefit per household B_i is substituted for the product $(\Delta NOX_i)(a_P)$. B_i is calculated as follows:

$$B_i = \int_{NOX_{90}}^{NOX_{70}} W_i dNOX_i, \tag{6–20}$$

where W_i is $f(NOX_i, INC_i)$.

Source: Harrison and Rubinfeld (1978).

1. That there is a large continuum of different individuals located in homogeneous communities (if communities are nonhomogeneous, property values capture willingness to pay for variables other than environmental quality);
2. That the price of land is based on expectations about future environmental quality, while the method depends on correlations with current environmental quality;
3. That people can perceive differences in environmental quality;
4. That people are willing to pay for environmental quality improvements in the neighborhood in which they are now living;
5. That perfect information on real estate prices exists;
6. That households continually reevaluate their locational decisions; and
7. That people do not cluster in areas with the same level of environmental quality for social reasons or transportation purposes.

Most of these assumptions place unrealistic requirements on the real estate market. If perfect information is not present, or if intraurban mobility is low, results may be biased.

Segmentation of the housing market distorts a property value analysis of the shadow price of environmental amenities or disamenities. The implicit hedonic price for the entire urban area will be wrong if, as some theorists believe, the housing market stratifies into separate segments (Hyman 1981).

In addition to the conceptual problems involved, the application of the technique raises many problems of measurement of the dependent and independent variables. Since owner-occupied housing may be only infrequently exchanged, it may be difficult to obtain enough housing-market data. Multicollinearity may prove to be a serious problem in estimating regression coefficients. These and other possible shortcomings need to be recognized before applying the technique (Hyman 1981, Pearce 1978).

Given all of these caveats, Freeman (1979d) argued that the hedonic price technique, while involving substantial simplification and abstraction from a complex reality, still has a logical and consistent theoretical basis. Examining the theory, criticisms, and results of more than a dozen studies that used the technique, he argued that the hedonic price model has substantial explanatory power and can provide a useful way to relate changes in environmental quality and housing prices.

Conclusion. Throughout this discussion, answers have been sought to two fundamental questions:

1. Can the property value equation be used to predict correctly the new equilibrium property-value schedule (and therefore the change in aggregate property values) resulting from a change in the air quality (or any other variables such as noise, water quality, or quality of amenities) schedule?

2. Is the actual change in aggregate property values (whether or not predicted correctly by the equation) equivalent to the willingness to pay for cleaner air (less noise, cleaner water, or better amenities)?

The earlier discussions lead to the conclusion that the answer to the first question depends on the circumstances. The circumstances necessary for an affirmative answer are those of equilibrium in the housing market and an open city with free mobility of labor and other factors (White 1979). The answer to the second question depends on the assumptions one makes about the demand and supply of housing characteristics and the utility of the people involved.

For marginal changes in the level of environmental quality, the technique can be used to give some indication of the magnitude and direction of benefits. However, as soon as the changes become nonmarginal (i.e., other prices and variables change), additional stages of analysis are required, which in turn require more assumptions, some of which may be unrealistic.

The method places great demands on data and may therefore be of limited use in some developing countries. It could become more useful, however, as more property market data become available and experience is gained through application of the technique. Because the technique is based on actual market data, it is less prone to systematic biases than are hypothetical valuation methods. Also, the fact that it can be applied to problems for which few alternative valuation techniques exist should be an encouragement for further research.

Other Areas of Application.

Property Values and Water Pollution.   One of the few studies that has treated this problem is that by David (1968). According to Freeman (1975), the two reasons for such a dearth of applications in the water pollution field are limited data and the fact that property value studies measure only those benefits that accrue to landowners adjacent to the improved body of water. For major bodies of water, however, this is likely to represent only a relatively small portion of the total benefits, and for small bodies of water the outlay of time and labor required to do a competent property value study is probably not warranted.

Property Values and Air Pollution.   Many other applications of the property value approach to air pollution exist. Important surveys of such applications can be found in Freeman (1979a,d), Pearce (1978), Pearce and Edwards (1979), Anderson and Crocker (1971), and Waddell (1974).

Property Values and Neighborhood Amenities.   Studies of this kind have been conducted by Abelson (1979), Polinsky and Shavell (1976), and Freeman (1979c).

Property Values and Aesthetic Benefits.   Sinden and Worrell (1979) discussed an application of the approach by Armstrong (1974) to quantify the aesthetic value of forests in two counties in Vermont, United States.

Other Land Value Approaches

Other approaches using market prices for land to determine the value of environmental quality benefits exist. Conceptually, these methods are related to the property value approach; they are much simpler, however, and attempt to estimate total values rather than marginal willingness-to-pay values.

Although these methods are less attractive theoretically than the hedonic price approach, they are much more straightforward and may be more applicable for use when data are limited. One needs to be careful when interpreting the results, but each of these methods may prove very useful as a first step toward estimating environmental quality benefits.

Valuation of Nonuser Benefits of Preservation.   Preservation benefits of a historical, educational, cultural, scientific, or ecological nature are difficult to value. Often such benefits accrue to people only in the future, and many of these benefits are hard to identify and estimate. However, when decisions are made that involve the purchase of land explicitly for preservation, the prices paid can be used to quantify the implicit valuation placed on the benefits from that land (Sinden and Worrell 1979). The following example illustrates such a valuation.

Example.   An analysis by Gupta and Foster (1975) valued the net benefits of preserving wetlands. The alternative uses of the wetlands are either to preserve them in their natural state or to allow development to proceed. To determine the economic desirability of either alternative, a comparison must be made between the opportunity cost of preservation and the economic benefits of that preservation.

As discussed earlier, the opportunity costs associated with preserving a natural resource are the benefits society would receive from the resource under the alternative uses that must be foregone to achieve preservation. In this example, market prices of wetlands are used as indicators of the opportunity cost of wetland preservation. With this approach, the economic benefits of preserving specific wetlands are implicitly derived from the prices paid for similar wetlands by public agencies, with due regard for the natural systems attributes of the land.

Data Requirements.   In this approach, two sets of data are required: prices paid by government or other agencies for land for wildlife, water supply, aesthetic, or other purposes; and market prices paid for wetlands for purposes of development.

If no transactions for preserving wetlands have taken place, this approach cannot be used. If no market price data are available, alternative sources of information can still be tried. One such source is estimates from local real estate appraisers of the value of the wetlands if they could be developed. Such estimates would provide reasonable substitutes for market prices and would reflect the social opportunity cost foregone if the area were preserved.

Application of the Example.   Market prices were obtained for wetlands sold for development in Massachusetts in 1970–71. The prices varied from US$300 to $70,000 an acre. Using a 5.375% capitalization rate, the annual economic rent from, or opportunity cost of, preserving wetlands varied from US$16 to $3,762 per acre.

Wetland benefits, on the other hand, can be divided into four groups:

1. wildlife production;
2. visual-cultural effects (i.e., recreational, educational, and aesthetic benefits);
3. water supply; and
4. flood control potential.

To place monetary values on these benefits, data gathered by wildlife biologists, landscape architects, and hydrologists for wetlands of differing productivity are used along with economic data to estimate monetary values for the four categories of wetlands.

Wildlife Values. Data on more than 8,000 acres of wetlands acquired by public agencies were analyzed. Based on the five highest prices, ranging from US$2,387 to $587 per acre, a figure of $1,200 per acre was selected as the capitalized value of wildlife benefits from the wetlands with the highest quality wildlife characteristics. Adding the cost of operation, capitalized at 5.375%, raised the value to about $1,300 per acre. On an annual basis, such wetlands produce nearly $70 worth of wildlife benefits per acre.

Next, wildlife biologists developed a quality-scoring model that considers ten natural resource variables including wetland class richness, size, surrounding habitat types, and diversity. Using this model, a wetland considered ideal as a wildlife habitat is expected to score a maximum of 100 points and have an annual value of benefits of $70. Hence, in taking any area of wetland, the quality of its wildlife benefits is scored and value of these benefits is calculated as

Total annual wildlife benefit per acre = US$70 × point score (expressed as a decimal).

Visual-Cultural Values. These values are measured in a similar way. Data on land purchases made by town conservation commissions for open spaces were collected for twenty-nine municipalities. The total area was 1,567 acres and the range of prices was US$5,769 to $3,684 per acre. A figure of $5,000 per acre was selected as the capital value of open-space land with high productivity of visual-cultural benefits. Annual benefits, using a capitalization rate of 5.375% were US$270 per acre. With the help of landscape architects, a point-scoring index similar to the one for wildlife habitat was developed. Benefits for any area of open space are then calculated as

Total annual open space benefit per acre = US$270 × point score (expressed as a decimal).

Water-Supply Benefits. The approach used here compared the cost of water from wetlands with that of the most economical, available alternative water source. The cost of producing water from a wellhead in the wetland was estimated at an average of $0.0427 per 1,000 gallons (gal) per day. An alternative water supply was one from the Boston Metropolitan District Commission, which charged $0.1200 per 1,000 gal per day. The $0.0773 cents difference between the two delivery costs was assumed to be the value of wetland water. This assumes that the $0.1200 per 1,000 gal per day represented the most economical incremental cost of an alternative supply, and that the per capita demand for water would be the same at the two levels of cost. In annual terms, the value was $28 per 1,000 gal per day. A typical wetland acre was assumed to supply 1 million gal per day. Therefore, a 10-acre wetland area supplying 1 million gal per day would have annual benefits of $2,800 per acre. Capitalized at 5.375%, the estimated value of such a wetland was US$52,000 per acre.

Flood Control Benefits.   These are based on a study that calculated benefits as losses avoided by flood control measures. On a per acre basis, this was US$80 annually, or $1,488 on a capitalized basis using a 5.375% interest rate.

The overall results of these calculations are shown in table 6.10. Because the four types of benefits were added to obtain an estimate of total benefits, the possibility of double counting of some benefits must be raised. The main source of possible double counting is between the visual-cultural and the wildlife benefits. The concept of open space is, however, sufficiently distinct from that of wildlife characteristics and values that serious concern about double counting of these benefits is not warranted.

Some questions can be raised about the water supply values, which are very large and account for more than 85% of total land values. This analysis assumed that the wetlands would in fact be used to supply water and that the additional water would be in demand at the higher price. The fact that the estimated value of a wetland acre from water alone ($52,000 at a capitalization factor of 5.375%) was ten times the highest price actually paid for wetland preservation casts doubt on this figure. Both wildlife and visual-cultural values are based on prices actually paid to preserve wetlands that had the desired characteristics, not the costs of providing these characteristics in another location. It appears, therefore, that water supply values should be interpreted with caution.

Using all combinations of high, medium, and low productivity values for the four types of benefits, the capitalized values of total wetland benefits per acre are calculated. These total values can now be compared with the prospective returns from developing the wetlands.

It is important to remember that because of the irreversible nature of wetland alteration and the scarcity of wetlands in the United States, the social value of preserved wetlands is likely to increase significantly over time relative to the general price level. Comparing current costs and benefits could

Table 6.10. Assumed Annual Value per Acre of Wetlands in Massachusetts at High, Medium, and Low Productivity Levels, 1972

	Annual per acre values		
	Benefit productivity level		
Type of benefit	High	Medium	Low
Wildlife	$ 70	$ 35	$ 10
Visual-cultural	270	135	20
Water supply	2,800	1,400	400
Flood control	80	40	10
Total	3,220	1,610	440

Source: Gupta and Foster (1975).

favor development of certain wetlands, while an analysis that considered values thirty years hence could favor their preservation. This uncertainty should be incorporated in current decisions.

This wetland study shows how land values, some of which are determined politically, could be used to establish values for wildlife and visual-cultural benefits. Benefits of water supply from wetland areas were based on the cost of alternative sources, while flood control benefits were established by calculating losses avoided.

If data on prices paid by public agencies for wetlands or other natural areas are available, the above technique may be very useful for placing annual values on the benefits from these lands. Of course, annual values are also a function of the interest rate that is assumed. If such price data are not available, however, the first two benefit estimation techniques (for wildlife and visual-cultural values) will be of no use. The last two techniques (for water supply and flood control) are standard methods used in cases of this type.

Valuation of a Soil Conservation Project.   In another type of land value approach, a two-step process was used to estimate the benefits from improved environmental quality for a soil conservation project. In this example, a with and without project analysis was done of the value of production (in this case, range-fed livestock). The increased value per hectare from improved pasture productivity was easily calculated. The difference in retail land prices between the improved and unimproved land was larger, however, than the value of the increased productivity. The extra value was attributed to environmental quality benefits (Australia, Department of Environment, 1978).

This land value technique permitted quantification of benefits and a division between productivity-related and aesthetic benefits. Since the land was privately owned, and the increased land values therefore were captured by individuals and not by society, the question arises as to who should pay the costs of the soil conservation project.

Conclusion.   The land value approaches discussed here are indicative of the types of analysis that can be done if data are available on actual market prices or on expert opinions about market values of land. It must be emphasized that land values may not reflect total benefits; rather, they should be considered estimates of the minimum values of benefits from preservation or environmental improvements.

The Wage Differential Approach

Theoretical Concept.   The wage differential approach is very similar to the property value approach. It rests on the theory that in a perfectly competitive equilibrium, the demand for labor equals the value of the marginal product of the workers, and that the supply of labor varies with working and living conditions in the area. A higher wage is therefore necessary to induce workers to locate in polluted areas or to undertake risky occupations. Workers are supposedly able to move freely among jobs and are therefore able to choose a particular job in a particular area at a certain wage that will maximize their utility. If wages are centrally set, this approach cannot be used unless wages are systematically varied to achieve equilibrium in the labor market and unless laborers have freedom of movement.

Differences in wage levels for similar jobs can be conceived of as a function of different levels in job attributes that relate to working conditions and living conditions in the area where the job is. If such a relationship between wage levels and attributes could be estimated, implicit prices (as in the property value approach) could be determined. Assuming constant implicit prices (reflecting marginal willingness to pay or acceptance of lower or higher wages for lower or higher levels of the particular attribute), benefits could be estimated for improvements in levels of attributes.

Many attributes that affect wage differentials can be identified. The two attributes of interest, however, and to which most examples refer, are *risk* to life and health and *urban amenities* or disamenities, especially air pollution. The implicit price of the latter attribute would provide a trade-off value between air pollution and income.

Applications. Few good examples of the application of this technique exist. This may reflect the fact that the technique is not well developed as yet and suffers from many theoretical and practical difficulties. No example will be described in detail in this section, but a few applications will be briefly mentioned.

The pioneering study using wage differentials is that of Meyer and Leone (1977). In it, differences in wages among cities were interpreted as reflecting workers' willingness to pay (in the form of lower wages) to work and live in cities with higher levels of environmental and other amenities. The authors estimated the air quality benefits associated with a 45% reduction in levels of particulates, sulfur dioxide, and nitrogen dioxide. In the conclusion to the paper, they asked: "Should wage differential analysis proceed and, if so, in what direction?" In their answer, they indicated that alternative approaches may be much more promising because of the theoretical and practical difficulties associated with the wage differential technique.

Cropper (1979) developed a labor-supply model that takes into account interurban differences in amenities, locations of housing sites within the urban area, and wages. Under certain assumptions, knowledge of the labor-supply function makes it possible to estimate the coefficients of the utility function and to compute willingness to pay for changes in the level of urban amenities. Cropper estimated the model, using 1969 wage data. Sulfur dioxide was one of the amenity variables. She estimated that a laborer with an income of $9,000.00 per year would be willing to pay $55.65 per year for a 20% decrease in SO_2 levels. She did not estimate aggregate or national benefits.

Thäler and Rosen (1976) provided estimates of individuals' revealed willingness to trade off income for safety. Using data on occupational risks and pay differentials, they found that workers were willing to accept an additional $390 per year to work on jobs that would increase their annual risk of death by one in one thousand. From this the authors observed that a "statistical life" was implicitly valued at $390,000 because a thousand such individuals would be willing to pay the appropriate premium to reduce the annual risk of death to each by 0.001 (Portney 1981). An example of this technique applied to air pollution control benefits was given in a report by the U.S. National Academy of Sciences (1974).

M. W. Jones-Lee (1976), in his book on economic valuation of human life, referred to an earlier paper by Thäler and Rosen (1973), in which wage premiums were used to analyze risky work situations. The authors estimated the equilibrium marginal rate of substitution between income and risk (which is tantamount to a "value of life") to be about $200,000 for risk changes effective over a period of one year.

Assumptions and Shortcomings.   The wage differential approach suffers from many of the same drawbacks as the property value approach. It assumes that people can make free choices with perfect information in the absence of discrimination, monopsony, union market power, involuntary unemployment or barriers to mobility. The assumption of a perfectly competitive labor market is not very realistic and is even less tenable than the assumption of a perfectly competitive real estate market in the property value approach. The assumption of perfect information implies that the individual has a reasonable notion of what the risks or attribute levels of alternative choices are. These may actually be very difficult to perceive. One can hardly learn about the risk of death by personal experience, and learning from the experience of others is often unsatisfactory.

In applying the technique, *all* attributes will have to be identified and measured because the underlying utility function is defined by a multitude of attributes. This is a very difficult task, and one that demands thorough data. Incomplete equations, however, will give erroneous results.

The results obtained for the trade-offs between risk and money—from, for example, coal miners—tell us something only about their preferences. Some occupations are relatively dangerous and are likely to attract individuals with unusually low aversion to risk. Therefore, the results obtained from analyzing the trade-offs of "risk-lovers" give us little useful information about the amount of compensation that other individuals must be offered to accept added risk (or the amount they would be willing to pay to avoid it). Therefore, estimates of trade-offs must be obtained for all occupational groups, and for men, women, and children (Bishop and Cicchetti 1975). Also, even if one has determined the trade-off between income and risk in one occupation, it does not necessarily follow that these values hold for other kinds of occupations.

Conclusion.   The wage differential technique could be applied in the field of air pollution control, for improving urban amenities, and for reducing risks to life and health. The approach is appealing because it uses values derived from the real world of the labor market. It suffers, however, from many theoretical and practical drawbacks. The assumption of perfect competition is not very tenable in most countries. Also, the poor in many countries may have no choice about the quality of their living or working conditions. Because of the gap between their theoretical willingness to pay and their actual ability to pay, their attitudes toward amenities and risks are unlikely to reflect the attitudes of the rest of the population.

Further empirical work is required to determine whether there is, in fact, a significant association between wages and environmental degradation (such as air pollution) in a properly specified model. In the meantime, alternative techniques should also be considered when attempting to estimate the benefits of reduced levels of air pollution on risk to life and health.

The Travel-Cost Approach

The travel-cost approach is a way to value unpriced goods. In developed countries, this approach has been extensively used to derive a demand curve for recreational goods (Clawson and Knetsch 1966). Outdoor recreation is a typical example of such an unpriced good. Although the approach seems associated solely with recreational analysis, there is no reason why it could not be applied to a broader range of problems.

The discussion of the theoretical concept of the travel-cost approach is in terms of recreation analysis, but the focus is actually on the valuation of an unpriced good. A recreational good is just one of a number of goods in this category.

Theoretical Concept.   The travel-cost approach was initially developed to value the benefits received by consumers from their use of an environmental good. Most examples of the approach use outdoor recreation facilities—a lake, a river, or a campground—as the environmental good being considered. Because users of these recreation sites frequently pay nothing or, at most, nominal admission fees, the revenue collected for use of these facilities is not a good indicator of the value of the site or the actual willingness of users to pay. The real value of the site, which includes both user charges and the total consumer surplus enjoyed by users, becomes important when decisions must be made about committing resources to preserve an existing site or create a new one.

Survey techniques could be used to find out consumers' hypothetical valuation of a recreation site, and such techniques are discussed later. In outdoor recreation, however, there is another way to determine consumers' implicit valuation of a site. We assume that the recreation site charges no admission or user fee and is a desirable environmental good. Users come from various places to spend time at the site. Although no entrance fee is charged (or only a nominal one), demand for the good is not infinite because there is a cost involved in getting to and from the site. This is where the travel-cost approach begins.

The farther away potential users of the recreation site live, the less is their expected use of (demand for) the site (the environmental good). Those users who live close by would be expected to demand more of the environmental good because its implicit price, as measured by travel costs, is lower than for users more distant from the good. In terms of consumer's surplus, the user most distant with the highest travel cost is assumed to have the lowest (or no) consumer's surplus. Likewise, those who live closer and have lower travel costs also have larger consumer's surpluses.

In actual practice, the travel-cost approach is site-specific and measures the benefits from one particular site and not from recreation in general (Freeman 1979). The recreation site is identified, and the surrounding area is divided into concentric zones of increasing distance, which represent increasing levels of travel costs. A survey of users is conducted at the recreation site to determine zone of origin, visitation rates, travel costs, and various socioeconomic characteristics. The information from this sample of visitors is then analyzed, and the data generated are used to regress visitation rates on travel cost and the various socioeconomic variables.

$$Q_i = f\,(TC,\,X_1,\,.\,.\,.\,,\,X_n) \tag{6-21}$$

where Q_i is the visitation rate (number of visitors from zone i per 1,000 population in zone i), TC is travel cost, and $X_1 \ldots X_n$ are a number of socioeconomic variables including income, level of education, and other appropriate variables.

This regression will test the hypothesis that travel costs do in fact have an impact on visitation rates. The inclusion of the other variables helps to eliminate the effects of non-travel-cost-related components of total visitation rates.

This first step leads to the creation of a so-called "whole experience" demand curve based on visitation rates, not the actual number of visitor-days spent at the site. To estimate the consumer surplus, or benefits, from the site, this demand curve can be used to estimate actual numbers of visitors and how the numbers would change with increases in admission price—in effect, creating a classic demand curve.

As Freeman points out (1979), the base information about total visitation from all travel-cost zones defines one point on the demand curve for the recreation site under study. That is, it defines the point of intersection of the present nominal or zero price line with the true economic demand curve. In figure 6.9 this would be point A if the admission charge were zero. The remainder of the demand curve is derived by assuming that visitors would respond in the same way to increases in admission costs as to equal increases in travel costs. For each incremental increase in admission cost, the expected visitation rate from each travel origin zone is calculated. These values are summed across all travel origin zones to find the predicted total number of visitors at the new admission price. A $1 increase in admission charge may lead to point B in figure 6.9. This calculation is repeated for higher and higher admission charges until the entire demand curve, AM, is traced. The area

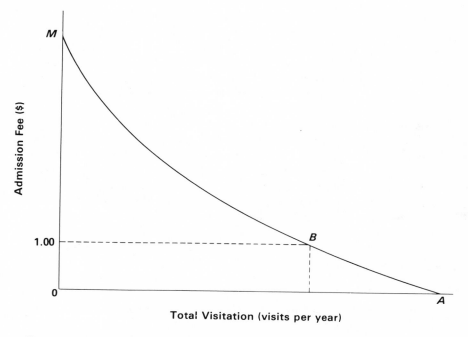

Figure 6.9 Demand curve for outdoor recreation at a specific site.

under the curve is an estimate, therefore, of the total consumer's surplus enjoyed by present users of the recreation site, assuming an original access price of zero.

To use the travel-cost approach, a number of assumptions must be made about individual behavior and about the variables measured. Sinden and Worrell (1979) specified the following:

1. All users must obtain the same total benefit from the use of the site, and this is equal to the travel cost of the marginal user (most distant).
2. The consumer's surplus of the marginal user is zero.
3. Travel cost is a reliable proxy for price. This, in turn, rests on an assumption that the disutility of overcoming distance derives from monetary costs alone.
4. People in all distance zones would consume the same quantities of the activity at given monetary costs. That is, the demand curves for all distance zones have the same slope.

These assumptions will be discussed later; but first, a simple hypothetical example of the technique will be given.

Hypothetical Example (Knetsch and Davis 1966).   Assume a free recreation area, such as a public park or lake. People arriving at the area have been

Table 6.11. Visitors to a Recreation Area (Hypothetical Example)

Zone	Population	Average travel cost of visit ($)	Visits made	Visits/1,000 population
I	1,000	1	400	400
II	2,000	3	400	200
III	4,000	4	400	100
Beyond III			0	
Total			1,200	

Source: Adapted from Knetsch and Davis (1966).

interviewed to obtain information about the distance traveled, travel costs, purpose of the trip, and other socioeconomic characteristics. The total area of visitor origin is then divided into zones of increasing travel costs. For each zone, the total population is determined. All of this information is shown in table 6.11.

With no admission fee to the site, the number of visits made from each zone over a specified time period will be a function of travel costs and other determinants of recreational visits. Travel costs include outlays for such items as transportation, lodging, and food greater than those incurred if the trip were not made.*

The visits per unit of population V, in this case per thousand population ($V/1,000$), may then be plotted against the average cost per visit, C. Or, by using statistical procedures, a relationship between visits per thousand population and travel cost could be determined. In this example, the relationship is linear and is given by

$$V/1,000 = 500 - 100C. \qquad (6\text{--}22)$$

This demand curve is called the whole-experience demand curve. Sinden and Worrell (1979) showed how consumer's surplus is calculated from this curve. Estimating the whole experience, however, gives only a minimum value. Users from the most distant zone are assumed to have no consumer's surplus. In addition, other visitors have no opportunity to demonstrate their maximum willingness to pay for the use of the site.

In order to estimate the total value of the on-site experience, Clawson (1959) suggested extending the whole-experience method. This approach is based on the assumption that the differences in costs between zones can be used to simulate an entrance fee and that people's reaction to entrance fees is

---

*What should be included in the travel-cost item requires some judgment. With respect to automobile costs, only the variable cost of the round trip should be counted. Some applications have used perceived cost instead of real cost. The cost of a visit includes the money spent at a site plus the per visitor-day costs of recreational supplies, fees for camp or trailer, sites and boat launching, fish bait, and *extra* cost of food, lodging, and other services beyond those that would be incurred at home.

Table 6.12. Visits to a Recreation Area, Assuming $1 Entrance Fee

Zone	New cost ($) (C)	Visits/1,000[a] population	Population (thousands)	Visits
I	2	300	1	300
II	4	100	2	200
III	5	0	4	0
				500

[a] Visits/1,000 population calculated from equation 6–22: $V/1,000 = 500 - 100C$.

the same as their reaction to higher travel costs. Using this assumption and the data in tables 6.11 and 6.12, the demand curve for the on-site experience is established as follows:

1. At present, no entrance fee is charged to visit the site, and the total number of visits made is 1,200 for a specified time period. This gives point A on the demand curve in figure 6.10.
2. Assume a $1 entrance fee. This is added to the travel cost so that the cost per visit for visitors from zone I becomes $2 ($1 travel cost plus $1 admission). Using formula 6–22, the new visitation rate can be calculated for each zone. As shown in table 6.12 and point B in figure 6.10, total visits now drop to 500.
3. Repeat step 2 for entrance fees of $2, $3, and $4. Thus, by using the visit rate-travel cost relationship, we can calculate the total number of visits that would be made *if people treat an increment in travel cost the same as admission fees*. Total visits are shown in table 6.13 and plotted in figure 6.10.

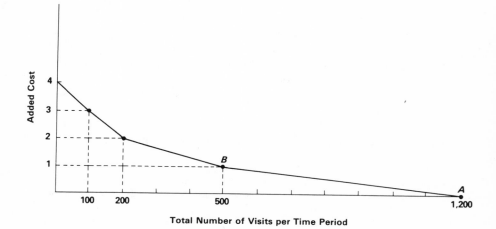

Figure 6.10 On-site experience demand curve for recreation area.

Table 6.13. Total Visits to a Recreation Area, with Entrance Fee as a Variable

Added cost (entrance fee)	Total number of visits
$0	1,200
1	500
2	200
3	100
4	0

Source: Knetsch and Davis (1966).

4. Total consumer's surplus, calculated from the area under the demand curve in figure 6.10, in this hypothetical example is

$$\frac{(1,200 - 500)}{2} \times \$1 = 350$$

$$\frac{(500 - 200)}{2} \times \$1 = 150$$

$$(500 - 200) \times \$1 = 300$$

$$\frac{(200 - 100)}{2} \times \$1 = 50$$

$$(200 - 100) \times \$2 = 200$$

$$\frac{(100 - 0)}{2} \times \$1 = 50$$

$$(100 - 0) \times \$3 = \underline{300}$$

$$\text{Total} \quad \overline{1,400}$$

or $\dfrac{1,400}{1,200} = \$1.17$ per on-site visit.

This example presents the basic travel-cost method. Many shortcomings can be found in this approach. The underlying assumption, that the visitation rate is solely a function of travel cost, is simplistic. Other factors will influence people's demand for recreation. Also, the assumption that people in the same zone have identical preferences is difficult to accept. Furthermore, travel time is ignored, and experience has shown that not all trips are single-purpose trips.

All of these problems and others have been recognized, and attempts have been made to overcome them. Before discussing these issues, however, a more realistic example of application of the travel-cost approach will be presented. It will show the steps required for a travel-cost analysis and will demonstrate some of the extensions of the technique.

Actual Example. The following example, taken from an analysis of reservoir recreation benefits (Tussey 1967), was chosen for two reasons: the subject matter is relevant to situations in both developed and developing countries, and the example clearly shows the steps required to apply the travel-cost approach. Emphasis in this section is on the mechanics of application and on data sources and problems. Little time will be spent on the statistical significance or the substance of the results.

The example deals with the analysis of a popular recreation reservoir in the state of Kentucky in the United States. The origin areas from which visitors came to the site were defined as the 120 Kentucky counties plus the 47 remaining states of the mainland United States and the District of Columbia. This provided 168 possible origin areas.

Visitation Data.   Annual reservoir attendance data collected by the U.S. Army Corps of Engineers are shown in table 6.14. To determine the number of visitors by origin area, two types of visitation data were utilized. The first type was data collected by the Corps of Engineers through visitor-origin surveys conducted during the years 1963 through 1966. The second was from a motor vehicle origin survey. Data were collected by driving a consistent route through the recreation area and recording state and county origins from the vehicle license plates.

After they were tested for compatibility, these two data sets were combined. The distribution of visitors by origin area was based on the interview data as well as on the visitor estimates taken from the drive-through survey for the months of March, April, May, June, and July. The total number of audited visitors (from interviews and drive-through surveys) was estimated at 71,000.*

Total Population Data.   These data were taken from the 1960 nationwide census. Later population figures could have been used, but population estimates between census years are less accurate and more difficult to obtain. A quick check showed that the populations in the counties immediately surrounding the reservoir had changed little since 1960.

Travel Distance Data.†   Travel distance was calculated from a point within the origin area (the center of the area) to the main entrance of the reservoir. Three measures were calculated: air distance and road distance (in miles) and time (in hours).

---

*Data collection is a difficult and time-consuming task. Many different survey techniques are available. The choice of a particular technique will depend very much on the actual recreation site and its facilities, access, size, and geographic location. Brown, Lyon, and MacMillan (1976) discussed some of these techniques.

†Sometimes (as in this example) travel distance may be more closely related to use of a site than travel cost. In one study, Sinden (1974) found that use of a recreation site varied with distance but that travel cost was not a statistically significant variable. If the monetary costs of travel are small, distance may act as a rationing device for recreation and may serve as a proxy for price in a travel-cost analysis (Sinden and Worrell 1979). The use of distance as a price proxy is found in studies by Merewitz (1966) and Mansfield (1971). Distance, of course, cannot be directly compared with monetary values. To make it comparable, the distance units must be converted to monetary units by a cost-per-mile multiplier (Smith and Kavanagh 1969, the example in the next section). Such a procedure assumes that the marginal disutility of time is constant and that all users incur the same monetary cost per mile (Sinden and Worrell 1979).

Table 6.14. Annual Attendance at Reservoir in Kentucky, United States, 1963–1966 (Thousands)

Year	Attendance
1963	554,000
1964	695,000
1965	778,000
1966	824,000

Source: Tussey (1967).

Population Characteristics. A fairly large number of socioeconomic characteristics were examined, and those with the greatest degree of statistical correlation to the visitation data were selected. Three variables were chosen for further analysis: median family income (seven income classes), urbanization of the origin area, and median individual age (seven age ranges).

Route Characteristics Data. Four variables characterizing travel routes were considered: the ratio of air distance to road distance, the percentage of the road distance with four or more highway lanes, the percentage of the road distance with federal-standard two-lane highways, and the percentage of the road distance with state-standard two-lane highways.

Competing Recreational Reservoir Data. The computation factor used in this study was defined as *the air distance from an origin area to the nearest selected competing reservoir* divided by *the air distance from the same origin area to the reservoir studied.* All state origin areas were assumed to have competing reservoirs nearer their populations and therefore were given a ratio value equal to zero.

Effective Distance Data. In general, the total travel distance from an origin area to the reservoir cannot be attributed to the reservoir studied. Only the out-of-the-way distance traveled to the site can be considered as determining the cost the visitor paid to reach the project. One might hypothesize that visitors traveling short distances to the reservoir had the sole purpose of visiting the reservoir, while visitors traveling greater distances might have stopped at intermediate points of interest or to visit friends or relatives and, thus, their out-of-the-way travel distance to the reservoir would have been only a portion of the distance from their homes to the reservoir.

To determine effective distance, visitors were queried by means of postcards and letters distributed at the site during the summer of 1966. Visitors were asked: "Does your trip away from home have any purpose other than to visit the reservoir?" If the answer was "yes," they were then asked: "How far out of your way, one way, did you go to come here?"

Results from the survey were translated into a curve relating road distance to out-of-the-way distance, which was used by the analyst to translate road distance observations into effective distance data.

Application of the Example. The data described above were used in a multiple regression analysis to estimate coefficient values for several equations. The first equation that was estimated was of the following form:

$$V = KP/d^n, \tag{6-23}$$

where V is the estimated annual number of visitor-days spent at the site, P is the population of the origin area, d is the distance of the reservoir from the origin area, n is the exponent describing the relationship between distance and visitation, and K is a constant describing the propensity of the individuals in the origin areas to visit the reservoir.*

The total number of audited visitors obtained from the data was 70,976 in 1966. Total actual visitation for that year was 824,000 (table 6.14), and these visitors were assumed to be distributed in the same manner as the 70,976 audited visitors (table 6.15, columns 1 and 2). Rearranging equation (6–23) yields

$$\frac{V}{P} = \frac{K}{d^n} ; \tag{6-24}$$

taking common logs of both sides yields

$$\log \frac{V}{P} = \log K - n \log d. \tag{6-25}$$

This equation was estimated as follows:

$$\log \frac{V}{P} = 3.411 - 2,445 \log d , \tag{6-26}$$

$$\text{or } V = 2577 \, \frac{P}{d^{2.445}} .$$

This equation can be used to estimate the annual visitation from each origin area to the reservoir (table 6.15, column 3).

The next step was to try to improve the correlation of equation 6–26 by adding new variables. Other variables were included on the hypothesis that they accounted for at least part of the difference between visitation predicted by equation 6–26 and actual visitation. Of all the variables tested, including the different income and age classes, only seven were retained for further analysis. These were:

1. median family income (x_1);
2. percentage of families with annual incomes between \$15,000 and \$20,000 (x_2);

*Throughout the literature, many equations relating V, P, d, and other variables have been used. Everett (1978) used $V = a + \dfrac{b}{(c + k)}$ where a, b, and k are constants and c is the cost of travel. Knetsch (1963) included several socioeconomic variables, as did Merewitz (1966) and Sinden (1978). Shucksmith (1979) briefly discussed different forms and compared results from using a semilog and a doublelog function. The doublelog function, however, predicted that if there were no cost the visitation rate would be infinite. To get an intercept term, some analysts have added an arbitrary constant to the equation. Common (1973) criticized this approach.

Table 6.15. Various Estimates of Annual Visitation at Reservoir in Kentucky

Origin area	Audited visits	Actual visits	Equation 6–26 estimate	Adjusted equation 6–26[a] estimate
1 Adair County	72	836	985	1,327
2 Allen County	88	1,022	1,167	1,541
56 Jefferson County	28,198	327,445	70,646	319,204
121 Alabama State	145	1,684	7,380	22,569
168 Wyoming State	4	46	31	0

[a] Estimates of K from equation 6–27 were inserted in equation 6–26 to obtain visitation rates.
Source: Tussey (1967).

3. percentage of people between the ages of ten and nineteen (x_3);
4. percentage of residents living in cities having more than 50,000 people (x_4);
5. median individual age (x_5);
6. a recreation competition factor (x_6); and
7. percentage of the road distance from the reservoir to the origin area in four-lane highway (x_7).

An imputed K for each origin was calculated from known values of V, P, and d. These 168 imputed values were regressed on the seven variables (K was weighted to correct for the differences in audited visitors in origin areas).

$$K = a + bX_1 + cX_2 + dX_3 + eX_4 + fX_5 + gX_6 + hX_7$$

$$K = 1116.31744 + 221.33237\, X_4 - .40325\, X_1$$
$$- 1684.04123\, X_2 + 382.38046\, X_5, \quad R^2 = .8367. \tag{6–27}$$

These estimates of K were inserted in equation 6–26 to obtain revised visitation estimates (column 4 of table 6.15).

Estimation of Benefits.   Equations 6–26 and 6–27 provide estimates of visitation that correspond to the combination of distance, population, route, and competition characteristics applying to a particular origin area. If all characteristics are held constant and distance is increased by increments, estimated visitation decreases. The cost of traveling the incremental distance is calculated as the product of the incremental distance, the fraction of the total distance that is out-of-the-way distance, obtained from the curve described under the earlier heading *Effective Distance Data,* and a unit cost per mile. Plotting visitation for each increment as a function of cost for that increment produces the demand curve. The area under the curve is calculated and is taken as the estimated recreation benefits.

An Example of Calculating Benefits.   The calculation of estimated annual benefits for one origin area—Jefferson County—was as follows:

1. The population of the origin area was 610,947; air distance to the reservoir is 60 miles; actual 1966 visitation to the reservoir was 327,445.

Using the imputed value of K for Jefferson County in equation 6–26, the estimated visitation to the reservoir would be 319,204 people.
2. The cost per additional mile of travel to the reservoir would be $0.034.

Two demand curves could be drawn by plotting either columns 3 versus 5 or 3 versus 6 from table 6.16. Figure 6.11 shows the first of these two. Estimating benefits as the area under the demand curve yielded an annual benefit of US$381,537 to Jefferson County visitors, or approximately $1.16 per visitor-day.

This calculation was then repeated for all 168 origin areas. Summing the visitation from all origin areas for a given distance increment gave a single point on the total demand curve. Repeating this step for each incremental distance yielded the total reservoir demand curve expressing visitation as a function of cost.

Total annual benefits for all 168 origin areas for the two demand curves were:

US$1,573,540 as in cols. 3 vs. 5, table 6.16.

US$1,043,839 as in cols. 3 vs. 6, table 6.16;

As the distance from the origin area to the reservoir increased, average benefits per visitor-day increased from $0.36 to $4.61, with most of the values lying in the range of from $0.50 to $2.50.

Conclusion.   The example has demonstrated what is involved in a travel-cost analysis. The approach used to estimate the visitation equation will, of course, differ from analyst to analyst and from situation to situation. Although

Table 6.16. Data for Computation of the Marginal Benefit Curves for Origin Area 56, Jefferson County, Kentucky

(1) Added distance (miles)	(2) Effective distance (miles)	(3) Cost ($)	(4) Visitation distance (miles)	(5) Actual K	(6) Estimated K
0	0		60	327,445	319,204
10	10	0.340	70	224,615	218,962
20	20	0.680	80	162,045	157,966
80	77	2.533	140	41,243	40,205
1,200	150	5.100	1,260	191	187
2,400	150	5.100	2,460	37	36

Notes:
Column (5): *KP* was calculated for visitors actually counted by solving equation 6–23 to get Vd^n, where *n* was taken as 2.445. Hence, $KP = Vd^n = 327,445 \times 60^{2.445} = 7,297,000,000$. The reduction in visitation with increasing distance was estimated from the product $KPd^{-2.445}$.

Column (6): *KP* is now based on equation 6–27 and is calculated as $KP =$ estimated $K \times$ Population $- 11,643 \times 610,947 = 7,113,000,000$.

Source: Tussey (1967).

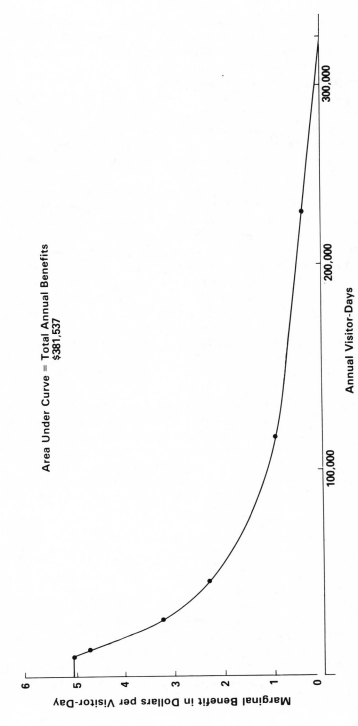

Figure 6.11 Demand curve for reservoir use by Jefferson County, Kentucky, visitors (annual visitor-days). (*Source:* Tussey, 1967.)

most of the socioeconomic variables were not found to be significant, the substitution of effective for total travel distance was significant. Furthermore, the example has shown the type of data needed to undertake a travel-cost analysis.

Shortcomings and Further Developments.

Travel Cost vs. Entrance Fees.   A basic assumption of the Clawson-Knetsch method is that visitors will react in the same way to increases in cost whatever their source; that is, they will be indifferent to the cause of the increases, whether from a rise in entrance fees or from a rise in travel costs. Some writers have regarded this as a strong assumption (Common 1973), but no alternative suggestions have been made.

Time Bias.   Both direct expenses in traveling and the time spent in traveling can be considered as part of the total travel cost. The basic travel cost approach focuses on actual monetary costs and assumes that the behavior of individuals in different zones (with different monetary travel costs) can be used to predict changes in use rates resulting from changes in travel cost. For example, monetary travel cost in 1966 for a visitor from zone 1 might have been $3 while the cost for a visitor from a more distant zone 2 might have been $5. The assumption usually made is that a $2 increase in the travel cost to a zone 1 visitor would have reduced use rates from zone 1 to the same level previously measured for zone 2. However, since travel time for zone 1 visitors would still have been less than from zone 2, the new use rate would have been lower than before but higher than from zone 2 (Sinden and Worrell (1979). The demand curve that excludes time would tend to underestimate total benefits.

Cesario and Knetsch (1970) suggested explicit inclusion of time as a separate variable in the trip generation function. But if the only money costs that vary among individuals are those associated with travel, then money costs and time costs are likely to be too highly correlated statistically to permit the separate estimation of their effects. Cesario and Knetsch (1976) recognized this and suggested instead the use of assumed trade-off functions between time and money. They suggested two approaches:

$$\text{Method I:} \quad C_i = (\$0.06 \, D_i) \, (t_i Ti); \tag{6-28}$$

$$\text{Method II:} \quad C_i = \$0.06 \, D_i + t_i T_i; \tag{6-29}$$

where C_i is the generalized cost of traveling from i to the park, D_i is the distance in miles, t_i is the value of travel time, and T_i is time.

The choice of the shadow price of time is critical to the estimation of the elasticity of demand for, and calculation of the benefits of, the site. Freeman (1979) discussed in detail the components of the time cost. At the end of his discussion, he stated that although it is known that failure to account for time costs biases the estimate of benefits, there is little guidance on how to assign a value of travel time for empirical purposes. Cesario (1976) reviewed a number of travel-time and transportation-cost studies in an effort to determine a shadow price for time. His conclusion suggested that the value of time with respect to nonwork travel should be between one-quarter and one-half of the wage rate.

In conclusion, time is an important variable, and ignoring it can bias the final results (Bishop and Heberlein 1979). In theory, the problem can be overcome by observing actual trade-offs between time and monetary costs, but "no universally accepted formulation of this tradeoff has been established and empirically tested" (U.S. Water Resources Council 1979). Thus, the least that should be done is to incorporate the value of time in the cost variable and determine the sensitivity of the results to various time values.

The Single-Purpose Excursion Assumption. If visitors come from some distance, there may be other recreational sites between the zone of origin and the site being studied. A trip to the site may therefore not be for a single purpose, and the travel costs should be divided between the different sites (Smith and Kopp 1980). In addition, the journey itself may give utility or disutility beyond the directly measurable money and time costs.

Cheshire and Stabler (1976) defined three categories of visitors:

1. *Pure visitors,* who are site-oriented and whose journey involves pure costs;
2. *Meanderers,* who derive utility from the journey; and
3. *Transit visitors,* whose journey is made for another purpose or joined purpose and who call in at the site.

Only group 1 fits the basic assumption underlying the travel-cost approach. Inclusion of groups 2 and 3 may lead to over- or underestimation of benefits. Problems of valuation of non-site-specific recreational travel were considered in the reservoir example and, in general, can only be overcome by more extensive data collection (Gibson 1978).

Effect of Income on Valuation. Another basis assumption underlying the travel-cost approach is that of constant tastes; that is, that people in different distance zones take the same quantity of recreation at the same monetary cost. This assumption was criticized by Seckler (1966), who argued that the demand curves of users from different zones might not be comparable if there were systematic variations of income and utility functions between zones. Stoevener and Brown (1967, 1968) showed that the aggregation of separate demand curves for income groups may well be necessary to adjust for the effects of incomes.

Income can be related to quantity of use in at least two ways. One contains the assumption that the response to travel cost or distance, D, as a proxy for price, is the same at any income level, I. The following regression model is then applicable:

$$Q = a - b_1 D + b_2 I, \tag{6-30}$$

where a is the regression constant, and b_1 and b_2 are the regression coefficients.

The other way contains the assumption that the response to distance differs at different income levels. A different model,

$$Q = a - bD , \qquad\qquad (6-31)$$

would then apply and would be built for each income group. In this second equation, the reaction to travel cost is itself affected by income; hence, the slopes of the demand curves will vary for different levels of income.

In a similar vein, Pearse (1968) proposed an alternative way of grouping users so that the assumption of constant tastes across zones is no longer required (Sinden and Worrell 1979):

1.   Subjects are classified by income group;
2.   The marginal costs of all subjects are considered, and the higher one in each income class is noted;
3.   The consumer's surplus for each subject is calculated as the highest marginal cost in his or her income class minus the individual's own marginal cost;
4.   Consumers' surplus for all subjects is summed to give the estimate of value.

Pearse's basic assumption was that visitors from a given income class are more likely to have common tastes and preferences than travelers originating from a zone based on distance.

In conclusion, the treatment of income has resulted in varying degrees of success. Therefore, when using a travel-cost approach it would be wise to test whether or not income may have a significant effect on the results.

Other Shortcomings.   It is possible to criticize the travel-cost approach on several other grounds (Hyman 1981). Often, criticism is leveled at the omission of important variables. Such shortcomings can be at least partially corrected. An example of criticism is that the approach nowhere accounts for the intensity or quality of the recreational experience. Some analysts therefore reject the approach for such problems as the preservation of wild rivers. Others, such as Sinden (1978), incorporate taste variables to account for experience. Similar arguments hold for congestion; congestion decreases the quality of a site and, hence, the recreational experience (Cicchetti and Smith 1973; McConnell 1977; Shelby 1980).

Flegg (1976) raised the issue of equity. The travel-cost approach is based on calculating consumers' willingness to pay. This criterion is based on two value judgments: that individuals' preferences count, and that these preferences should be weighted by individuals' incomes. In particular, the second of these value judgments is highly controversial. Flegg, who attempted to change the procedure to a more equally based preference weighting, found that the results were insensitive to change.

With some thought and ingenuity, however, all of these shortcomings can be dealt with in the approach. Often, the limiting factor will be the available data.

Conclusion. The travel-cost approach as described in this section is a technique that enables one to calculate a demand curve for an unpriced good. The value of the unpriced good is estimated from the area under the demand curve; this area is the consumer's surplus, or willingness to pay for the good.

Using the measure of consumer's surplus raises two points. First, the results of this technique are not directly comparable with other monetary measures, which often ignore consumer's surplus. In our opinion, the calculation of consumer's surplus is essential when dealing with environmental goods, but the fact that other techniques ignore consumer's surplus should make one careful when making comparisons.

Second, the estimates of value derived from the analysis are site-specific. Hence, an estimate of x dollars per person per year of consumer's surplus applies only to a particular site and not to sites in general.

The philosophy underlying the approach needs to be recognized; that is, benefits are a direct reflection of the utility derived by those who are able to pay. Hence, benefits are a function of the current income distribution. Those people who do not visit the recreation site because of low incomes do not derive any benefit from it. But if these people had more income, they could visit and thereby derive benefits.

In view of these points, we should be aware of two more if we wish to apply the travel-cost approach:

1. Because the results are a function of the current distribution of income, and if current opinion is that this distribution, however it is determined, is not equitable, then the results should be used with great care. This point will be important in countries with a very skewed distribution of income.
2. The benefits calculated must be considered as a *minimum estimate* of total benefits derived from a recreational facility under the assumptions used in the analysis. Other values associated with the site-specific recreation experience may not be captured in the analysis. For example, even though people do not visit the site, they may still derive benefits from knowing that the site exists. When the purpose of the analysis is to place a value on a park, reservoir, or other recreation site, values other than travel cost—such as option values and benefits derived by those living near the park who do not visit it—must be accounted for.

Clearly, the technique must be applied with great caution. Biases can easily creep into the analysis if some of the basic assumptions are violated. We have shown that failure to account for access to substitutes, multipurpose trips, and variations in income levels and travel time can lead to biased results. Some of these variables can be controlled statistically, but others create problems.

Bishop and Heberlein (1979) looked at some of these biases in more detail and reported an experiment to define the magnitude of some of them. They concluded that more research is needed to develop and refine the travel-cost approach further. For successful applications, one needs a careful specification of the problem to be analyzed plus a sensitivity analysis of the results in terms of the included and excluded variables. If recreational benefits are an important factor in a resource development program, the travel-cost technique described here is one of the most useful for systematically evaluating those benefits.

Other Applications.

Recreation and Water Quality. Stevens (1966); and Reiling, Gibbs, and Stoevener (1973).

Sport Fishing. Brown, Singh, and Castle (1965); Smith (1971); Shucksmith (1979); and Smith and Kavanagh (1969).

Wildlife. Everett (1978).

Recreation from Sites with Many Activities. Flegg (1976); and Sinden (1978).

New Recreational Facilities. Mansfield (1971); and Merewitz (1966).

Congestion. Cicchetti and Smith (1973); Fisher and Krutilla (1972); and McConnell (1977).

LITIGATION AND COMPENSATION

Sometimes compensation for environmental damages is decided by court order. Such an award reflects the estimated total amount of damage inflicted on people. For example, reclamation of land in Tokyo Bay has destroyed the seaweed and shellfish industries in the reclaimed areas. During the years of reclamation, fishermen's unions gave up their fishing rights in exchange for some pecuniary compensation, which was based on capitalization of average annual profits (Hanayama and Sano 1981). The compensation payments could be taken as a measure of the cost of losing a resource. If the payments were based on capitalized annual profits, however, it might have been more straightforward to use production figures and market prices to determine the social cost.

Compensation and litigation results vary from case to case. This variability in awards suggests that it may be difficult to attach a meaningful value to environmental damage from such awards. And, even if the value were meaningful, legal compensation is awarded in lump sums, and often there is no indication of how a sum has been derived or what it represents. Frequently, it includes other considerations than environmental damage (Mäler and Wyzga 1976). Therefore, as an approach to estimating environmental benefits or costs, litigation results may be of little use.

SURVEY-BASED VALUATION TECHNIQUES

A number of other valuation methods have been developed to meet the need for obtaining benefit or demand information in the absence of data on market prices. These methods rely on direct surveys of consumer willingness to pay or consumer willingness to choose quantities of goods or services. As such, they seek to measure consumer *preferences* in hypothetical situations rather than consumer *behavior* in actual situations, as is done, for example, in the travel-cost approach. Survey-based valuations have been applied to common-property resources or nonexcludable goods, such as air and water quality, to amenity resources with scenic, cultural, ecological, historical, or uniqueness characteristics, and to other situations in which market price data are absent.

A useful classification of these valuation methods is shown in figure 6.12.

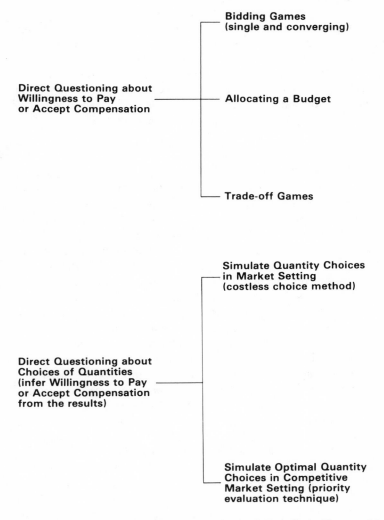

Figure 6.12 Classification of survey-based valuation methods. (*Source:* Adapted from Sinden and Worrell, 1979.)

Of the two groups of valuation methods used to obtain estimates of benefits, the first relies on questions about willingness to pay or to accept compensation, while the second group uses questions about quantities of goods and services demanded to infer consumer willingness to pay or to accept compensation.

Basic Theory

Survey-based valuation methods rely on the theory of individual demand curves (the Marshallian demand curve) and on the two Hicksian measures of consumer's surplus, compensating variation and equivalent variation, as discussed in the Appendix to Chapter 3. To measure benefits, these methods rely on estimating either consumer willingness to pay for a good or service or consumer willingness to accept compensation for the prospective loss of a good or service. These estimates either are derived from a direct bidding-game approach or are inferred from choices made among various bundles of goods. Because the methods attempt to define consumer demand curves, they take full account of consumer's surplus in estimating benefits.

The Bidding-Game Approach

Bidding games are based on the assumption that the prices of goods or services vary in response to a change in the equilibrium quantity or quality of the goods supplied (Bohm 1971, 1972; Sinden and Worrell 1979). Often, pure public goods are involved, so the same amount of a good of a given quality is available to everyone. Examples of such public goods are clean air in a city or an unobstructed view of a mountain range. In this approach, individuals are asked to evaluate contingencies—hypothetical bundles composed of various quantity or quality levels of the good. The evaluations are made on the basis of willingness to pay for an improved bundle of goods (compensating variation) or willingness to accept payment in return for an inferior bundle of goods (equivalent variation). For pure public goods, individual bid curves are summed vertically to obtain an aggregate bid curve because, except for congestion effects, the marginal cost of provision of the bundle of goods for an additional user is zero once the good has been provided. The aggregate bid curve is a surrogate for an income-compensated demand curve. An article by Rowe, d'Arge, and Brookshire (1980) provides a thorough review of the state of the art of bidding games and the various biases that may enter into the analysis.

One method of estimating the maximum amount individuals will pay or the minimum compensation they will accept is through the use of an iterative bidding process in a personal interview. First, the interviewer carefully describes the quantity, quality, time, and location dimensions of the good and defines the right to use the good for a fixed period of time—for example, one year. In return, respondents are given a starting-point bid and asked whether they would pay that amount for the good. If the answer is "yes," the interviewer records the information and raises the bid. The bid increases until the respondents are no longer willing to pay it. Then, the interviewer progressively lowers the bid to approach the exact amount that respondents are willing to pay. This is called a converging-bid approach.

Similarly, respondents could be faced with the potential loss of a good and are asked how much they are willing to pay each year to avoid the loss of an additional unit of the good. In an alternative method, the interviewer could ask respondents about the minimum amount of compensation they are willing to accept in exchange for the loss of the good. Willingness to pay in order to avoid a loss of a good and willingness to accept compensation for that loss are usually not the same. People are usually willing to accept a higher compensation for a loss than they are willing to pay to prevent the same loss. These points are discussed later.

The converging-bid approach allows finer tuning of the final individual bids. A single bid game, one in which individuals are asked to state how much they are willing to pay or to accept in compensation, tends to result in answers with much higher standard deviations around the mean. This is especially true if no indication is given of the expected range of answers. In the converging-bid approach, however, the opening bid is an indication to the individual being interviewed of the expected order of magnitude of the response. This does allow a certain bias to enter into the results, the so-called starting-point bias. No agreement exists, however, on the extent of this bias; Thayer (1981) found little evidence of it. The presence or absence of this bias is probably dependent on the interviewer's understanding of the context and the appropriate range of possible bids. In Thayer's case, individuals finished with a final bid of about $2.40 irrespective of whether they started the bidding process at $1 or $10. If the range had been between $1 and $500, the end result might have been different.

The way in which the money is to be collected is also important. Typically, the interviewer suggests some neutral vehicle or way of collecting or disbursing the money. Most studies employ a monthly or annual tax or utility bill charge as the vehicle. It should be made clear that the collected money is placed in a trust fund used only for the purpose of providing or maintaining the public good. The problem of the respondent's personal discount rate (the trade-off between consumption now and consumption later) is circumvented in the bidding process because, in theory, respondents consider that factor in deciding how much to bid. When bidding games are conducted for several environmental quality attributes in the same analysis, one can derive the implied trade-offs among the attributes.

A Simplified Example.   This example deals with a recreation area along a free-flowing stream in a forest. The area has regularly been used for recreation at no charge to the population of the surrounding region. A proposal exists to develop the area in such a way that the population no longer could have access to the recreation area. This case, therefore, illustrates finding the value of an existing recreational good, not the value of increasing the quantity of the same good.

Prior to developing a management plan for the area, a survey is made of people using the area. The survey is designed so that the sample of users interviewed is representative of the entire population of users over the annual recreation season, within an acceptable sampling error (e.g., 4%).

The survey is conducted by personal interview of each adult visitor to the recreation area. Questions asked include purpose of trip, duration of visit, age, size of family, range of family income, occupation, home address, and other socioeconomic variables (Brookshire, Ives, and Schulze 1976).

To ascertain willingness to pay or willingness to accept compensation, the interviewer asks a series of converging questions. For example, the interviewer starts with a trial amount (perhaps $5 per year). If the answer is "yes," the interviewer raises the amount (perhaps to $10 per year) and continues until the response is "no." The amount is then lowered until a final figure on willingness to pay is determined for the visitor being questioned.

The two types of questions are of this form:

1. Would you pay $X per year to continue to have access to this recreation area?
2. Would you give up access to this recreation area for a payment to you of $X per year?

From these interviews, sample and population data on willingness to pay are obtained for the first type of question (table 6.17). This information can be plotted in the form of an aggregate bid schedule (fig. 6.13). The total area under the curve is a measure of the total consumers' surplus of those using the recreation area. In this example, the value of benefits is $685,000 per year.

Table 6.17. Willingness to Pay for Access to Recreation Area (Hypothetical Example)

		Number of individuals		
Willingness to pay		Sample of 5%	Total population	Total willingness to pay[a]
0	to $10	50	1,000	$5,000[b]
10.01	to 20	100	2,000	30,000
20.01	to 30	200	4,000	100,000
30.01	to 40	450	9,000	315,000
40.01	to 50	150	3,000	135,000
more than	50	50	1,000	100,000
Total		1,000	20,000	685,000

[a] Total population × midpoint of willingness-to-pay range. For over $50 range, midpoint is taken at $100.

[b] $1,000 \times \dfrac{0 + \$10}{2} = \$5,000.$

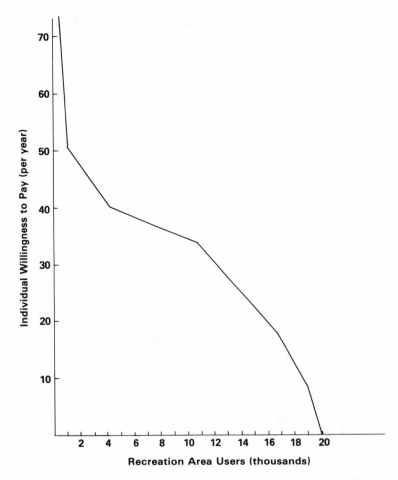

Figure 6.13 Aggregate bid schedule for access to recreation area based on survey data on willingness to pay.

Similar data on willingness to accept compensation are also obtained from the interviews. Studies have shown that respondents typically quote willingness to accept compensation values that are considerably in excess of willingness to pay values for the identical good (Meyer 1976, Bishop and Heberlein 1979). Thus, the data in table 6.18 can be considered as reasonable. The aggregate bid schedule based on willingness to accept compensation is shown in figure 6.14; the aggregate value of these benefits is $2,980,000.

In this simplified example, the annual economic benefits of the recreation site range from the willingness-to-pay value of $685,000 to the willingness-to-accept-compensation value of $2,980,000. Annual per person values range from $34.25 to $149.00. These values can be considered as lower and upper

Table 6.18. Willingness to Accept Compensation for Loss of Access to Recreation Area (Hypothetical Example)

| | Number of Individuals | | |
Willingness to accept compensation	Sample of 5%	Total population	Total willingness to accept compensation[a]
0 to $ 20	50	1,000	$ 10,000[b]
20 to 50	100	2,000	70,000
50 to 100	200	4,000	300,000
100 to 200	450	9,000	1,350,000
200 to 300	150	3,000	750,000
more than 300	50	1,000	500,000
Total	1,000	20,000	2,980,000

[a]Total population × midpoint of willingness-to-accept-compensation range. For over $300 range, midpoint is taken at $500.

[b]$1,000 \times \dfrac{0 + \$20}{2} = \$10,000$

bounds, with more realistic estimates likely to be closer to the lower willingness-to-pay value.

An Actual Application. The following example of the use of the bidding-game technique is taken from Brookshire, Ives, and Schulze (1976). The technique was used to estimate the value of aesthetic damages that would result from the proposed construction of a large coal-fired power plant near Lake Powell, a lake formed in 1965 after completion of the Glen Canyon Dam in Arizona in southwestern United States.

While the direct costing of physical damage and losses in productivity, property, and health is a fairly well-developed methodology, the aesthetic losses associated with deteriorating environmental quality are hard to quantify. In the Lake Powell example, these aesthetic losses are of two main types—the visual impact of tall smokestacks, some more than 700 feet high, and the reduced visibility as a result of stack emissions.

The principal users of Lake Powell are individuals who come to boat and camp along the lake's periphery. To determine the users' willingness to pay for a reduction in negative environmental effects, a bidding game was set up in which an entrance fee was used as the instrument to collect bids. This is a fairly neutral instrument—entrance fees are an accepted form of payment, and only those using the lake, and therefore directly affected by the proposed power plant, would pay.

The questionnaire designed for this bidding game closely followed the one of Randall, Ives, and Eastman (1974). In each interview, the respondent was shown three sets of drawings and photographs, which represented different possible development options (fig. 6.15). In situation A, the lake and the canyon were shown as is, without the proposed power plant. Situations B and C showed the power plant and stacks clearly visible from the lake. In B, no

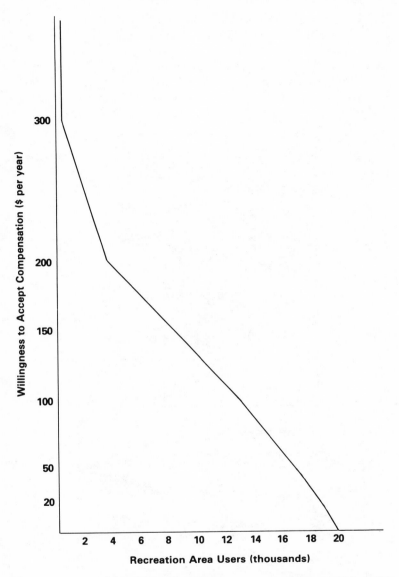

Figure 6.14 Aggregate bid schedule for access to recreation area based on survey data on willingness to accept compensation.

visible emissions appeared, so visibility was not affected; in situation *C*, the power plant emissions were visible, and visibility in the whole area was reduced.

The respondents were chosen from four distinct groups: (1) nearby residents, (2) motel visitors and passersby, (3) visitors to developed campgrounds, and (4) campers in remote, undeveloped areas. Each respondent was

Situation *A*.

Figure 6.15 Visual aids used in the Lake Powell bidding game experiment. (*Source:* Brookshire, Ives, and Schulze, 1976.)

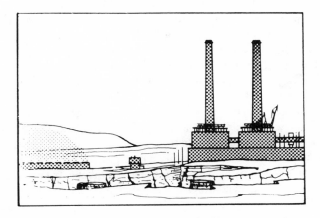

Situation *B*.

Situation *C*.

given an explanation of the proposed development and the proposed collection instrument (an entrance fee) and was shown the three sets of drawings and photographs. Situation *A* was the predevelopment state. The respondents were then asked if they would be willing to pay $1.00 per day as a family entrance fee to prevent situation *C* (or *B*) from occurring, thereby preserving situation *A*. The initial bid was increased by $1.00 increments until a negative response resulted; the amount was then decreased by $0.25 increments until a positive result was obtained. This converging-bid approach was used on all categories of respondents. In addition, socioeconomic information was obtained about the number of family members present, income, and length of stay. The sample group characteristics are given in table 6.19 and the bidding results in table 6.20. Standard errors are shown in parentheses.

The division of the sample into four groups allows comparison among group characteristics. The nearby residents had the lowest yearly income and also offered the lowest average bid (with the smallest standard error). In discussions, members of this group believed that the ultimate users of the power generated should be taxed (perhaps by a utility bill surcharge); this local resident group also saw the proposed project as a source of income for the area. The other three sets of respondents all came from some distance to use the lake, stayed much longer than the local residents, had higher incomes, and were willing to pay more. All groups were willing to pay more to prevent situation *C* (power plant with reduced visibility) than to prevent situation *B* (power plant without reduced visibility).

The aggregate bids presented in table 6.20 are based on the different group means and on the estimated total number of visitors per year from each group. The present value over some time period of the aggregate bids can also be calculated. This example illustrates how one type of survey-based valuation can be used to evaluate an unpriced good—in this case, an unobstructed view and clear air. The aggregate bid derived from the analysis does not answer the question of whether or not the power plant should be built. This analysis does

Table 6.19. Sample Group Characteristics, Lake Powell Bidding Game

	Sample group means			
Characteristics	Residents	Remote	Developed	Motels
		(Standard errors in parentheses)		
Family size	3.00	4.20	3.80	3.40
	(0.30)	(0.42)	(0.41)	(0.33)
Visit length (days)	1.20	8.70	4.90	5.40
	(0.13)	(0.86)	(0.82)	(1.05)
Year's income ($)	16,000.00	23,500.00	20,000.00	28,600.00
	(2,035.00)	(2,521.00)	(2,067.00)	(4,696.00)
Sample size (*n*)	19	21	22	20

Source: Adapted from Brookshire, Ives, and Schulze (1976).

Table 6.20. Lake Powell Bidding Game Results

	Bid ($ per family per day)	
	For situation A over C	For situation A over B
	(Standard errors in parentheses)	
Group means		
Residents	1.75 (0.22)	0.87 (0.20)
Remote	3.38 (0.50)	2.11 (0.54)
Developed	2.60 (0.41)	1.08 (0.29)
Motels	3.11 (0.33)	1.94 (0.48)
Population sample means	2.77 (0.19)	1.58 (0.24)
Estimated aggregate bid	727,600 (50,270)	414,000 (62,400)

Source: Adapted from Brookshire, Ives, and Schulze (1976).

allow some estimate of the order of magnitude of benefits derived by present users from the existing natural system. The estimated aggregate bids ranged from over $400,000 to over $700,000 per year. Probably what is significant is not these numbers as such, but that they are not $50,000 or $5,000,000 per year. The order of magnitude of the benefits can be compared to the costs of different methods of reducing environmental damages. In this case, defensive expenditure options would include resiting the power plant and installing scrubbers.

The various biases that may occur in bidding games or in the other survey techniques are discussed later in this chapter. In the Lake Powell study, the researchers tested for the various biases and found them to be insignificant.

Trade-off Games

Trade-off games are used to determine individual preferences among various outcomes. In a simple case, each outcome will have two components—a certain quantity of money and a certain quantity of an environmental good. This is the single trade-off game (table 6.21), adapted from Sinden and Worrell (1979).

As in the bidding game, the type, quantity, and other attributes of the environmental good are described in detail. The base outcome (Outcome I) will combine no money with some quantity of the environmental good. The second possible choice, Outcome II, will have some amount of money to be paid by the individual (e.g., $10 per year) and a changed amount of the environmental good. The individual then is asked to specify a preference between the two outcomes. The value of the money donation in Outcome II is

Table 6.21.   Example of a Single Trade-off Game

	Outcomes	
Object	I	II
Money donation ($)	$0.00	$10.00
Quantity of environmental good	2	3

Note: The money value in Outcome II is varied until the individual is indifferent between Outcomes I and II.
Source: Adapted from Sinden and Worrell (1979).

then varied systematically until the individual is indifferent between the two outcomes. This value is the trade-off in money that the individual would make for the increase in the quantity of the environmental good between Outcomes I and II. The value can be interpreted as the individual's willingness to pay for this increase. By interviewing an adequately sized, representative population sample, an estimate of aggregate willingness to pay for the increase in quantity of an environmental good can be obtained, subject to the usual tests of statistical significance.

A Simplified Example. A reservoir used primarily for hydroelectric power generation can be operated to provide a constant water level in the reservoir during the dry summer recreation season. This can be done only at some cost in the amount of electric energy produced, because water drawdown for power generation will have to be curtailed. It is therefore important to have some indication of the value to the users of the reservoir and its shoreline of maintaining the constant water level. The users include swimmers, boaters, picnickers, campers, and hikers. During a recreation season of twelve weeks, the water can be maintained at a constant, full level for six weeks, with essentially no cost to electric energy output. Maintaining this level for each additional week, however, would entail substantial losses in electric energy.

The trade-off analysis is set up to test the willingness of reservoir users to pay for each week of full water level beyond the six-week base. The analysis begins with the assumption of a one-week extension (table 6.22).

Six weeks of constant full water level is the base, costless situation, and no money donation is involved. If the time of full water level is lengthened by one week in Outcome II, we wish to estimate the willingness of respondents to pay for the one-week extension.

To begin the analysis, an arbitrary initial money donation (e.g., $10 per year) is entered in Outcome II and the respondent is asked: Which outcome (I or II) do you prefer, or are you indifferent to them? If Outcome I is preferred, the donation level is lowered (e.g., to $9); if Outcome II is preferred, the donation level is raised (perhaps to $11), and the questions are repeated. The process continues until the respondent is indifferent to the outcomes. In this example, we assume that the donation level of $15 in Outcome II is the point

Table 6.22. Single Trade-off, Money for Extension of Time for Full Reservoir Water Level

	Outcomes	
Item	I	II
Money donation ($)	0	10
Weeks of constant water level	6	7

of indifference. We can interpret this as the respondent's willingness to pay $15 for a one-week extension of the full water level.

The game can be repeated to obtain the respondent's willingness to pay for extensions of the full water level for two through six weeks. In each repetition of the game, Outcome I of table 6.22 remains the same, and only the values in Outcome II are changed. For each trial, one week is added to the weeks of full level, and the money donation value that makes the respondent indifferent between Outcomes I and II is systematically determined as described.

In this example, hypothetical results are shown in table 6.23 for a sample of six respondents.

If the assumption were made that the average individual willingness to pay was applicable to the entire population of reservoir users, then this figure could be used to calculate total willingness to pay for extensions of the period of full reservoir water level. This total benefit could be compared with the expected economic loss of electric energy output associated with maintenance of a constant, full level from the seventh through twelfth week.

Assuming a population of 20,000 potential users, the benefits for extending the period of full level are shown as curve A in figure 6.16. Assuming

Table 6.23. Willingness to Pay to Extend Time of Full Water Level from 6 through 12 Weeks ($)

Period of full water level (weeks)	Respondents						Average of 1–6
	1	2	3	4	5	6	
6	0	0	0	0	0	0	0
7	15	18	11	8	22	13	14.5
8	22	27	15	12	33	20	21.5
9	26	32	18	15	40	26	26.2
10	29	36	20	17	45	31	29.7
11	31	39	21	18	48	34	31.8
12	32	40	21	18	50	35	32.7

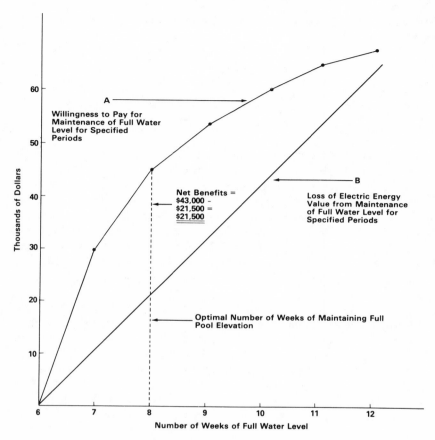

Figure 6.16 Economic benefits and losses of weeks of maintenance of full water level, hydroelectric reservoir project.

arbitrary values for electric energy losses as shown in curve *B*, we can define the optimal period of extending the full level as eight weeks. At this point, net benefits (gross willingness of reservoir users to pay minus energy costs) are greatest ($21,500). For periods of more or less than eight weeks of full reservoir level, the net benefits will be less.

Costless Choice

Costless choice methods were first proposed by Romm in 1969. In this technique, direct questioning is used to determine preferences between various quantities of goods. This approach provides quantity data from which willingness to pay can be inferred. The choice is costless in the sense that the comparison is between two or more alternatives, each of which is desirable, and all of which are free. One of the alternatives can be an unpriced, environmental good, while the other alternative can be a sum of money or various physical goods that the individuals would purchase if they had enough money.

In a two-alternative model, the choice may be between a sum of money and an environmental good; if the individual chooses the environmental good, it must be valued at least as much as the money foregone. This places a minimum valuation on the good. If the amount of money is varied and the quantity of the environmental good is held constant, this becomes a type of bidding game. The principal difference, however, is that the individual will not have to pay anything to receive the good (other than the money foregone), nor will the individual lose any presently existing environmental good if the money is taken. The individual therefore gains in both cases, and the costless choice allows an estimate to be made of the minimal valuation placed on an environmental good while minimizing some of the biases found in bidding games, which combine a desirable with an undesirable outcome.

A Simplified Example. A large city uses vacant land to dump household garbage and other refuse. The areas are not regularly covered with soil or treated, and therefore become a source of odors, flies, and rats. Proper landfill techniques could be used but are expensive. To value the benefits nearby residents would receive from use of these landfill techniques, a costless choice experiment is conducted.

The dump site under study is in a poor squatters' area. The geographical extent of environmental damage resulting from the dump is determined, and a random sample of households is chosen within the area. Two separate experiments are conducted.

In the first experiment, a simplified two-option costless choice technique is used. The environmental effect of the refuse dump is described in detail (rats, smell, and flies) and the individual is offered a choice between a yearly sum of money and a 90% reduction in the level of the various noxious effects coming from the dump. Each individual is offered only one choice of the amount of the cash gift that could be taken in place of the 90% reduction described. If an individual takes the 90% reduction, it means that the environmental good is valued at least as much as the cash foregone. If, at a higher level cash offer, no one chooses the 90% reduction, it means that the maximum value placed on the environmental good is less than the cash amount. Fifty individuals were interviewed; the results are presented in table 6.24.

The ten individuals who were offered $5 all chose the 90% reduction; this places a minimum value on the proposed environmental improvement. The ten individuals who were offered $25 all accepted the cash; this is therefore more than the maximum value they placed on the 90% reduction. This method, however, does not clearly define the average value placed on the 90% reduction by the sample population. The people offered $5 were all willing to forego that much cash for the environmental improvement, but one cannot say that they will be willing to forego $10 or $15. If each individual were offered

Table 6.24. Costless Choice Decisions between 90% Reduction of Dump Effects and a Money Gift

	Choices made	
Number of individuals interviewed	90% reduction in dump effects	Number of individuals accepting cash offer of ($)
10	10	0 ($5)
10	7	3 (10)
10	5	5 (15)
10	2	8 (20)
10	0	10 (25)

a series of cash amounts that raised the offer to the point at which the cash was accepted in place of the environmental good, the estimated maximum value placed on the environmental good could be more easily determined. This modified bidding-type game, however, could lead to strategic game playing on the part of individuals as they hold out for higher cash offers than they would really require to be indifferent between the two choices.

To simulate a range of offers without involving this iterative process, a second approach could be tried. In this case, each individual is offered a choice between several different goods and the same 90% reduction in the dump's effects. The various goods are described in detail, and estimates are made of the local values of these goods. In this way, each individual can respond to a choice between a set of goods that has definite value and an unpriced good (the 90% reduction). The individual is asked to consider each good separately and to specify a preference between that good and a 90% reduction. This approach differs from a bidding game in that the entire range of possible bids (the goods) is presented at one time.

Several problems of valuation and consistency arise with this approach. The individual may place a subjective value on a good that is considerably different from the actual market price. The goods offered, therefore, should be items that are in common demand and that might reasonably be purchased if the individual had sufficient money. Table 6.25 presents the hypothetical responses of several individuals to a set of choices of this type.

For consistent responses, such as numbers 1, 2, and 3 in table 6.25, a cutoff value can be placed on the 90% reduction in the dump's ill effects. For respondent 1, this is between $15 and $25; for respondent 3, it is between $25 and $50. Inconsistent choices, such as those made by respondent 4, or reversed choices, such as those made by respondent 5, cannot be evaluated and would not be included in the analysis (Sinden and Worrell 1979).

The costless choice technique can be used, therefore, to place approximate values on various environmental goods. This technique is simple and quite direct, yet it removes some of the strategic bias found in other techniques. The

Table 6.25. **Costless Choice between a 90% Nuisance Reduction and a Set of Goods for Five Respondents**

Alternatives	Value ($)	Respondent number				
		1	2	3	4	5
Pair of leather sandals	5	−	−	−	−	+
Tin of cooking oil	10	−	+	−	+	+
Set of clothing	15	−	+	−	+	−
Portable radio	25	+	+	−	−	−
Bicycle	50	+	+	+	−	−

Note: + = the good is taken in preference to the 90% reduction in nuisance.
  − = the good is not taken in preference to the 90% reduction in nuisance.

results have to be evaluated with caution, however, especially in the case of inconsistent choices.

Priority Evaluator Technique

The priority evaluator technique is another method that, through interviews, attempts to simulate the workings of a perfectly competitive market and thus to arrive at values or expressions of willingness to pay for nonpriced goods, such as environmental quality. The technique is similar to the costless choice method described earlier in which the respondent chooses among various alternative goods. The unique feature of the priority evaluator technique is that starting values, or prices, are assigned to a set of goods, and then these values are adjusted in such a way as to encourage convergence to a set of equilibrium values.

Originally developed by Hoinville and Berthoud (1970), the technique is based on the principle of an individual's utility maximization within a budget constraint. Individuals will maximize their utility if they can allocate their total budgets in such a way that the marginal utility of the last dollar spent on any good equals the marginal utility of the last dollar spent on any other good. Where there are n goods, this is demonstrated as follows:

$$\frac{MU_1}{P_1} = \frac{MU_2}{P_2} = \cdot \cdot \cdot = \frac{MU_n}{P_n}, \tag{6-32}$$

If this condition is not met, an individual could switch expenditures between goods (reallocate the budget) and thereby increase total utility. Total utility can be increased by such rearrangements until the condition in equation 6–32 has been reached. After that, further increases in total utility are no longer possible, given existing prices and the budget constraint.

The two requirements for consumers to maximize their utility within a given budget are that all of the budget is spent or allocated and that the equal marginal utility condition is satisfied. The first condition is easy to test and verify and can be controlled within the technique. The second condition, equalizing marginal utilities, is much more difficult to implement and verify. This is the condition that the technique is designed to meet.

In a stylized format, the priority evaluator approach proceeds as follows: A number of goods are chosen, and for each good several different quantity levels are specified; for example, for new clothing the alternatives would be one, two, or three complete sets for an adult male. One of the goods is an unpriced environmental good (e.g., water quality), while the others are common market items (e.g., clothing, food, transportation, or housing). In order to simulate a competitive market, the various goods must meet certain conditions—they must be independent of each other in production, they must be continuously variable in both production and consumption, and their utility must be independent of any other consumption (Sinden and Worrell 1979).

Several different approaches may be used in applying the technique, but the general format is similar (Hoinville and Berthoud 1970; Pendse and Wyckoff 1974a,b). If there are five goods with three levels of each, each of the fifteen choices is described in detail to the individuals being interviewed. An initial price for each of the fifteen choices has been previously determined, and the respondent is given a budget within which to make choices. The prices may be determined by using prevailing market prices for the priced goods or by taking the total social cost of supplying the good and dividing by the likely number of purchasers (Sinden and Worrell 1979). The budget is large enough so that some level of each good can be chosen, but not large enough to buy the maximum level of all five goods. The subject is also instructed to choose only one level from each of the five goods, to make at least one choice in each group, and to exhaust the budget (a dummy variable for "all other things" may be entered as one of the choices).

The key to satisfying the marginal-utility condition is the assumption that if the separate prices are correct, the individual will be indifferent among *any* of the fifteen choices in our example, and therefore the expected frequency of any of the fifteen items being chosen is random. For example, if 100 people are interviewed, the expected frequency of choice of any one of the three levels of a good is 33⅓ because each individual will choose one of the three levels available for any type of good. The expected frequency of choice of any level of a good is therefore 33⅓%. When the actual choices are made, therefore, the observed number of times one of the fifteen choices is selected is compared to the a priori expected frequency. If the prices have been chosen correctly, this ratio will equal 1.0. If the actual distribution of choices appears to be different from a random distribution, then some of the original prices chosen are not equilibrium values. For example, if the second level of good number 3 is chosen 50 times rather than 33⅓ times by the sample of 100 respondents, this indicates that the price chosen for this good was too low and that individuals chose more of that good in order to increase total utility. In the second round of interviews, the price of this good is raised. For each of the fifteen choices, the ratio of observed quantity chosen (OQ) to expected quantity (EQ) is examined. If the ratio OQ/EQ > 1, then the initial price was too low and should be raised for the next round; if OQ/EQ < 1, the reverse holds. As the individuals are reinterviewed with new prices and the OQ/EQ ratio approaches 1.0, the second condition of utility maximization is met. To test if the observed frequency is significantly different from the expected frequency, one can use the chi-square test of significance. The first condition, complete budget allocation, is also easily verified. When the equilibrium stage has been reached, the previously unpriced environmental good has received an explicit value or price as the various individuals have evaluated the trade-offs of this environmental good with other market-priced goods.

In most cases, these equilibrium prices will be relative prices (remember, the process started off with arbitrary relative prices). To convert these relative prices to absolute values, one of the prices will have to be pegged. The simplest process would be to take the relative price of a market good (for example, new clothes) and compare it to the actual market price, calculate the ratio of relative to actual price, and then use this ratio to adjust all other relative prices resulting from the approach. The absolute price for the non-market good (e.g., levels of water quality) can now be used to estimate the benefits (as expressed by willingness to pay) of water quality improvements.

Many problems occur in actually using this approach. Some authors suggest the use of points and a point budget in place of dollar values. There are no firm rules for the magnitude of price adjustments after the initial interview, and considerable care has to be taken with the selection, specification, description, and pricing of the various choices so that the actual responses reflect real-world decisions. The priority evaluator technique is still too unproved to be used in most situations, but it is an intriguing attempt to meld the economic theory of utility maximization with survey techniques to value an unpriced environmental good.

Delphi Techniques

Delphi techniques incorporate a group of survey approaches which, through the direct questioning of "experts," attempt to place a value on a particular good. Originally developed by Dalkey and Helmer (1963) at the Rand Corporation, the technique consists of assembling a group of experts who are asked independently to place values or prices on one or several groups of goods.

The initial set of values is obtained from the group and presented in graphic or tabular form. Outlying values are noted, and explanations for them are provided by the relevant expert. This information is then fed back to the entire group, each member of which independently reevaluates the estimates and makes new value judgments. Through successive rounds, the hope is that the distribution will concentrate around a group mean.

The essence of the technique is that the group is not assembled face-to-face; rather, indirect communication is used to avoid the influence of personalities in the decision process. This neutrality can also be achieved by bringing all of the experts together and using written, not oral, communication. Estimates of values are written out and passed to the group leader who will tabulate the results and display the distribution. Reasons given to explain outlying estimates can also be read before each successive iteration.

This approach is commonly used for forecasting, but is also applicable to the pricing of environmental goods. The degree of accuracy will depend on the quality of the panel, the panel's ability to reflect societal values, and the skill with which the process is carried out.

The principal strengths of the Delphi technique are its nonconfrontational nature and its systematic reinterviewing of a group of experts. It can be a useful means of checking the results obtained from more conventional surveys.

Potential Biases and Shortcomings in Survey-Based Valuation Techniques

Survey-based techniques rely on an individual's placement of hypothetical values on various changes in environmental quality. These hypothetical valuations can be used in attempts to measure either the compensation required by an individual to accept a deterioration in environmental quality or the payment the individual is willing to make to prevent the same deterioration. Willingness-to-accept-compensation measures of welfare have as much theoretical validity as willingness-to-pay measures for common-property environmental resources. If implicit property rights for use are given to polluters, the willingness-to-pay measure is the appropriate method to determine the value of abating pollution. On the other hand, willingness to accept compensation is more appropriate if consumers are considered to have a right to a pristine environment and, therefore, would have to be compensated for a negative change in environmental quality.

The primary difficulty with hypothetical valuations is their synthetic character. Unlike other measures of costs or benefits based on physical measurements and market prices, survey-based techniques attempt to measure the implied values placed on the preservation or deterioration of some environmental quality. Such qualities are frequently quite intangible (e.g., the natural character of a vista, the clearness of air, or quiet).

Many authors have discussed the various biases that may be important in survey-based techniques (Schulze, d'Arge, and Brookshire 1980; Bishop and Heberlein 1980; Hyman 1981). The four principal biases are (1) *strategic bias,* whereby individuals attempt to influence the outcomes or results by not responding truthfully; (2) *information bias* resulting from the type of information supplied to the individual; (3) *instrument bias* from the types of questions asked or the vehicle proposed for collecting payment or making compensation; and (4) *hypothetical bias,* which is the potential error inherent in a process that is not an actual situation. Each of these biases may be more or less important in different situations. Much of the following discussion is based on Schulze, d'Arge, and Brookshire (1980).

Strategic bias occurs when individuals believe their answers can help influence decisions in such a way that their actual costs are decreased or their actual benefits are increased in relation to the expected result in a normal market situation. For example, if nearby residents were asked about their willingness to pay to clean up the air near a power plant, and if they believed that the control costs would be paid by power consumers elsewhere, the local residents would have an incentive to overstate their willingness to pay. Conversely, if residents believed that they would be individually taxed based on their separate willingness to pay, then a clear incentive would exist to understate their willingness to pay with the hope that others would bid more and thereby promote the desired change. If the good in question is a public good (e.g., an unobstructed view or clean air), the individual may try to give the lowest possible bid that would insure the good would be provided and, therefore, available to all. The extent of strategic bias, if it exists, will depend on how much an individual believes her or his bid will influence the desired change and the costs involved. Empirical tests of strategic bias have not, so far, found it to be a major problem (Bohm 1972; Scherr and Babb 1975; Smith 1976).

Information bias results from incomplete or misleading statements about the proposed changes. Detailed information may be needed to explain clearly the changes as well as the available alternatives. This is essential, given the hypothetical nature of survey-based techniques, and the bias can be reduced by the use of visual or other aids in explaining the various options (e.g., the use of photographs and drawings in the Lake Powell example).

Instrument bias may result from the choice of method used to collect money or make payments. Some taxes, for example, are considered more onerous than others, and their use will influence statements by respondents. The payment vehicle needs to be realistic, however, and therefore, for recreation problems, an entrance fee or user tax is often proposed.

Another type of instrument bias is the starting-point bias. Surveys usually rely on "yes" or "no" answers to the question "Are you willing to pay *x* dollars to prevent the proposed change?" rather than on answers to "How much are you willing to pay to prevent the proposed change?" The bias results from the choice of a starting bid—the value chosen gives an indication of the expected level of response (e.g., $0.10 or $10.00 or $100.00). If a lengthy bidding process ensues whereby the bid is changed in small increments, the respondent may become bored. Some researchers have found that this starting-point bias is not a major problem, given a reasonable range of initial values—respondents have usually ended with a similar final bid whether they started at $1 or $10.

The last major bias mentioned here is hypothetical bias. This is unavoidable in a process in which actual market behavior is not measured. For instance, willingness to pay for existing public amenities that have been supplied to users at zero or nominal cost may not indicate the real value of the amenity to the user. Respondents become accustomed to the historically low fee and consider the amenity as part of their birthright; thus, they rebel at paying anything if the good has been free. For these reasons, it is important to be clear about the various options and alternatives available. This should help the individual to evaluate the choices and to make estimates that are as realistic as possible.

Existence of these biases does not mean that the results obtained from the survey-based technique should not or cannot be used. Rather, it indicates why care should be taken in presenting information and options so that realistic decisions can be made. If people are not willing to play the games involved with these techniques, the results will also be unreliable.

A final major problem with these techniques is that they are labor intensive and time consuming. They are costly to carry out, and the examples described in the literature are frequently based on interviews of only 20 to 40 respondents rather than on more realistic numbers such as 500 to 1,000. Sampling biases may enter in, and efforts must be made to select respondents from a representative cross-section of the relevant population. For example, in the Lake Powell study, the potential recreation users were divided into four groups, and each group was sampled differently.

Applying these techniques in many developing countries will be challenging. Greater suspicion toward interviewers may exist, as well as greater difficulty in understanding hypothetical alternatives. Making clear presentations of the problem, the choices, and the method of payment or compensation will be essential. Different techniques can be applied in the same setting to see if the results are similar. In any event, considerable experimentation with the techniques will be required in developing countries before the utility of these survey-based techniques can be determined.

REFERENCES

Market Value or Productivity Approaches

Fleming, W. M. *Phewa Tal Catchment Management Program: Benefits and Costs of Forestry and Soil Conservation in Nepal.* Unpublished Case Study. Honolulu: East-West Environment and Policy Institute, 1981.

Squire, L., and H. van der Tak. *Economic Analysis of Projects.* Baltimore: Johns Hopkins University Press, 1975.

Human Capital Approach

Cooper, B. S., and D. P. Rice. "The Economic Cost of Illness Revisited." *Social Security Bulletin* 39 (1976): 21.

Freeman, A. M. III. *The Benefits of Environmental Improvement: Theory and Practice*. Baltimore: Johns Hopkins University Press, 1979.

Hyman, E. L. "The Valuation of Extramarket Benefits and Costs in Environmental Impact Assessment." *Environmental Impact Assessment Review* 2, 3 (1981): 227–64.

Jones-Lee, M. W. *The Value of Life: An Economic Analysis*. London: Martin Robertson, 1976.

Kneese, A. V. "Research Goals and Progress Towards Them." In *Environmental Quality in a Growing Economy*, ed. H. Jarrett. Baltimore: Johns Hopkins Press, 1966.

Lave, L. B., and E. P. Seskin. "Air Pollution and Human Health." *Science* 169 (August 1970): 723–33.

————. *Air Pollution and Human Health*. Baltimore: Johns Hopkins University Press, 1977.

Mäler, K. G., and R. E. Wyzga. *Economic Measurement of Environmental Damage: A Technical Handbook*. Paris: OECD, 1976.

Mishan, E. J. "The Value of Life." *Cost-Benefit Analysis*, ed. R. Layard. New York: Penguin Books, 1972.

Mooney, G. H. *The Valuation of Human Life*. London: Macmillan & Co., 1977.

Needleman, L. "Valuing Other People's Lives," *Manchester School of Economic and Social Studies* 44, 4 (1976): 309–42.

————. "The Valuation of Changes in the Risk of Death by Those at Risk." *Manchester School of Economic and Social Studies*. 48, 3 (September 1980): 229–54.

Pearce, D. W., ed. *The Valuation of Social Cost*. London: Allen and Unwin, 1978.

Rice, D. P. "Estimating the Cost of Illness." In *U.S. Department of Health, Education and Welfare, Health Economic Series No. 6*. Washington, D.C.: U.S. Government Printing Office, 1966.

Ridker, R. G. *Economic Costs of Air Pollution: Studies in Measurement*. New York: Praeger, 1967.

Schelling, T. C. "The Life You Save May Be Your Own." *In Problems in Public Expenditure*, ed. S. B. Chase, Jr. Washington, D.C.: Brookings Institution, 1968.

Schwing, R. C.; B. W. Southworth; C. R. von Buseck; and C. J. Jackson. "Benefit-Cost Analysis of Automotive Emission Reductions." *Journal of Environmental Economics and Management* 7, 1 (1980): 44–64.

Schwing, R. C., and G. C. McDonald. "Measures of Association of Some Air Pollutants, Natural Ionizing Radiation and Cigarette Smoking with Mortality Rates." *Science, Total Environment* 5 (1976): 139–69.

Opportunity-Cost Approach

Commonwealth of Australia. *Economic and Environmental Aspects of the Export Hardwood Woodchip Industry*. Report of a Working Group Set Up by the Australian Ministers for the Environment and Agriculture. Canberra, Australian Government Printing Service, 1975.

Hitchens, M. T.; D. J. Thampapillai; and J. A. Sinden. "The Opportunity Cost Criterion for Land Allocations." *Review of Marketing and Agricultural Economics* 46, 3 (December 1978): 275–93.

Krutilla, J. V. *On the Economics of Preservation or Development of the Lower Portion of the Hells Canyon*. Draft Report to the Federal Power Commission. Washington, D.C., 1969.

Krutilla, J. V., and A. C. Fisher. *The Economics of Natural Environments*. Baltimore: Johns Hopkins University Press, 1975.

Property Value Approach

Abelson, P. W. "Property Prices and the Value of Amenities." *Journal of Environmental Economics and Management* 6 (1979): 11–28.

Anderson, R. J., and T. D. Crocker. "Air Pollution and Residential Property Values." *Urban Studies* 8 (1971): 171–80.

Armstrong, F. H. "Valuation of Amenity Forests." *The Consultant* 19 (1974): 13–19.

David, E. "Lake Shore Property Values: A Guide to Public Investment in Recreation." *Water Resources Research* 4 (1968): 697–707.

Freeman, A. M. III. "On Estimating Air Pollution Control Benefits from Land Value Studies." *Journal of Environmental Economics and Management* 1, 1 (May 1974): 74–83.

————. "A Survey of the Techniques for Measuring the Benefits of Water Quality Improvement." In *Cost-Benefit Analysis and Water Pollution Policy*, ed. H. M. Peskin and E. P. Seskin. Washington, D.C.: Urban Institute, 1975.

————. "The Hedonic Price Approach to Measuring Demand for Neighborhood Characteristics." In *The Economics of Neighborhood*, ed. D. Segal. New York: Academic Press, 1979a.

————. *The Benefits of Environmental Improvement: Theory and Practice*. Baltimore: Johns Hopkins University Press, 1979b.

————. *The Benefits of Air and Water Pollution Control: A Review and Synthesis of Recent Estimates*. Report for the U.S. Council on Environmental Quality. Washington, D.C., December 1979c.

————. "Hedonic Prices, Property Values and Measuring Environmental Benefits: A Survey of the Issues." *Scandinavian Journal of Economics* 81, 2 (1979d): 154–73.

Harrison, D., Jr., and D. L. Rubinfeld. "Hedonic Housing Prices and the Demand for Clean Air." *Journal of Environmental Economics and Management* 5 (1978a): 81–102.

————. "The Distribution of Benefits from Improvements in Urban Air Quality." *Journal of Environmental Economics and Management* 5 (1978b): 313–32.

Hyman, E. L. "The Valuation of Extramarket Benefits and Costs in Environmental Impact Assessment." *Environmental Impact Assessment Review* 2, 3 (1981): 227–64.

Mäler, K. G. "A Note on the Use of Property Values in Estimating Marginal Willingness to Pay for Environmental Quality." *Journal of Environmental Economics and Management* 4 (1977): 355–69.

Pearce, D. W., ed. *The Valuation of Social Cost*. London: Allen and Unwin, 1978.

Pearce, D. W., and R. Edwards. "The Monetary Evaluation of Noise Nuisance: Implications for Noise Abatement Policy." In *Progress in Resource Management and Environmental Planning*, vol. 1, ed. T. O'Riordan and R. C. d'Arge. New York: Wiley, 1979.

Polinsky, A. M., and S. Shavell. "Amenities and Property Values in a Model of an Urban Area." *Journal of Public Economics* 5 (1976): 119–29.

Rosen, S. "Hedonic Prices and Implicit Markets: Product Differentiation in Perfect Competition." *Journal of Political Economy* 82, 1 (1974): 34–55.

Sinden, J. A., and A. C. Worrell. *Unpriced Values: Decisions Without Market Prices*. New York: Wiley, 1979.

Waddell, T. E. *The Economic Damage of Air Pollution*. Report No. EPA-600/5-74-012. Washington, D.C.: U.S. Environmental Protection Agency, 1974.

White, M. J. "Measuring the Benefits of Environmental and Public Policy Changes in Cities: Short-Term and Long-Term Considerations." *Journal of Public Economics* 11 (1979): 247–60.

Other Land Value Approaches

Australia, Research Directorate, Department of Environment, Housing and Community Development. *Economic Evaluation of the Eppalock Catchment Soil Conservation Project*. Report No. 9. Canberra: Australian Government Publishing Service, 1978.

Gupta, T. R., and J. H. Foster. "Economic Criteria for Freshwater Wetland Policy in Massachusetts." *American Journal of Agricultural Economics* 57, 1 (1975): 40–45.

Wage Differential Approach

Bishop, J., and C. Cicchetti. "Some Institutional and Conceptual Thoughts on the Measurement of Indirect and Intangible Benefits and Costs." *Cost Benefit Analysis and Water Pollution Policy,* ed. H. M. Peskin and E. P. Seskin. Washington, D.C.: Urban Institute, 1975.

Cropper, M. L. "The Valuation of Locational Amenities, an Alternative to the Hedonic Price Approach." In *Methods Development for Assessing Air Pollution Control Benefits.* Studies on Partial Equilibrium Approaches to Valuation of Environmental Amenities, vol. 4. Washington, D.C.: U.S. Environmental Protection Agency, 1979.

Jones-Lee, M. W. *The Value of Life: An Economic Analysis.* London: Martin Robertson, 1976.

Meyer, J., and R. Leone. "The Urban Disamenity Revisited." In *Public Economics and Quality of Life,* ed. L. Wingo and A. Evans. Baltimore: Johns Hopkins University Press, 1977.

Portney, P. R. "Housing Prices, Health Effects and Valuing Reductions in Risk of Death." *Journal of Environmental Economics and Management* 8, 1 (March 1981): 72–78.

Thäler, R., and S. Rosen. *The Value of Saving a Life: Evidence from the Labor Market.* Working Paper No. 7401. Rochester, N.Y.: University of Rochester Graduate School of Management, December 1973.

————. "The Value of Saving a Life: Evidence from the Labor Market." In *Household Production and Consumption,* vol. 40, ed. Nelson Terleckyj. Washington, D.C.: National Bureau of Economic Research, 1976.

U.S. National Academy of Sciences. *Air Quality and Automobile Emission Control.* Report by the Coordinating Committee on Air Quality Studies, vol. 4. Washington, D.C., September 1974.

Travel-Cost Approach

Bishop, R. C., and T. A. Heberlein. "Measuring Values of Extramarket Goods: Are Indirect Measures Biased?" *American Journal of Agricultural Economics* 61, 5 (December 1979): 926–30.

Brown, N.; S. Lyon; and J. A. MacMillan. *Hecla Provincial Park: Data Collection Procedures and Analysis of Recreation Usage.* Research Bulletin No. 76–2. Winnipeg: Department of Agricultural Economics and Farm Management, Faculty of Agriculture, University of Manitoba, August 1976.

Brown, W. G.; A. Singh; and E. N. Castle. *An Economic Evaluation of the Oregon Salmon and Steelhead Sport Fishery.* Technical Bulletin 78. Corvallis, Oreg.: Oregon State University Agricultural Experiment Station, 1964.

————. "Net Economic Value of the Oregon Salmon-Steelhead Sport Fishery." *Journal of Wildlife Management* 29, 2 (April 1965): 266–79.

Cesario, F. J. "Value of Time in Recreation Benefit Studies." *Land Economics* 55, 1 (February 1976): 32–41.

Cesario, F. J., and J. L. Knetsch. "Time Bias in Recreation Benefit Estimates." *Water Resources Research* 6 (1970): 700–4.

————. "A Recreation Site Demand and Benefit Estimation Model." *Regional Studies* 10 (1976): 97–104.

Cheshire, P. C., and M. J. Stabler. "Joint Consumption Benefits in Recreation Site Surplus: An Empirical Estimate." *Regional Studies* 10 (1976): 343–51.

Cicchetti, C. J., and V. K. Smith. "Congestion, Quality Deterioration, and Optimal Use: Wilderness Recreation in the Spanish Peaks Primitive Area." *Social Science Research* 2 (March 1973): 15–30.

Clawson, M. *Methods of Measuring Demand for and Value of Outdoor Recreation.* RFF Reprint No. 10. Washington, D.C.: Resources for the Future, 1959.

Clawson, M., and J. L. Knetsch. *Economics of Outdoor Recreation.* Baltimore: Johns Hopkins Press, 1966.

Common, M. S. "A Note on the Use of the Clawson Method for the Evaluation of Recreation Site Benefits." *Regional Studies* 7 (1973): 401–6.

Everett, R. D. "The Monetary Value of the Recreational Benefits of Wildlife." *Journal of Environmental Management* 8 (1978): 203–13.

Fisher, A. C., and J. V. Krutilla. "Determination of Optimal Capacity of Resource-Based Recreation Facilities." *Natural Resources Journal* 12 (1972): 417–44.

Flegg, A. T. "Methodological Problems in Estimating Recreational Demand Functions and Evaluating Recreational Benefits." *Regional Studies* 10 (1976): 353–62.

Freeman, A. M. III. *The Benefits of Environmental Improvement: Theory and Practice.* Baltimore: Johns Hopkins University Press, 1979.

Gibson, J. "Recreational Land Use." In *The Valuation of Social Cost,* ed. D. W. Pearce. London: Allen and Unwin, 1978.

Hyman, E. L. "The Valuation of Extramarket Benefits and Costs in Environmental Impact Assessment." *Environmental Impact Assessment Review* 2, 3 (1981): 227–64.

Knetsch, J. L. "Outdoor Recreation Demands and Benefits." *Land Economics* 39, 4 (1963): 328–37.

Knetsch, J. L., and R. K. Davis. "Comparison of Methods for Recreation Evaluation." In *Water Research,* ed. A. V. Kneese and S. C. Smith. Baltimore: Johns Hopkins Press, 1966.

Mansfield, N. W. "The Estimation of Benefits From Recreation Sites and the Provision of a New Recreation Facility. *Regional Studies* 5 (1971): 55–69.

McConnell, K. E. "Congestion and Willingness to Pay: A Study of Beach Use." *Land Economics* 53 (1977): 185–95.

Merewitz, L. "Recreational Benefits of Water Resource Development." *Water Resource Research* 2, 2 (1966): 167–82.

Pearse, P. H. "A New Approach to the Evaluation of Non-Priced Recreation Resources." *Land Economics* 44, 1 (1968): 87–99.

Reiling, S. D.; K. C. Gibbs; and H. H. Stoevener. *Economic Benefits from an Improvement in Water Quality.* Washington, D.C.: U.S. Environmental Protection Agency, 1973.

Seckler, D. W. "On the Uses and Abuses of Economic Science in Evaluating Public Outdoor Recreation." *Land Economics* 42, 4 (1966): 485–94.

Shelby, B. "Crowding Models for Background Recreation." *Land Economics* 56, 1 (February 1980): 43–55.

Shucksmith, D. M. "The Demand for Angling at the Derwent Reservoir, 1970 to 1976." *Journal of Agricultural Economics* 30 (1979): 25–37.

Sinden, J. A. "A Utility Approach to the Valuation of Recreational and Aesthetic Experiences." *American Journal of Agricultural Economics* 56, 1 (1974): 61–72.

————. "The Application of Benefit-Cost Principles of Recreation Management: Case Study of Coloshire, N.S.W." In *Australian Project Evaluation,* ed. J. C. McMaster and G. R. Webb. Sydney: ANZ Book Co., 1978.

Sinden, J. A., and A. C. Worrell. *Unpriced Values: Decisions Without Market Prices.* New York: Wiley, 1979.

Smith, R. J. "The Evaluation of Recreational Benefits: The Clawson Method in Practice." *Urban Studies* 8 (1971): 89–102.

Smith, R. J., and N. J. Kavanagh. "The Measurement of Benefits of Trout Fishing: Preliminary Results of a Study of Grafham Water, Great Ouse Water Authority, Huntingdonshire." *Journal of Leisure Research* 1, 4 (1969): 316–32.

Smith, V. K., and R. J. Kopp. "The Spatial Limits of the Travel Cost Recreational Demand Model." *Land Economics* 56, 1 (February 1980): 64–71.

Stevens, J. V. "Recreation Benefits from Water Pollution Control." *Water Resources Research* 2, 2 (1966): 167–82.

Stoevener, H. H., and W. G. Brown. "Analytical Issues in Demand Analysis for Outdoor Recreation." *Journal of Farm Economics* 49, 5 (1967): 1295–1304.

————. "Analytical Issues in Demand Analysis for Outdoor Recreation: Reply." *American Journal of Agricultural Economics* 50, 1 (1968): 151–53.

Tussey, R. C., Jr. *Analysis of Reservoir Recreation Benefits.* Research Report No. 2. Lexington: University of Kentucky Water Resources Institute, 1967.

U.S. Water Resources Council. "Procedures for Evaluation of National Economic Development (NED) Benefits and Costs in Water Resources Planning (Level C)." In *Final Rule Federal Register,* 14 December 1979. Washington, D.C.: U.S. Government Printing Office, 1979.

Litigation and Compensation

Hanayama, Y., and I. Sano. *Valuation of Losses of Marine Product Resources Caused by Coastal Development of Tokyo Bay.* Tokyo Institute of Technology, 1981.

Mäler, K. G., and R. E. Wyzga. *Economic Measurement of Environmental Damage: A Technical Handbook,* Paris: OECD, 1976.

Survey-Based Valuation Techniques

Bishop, R. C., and T. A. Heberlein. "Measuring Values of Extramarket Goods: Are Indirect Measures Biased?" *American Journal of Agricultural Economics* 61 (December 1979): 926–30.

————. *Simulated Markets, Hypothetical Markets, and Travel Cost Analysis: Alternative Methods of Estimating Outdoor Recreation Demand.* Agricultural Economics Staff Paper No. 187. Madison: University of Wisconsin, 1980.

Bohm, P. "An Approach to the Problem of Estimating the Demand for Public Goods." *Swedish Journal of Economics* 73 (1971): 55–66.

————. "Estimating the Demand for Public Goods: An Experiment." *European Economic Review* 3 (1972): 111–30.

Brookshire, D. S.; B. C. Ives; and W. D. Schulze. "The Valuation of Aesthetic Preferences." *Journal of Environmental Economics and Management* 4 (1976): 325–46.

Dalkey, N. C., and O. Helmer. "An Experimental Application of the Delphi Method to the Use of Experts." *Management Science* 9 (1963): 458–67.

Hoinville, G., and R. Berthoud. *Identifying and Evaluating Trade-Off Preferences: An Analysis of Environmental Accessibility Priorities.* Publication P-117. London: Social and Community Planning Research, 1970.

Hyman, E. L. "The Valuation of Extramarket Benefits and Costs in Environmental Impact Assessment." *Environmental Impact Assessment Review* 2, 3 (1981): 227–64.

Meyer, P. *A Comparison of Direct Questioning Methods for Obtaining Dollar Values for Public Recreation and Preservation.* Vancouver: Environment Canada, 1976.

Pendse, D., and J. B. Wyckoff. "Scope for Valuation of Environmental Goods." *Land Economics* 50 (1974a): 89–92.

————. *A Systematic Evaluation of Environmental Perceptions, Optimum Preferences and Trade-Off Values in Water Resource Analysis.* Bulletin WRRI-25. Corvallis, Oreg.: Oregon State University, Water Resource Research Institute, 1974b.

Randall, A.; B. Ives; and C. Eastman. "Bidding Games for Valuation of Aesthetic Environmental Improvements." *Journal of Environmental Economics and Management* 2 (1974): 132–49.

Romm, J. *The Value of Reservoir Recreation.* Water Resources and Marine Sciences Center Technical Report 19; Agricultural Experiment Station Report AE Research 296. Ithaca, N.Y.: Cornell University, 1969.

Rowe, R. D.; R. C. d'Arge; and D. Brookshire. "An Experiment on the Economic Value of Visibility." *Journal of Environmental Economics and Management* 1 (1980): 1–19.

Scherr, B. A., and E. M. Babb. "Pricing Public Goods: An Experiment with Two Proposed Pricing Systems." *Public Choice* 23 (1975): 35–48.

Schulze, W. D.; R. C. d'Arge; and D. S. Brookshire. *Valuing Environmental Commodities: Some Recent Experiments.* Laramie: Department of Economics, University of Wyoming, 1980 (unpublished manuscript).

Sinden, J. A., and A. C. Worrell. *Unpriced Values: Decisions Without Market Prices.* New York: Wiley, 1979.

Smith, V. L. "The Principle of Unanimity and Voluntary Consent in Social Choice." *Journal of Political Economy* 6 (1976): 1125–39.

Thayer, M. A. "Contingent Valuation Techniques for Assessing Environmental Impacts: Further Evidence." *Journal of Environmental Economics and Management* 8 (1981): 27–44.

7
Environmental Quality Valuation from the Cost Side

COST ANALYSIS TECHNIQUES

Estimating fully the benefits of environmental quality protection or improvement may be difficult in many situations. Governments with limited funds and restricted research skills and data may not, in general, be able to apply the techniques discussed in Chapter 6. Theoretical reasons exist as well for not relying completely on benefit estimation methods that are based on a willingness-to-pay approach. Some of these reasons have already been outlined in Chapter 3. In reality, many decisions about environmental quality are made in the absence of monetary estimates of benefits. Monetary benefits are replaced by specific goals or some kind of physical indicator, such as emissions, ambient concentrations of pollutants, or measures of community health. Desirable standards can be determined in an arbitrary manner and attention can be focused on the relevant resource costs. As shown in Chapter 3, such costs can arise in development planning, at the project and program levels, and in programs for improving environmental quality. The concern is with *economic* as distinct from *financial* costs; economic costs reflect the opportunity costs of resources allocated for environmental quality purposes instead of for other economic uses.

Exactly who makes the assessment of desirable levels of costs and environmental quality is a critical factor from a policy viewpoint. Sometimes producers or individuals may be prepared to protect themselves from environmental damage on a voluntary basis, as discussed under the preventive expenditures method. The implicit values of environmental quality benefits obtained are revealed in the willingness to incur defensive costs. The economic value of resources committed provides, according to those incurring the costs, a minimum estimate of the benefits generated.

At other times, as in programs for protecting or improving environmental quality, government authorities need to determine the "best" level of protection and are responsible for assessing the size and the distribution of the cost

261

burden. Similar decisions are required at the project level when design standards and management practices that protect or enhance ambient environmental quality need to be incorporated in project plans. Policymakers must make subjective (although, it is hoped, well-informed) judgments about benefits bestowed on the community. Once standards for environmental quality have been set, cost-effectiveness analysis can help environmental decision makers to minimize resource inputs.

One approach to valuation of the economic benefits foregone through the environmental damages caused by economic activity is to measure the cost of replacing the environmental services destroyed. Examples are water treatment schemes to replace the cleansing effects of natural ecosystems, air conditioners as substitutes for trees for cooling purposes, and the costs of fish produced from artificial ponds as a replacement for fish in the natural environment. The "shadow-project" approach is a special version of the replacement-cost valuation technique. Such approaches again provide only minimum estimates of the presumed value of environmental services foregone.

The Preventive Expenditures Method

Theory.   Estimates of individuals' minimal valuations of environmental quality can sometimes be obtained from empirical data showing their willingness to incur costs for eradicating or reducing adverse effects on the environment. This approach to valuation is known as the "defensive expenditures," or "exclusion facilities," method. It has been applied to noise control in domestic dwellings (Starkie and Johnson 1975).

Many of the attempts to place an economic value on the disutility caused by noise have relied upon the willingness to move or stay as an indicator of willingness to pay (Metra 1970, Paul 1971, Walters 1975, Pearce 1978). Each household has a subjective assessment, N, of the disutility (nuisance) caused by noise. Certain costs are incurred, however, if the household decides to move to a quieter area. These comprise:

1. Consumer's surplus, S, reflecting the value of additional services or economic rent yielded by the house to its owner in excess of its market value;
2. Depreciation in property value, D, caused by noise; and
3. The costs of moving, R, such as parking, haulage, and legal fees.

A rational houseowner will move if

$$N > S + D + R, \qquad\qquad (7\text{--}1)$$

and will stay and tolerate the noise if

$$N < S + D + R. \qquad\qquad (7\text{--}2)$$

The preferred alternative will minimize the owner's total cost, both real and subjective.

Starkie and Johnson argue that noise alone is rarely sufficient to induce a household to move. A third alternative is to stay and insulate the house against noise. The willingness to accept the costs of noise control can then be interpreted as a demand for peace and quiet.

Letting the cost of sound insulation be represented by G and residual noise (remaining after sound improvement measures have been taken) by N', the basic decision model can be extended. Owners who decide to stay, take no defensive measures, and tolerate the noise must obey the restriction

$$S + D + R > N < G + N'. \tag{7-3}$$

Those who stay and decide to install noise insulation must obey the inequality

$$N > G + N' < S + D + R. \tag{7-4}$$

The rational household will continue to purchase sound insulation until the following equality holds:

$$(N - N') = G. \tag{7-5}$$

The demand curve for noise exclusion facilities, shown in figure 7.1, becomes a surrogate demand curve for noise prevention or for peace and quiet. Following the theory outlined in Chapter 3, the economic benefits of

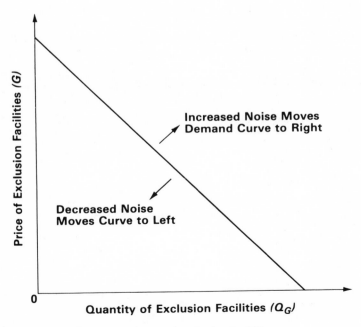

Figure 7.1 The demand for noise exclusion facilities.

noise insulation comprise the total area lying under the demand curve, measuring the total willingness to pay, or Marshallian consumer's surplus.

An Example: Heathrow Airport.   Starkie and Johnson tested their noise exclusion facilities approach for a sample of Hounslow households in the vicinity of London's Heathrow Airport. Insulating Hounslow houses against sound by means of double-glazed windows was encouraged in 1966 by introducing a subsidy scheme. By 1972 the market saturation point had been reached. Firms supplying windows resorted to an average-cost pricing policy after a scale of "allowable" charges was fixed by local authorities. The costs of insulation could thus be related to the number of rooms glazed rather than to the area of glazing itself.

Noise levels were measured in terms of average peak PNdB (perceived noise level in decibels), peak PNdB, and the number of heard aircraft, N (those with a noise value exceeding 80 PNdB). Explanatory variables used by Starkie and Johnson are given in table 7.1.

The dependent variable estimated in the study is the number of rooms that are fitted with double glazing. From this, and from existing data on the cost of glazing, the cost of noise exclusion facilities—hence, the demand for peace and quiet—is ascertainable. Several types of model specification were tried, including a binary regression model. The results of the binary regression model are reported here because the authors concluded that this model was satisfactory.

The usual linear regression model has the form

$$E(y_i) = \alpha + \sum_{j=1}^{k} \beta_j x_{ij}, \tag{7-6}$$

Table 7.1. Basic Explanatory Variables Used in the Noise Analysis, Heathrow Airport Neighborhood

Independent variables	Means
Distance from Heathrow Airport center (10^4 feet)	1.376
Traffic noise dummy variable	55% (=1)
Rail noise dummy variable	11% (=1)
N day	123
PNdB day	95
N evening	28
PNdB evening	94
Peak PNdB evening	102
ΔPNdB evening	8
N night	27
PNdB night	93
Peak PNdB night	103
ΔPNdB night	10
Net cost of insulating five rooms (£)	89.3

Source: Starkie and Johnson (1975).

Table 7.2. Stepwise Regression: Five Rooms Insulated

Independent variables	β	St error	t values
Rail noise	0.186	0.095	1.948
ΔPNdB evening	0.028	0.008	3.510
Net total cost	−0.023	0.004	5.256

Source: Starkie and Johnson (1975).

where $E(y_i)$ is the expected value of the dependent variable y_i, x_{ij} are given values of k independent variables, β_j are the regression coefficients, and α is the intercept term.

Whether or not glazing takes place is indicated by binary observations 1 or 0. The model can thus be extended to the following form (Cox 1970):

$$\phi = 0 \le \phi \le 1 = E(y_i) = \alpha + \sum_{j=1}^{k} \beta_j x_{ij}. \tag{7-7}$$

The results displayed in table 7.2 are confined to houses with five rooms and show the proportion of households opting for full insulation or none at all. The price variable in the demand function comes from the cost (excluding the subsidy) that must be paid to insulate five rooms. Each coefficient indicates the change in the proportion of households that would demand full insulation following a one-unit change in the associated independent variable. If PNdB increased by one unit, an additional 2.8% of the households in the sample could be expected to install double glazing.

Other regression equations used by Starkie and Johnson determined the proportion of two-story-house owners that would insulate the upstairs section (three bedrooms) and downstairs section (two living rooms) separately. The results are shown in tables 7.3 and 7.4 and are interpreted in the same way as those in table 7.2.

The ultimate findings of the study were that the average household would be willing to pay £45 for the insulation of all bedrooms and £33 for living rooms. The average household income was £1800; thus, the willingness to pay represents 2.6 and 1.8% of income for upstairs and downstairs sound

Table 7.3. Stepwise Regression: Insulation of Two Living Rooms

Independent variables	β	St error	t values
Distance from Heathrow	−0.174	0.063	2.773
Downstairs cost	−0.029	0.007	4.240
Traffic noise	−0.113	0.074	1.526[a]
Rail noise	0.176	0.119	1.480[a]

[a] Not significant at the 0.1 level in a two-tailed test.
Source: Starkie and Johnson (1975).

Table 7.4. Stepwise Regression: Insulation of Three Bedrooms

Independent variables	β	St error	t values
ΔPNdB night	0.024	0.006	4.058
Upstairs cost	−0.045	0.008	5.515

Source: Starkie and Johnson (1975).

insulation, respectively. The reduction in noise achieved was 14 decibels (dBA), slightly more than half of the initial noise level. This is comparable to the reduction that would be achieved by modifying aircraft engines or changing flight procedures. Cost-effectiveness analysis would make it possible to determine the most economically efficient strategy for noise control.

Critique of the Method. Pearce (1978) has noted several drawbacks to Starkie and Johnson's approach. First, the method breaks down if there is sufficient noise to induce a significant number of people to move. Second, the measure of noise is restricted to indoor rather than outdoor levels, so the full nuisance effect would not be captured. Third, the results indicate only the average willingness to pay. Marginal valuations of further changes in noise levels remain unknown. Finally, double glazing may have secondary benefits, such as heat insulation and an increase in property value. The willingness to pay separately for these improvements is not distinguished in the analysis.

Other Applications. Apart from applications to noise prevention, the exclusion facilities approach has not been widely used. Other areas of application, however, are possible. In a case study of soil erosion in the upland areas of Korea, various methods of dealing with the damage to lowland paddy fields were examined (Kim and Dixon 1982). One involved defensive measures by lowland farmers (construction of water diversion dikes) to prevent siltation of their paddy fields. Another example is the widespread practice—in countries where streams are polluted by raw sewage—of treating the water, either in households or in centralized purification plants, before using it for cooking and drinking. Implied benefits in both of these examples would be at least as great as the defensive expenditures incurred.

The Replacement-Cost Approach

Theory. The costs of replacing productive assets damaged by lowered environmental quality or by improper on-site management practices can be taken as a minimum estimate of the presumed benefits of programs for protecting or improving the environment. Relevant examples are the costs of replacing trees damaged by water pollution and the buildings lost through land subsidence associated with underground mining.

A Case Study: Soil Conservation in Korea. In the Korean case study by Kim and Dixon (1982), various mulching and land preparation techniques were examined as means of reducing soil erosion from upland farming areas. Some of the benefits of this program were increased crop yields from upland areas and reduced payments to lowland paddy farmers to compensate for lost rice production from silted fields. The primary benefit, however, was a substantial reduction in the costs of replacing soil and nutrients that otherwise would have been required in the absence of the soil conservation program. Replacement costs are indicated in table 7.5, measured in *won* per hectare (ha) (US$1 equals W690). To offset physical erosion losses, it would have been necessary to recover and replace 40.35 tons of soil per ha per year. Costs of truck service and spreading per ha would have been W80,700.

Other costs of replacement were for nutrients lost through erosion. As shown in table 7.5, estimates were obtained by multiplying the quantity of each chemical element needed per ha by the corresponding market price. Application costs are another cost component. Additional expenditures were required for supplemental irrigation, field maintenance and repair, and compensation payments to lowland farmers whose farms were affected by the eroded soil. These costs totaled more than W150,000 per ha per year. This study was able to show that the economic benefits of the mulching program far exceeded the resource costs and recommended introducing such practices in upland farming areas.

The "Shadow-Project" Approach

Theory of the Shadow Project.   The shadow-project approach is a special version of the replacement-cost technique. When environmental services are difficult to value and could be lost because of development proposals, a ranking of alternatives is often assisted by determining the economic cost of a supplementary project that provides substitute environmental services. For example, if recreational amenities or fisheries production are destroyed or impaired, an alternative investment can, in principle, provide the same output of goods and services. This has been described as the shadow-project approach. The total costs of an alternative that provides substitute environmental

Table 7.5. Replacement Costs of Soil Lost through Erosion

Item	Price/kg (won)	Quantity (kg)	Cost (won/ha)
Soil recovery and spreading			80,700
Replacement of nutrients			
Nitrogen	480 ×	15.72 =	7,546
Phosphorus	345 ×	3.58 =	1,235
Potassium	105 ×	14.59 =	1,532
Organic matter	175 ×	75.35 =	13,186
Calcium	60 ×	10.61 =	637
Magnesium	1,400 ×	1.62 =	2,268
Application cost	40 ×	121.5 =	4,860
Subtotal			31,264

Source: Kim and Dixon (1982).

services comprise the basic resource costs of the main project plus the costs of the shadow project itself. By examining the respective total costs, comparisons can be made with alternative schemes that still preserve environmental services.

A Case Study: Flood Control in the Oosterschelde.   The shadow-project concept was used in the planning of flood prevention schemes for part of the Rhine Delta (the Oosterschelde) in the Netherlands (Commissie Oosterschelde 1974). In 1953, as a result of severe storms and high tides, the sea broke through the dike system in southwest Netherlands and caused widespread damage, including the loss of 1,835 lives. The greatest losses occurred in the Oosterschelde region. A bill calling for intensive research into ways of preventing a similar disaster was quickly passed by the parliament. Closing off the estuary with a large new dike (the Delta Plan) was initially thought the best solution to the problem. Public objections to the proposal, however, led to its reconsideration. The Oosterschelde in its natural state provided valuable environmental services: as an important water resource for commercial fisheries and shellfish production, yielding large quantities of flatfish, anchovies, flounder, eel, shrimp, crabs, oysters, periwinkles, and mussels; as the major sportfishing area in southwest Netherlands and a popular site for other water-based recreational activities; and as a nursery for small fish (of significance to North Sea fisheries) and a habitat for migratory and breeding birds. The Delta Plan would have destroyed all of these ecological services. By the early 1970s, the plan was publicly described as an environmental disaster.

In 1973, the Oosterschelde Commission was established to report on all safety and environmental aspects of the Delta Plan, and to advise on the extent to which the original proposal ought to be carried out, or on modifications that might be needed. The commission ultimately recommended that the dike closing the estuary should not be built. It advocated instead the construction of a special dam with large gates, which would generally be left open to permit normal tidal flows but which would be closed to block off the sea when dangerous storm conditions prevailed.

The commission considered five basic plans with different variants and carried out detailed benefit-cost analyses of six selected plans. Four of the plans are reported here. Costs and benefits appear in table 7.6.

The original Delta Plan, Plan A, is sketched in figure 7.2. The required dike was only 9 km long. It could have been built in only four years, and together with the existing dike system would have provided almost absolute safety. Benefits from reducing flood damage were estimated as the value of property and agricultural production that would no longer be lost through expected storm damage. The direct construction and operating costs of the scheme were quite low. Loss of income from fisheries, however, would have led to substantial indirect monetary costs, as shown in the table. With a low discount rate, Plan A would have yielded positive net benefits in monetary terms. With a 6% discount rate, Plan A was uneconomic and was only barely

Table 7.6. Benefit-Cost Comparisons of Alternative Plans for the Oosterschelde, Netherlands (Billions of 1974 Guilders)

Plan	A			B			C			D		
Discount rate (%)	2	4	6	2	4	6	2	4	6	2	4	6
Construction costs	1.31	1.31	1.31	2.81	2.81	2.81	1.70	1.70	1.70	2.95	2.95	2.95
Operating costs	0.03	0.02	0.02	0.03	0.02	0.02	0.09	0.08	0.07	0.03	0.02	0.02
Damage to fisheries and shellfish production	0.62	0.47	0.38	0.62	0.47	0.38						
Costs of water management	0.12	0.10	0.09	0.12	0.10	0.09	0.07	0.06	0.05	0.07	0.06	0.05
Total costs	2.08	1.90	1.80	3.58	3.40	3.30	1.86	1.84	1.82	3.05	3.03	3.02
Flood prevention benefits	4.08	1.92	1.21	4.08	1.92	1.21	3.40	1.37	0.74	4.03	1.89	1.18
Net monetary benefits	2.00	0.02	−0.59	0.50	−1.48	−2.09	1.54	−0.47	−1.08	0.98	−1.14	−1.84

Note: A: Complete closure of estuary; B: Complete closure plus *haff* (artificial lagoon); C: Strengthening existing dikes; D: Partial closure plus flood control.
Source: Rapport Commissie Oosterschelde (1974).

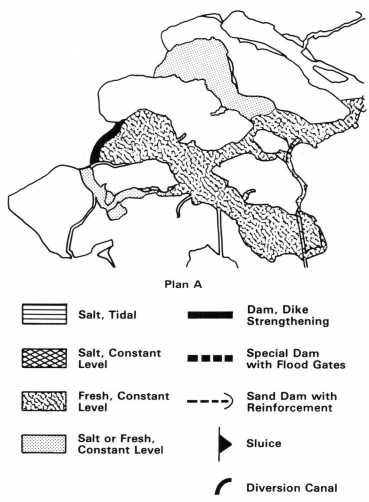

Plan A

☰ Salt, Tidal		▬	Dam, Dike Strengthening
⊠ Salt, Constant Level		▪ ▪ ▪	Special Dam with Flood Gates
Fresh, Constant Level		– – –➤	Sand Dam with Reinforcement
Salt or Fresh, Constant Level		▶	Sluice
		⌐	Diversion Canal

Figure 7.2 Complete closure of the estuary—Plan A. (*Source:* **Commissie Oosterschelde, 1974.**)

economic when the rate was 4%. Other unpriced adverse impacts on environmental quality, not explicitly stated in the monetary analysis, were considered sufficiently large to reject the Delta Plan.

Plan B included the costs of a shadow project. The scheme involved building the 9-km dike as in Plan A and, in addition, an artificial lagoon (*haff*) in the North Sea to provide substitute fishing and ecological and recreational services. Cost of the haff was estimated at between 1.0 and 2.0 billion guilders (fl). The mean figure (fl1.5 billion) is included in Plan B construction costs at a 4% discount rate in table 7.6. Some doubt was expressed by fisheries experts about the ability of a haff to compensate for fishery losses. The net monetary benefits of Plan B for discount rates of 4 and 6% were negative. They would have been negative at these rates even if the full value of fishery losses were restored by the haff. This can be verified by adding the figures for fishery damage costs to the estimates of net monetary benefits for the proposal. Only with a discount rate of 2% could positive net benefits have been yielded. Plan B was also rejected by the commission.

In Plan C the existing dike system was retained, but the walls were to be strengthened (fig. 7.3). The construction and operating costs were higher than for Plan A, but no fishery losses would have been incurred. Because approximately 250 km of dike walls would remain, the probability of a breakthrough by flood waters would be quite high, so the expected monetary benefits from reduced flood damage were much lower than for Plans A and B. This led to negative net benefits for the scheme as a whole with discount rates of 4 and 6%. Positive net benefits arise with a discount rate of 2%. Given the importance of preventing future flood disasters (with their additional nonmonetary costs in loss of life and human suffering), Plan C was considered an unsatisfactory solution to the problem.

The alternative recommended by the commission and carried out by the Netherlands government was Plan D (fig. 7.4). The special dam with flood gates, combined with the existing dike system, was superior to Plan C and equivalent to Plans A and B in terms of safety. Although the net monetary

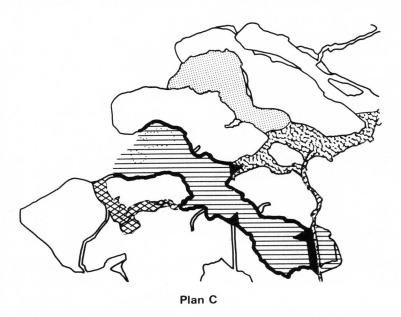

Plan C

Figure 7.3 Strengthening of existing dike system—Plan C. (*Source:* Commissie Oosterschelde, 1974.)

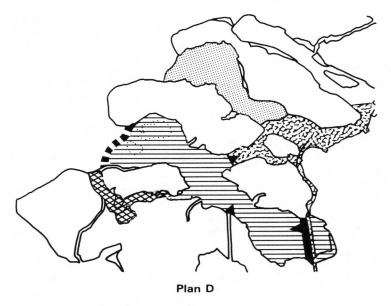

Plan D

Figure 7.4 Dike with storm gates—Plan D. (*Source:* Commissie Oosterschelde, 1974.)

benefits of Plan D were less than Plan A, the difference would, in the commission's judgment, be more than offset by the unpriced environmental benefits that Plan D would provide. Plan B would yield monetary net benefits lower than those from Plan D. (The negative net benefits for Plan B were greater than those for Plan D.) For Plan B to be superior to Plan D, the monetary and nonmonetary benefits of the shadow project would have needed to exceed the difference in net benefits between the two plans. The commission judged that this would not happen because the environmental services provided by a human-built alternative were not likely to be as beneficial as those of the natural environment. Inclusion of shadow-project costs in Plan B gave some indication to the commission of how large the benefits of a haff would need to be to equate its net benefits with those provided by the special dam proposed under Plan D. Subjective assessment led to selection of Plan D as the best alternative.

COST-EFFECTIVENESS ANALYSIS

Cost-effectiveness analysis is used to assess trade-offs between benefits, measured in some unit other than money, and resource costs. It can indicate the least-cost method of reaching a prescribed objective, such as a given level of emissions or ambient air quality, as well as ways of maximizing (or minimizing) some physical environmental effect with available resources.

The concept is applicable at all levels of economic-environmental quality assessment, ranging from individual production plants or activities to regional and national economic systems.

Cost-effective Measures to Reduce Discharges from Individual Plants

Theoretical Aspects.   Correct costing of physical measures taken to reduce discharges from individual plants is of major policy significance in programs to improve ambient environmental quality. Although the ultimate goal may be efficient management of ambient environmental quality, the costs of meeting prescribed discharge standards are incurred at the individual plant and activity level.

From a policy viewpoint, two reasons exist for compiling data on discharge reduction costs for individual plants and activities. First, for production enterprises owned by government, such data are a necessary input to decisions about committing public funds and about setting appropriate discharge standards. Second, where the relevant production activities take place under private ownership, those in charge of managing environmental quality should obtain detailed information about technical and cost conditions before imposing standards or charges or before issuing discharge permits. Any attempt to introduce such measures without careful examination of these cost factors carries the risk of creating economic inefficiencies and legal entanglements, antagonizing industry, and undermining the credibility of the authorities who must devise workable strategies for managing environmental quality.

Even though the significant control target variables, such as plant emissions, may be clearly specified by control authorities, estimating costs does have its complications. Emissions can be reduced by a variety of technologies and management practices. Some are mutually exclusive, whereas others may be implemented in combination. The capacity to reduce the discharge of several residuals simultaneously is frequently a characteristic of discharge reduction technologies. Sometimes attempts to reduce discharges of one residual can exacerbate discharges of another. Discharge reduction costs can vary considerably depending on, among other things, specific residuals to be reduced; required levels of discharge reduction; factor input prices; spread of costs between the basic production plant and the additional discharge reduction equipment; plant size; possible production of saleable by-products and recovery of materials and energy; and whether the discharge reduction technology is being built into a new plant or retrofitted to an old one. Also, differences in plant location can affect both capital and operating costs. With newer discharge reduction technologies, many of which are still in the research and development or pilot-plant stage, cost estimates can vary because of uncertainty about future cost components and factor input prices and about the efficiency of future plant performance once it is in full-scale commercial operation.

In complex situations, a set of cost-effective discharge reduction measures for an individual plant can be determined by optimization techniques. Typically, the aim is to meet conventional output targets, such as for steel, electric energy, or petroleum products, and discharge standards at minimum total cost. One approach toward identifying the minimum-cost alternative is the search method, under which appropriate sets of discharge reduction measures are identified and the costs of each are ascertained. The best combination is chosen from the tabulated results by using a cost-effective increment approach. Other approaches are various forms of mathematical programming.

An Electric Power Plant Example.   The search method can be illustrated with a U.S. electric power plant example developed by North and Merkhofer (1975). The focus is on the costs of using alternative methods of reducing sulfur dioxide discharges from "representative" new, coal-fired power plants. Table 7.7 shows the average total costs of producing electricity and of reducing sulfur dioxide emissions for a 600-megawatt (MW) plant. Costs are estimated for five alternative methods of reducing discharges. Total costs include capital, fuel, and other operating costs and are expressed on a mills per kilowatt-hour basis (1 mill = $0.001). The results are displayed in figure 7.5. The rate of sulfur dioxide (expressed as sulfur) emitted is measured from right to left; the sulfur removal rate can be read in the opposite direction. The cost curve slopes upward, indicating that unit costs of generating electric energy rise as discharges are progressively reduced.

As shown in table 7.7 and figure 7.5, the lowest generating costs are incurred when the only controls are tall stacks and intermittent emission reductions, but when sulfur emissions are very high. For a relatively modest increase in costs, coal preparation can be used to reduce the sulfur content of the fuel, which would cut sulfur emissions by one-third. Further gains are obtained at low incremental cost by switching to low-sulfur eastern coal.

The critical decision is whether to reduce emissions further by using flue-gas desulfurization or by switching to low-sulfur western coal. Generating

Table 7.7. Electricity Production Costs and Sulfur Emissions for a Representative New Power Plant, East Coast, United States

Alternative	Total cost per unit of electricity (mills/kwh, 1975 prices)	Sulfur emitted ($\times 10^{-3}$ lbs/kwh)
1. High-sulfur coal with tall stacks and intermittent emission reductions	21.6	22.5
2. Coal preparation	23.6	15.0
3. Flue-gas desulfurization	26.2	2.4
4. Switch to low-sulfur western United States coal	25.5	6.0
5. Switch to low-sulfur eastern United States coal	24.6	6.7

Source: Adapted from North and Merkhofer (1975).

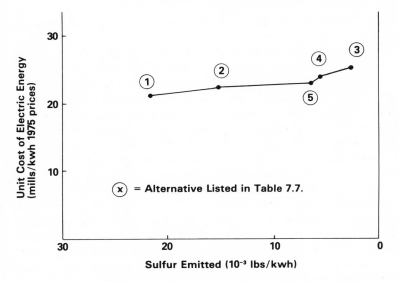

Figure 7.5 Cost curve for reduction in sulfur oxide discharges, for a representative new coal-fired electric power plant. (*Source:* Compiled from data in North and Merkhofer, 1975.)

costs are greater for both of these alternatives than for the switch to low-sulfur eastern coal, yet the reduction in sulfur emissions is rather small. Strong assumptions about the relationship between sulfur emissions and ultimate damage (e.g., a nonlinear function or one involving a threshold damage effect) would need to be made to justify these alternatives. If a high degree of discharge reduction is desired, it is apparent that flue-gas desulfurization is probably the better choice. A switch to western coal leads to only a small reduction in emissions, whereas flue-gas desulfurization gives greater benefits for roughly the same incremental cost.

Petroleum Refinery Example: A Mathematical-Programming Approach. The petroleum refinery study by Russell (1973) is a classic example of the application of mathematical programming (see Chapter 8) to the problem of residuals management in an industrial operation. Linear programming has a long history in industry as a way of helping managers achieve private economic efficiency of operations. Russell's study represents an extension of the basic linear-programming model by incorporating social costs for nonproduct outputs (residuals) arising from production. The approach analyzes the response of plants to effluent charges. Plants (activities) will reduce discharges to the point at which the marginal cost of reduction for each residual is equal to the effluent charge (OECD 1980). Sensitivity analysis can be carried out by varying the charge for each residual and by modeling the outcomes in terms of the activity's responses. Changes in discharges of each residual can then be plotted against the costs of reduction to obtain trade-off curves.

Russell's model minimizes the total social costs of production and discharge reduction, subject to output, technological, and other resource constraints. Residuals charges appear as cost components in the objective function. The model also simulates residuals discharge reduction by emission standards. The shadow prices of the relevant constraints correspond to the alternative system of effluent charges. Because the model is linear, however, this correspondence is not continuous. Constraint levels and effluent charges need to vary over a range before a jump from one process technology to another occurs (fig. 7.6). When effluent charges are used, only the dotted lines in the diagram will be observed. If discharge constraints are simulated, only the solid vertical lines will be apparent.

The costs estimated in Russell's analysis are actual resource or social costs and do not necessarily represent the costs that would be borne by the dischargers. In the United States and elsewhere, dischargers may have subsidies—such as tax credits and rapid depreciation—available to reduce their actual costs below the resource or social costs. This cost difference is important because the response of a discharger to constraints or incentives directed toward reducing discharges will be in terms of actual financial costs rather than social economic costs.

The model is too detailed to discuss here in its entirety. A sample of results can be presented, however. Operation of the basic refinery without controls on discharges leads to a given pattern of product outputs and residuals discharges. Technologies to reduce residuals discharges from the basic plant are specified next, and charges for residuals discharges are introduced. The re-

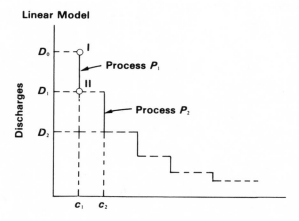

Linear Model

Effluent Charge or Shadow Price

Figure 7.6 Effluent charges, discharge constraints, and shadow prices. (*Source:* Russell, 1973.)

sponse to BOD_5 effluent charges is shown in figure 7.7. In the range of $0.01 to $0.07 per pound, there is rapid reduction of BOD_5—almost 70%. Raising the charge has no further effect until the $0.16-per-pound level, where 80% BOD_5 reduction is reached. A 95% removal rate is attained when the charge equals $0.25. The model shows that other residuals are also reduced as a side effect of reducing BOD_5 discharges.

Other technological options for the refinery include a hydrocracking (hydrogen intensive) process and a reduced crude process known as H-oil. A refinery equipped with these technologies is described by Russell as "advanced." Cost functions for reducing BOD_5 discharges in basic and advanced refineries are shown in figure 7.8. Total and marginal costs rise dramatically when high levels of control are sought.

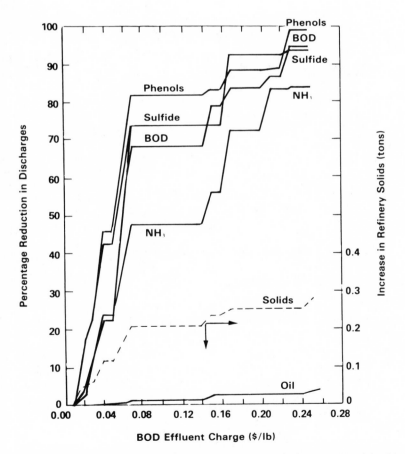

Figure 7.7 Response to BOD_5 effluent charges: basic refinery, benchmark product mix. (*Source:* Russell, 1973.)

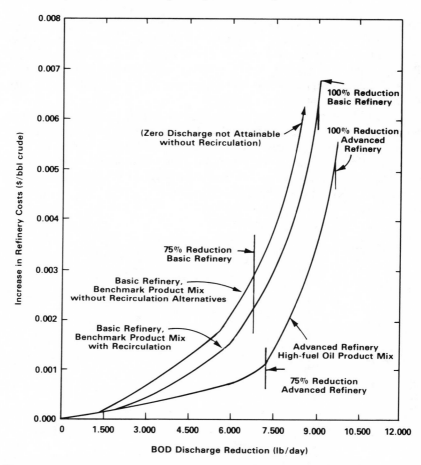

Figure 7.8 Total cost of BOD$_5$ discharge reduction. (*Source:* Russell, 1973.)

A Regional Ambient Air Quality Example

Cost-effective methods of attaining desired ambient concentrations of NO$_x$ were recently investigated in the United States for the Chicago region (U.S. CEQ 1979). Cost estimates (table 7.8) are for different approaches to the reduction of NO$_x$ emissions from 797 stationary sources in the Chicago Air Quality Control Region. A hypothetical short-term ambient standard of 250 μg(micrograms)/m^3 was assumed. The following strategies were examined: *baseline,* characterized by no emission reduction; *reasonably available control technology* (RACT), installed by all sources; *least cost,* based on an economically efficient method of assigning reductions to specific sources, taking into account the costs of reduction and individual contributions to ambient concentrations of NO$_x$; *selective emissions reduction,* a less sophisticated version of the least-cost approach; *simple rollback,* whereby all sources reduce emissions by an equal percentage; *maximum feasible reduction,* under which all sources install the best available technology regardless of cost; and *uniform charges,* imposed on NO_x emissions from all sources.

The most efficient way of meeting the ambient standard is to reduce emissions from a relatively small number of "worst offenders." Under the least-cost approach, only a minimal quantity of NO_x is removed. All other methods remove more NO_x than is really necessary—in some cases, more than twenty times the minimal level of emissions required to achieve the ambient standards. Possible errors in dispersion model predictions, however, may exaggerate this difference. Table 7.8 shows that the 90% simple rollback and maximum feasible reduction approaches both involve twelve times the total cost of the least-cost approach, eleven times that of RACT, and three times that of selective emission reduction.

Because emission rates differ significantly under the alternative strategies, the average costs of emissions reduction show considerable variation, and the ranking of strategies based on average emissions reduction costs is quite different from that based on the total costs of meeting the ambient standard. The least-cost strategy, for example, involves the highest average cost of reducing emissions, presumably because at such low rates of emission reduction it is not possible to take advantage of economies of scale in abatement activity. The least-cost method nevertheless minimizes the total costs of attaining the ambient standard.

It is easy to prove that to reduce total emissions within a region by a predetermined amount, a system of equal charges will achieve the desired

Table 7.8. Cost and Effectiveness of Strategies to Reduce Nitrogen Dioxide Discharges, Chicago Air Quality Control Region

Reduction strategy	Number of sources reducing discharges	NO_x Emissions removed (thousands of lbs/hr)	Number of receptors in violation	Annual reduction cost (millions of \$/yr)	Average annual dollar cost of NO_x removal (1 lb/hr)
No reduction baseline	0	0	104	0	0
RACT	797	37	80	23	622
Least cost	96	5	0	21	4200
Selective emissions reduction	741	39	0	94	3240
Simple rollback					
90%	797	106	0	254	2400
80%	792	104	6	243	2340
Maximum feasible reduction	797	106	0	254	2400
Uniform charges	790	105	0	239	2280

Source: U.S. Council on Environmental Quality (1979).

result at minimum total cost (OECD 1980). In general, this approach will not yield the least-cost solution to meeting ambient environmental quality standards. (The exception is a "mixing bowl" situation in which emissions contribute proportionately to ambient pollution.) When emissions from individual sources do not contribute proportionately to ambient concentrations, as in the Chicago study, charges should be specifically calculated for each activity to reach the standard at least total cost. In principle, and depending on administrative costs, a system of differential charges could yield the least-cost solution appearing in table 7.8. Penalties for "worst offenders" under an ideal system might need to be as high as $40,000 per pound per hour, as compared with charges to less significant polluters of $60 per pound per hour. Whether such a system would be administratively feasible is, of course, another issue. The results in table 7.8 nevertheless reveal that in this particular instance, a system of uniform charges would not be an economically efficient way of meeting the hypothetical ambient concentration standard.

Effects on Humans as Receptors: Water-borne Diseases

In a number of areas of the world, one or more types of water-borne diseases are endemic. Water development projects in such areas, particularly irrigation projects, often exacerbate the problems and result in increased prevalence of disease. Thus, before implementing water development projects it is essential to analyze their effects on human receptors. Policy makers whose objective is to reduce the existing prevalence of a water-borne disease should also look at proposed projects. Because the economic benefits of health improvements are difficult to measure in such cases, a cost-effectiveness approach to the control of disease can be taken. Schistosomiasis, a water-borne disease transmitted by snails, is used here to illustrate the approach (Rosenfield and Bower 1978).

The first step in the analysis is construction of a model to determine incidence and prevalence of the disease. The *incidence* of schistosomiasis in a given population is defined as the rate of change in the proportions of infected and uninfected individuals over a given period in time. *Prevalence* is the fraction of the population infected with schistosomiasis at any point in time. Incidence is a function of the amount of snail habitat, of the amount of human water contact (contact with snail habitat), and of prevalence in the given population. Conceptually, an equation for estimating incidence would be

$$A = f(H, W, P) \tag{7-8}$$

where A is the incidence rate of schistosomiasis, H is snail habitat, W is human water contact, and P is the prevalence of schistosomiasis. The problem is to develop an operational estimating equation from the conceptual model.

Several operational versions have been developed, each applied to empirical data from specific areas in two different countries. Two are presented here. One included the two variables H and P to estimate prevalence as follows (Rosenfield, Smith, and Wolman 1977):

$$P = (Y_t) \text{ (total population)}, \qquad (7\text{--}9)$$

$$A = b_0 \, (H^{b_1}) \, (P^{b_2}), \text{ and} \qquad (7\text{--}10)$$

$$Y_{t+dt} = \left(Y_t - \frac{A}{A+B} \right) e^{-(A+B)dt} + \frac{A}{A+B}, \qquad (7\text{--}11)$$

where P is the number of infected persons in the population, Y is the fraction of the population infected, A is incidence (infection rate coefficient), b_0, b_1, b_2 are regression coefficients, H is meters of snail habitats accessible to the population, B is deinfection rate coefficient, and t is time.

Deinfection refers to the natural process by which individuals divest themselves of schistosomiasis. The coefficient B is thought to be specific for particular species of schistosomiasis.

Another version included the two variables W and P to estimate prevalence as follows (Rosenfield 1979):

$$P = (Y_t) \text{ (total population)}, \qquad (7\text{--}12)$$

$$A = b_0 \, (W^{b_1}) \, (P^{b_2}), \text{ and} \qquad (7\text{--}13)$$

$$Y_{t+dt} = \left(Y_t - \frac{A}{A+B} \right) e^{-(A+B)dt} + \frac{A}{A+B}, \qquad (7\text{--}11)$$

where all variables are the same as in equations 7–9, 7–10, and 7–11, and W is a water-contact parameter.

Table 7.9 shows the typical human-snail contact points in connection with an irrigation project. Given these possible contact points, empirical data are necessary in order to develop representative water-contact patterns for different age groups.

Using a model for predicting prevalence (such as one of the two described above), one can initially assume that no control measures are taken and can estimate the prevalence of schistosomiasis as a function of estimated changes in snail habitats and human water contact arising from the design and operation of a proposed irrigation project (figs. 7.9–10).

The second step in the analysis requires an examination of physical measures for reducing the prevalence of schistosomiasis (table 7.10). These measures include reducing snail habitats, modifying human activities associated with water, and providing medical treatment of infected individuals by chemotherapy.

The third step involves devising alternative strategies for reducing the prevalence of the disease, which incorporate various combinations of physical measures, implementation incentives, and institutional arrangements. Six

Table 7.9. Human Activity and Transmission of Schistosomiasis in Irrigation Projects

Human activity	Human-Snail contact points
Irrigation of fields	Standing water in fields; Manipulating siphons from secondary (field) laterals
Maintenance of irrigation system	All canals and drains
Washing (personal, laundry, dishes)	Secondary laterals, drains, rivers, sidepools
Recreation	Sidepools, rivers, canals, main laterals
Obtaining water	Secondary laterals, drains, rivers, sidepools
Drinking water	Secondary laterals, drains, rivers, sidepools
Residuals disposal:	
Personal	Fields, drains, main and secondary laterals, river
Garbage	Drains, main and secondary laterals, river
Livestock management	Flood plain of river, sidepools, ponds, swamps

Source: Adapted from Rosenfield and Bower (1978).

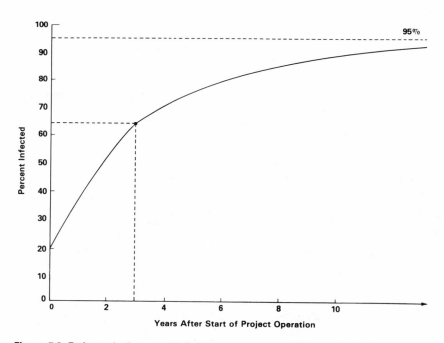

Figure 7.9 Estimated changes in *Schistosoma haematobium* prevalence over time after prototype irrigation development, assuming no schistosomiasis management. (*Source:* Adapted from Rosenfield and Bower, 1978.)

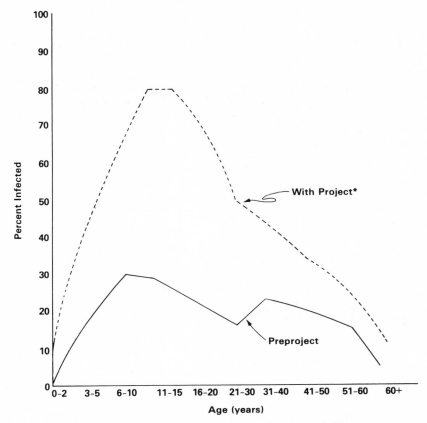

*Estimated overall with-project prevalence equals 65 percent.

Figure 7.10 Estimated age distribution of *Schistosoma haematobium* prevalence under preproject conditions and after three years of prototype irrigation project operation, assuming no schistosomiasis management. (*Source:* Adapted from Rosenfield and Bower, 1978.)

possible sets of physical measures are shown in table 7.11. The sets were developed for a particular situation and reflect increasing degrees of reduction in prevalence as one moves from Set I to set VI.

Finally, costs can be estimated for each of the alternatives and compared with levels of effect (table 7.12).

Estimating the prevalence of schistosomiasis is only part of the problem of assessing the effects on human receptors. The disease in and of itself is rarely fatal. Schistosomiasis must be considered as one part of a spectrum of low-grade infections. When combined with malaria, hookworm, roundworm, and other parasitic diseases, it contributes to synergistic effects. It is not possible as yet to separate the effects of a single disease in such a multi-disease

Table 7.10. Physical Measures for Reducing Prevalence of Schistosomiasis

I. Reducing Human-Snail Contact
  A. Reducing Snail Habitats and/or Snail Populations
    1. Mollusciciding
      (a) All habitats
      (b) Focal (treating only habitats that are known transmission sites)
    2. Constructing mechanical screening at diversion point to prevent entry of snails into irrigation system
    3. Lining of main canal
    4. Draining standing water in fields and from main canal and laterals
    5. Removing vegetation and silt from main canal, laterals, drains
    6. Introducing predator or competitor species
    7. Transporting water by pipe to secondary laterals
    8. Increasing efficiency of irrigation
  B. Modifying Human Activities
    1. Providing domestic water supplies by standpipes in courtyards
    2. Providing laundries
    3. Providing showers
    4. Providing swimming pools
    5. Protecting water recreation sites
    6. Locating canals and drains away from existing settlements
    7. Providing boots for irrigators and irrigation system maintenance workers
    8. Providing latrines and garbage disposal sites in closer proximity to village than canal, laterals, drains
    9. Protecting animal grazing areas
II. Treating Human Population with Drugs—Chemotherapy
  A. All Infected Population
  B. Specific Segments of the Population

Source: Adapted from Rosenfield and Bower (1978).

context. All appear to contribute to shortened life spans and decreased economic productivity. Quite possibly, the nutritional and health status of the human host may be important in terms of effect on prevalence and on the consequences of the disease for infected individuals.

Table 7.11. Illustrative Sets of Physical Measures for Reducing Prevalence of Schistosomiasis

Set No.
  I. No physical measures explicitly for schistosomiasis management
  II. Mollusciciding all sites (I.A.1.*a*)
  III. Chemotherapy for the whole infected population (II.A.)
  IV. Chemotherapy for the whole population before project construction (II.A.); mechanical screening at diversion point (I.A.2.); drainage facilities (I.A.4.); vegetation and silt removal (I.A.5.); and improved irrigation efficiency (I.A.8.)
  V. Focal mollusciciding (I.A.1.*b*); providing domestic water supplies (I.B.1.); protecting water recreation sites (I.B.5.); providing boots for irrigators and irrigation system maintenance workers (I.B.7.); chemotherapy for specific segments of the population (II.B)
  VI. Mollusciciding all sites (I.A.1.*a*); mechanical screening at diversion point (I.A.2.); drainage (I.A.4.); vegetation/silt removal (I.A.5); providing domestic water supplies (I.B.1.); providing laundries (I.B.2.); providing showers (I.B.3.); providing swimming pools (I.B.4.); providing latrines and garbage disposal sites (I.B.8.); targeted chemotherapy (II.B.)

Note: Refer to the specific physical measures listed in Table 7.10.
Source: Adapted from Rosenfield and Bower (1978).

Table 7.12. Relative Cost and Effectiveness of Sets of Physical Measures for Reducing Prevalence of Schistosomiasis

Set of physical measures	Net annual cost ($)	Steady-state prevalence (%)[a]	Incremental cost ($)	Incremental reduction in steady-state prevalence (%)	Incremental reduction in prevalence per unit cost (%/$)
I	0	90–100			
			1.2X	10.0	8.3/X
II	1.2X	80–90			
			0.8X	10.0	12.5/X
III	2.0X	70–80			
			1.5X	30.0	20.0/X
IV	3.5X	40–50			
			2.0X	34.5	17.2/X
V	5.5X	8–13			
			3.5X	8.5	2.4/X
VI	9.0X	1–3			

[a] After project operation at design level for at least three years.

REFERENCES

Commissie Oosterschelde. *Rapport.* 's Gravenhage: Staatsuitgeverij, 1974.

Cox, D. R. *Analysis of Binary Data.* London: Methuen, 1970.

Kim, S. H., and J. A. Dixon. *A Case Study of Economic Valuation of Environmental Quality Aspects of Upland Agricultural Projects in Korea.* Honolulu: East-West Center, Environment and Policy Institute, March 1982.

North, D. W., and M. W. Merkhofer. "Analysis of Alternative Emissions Control Strategies." *Air Quality and Stationary Source Emission Control.* U.S. Senate Committee on Public Works, No. 94–4. Washington, D.C.: U.S. Government Printing Office, 1975.

OECD. *Pollution Charges in Practice.* Paris, 1980.

Paul, M. E. "Can Aircraft Noise Be Measured in Money?" *Oxford Economic Papers* 23, 3 (1971): 297–322.

Pearce, D. W., ed. *The Valuation of Social Cost.* London: Allen and Unwin, 1978.

Plowden, S.P.C. "The Cost of Noise." *Metra* 10, 1 (1970): 65–78.

Rosenfield, P. L. *The Management of Schistosomiasis.* Research Paper R–16. Washington, D.C.: Resources for the Future, 1979.

Rosenfield, P. L., and B. T. Bower. *Management Strategies for Reducing Adverse Health Impacts of Water Resources Development Projects.* Discussion Paper D–3. Washington, D.C.: Resources for the Future, 1978.

Rosenfield, P. L.; R. A. Smith; and M. G. Wolman. "Development and Verification of a Schistosomiasis Transmission Model." *American Journal of Tropical Medicine and Hygiene* 26, 3 (1977): 505–16.

Russell, C. S. *Residuals Management in Industry: A Case Study of Petroleum Refining.* Baltimore: Johns Hopkins University Press, 1973.

Starkie, D.N.M., and D. M. Johnson. *The Economic Value of Peace and Quiet.* Lexington, Mass.: Heath, 1975.

U.S. Council on Environmental Quality. *Environmental Quality—Tenth Annual Report.* Washington, D.C., 1979.

Walters, A. A. *Noise and Prices.* Oxford: Clarendon Press, 1975.

8

Multiactivity Economic-Environmental Quality Models

Valuation of natural systems and environmental quality effects can be carried out only after the physical, chemical, and biological impacts of economic activities have been identified. One of the difficulties of assessing ambient environmental quality is the correct selection of the boundaries of analysis. Many effects on environmental quality occur in a regional rather than a site-specific context. Others may have national or global significance. Secondary economic and environmental quality effects of development projects, programs, and residuals management practices have already been discussed in Chapter 3. General-equilibrium models can help to overcome the analytical problems involved in accounting for secondary effects.

Normal production and consumption activities are not always the driving force in economic-environmental systems. Causal relationships can also run in the opposite direction. Policy makers may not recognize that the arbitrary application of ambient environmental quality standards without regard to economic cost can create considerable economic dislocation. If technologies to reduce discharges are unavailable or are prohibitively expensive, economic activities may be forced to reduce production or to close down. This can have widespread regional and perhaps even national economic consequences. Broad boundaries need to be prescribed to measure the costs and benefits under such circumstances.

Time as well as space can create problems in defining the limits of analysis. Benefit-cost analysis is often restricted to a steady-state approach—for example, estimating annually recurring costs and benefits of an air quality management program. But some effects on ambient environmental quality and receptors are cumulative, such as the concentration of heavy metals, pesticides, or radionuclides in animals and humans, or the accumulation of solid residuals from industrial and household activities. The time profiles of such variables should be identified to account for possible long-term damage. The time profiles can also be incorporated into certain types of general-equilibrium models.

INPUT-OUTPUT MODELS

Basic Features of Input-Output Models

Input-output analysis was developed by Wassily Leontief in the late 1930s. The approach is based on the fact that in modern economic systems, production activities are closely interrelated. Each producing activity acts in a double capacity: first, as a supplier, selling its output to other industries and to final buyers; second, as a buyer of inputs, purchasing the products of other producing activities, as well as labor skills, capital services, natural resources, land, managerial expertise, and imported materials. The value of output comprises the value of materials and services purchased from other sectors plus the value of primary inputs used directly in the production process.

Demands for final outputs of the economic system create chain reactions of production and factor use. To generate 100 megawatts (MW) of electricity, for example, coal must be produced. But electricity is needed in coal production. Thus, more than the initial 100 MW of electricity is required. This in turn creates extra demand for coal, more electricity, more coal . . . until the total direct and indirect requirements of both commodities have been produced. Labor, capital services, land, and managerial inputs are also used. The whole system is "driven" by final demands for economic goods and services. In a wider national or regional setting, this process takes place for many industries simultaneously. A regional model may have thirty or forty sectors, and a national model one hundred to three hundred sectors.

Discharges of residuals and demands for inputs from the environment are handled in a fashion similar to primary inputs, such as labor and capital. Each 100 MW of electricity produced will require a certain amount of water for steam production and for cooling. At the same time, residuals will be discharged; for example, gases and particulates in stack emissions, sludges and solid wastes, and liquid effluents. Each ton of coal produced has similar effects that can be encompassed by the model using the same methodology. Further natural-systems processes, such as dispersion in air and water systems and damage to ecosystems, are analyzed by adding natural-systems models. The extended system is again driven by final demand for economic goods and services.

The general form of an economic-environmental quality input-output model is shown in figure 8.1. This informational system can aid decision makers in a variety of ways. First, because input-output models are derived from a comprehensive data system for a given base year, setting up a model forces analysts to obtain an accurate historical record and a consistent set of estimates for major economic and natural-systems flows and their interconnections. This should lead to systematic monitoring, estimating, and data collecting and provides a framework within which to assemble all results.

Second, once the model has been established it can be used to simulate

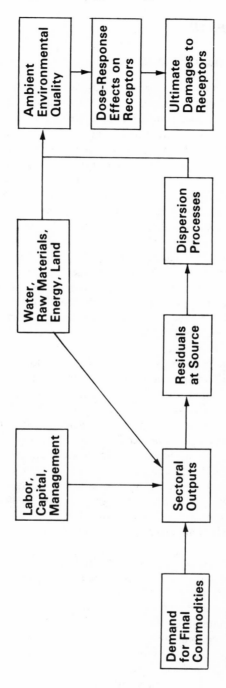

Figure 8.1 Economic-environmental quality input-output model.

different economic development scenarios. To construct such a scenario, exogenous sets of final demands are postulated for future time periods. Each time period, with its postulated final demand set, has a corresponding set of simultaneous equations and a solution set for economic and environmental quality variables. By means of computer simulation, the environmental quality effects of any planned pattern of economic development can be predicted in both temporal and spatial terms.

Third, by changing final demand patterns and structural relationships in the model, different options for economic development, residuals discharges, and ambient environmental quality can be generated, assisting policy makers in choosing what they consider to be the best development plan. In this sense, an input-output model functions as a technique for rational choice. If a given scenario does not meet the multiple objectives of policy makers, required changes in the system can be simulated and the process repeated until conditions are acceptable. With this approach, evaluation of alternatives is still required, but this takes place outside the model. The best available alternative can be chosen only if decision makers attach values—either their own subjective judgments or values derived from additional benefit-cost analysis—to alternative outcomes generated by the model, so that an iterative assessment and design procedure is followed.

In terms of figure 8.1, the cutoff point in assessing system trade-offs will depend on where, within the total system, environmental quality constraints or objectives are introduced. If environmental policies are directly concerned with ultimate damages to receptors, such as damage to human health, the entire model structure must be used. If the analysis needs to proceed only as far as the determination of ambient environmental quality, the modules assessing dose-response relationships and ultimate effects will not be required. If interest centers only on residuals discharges, the model needs to determine discharges at source points; in that case, procedures for dispersion modeling and damage estimating are no longer relevant to the analysis. These distinctions are important in judging the appropriateness of various types of input-output models for environmental quality policy making. National models can be useful, for example, if constraints take the form of discharge standards. The effects on industry and the remaining residuals generated may not be spatially significant. If, however, ambient environmental quality standards are prescribed, source discharges estimated at the national level must be allocated to specific regions for subsequent analysis of dispersion and ambient environmental quality effects. Alternatively, regional economic-environmental quality input-output models would have to be built.

Construction of an Input-Output Model

Theoretical Aspects. Construction of an economic input-output model starts with a data system for a given base year, showing the annual sales of all

Table 8.1. Hypothetical Input-Output Flow Matrix ($)

	Agriculture	Manufacturing	Commerce	Final sales	Total output
Agriculture	0	3,000	700	2,300	6,000
Manufacturing	3,000	0	1,400	600	5,000
Commerce	600	1,000	0	5,400	7,000
Primary input costs	2,400	1,000	4,900	8,300	
Total costs	6,000	5,000	7,000		18,000

industries to each other and to final buyers. These transactions can be measured in physical units, but monetary units are normally used.

A simple three-sector system is described in table 8.1. The economy is disaggregated into only three sectors: agriculture, manufacturing, and commerce. This so-called flow, or transactions, matrix would be obtained from historical data collected in a chosen base year. The table shows that the agricultural sector produced $6,000 of output that was sold to the manufacturing sector ($3,000), to the commercial sector ($700), and to final buyers ($2,300). Inputs to the agricultural sector took the form of manufactured products ($3,000), commercial services ($600), and primary inputs (labor and capital) costing $2,400. The total value of output for the agricultural sector ($6,000) equals the total cost of all inputs. Similar conditions apply to the other sectors.

The input-output model is constructed from this data base by linearizing the input flows. Each sector is assumed to use inputs strictly in fixed proportions. Thus, a 10% increase in agricultural output will lead to a 10% increase in all inputs. Production technology is assumed to remain constant. No economies of scale apply, marginal and average input ratios are the same, and input substitution does not take place.

Direct requirements per unit of output are obtained for each sector by dividing each entry in table 8.1 by its corresponding column total. This gives a set of input coefficients, a_{ij}, calculated as

$$a_{ij} = y_{ij}/z_j \qquad i = 1, \ldots, n$$
$$j = 1, \ldots, n \qquad (8-1)$$

where y_{ij} is total sales by the i-th sector to the j-th sector in the base year, z_j is total output of the j-th sector in the base year, and a_{ij} is the amount of output of sector i directly required to produce one unit of output by sector j. There are n industries in the economy.

The direct requirements coefficients obtained from table 8.1 are displayed in table 8.2. To produce $1.0 of agricultural output, $0.5 of manufactured goods and $0.1 of commercial services are directly required.

Suppose we wished to determine what the total output would be for each sector in 1984 if consumers demanded $8,000 of agricultural products,

Table 8.2. Direct Requirements Matrix ($)

	Agriculture	Manufacturing	Commerce
Agriculture	0.0	0.6	0.1
Manufacturing	0.5	0.0	0.2
Commerce	0.1	0.2	0.0

$10,000 of manufactured goods, and $9,000 of commercial services. The set of simultaneous equations representing this situation is as follows. Total outputs for the three sectors are denoted by x_1, x_2, and x_3.

$$x_1 = 0.0x_1 + 0.6\,x_2 + 0.1x_3 + 8,000,$$

$$x_2 = 0.5x_1 + 0.0\,x_2 + 0.2x_3 + 10,000,$$

$$x_3 = 0.1x_1 + 0.2\,x_2 + 0.0x_3 + 9,000. \tag{8-2}$$

The first equation states that enough agricultural output (x_1) has to be produced to meet the input requirements of the manufacturing and commercial sectors, as well as the $8,000 of agricultural output demanded by consumers. The same interpretation applies to the second and third equations for the manufacturing and commercial sectors, respectively. Because of interindustry input requirements, total sectoral outputs greatly exceed the final demands of $8,000, $10,000, and $9,000. Using ordinary substitution and elimination methods, it is possible to solve for x_1, x_2, and x_3. The answer is $x_1 = $25,253$, $x_2 = $25,970$, and $x_3 = $16,718$.

When constructing a model with a realistic number of sectors, it is necessary to rely on matrix algebra and on an electronic computer to solve the system of equations (see Appendix to this chapter). The simultaneous equations can be solved making use of "Leontief inverse matrix" coefficients. These are frequently referred to as total requirements coefficients. The Leontief coefficients for the example developed here are shown in table 8.3. Using these coefficients, total outputs for the three sectors are ascertained by solving the following equations, giving a final answer of $x_1 = $25,253$, $x_2 = $25,970$, and $x_3 = $16,718$ as before.

$$x_1 = 1.5286 \times 8,000 + 0.9872 \times 10,000 + 0.3503 \times 9,000,$$

$$x_2 = 0.8280 \times 8,000 + 1.5764 \times 10,000 + 0.3980 \times 9,000,$$

$$x_3 = 0.3184 \times 8,000 + 0.4140 \times 10,000 + 1.1146 \times 9,000. \tag{8-3}$$

Table 8.3. Leontief Inverse Matrix

	Agriculture	Manufacturing	Commerce
Agriculture	1.5286	0.9872	0.3503
Manufacturing	0.8280	1.5764	0.3980
Commerce	0.3184	0.4140	1.1146

In general, for any prescribed set of final demands $f_1, f_2, \ldots, f_n$, an input-output model will predict the required outputs of all sectors by providing a solution to the equation system below. The Leontief inverse coefficients appear as a set of α_{ij}. Each α_{ij} indicates the amount of output of the i-th sector directly and indirectly required to meet final demand for one unit of output by the j-th sector.

$$x_1 = \alpha_{11}f_1 + \alpha_{12}f_2 + \ldots + \alpha_{1n}f_n,$$
$$x_2 = \alpha_{21}f_1 + \alpha_{22}f_2 + \ldots + \alpha_{2n}f_n,$$
$$\cdot$$
$$\cdot$$
$$\cdot$$
$$x_n = \alpha_{n1}f_1 + \alpha_{n2}f_2 + \ldots + \alpha_{nn}f_n. \tag{8-4}$$

Supplementary Economic Information. If detailed base-year data describing other economic variables are available, these can also be represented in coefficient form to provide further information about economic effects in future years. Suppose the data shown in table 8.4 had been collected for the base year. Coefficients are derived by dividing each entry by the corresponding base-year total output level (see table 8.1) for each sector. Coefficients for labor, capital, and land are shown in table 8.5.

The typical coefficient in table 8.5 can be denoted b_{gj}, indicating the number of units of the g-th economic variable associated with one unit of total output by the j-th sector. In general, the levels of associated economic variables $q_1, q_2, \ldots, q_m$ are calculated as follows:

$$q_1 = b_{11}x_1 + b_{12}x_2 + \ldots + b_{1n}x_n,$$
$$q_2 = b_{21}x_1 + b_{22}x_2 + \ldots + b_{2n}x_n,$$
$$\cdot$$
$$\cdot$$
$$\cdot$$
$$q_m = b_{m1}x_1 + b_{m2}x_2 + \ldots + b_{mn}x_n. \tag{8-5}$$

With postulated final demands in 1984 for agriculture, manufactured goods, and commercial services of $8,000, $10,000, and $9,000, respectively, the accompanying economic effects can be ascertained by substituting the 1984 sectoral output levels ($x_1 = \$25,253$, $x_2 = \$25,970$, and $x_3 = $

Table 8.4. Economic Data: Factor Inputs to Indicated Sectors

	Agriculture	Manufacturing	Commerce
Labor (persons)	250	600	1,200
Capital ($)	500	800	200
Land (acres)	1,000	100	50

Table 8.5. Direct Economic Input Coefficients

	Agriculture	Manufacturing	Commerce
Labor (persons)	0.0416	0.1200	0.1714
Capital ($)	0.0833	0.1600	0.0285
Land (acres)	0.1666	0.0200	0.0071

$16,718) and the coefficients from table 8.5 into the above equation system and solving for the q's. The results are that $q_1 = 7,032$ persons, $q_2 = \$6,735$, and $q_3 = 4,845$ acres.

Environmental Quality Dimensions. Demands for inputs from the natural system and discharges of residuals into the natural system are handled in the same way as supplementary economic variables. Base-year data on interactions of industries with the natural system are needed. A hypothetical data set is supplied in table 8.6. This table contains data describing only four environmental quality variables—land use, water inputs, emissions of sulfur oxides, and emissions of particulates. In an operational model, much greater detail would appear. Direct coefficients for environmental quality variables are derived from table 8.6 by dividing each entry by the corresponding base-year sectoral output figure (see table 8.1). The typical environmental quality coefficient e_{kj} indicates the average level of the k-th environmental quality variable per unit of output of the j-th sector (table 8.7).

The magnitudes of environmental quality variables accompanying any given set of sectoral output levels can be represented by $r_1, r_2, \ldots, r_s$ and are found by solving the set of equations below:

$$r_1 = e_{11}x_1 + e_{12}x_2 + \ldots + e_{1n}x_n,$$
$$r_2 = e_{21}x_1 + e_{22}x_2 + \ldots + e_{2n}x_n,$$

.

.

.

$$r_s = e_{s1}x_1 + e_{s2}x_2 + \ldots + e_{sn}x_n. \qquad (8-6)$$

For example, the hypothetical output levels obtained for 1984 would lead to this solution: $r_1 = 4,845$ acres, $r_2 = 1,060$ acre feet/year, $r_3 = 8,056$ tons/

Table 8.6. Base-Year Environmental Quality Variables

	Agriculture	Manufacturing	Commerce
Land (acres)	1,000	100	50
Water (acre ft/yr)	200	40	5
SO_x (tons/yr)	400	1,200	60
Particulates (tons/yr)	500	1,500	150

Table 8.7. Direct Coefficients for Environmental Quality Variables

	Agriculture	Manufacturing	Commerce
Land (acres)	0.1666	0.0200	0.0071
Water (acre ft/yr)	0.0333	0.0080	0.0007
SO_x (tons/yr)	0.0666	0.2400	0.0085
Particulates (tons/yr)	0.0833	0.3000	0.0214

year, and $r_4 = 10,252$ tons/year. Further analysis would, of course, be required to translate these numbers into ambient environmental quality and ultimate damage effects.

Because the x_j's are calculated in terms of Leontief inverse coefficients and final demands, it is possible to determine levels of environmental quality variables as a function of final demands, making use of so-called cumulated (direct and indirect) coefficients. These are found by multiplying the direct environmental quality coefficients (e_{kj}) into the Leontief inverse matrix coefficients (α_{kj}) to obtain a new set of coefficients, c_{kj}. The typical coefficient indicates the direct and indirect effect on the k-th environmental quality variable created by supplying one unit of the j-th sector's output to final buyers. The equation system for calculating levels of environmental quality variables with cumulated coefficients and given final demands appears below.

$$r_1 = c_{11}f_1 + c_{12}f_2 + \ldots + c_{1n}f_n ,$$
$$r_2 = c_{21}f_1 + c_{22}f_2 + \ldots + c_{2n}f_n ,$$

.

.

.

$$r_s = c_{s1}f_1 + c_{s2}f_2 + \ldots + c_{sn}f_n . \tag{8-7}$$

Cumulated coefficients derived from tables 8.3 and 8.7 are presented in table 8.8. If these coefficients, along with the set of hypothetical final demands for 1984, are substituted in the above equation system, we once again obtain this solution: $r_1 = 4,845$, $r_2 = 1,060$, $r_3 = 8,056$, and $r_4 = 10,252$.

New technologies for controlling flows of residuals from economic activities can be incorporated in input-output models. Various approaches have been tried. For example, investment in new pollution abatement technologies

Table 8.8. Cumulated Coefficients for Environmental Quality Variables

	Agriculture	Manufacturing	Commerce
Land (acres)	0.2734	0.1988	0.0742
Water (acre ft/yr)	0.0577	0.0457	0.0156
SO_x (tons/yr)	0.3038	0.4476	0.1283
Particulates (tons/yr)	0.3825	0.5640	0.1724

can be included as an extra cost in the primary inputs section of an input-output system, and the Leontief inverse matrix can then be used to simulate the resultant cost and price impacts on the whole economy. Secondary effects on final demands, sectoral outputs, and factor inputs can then be determined. In other studies, the input-output coefficients and residuals coefficients have been altered to reflect changes in technology. Under "the dummy industry" approach, antipollution activities are represented by new sectors in the input-output matrix, whose "outputs" comprise reductions in residuals discharged. Pollutants discharged by antipollution sectors, as well as factor inputs required in pollution abatement, can be analyzed under the dummy industry approach. The topic of input-output modeling of pollution abatement is too extensive to be covered adequately here. A survey of relevant literature can be found in James, Jansen, and Opschoor (1978), among others.

An Australian Input-Output Emissions Model

An economic-environmental quality input-output model of the Australian national economic system for 1968–69 has been constructed to simulate combustion emissions under alternative economic growth assumptions (James 1982). An eleven-sector version of the input-output flow matrix, based on official input-output tables issued by the Australian Bureau of Statistics, is shown in table 8.9. The model emphasizes the energy sectors, so these appear in some detail in the condensed system. The other sectors are in highly aggregated form.

Estimated emissions by each sector in 1968–69 are indicated in table 8.10. These refer to potential emissions from uncontrolled combustion rather than actual emissions. In reality, many sector activities would have implemented emission reduction measures. The estimates were made by taking the fuel-use pattern for Australian industry in 1968–69 (James 1980) and applying combustion emission factors to each specific type of energy product—coal, petroleum, natural gas—consumed.

Direct emission coefficients indicating the per unit discharges of carbon monoxide, nitrogen oxides, sulfur oxides, particulates, and hydrocarbons were derived by dividing the entries in table 8.10 by the corresponding column totals in table 8.9. The coefficients are measured in metric tons (MT) per million dollars (Australian). The direct coefficients appear in table 8.11. Cumulated emission coefficients were calculated by first deriving Leontief inverse coefficients from table 8.9, then combining these with the direct emission coefficients. The cumulated emission coefficients are shown in table 8.12.

This model was used to simulate the effects of changes in the final supply of electric power by the Australian economy on national income, and on total emissions without controls. It would be equally useful, however, in the construction of scenarios for different national energy-economic growth policies.

Table 8.9. Industry by Industry Flow Matrix, Australia 1968–1969 ($A Million)

	1. Coal and crude petroleum	2. Petroleum and coal products	3. Electricity	4. Gas	5. Iron and steel	6. Rural	7. Mining	8. Manufacturing	9. Building and construction	10. Transportation	11. Service	Intermediate usage	Final demand	Total supply
1. Coal and crude petroleum	0	281.4	43.2	8.9	32.4	0	0.1	29.8	2.4	9.9	14.3	422.4	89.2	511.6
2. Petroleum and coal products	1.3	0	4.0	1.4	8.5	75.7	12.3	75.1	61.0	87.6	99.1	426.0	188.6	614.7
3. Electricity	11.2	6.6	0	3.0	32.9	22.6	17.3	170.1	14.8	11.8	183.0	473.2	282.9	756.1
4. Gas	0	0.5	0.7	0	2.4	0.2	0	13.8	1.9	1.0	7.2	27.8	77.2	105.0
5. Iron and steel	3.5	0.1	0.5	0	0	2.1	4.1	674.0	111.2	0.4	14.0	809.9	174.3	984.2

6. Rural	11.0	0	0.6	0	0.2	67.3	4.6	1,806.2	0.2	7.6	7.6	1,905.5	1,674.2	3,579.6
7. Mining	0.1	2.2	0	0.1	76.1	0.4	2.2	310.4	53.7	0.8	1.2	447.3	273.4	720.8
8. Manufacturing	22.4	40.4	19.4	3.1	100.8	465.5	56.4	3,441.3	1,861.3	317.4	2,178.0	8,505.9	9,178.4	17,684.5
9. Building and construction	3.8	3.0	8.8	1.4	2.9	43.3	5.3	95.1	0	119.3	564.9	847.9	3,997.8	4,845.7
10. Transportation	7.2	26.3	23.6	4.7	80.4	68.7	14.4	448.1	148.8	24.6	408.4	1,255.4	1,572.0	2,827.3
11. Services	20.2	27.0	37.5	22.8	48.5	506.3	54.3	1,440.0	523.4	316.8	5,181.5	8,178.3	12,913.9	21,092.1
Intermediate usage	80.8	387.4	138.3	45.4	385.2	1,252.2	171.2	8,504.0	2,778.7	897.1	8,659.3	23,299.6	30,421.9	53,721.6
Primary inputs	195.6	171.7	617.8	59.6	518.5	2,262.6	526.8	6,559.3	2,067.0	1,713.9	12,366.2	27,059.0	0	27,059.0
Australian production	276.4	559.1	756.1	105.0	903.7	3,514.8	698.0	15,063.3	4,845.7	2,611.0	21,025.5	50,358.6	30,421.9	80,780.0
Competing imports	235.2	55.5	0	0	80.4	64.7	22.8	2,621.4	0	216.4	66.6	3,363.0	0	3,363.0
Total usage	511.6	614.7	756.1	105.0	984.2	3,579.6	720.8	17,684.5	4,845.7	2,827.3	21,092.1	53,721.6	30,421.9	84,143.5

Source: James (1982).

Table 8.10. Emissions, Australia 1968–1969 (MT)

	Carbon monoxide	Nitrogen oxides	Sulfur oxides	Particulates	Hydrocarbons
Coal and crude petroleum	2,537	3,277	2,173	17,124	1,073
Petroleum and coal products	1,012,209	7,791	44,350	5,554	17,702
Electricity	34,014	159,920	145,714	874,367	8,828
Gas	6,297	9,113	7,977	61,183	890
Iron and steel	23,363	30,115	47,700	159,912	8,097
Rural	313,458	55,490	9,500	21,583	50,844
Mining	39,419	9,045	2,027	3,796	7,552
Manufacturing	182,001	98,074	130,346	257,300	27,990
Building and construction	134,017	37,404	18,261	25,326	27,981
Transportation	430,366	54,172	35,543	47,083	56,719
Services	402,732	46,047	49,081	29,111	43,756
Sector totals	2,580,418	510,452	492,675	1,502,343	251,438
Australian totals	3,709,132	592,874	502,476	1,548,860	352,042

Source: James (1982).

Structural changes can be modeled by manipulating final demand flows over time. Effects of different energy technologies and fuel-use patterns on environmental quality are simulated by changing the input-output coefficients in the basic model.

Other Studies

National input-output models for residuals discharges have been constructed in several countries. Leontief and Ford (1972) made forecasts of air emissions in the United States with an environmental input-output model.

Table 8.11. Direct Emission Coefficients, Australia 1968–1969 (MT/$A million)

	Carbon monoxide	Nitrogen oxides	Sulfur oxides	Particulates	Hydrocarbons
Coal and crude petroleum	9.17	11.85	7.86	61.94	3.88
Petroleum and coal products	1,810.30	13.93	79.31	9.93	31.66
Electricity	44.98	211.51	192.72	1,156.44	11.67
Gas	59.97	86.79	75.97	582.72	8.48
Iron and steel	25.85	33.32	52.78	176.95	8.96
Rural	89.17	15.78	2.70	6.14	14.46
Mining	56.47	12.95	2.90	5.43	10.82
Manufacturing	12.08	6.51	8.65	17.08	1.86
Building and construction	27.65	7.71	3.76	5.22	5.77
Transportation	164.82	20.74	13.61	18.03	21.72
Services	19.15	2.19	2.33	1.38	2.08

Source: James (1982).

Table 8.12. Cumulated Emission Coefficients, Australia 1968–1969 (MT/$A million)

	Carbon monoxide	Nitrogen oxides	Sulfur oxides	Particulates	Hydrocarbons
Coal and crude petroleum	30.49	22.86	18.07	113.27	6.14
Petroleum and coal products	1,836.14	29.68	92.19	83.42	36.23
Electricity	63.43	214.11	195.16	1,165.16	13.14
Gas	100.76	97.02	85.77	628.70	11.43
Iron and steel	68.83	46.29	64.20	229.99	13.22
Rural	139.84	19.90	7.94	18.86	16.70
Mining	98.18	20.46	11.04	39.39	12.82
Manufacturing	68.01	19.87	21.37	60.59	7.92
Building and construction	87.64	18.73	16.19	40.32	10.72
Transportation	245.65	26.86	21.74	37.13	25.10
Services	59.10	10.16	10.54	28.44	5.46

Source: James (1982).

Other studies have been done for the United States by Ayres and Gutmanis (1972), Cumberland and Stram (1974), and Ridker (1972). The U.S. Environmental Protection Agency (EPA) SEAS model is based on an input-output system (House 1977). Models have been built for Japan (OECD 1978), the Netherlands (Jansen 1978), Canada (Victor 1972), and Norway (Försund and Strom 1976).

Regional models have emphasized air pollution, as in the Haifa Bay study by Shefer (1973), the Charleston Metropolitan Area model (Hite and Laurent 1972), and a pollution abatement model for West Virginia (Miernyk and Sears 1974).

Water requirements and effluent discharge coefficients appear in the Charleston model (Hite and Laurent 1972) and in Victor's (1972) model for Canada. The Ayres and Gutmanis study (1972) includes solid residuals discharge coefficients.

There has been extensive use of input-output models in the economic-energy-environmental quality policy-making area. Representative studies are those of Folk and Hannon, and Just and Istvan (Macrakis 1976).

Some Limitations of Input-Output Models

The major drawback of input-output models is the amount of time and effort involved in collecting the basic data. Many Asian-Pacific countries already possess national input-output tables but, as already explained, further extensive work on the compilation of environmental quality data is needed, and regionalization of effects is essential if realistic ambient environmental quality assessments are to be carried out. Even to construct a modest regional input-output model requires several work-years' effort and a great deal of cooperation by government and industry. Often, there is a risk that by the time the data have been compiled, the model is far too old to make accurate policy appraisals. If an input-output table already exists, it may be usefully extended for national and regional environmental quality planning and management. Serious thought should be given to probable resource commitments, however, if such a system is contemplated solely for the purpose of environmental quality management.

Other objections to the approach relate to the methodology and underlying assumptions. The adoption of fixed coefficients may not be a valid representation of production relationships or environmental quality effects, especially over large ranges of variation in output. If the linearity property is extended into diffusion modeling, the technique may be inadequate to handle background concentrations of pollutants, environmental antagonisms and synergisms, and threshold effects. Special care would be needed to account for the accumulation of pollutants in the environment.

Finally, even though the "best" strategy can, in principle, be found by iterative procedures, the process can become cumbersome and frustrating to decision makers, especially when large numbers of variables and diverse options are involved. When these difficulties are encountered, mathematical-programming models may be a more suitable analytical approach.

LINEAR-PROGRAMMING MODELS OF ENVIRONMENTAL QUALITY MANAGEMENT

The preceding section on input-output models has stressed the importance of using a general-equilibrium model for regional and national environmental quality policy making and management. In complex situations involving many choices, the limitations of the input-output approach are quickly reached and more sophisticated mathematical-programming methods are required.

One of the advantages of programming is that multiple policy objectives relating to economic and environmental quality variables can be specifically incorporated in the analysis. Not all decision criteria can be included in the analysis, however. For example, legal and administrative feasibility and the timing of costs and returns may be excluded. Also, policy makers cannot escape the need to make value judgments; thus, benefit-cost analysis can still play a role in appraising various economic and environmental quality effects. With prior specification of the relative weights that decision makers wish to attach to these effects, an optimum is sought through programming that achieves the best possible trade-off of conflicting objectives, consistent with physical, technical, and economic restrictions on the range of options available.

In theory, the determination of an optimum is a purely mechanical procedure once the system parameters and decision makers' values have been ascertained. A common misconception is that both the analyst and the decision makers themselves may become slaves of a model and fail to think flexibly when formulating planning and management strategies. As pointed out by Holling (1978), however, mathematical-programming methods are only intended to supply interesting starting points for policy making in an iterative process of evaluation and design. Sensitivity analysis (arbitrarily varying the parameters of the model) is valuable for assisting in judgments about sensible limits to economic activity, residuals discharges, and possible decline or improvement in environmental quality.

Programming models have had many applications in environmental quality planning and assessment, ranging from the management of natural resources such as forests for multiple use, the control of residuals from individual production plants in industries such as iron and steel (Russell and Vaughan 1976), petroleum refining (Russell 1973), and electric power generation (Bower 1975), to complex regional and national models for the optimal utilization of water resources (Spofford, Russell, and Kelly 1976), airsheds (Kohn 1975), and energy supply systems (Muller 1979). Various types of programming models have been applied to environmental quality problems (Meister et al. 1976), the most widely accepted technique being linear programming. Some of these models are discussed below.

Linear-Programming Theory

The Primal Problem.   Policy makers frequently wish to maximize the economic benefits of production while at the same time preserving or enhancing environmental quality. As a hypothetical example, suppose plans are being made for the possible development of two major industries in a given region: electric power generation and tourism. Investment funds of $900 million and a labor supply of 5,000 people are available. Electric power output can be measured in megawatts (MW) per year and represented by the variable x_1. Tourism is quantified in terms of the number of tourists visiting the area each year, represented by x_2.

Suppose each megawatt of electric power requires $0.3 million of investment expenditure and the labor services of one person. Each tourist is assumed to need an investment outlay of $0.2 million and the labor services of two people. Feasible activity levels for electric power generation and tourism are limited to the following set:

$$0.3\, x_1 + 0.2\, x_2 \leq 900,$$
$$1.0\, x_1 + 2.0\, x_2 \leq 5,000,$$
$$x_1, x_2 \geq 0. \tag{8-8}$$

Finally, assume that the marketable value of electric power is $8,000 per MW per year, and average annual revenue obtained from each tourist is $6,000. A strictly economic objective function is, thus,

$$\text{maximize } 8,000\, x_1 + 6,000\, x_2.$$

The optimal solution to this problem is $x_1 = 2,000$ and $x_2 = 1,500$. To maximize the returns to production, a power station to provide 2,000 MW per year should be built and a tourist trade of 1,500 persons per year established. Total financial receipts amount to $25 million per year.

Graphic solution of the problem is shown in figure 8.2. The feasible production set comprises the shaded region $0ABC$. The value of the objective function is maximized at point B.

The general form of a primal linear-programming problem is as follows:

$$\text{maximize } p_1 x_1 + p_2 x_2 + \ldots + p_n x_n$$

subject to

$$a_{11} x_1 + a_{12} x_2 + \ldots + a_{1n} x_n \leq b_1,$$
$$a_{21} x_1 + a_{22} x_2 + \ldots + a_{2n} x_n \leq b_2,$$

$$\begin{aligned} &\phantom{a_{m1} x_1 + a_{m2} x_2 + \ldots + a_{mn} x_n}\\ &a_{m1} x_1 + a_{m2} x_2 + \ldots + a_{mn} x_n \leq b_m, \\ & \qquad\qquad x_1, x_2, \ldots, x_n \geq 0 \end{aligned} \qquad (8-9)$$

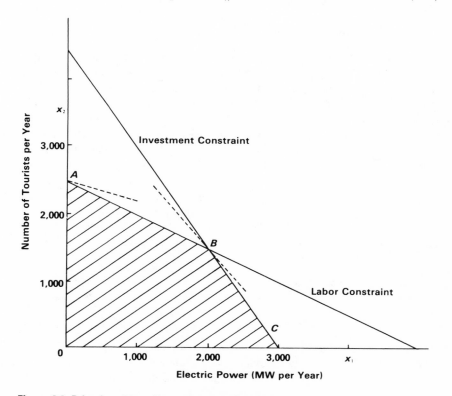

Figure 8.2 Primal problem, linear-programming example.

where x_j are activity levels, b_i available inputs, a_{ij} input requirements of the i-th resource per unit of activity level j, and p_j are the prices or weights in the objective function. There are n possible activities and m resource constraints. Large linear-programming problems are usually solved with an electronic computer.

The Dual Problem. Corresponding to the general primal problem is a dual, which (in the context of the example developed here) can be interpreted as minimizing the cost of resources used in production subject to output price constraints. Formally, the dual is specified by transposing the coefficients of the primal problem (writing rows as columns), introducing a new set of variables *(w_j)* known as "shadow prices," and interchanging the prices in the objective function with resource supplies. The dual problem takes the general form

$$\text{minimize } b_1 \, w_1 + b_2 \, w_2 + \ldots + b_m \, w_m$$

subject to

$$a_{11} \, w_1 + a_{21} \, w_2 + \ldots + a_{m1} \, w_m \geq p_1 \, ,$$
$$a_{12} \, w_1 + a_{22} \, w_2 + \ldots + a_{m2} \, w_m \geq p_2 \, ,$$
$$\cdot$$
$$\cdot$$
$$\cdot$$
$$a_{1n} \, w_1 + a_{2n} \, w_2 + \ldots + a_{mn} \, w_m \geq p_n \, ,$$
$$w_1, w_2, \ldots, w_m \geq 0 \, . \tag{8–10}$$

For the regional industrial development example, the corresponding dual is

$$\text{minimize } 900 \, w_1 + 5{,}000 \, w_2$$

subject to

$$0.3 \, w_1 + 1.0 \, w_2 \geq 8{,}000 \, ,$$
$$0.2 \, w_1 + 2.0 \, w_2 \geq 6{,}000 \, ,$$
$$w_1, w_2 \geq 0 \, . \tag{8–11}$$

The solution to this problem, illustrated in graphic form in figure 8.3, is $w_1 = 25{,}000$ and $w_2 = 500$ (point Y). The value of the objective function is $25 million—the same as in the primal problem. This will always be true if both exercises bave been correctly computed. In fact, the primal can be set up as a minimization problem. A common example is minimization of production costs subject to output target constraints. In the corresponding dual the objective function is maximized.

Calculated values of shadow prices are especially important for sensitivity analysis. The shadow price for investment funds (w_1) is \$25,000, indicating that if another unit of investment (\$1 million) were made available, the value of the objective function in the primal would rise by \$25,000. Similarly, increasing the labor supply by one person would increase the value of the primal objective function by \$500, since this is the shadow price for labor

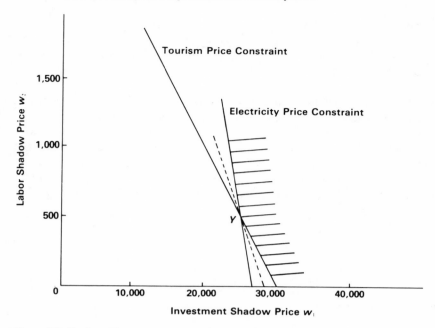

Figure 8.3 Dual problem, linear-programming example.

(w_2). The dual problem thus is useful in indicating to policy makers which particular constraints are exerting the greatest restriction on the attainment of primal objectives. The concept is particularly relevant to environmental quality planning and management because shadow prices often take the place of actual market prices as guides to valuation of environmental quality. As discussed in Chapter 3, market prices for environmental quality elements often do not exist.

Environmental Quality Objectives. Environmental quality effects can be incorporated into linear-programming models in several ways, depending on the nature of environmental quality objectives, technologies for discharge reductions, and implementation incentives. In situations in which economically feasible control technologies are unavailable, environmental quality effects can be regulated by *structural* methods, that is, by altering the composition of industrial outputs to meet environmental quality goals. If alternative technologies are available, *technical* means for reducing discharges can be implemented. Production methods can be modified to change the rates or composition of residuals discharged into the environment or, in situations in which demands for natural-systems inputs to production create a problem, different technologies can be used to lessen the effects. Discharges of particulates from electric power stations, for example, can be reduced by means of cyclones, electrostatic precipitators, or bag filters. Water requirements can be reduced by recycling cooling water rather than drawing water from a river on a "once through" basis. Some examples of the required modeling techniques are presented below.

Abating Pollution through Structural Changes

The Damage Cost Approach. This approach explicitly accounts for the social cost of damage to environmental quality caused by economic activity. Suppose, for the hypothetical example presented earlier, discharges of particulates and sulfur oxides shown in table 8.13 are estimated to occur when 2,000 MW of electricity are generated and 1,500 tourists visit the region.

Dividing each column entry by 2,000 and 1,500, respectively, yields the direct pollution coefficients per physical unit of output (table 8.14).

Suppose benefit-cost analysis reveals that the damage to environmental quality caused per ton of pollutant is $18.57 for particulates and $38.85 for SO_x. Each megawatt of electric power produced causes damage amounting to $6,400 (240 × 18.57 + 50 × 38.85). The true economic value of electric power output per megawatt is the market price minus damage costs—that is, $8,000 − $6,400, or $1,600. Similar calculations for tourism reveal that the net annual economic value to the community of each tourist is $5,000. These "true" economic values for x_1 and x_2 should be substituted for p_1 and p_2 in the primal problem, giving the following objective function:

maximize $1600 x_1 + 5,000 x_2$.

The new objective function has a flatter slope than the old one, and the best solution now is obtained at point A in figure 8.2. Damage to environmental quality caused by the generation of electricity is so great that the region should not produce any electricity at all. Instead, it should put all of its available resources into tourism. Labor supplies restrict the total trade to 2,500 tourists a year, yet this still leads to annual emissions of 30,000 tons of particulates and 50,000 tons of SO_x.

Emission Standards. Emission standards are a common practical approach to the management of environmental quality and can be administered at three different levels: first, for individual plants or industries; second, in terms of total regional source emissions; and third, as ambient environmental quality standards.

Plant emission standards based on structural abatement policies lead to

Table 8.13. Estimated Discharges of Pollutants (Tons per Year)

	Industries	
Pollutant	Electric power	Tourism
Particulates	480,000	18,000
SO_x	100,000	30,000

Table 8.14. Pollution Coefficients

Pollutant	Industries	
	Electric power (tons of pollutant/MW/yr)	Tourism (tons of pollutant/tourist/yr)
Particulates	240	12
SO_x	50	20

quite simple linear-programming treatments. If, for example, environmental quality authorities wished to reduce annual emissions from electricity generation to 192,000 tons for particulates and 80,000 tons for SO_x and were not concerned with discharges from tourist activities, the following constraints would have to be added to the original primal problem:

$$240 \ x_1 \ \leq \ 192,000,$$

$$50 \ x_1 \ \leq \ 80,000. \tag{8-12}$$

The new solution appears in figure 8.4. Only one of the environmental quality constraints (for particulates) is binding. Electric power generation should be restricted to only 800 MW and tourism expanded from 1,500 to 2,100 visitors per year (point D). Note that the total value of regional production will now be $\$8,000 \times 800 + 6,000 \times 2,100$, or \$19 million. Comparing

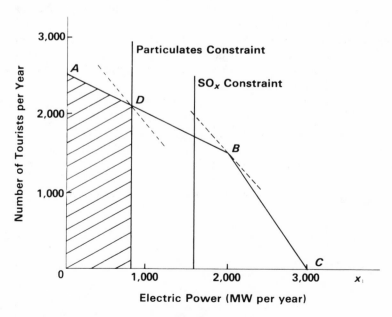

Figure 8.4 Power plant emissions constraints.

this with the unconstrained economic optimum, at which $25 million is earned, the model reveals that achievement of this level of environmental quality would cost the region $6 million per year. At least $6 million per year in environmental quality benefits would need to accrue before this policy could be judged desirable on the grounds of economic efficiency.

The second type of standard is total regional emissions. Policy makers might wish, for example, to restrict total particulate emissions from electricity and tourism to 430,000 tons per year and SO_x to 110,000 tons per year. To model this, one would take the original linear program and add the following environmental quality constraints:

$$240 \, x_1 + 12 \, x_2 \leq 430{,}000,$$

$$50 \, x_1 + 20 \, x_2 \leq 110{,}000. \tag{8-13}$$

The original objective function is still used, and a new solution is obtained where $x_1 = 1{,}500$ and $x_2 = 1{,}750$. Total regional revenue falls to $22.5 million. The outcome (point E) is described in figure 8.5.

The dual of this problem takes the form

$$\text{minimize } 900 \, w_1 + 5{,}000 \, w_2 + 430{,}000 \, w_3 + 110{,}000 \, w_4$$

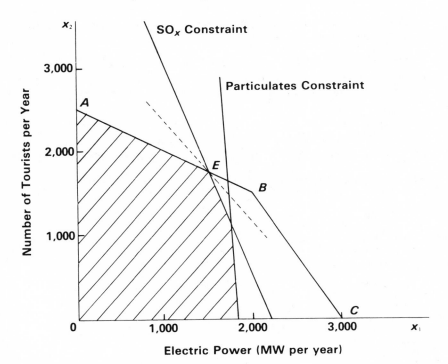

Figure 8.5 Regional emissions constraints.

subject to

$$0.3\ w_1 + 1.0\ w_2 + 240\ w_3 + 50\ w_4 \geq 8,000,$$

$$1.0\ w_1 + 2.0\ w_2 + 12\ w_3 + 20\ w_4 \geq 6,000,$$

$$w_1, w_2, w_3, w_4 \geq 0. \tag{8--14}$$

The solution values for the dual are $w_1 = 0$, $w_2 = 1,750$, $w_3 = 0$, and $w_4 = 125$. It will be seen that only two shadow prices are positive, reflecting the fact that only two constraints (for labor and for SO_x) are binding in the primal problem. The shadow price for SO_x is \$125, indicating that if the standard were relaxed by 1 ton, total regional revenue would rise by this amount. Sensitivity analysis would give decision makers further information about the trade-offs between regional revenue and standards for individual pollutants.

The third approach to standard setting—regional management of ambient environmental quality—requires adding special characteristics and a dispersion model to the basic framework. Because the mathematical treatment of this approach becomes very cumbersome unless matrix notation is employed, the topic will not be developed further here. Good descriptions of such models can be found in Kneese and Bower (1979) and Muller (1979), among others.

An Application of Linear Programming: Air Quality Management in the Rijnmond Region, Netherlands

Linear programming has been used extensively to devise air quality management programs for the Rijnmond Region in the Netherlands. In a study by Muller (1979), the optimal economic structure of production for the region was found by maximizing income from existing activities. Constraints were introduced for the labor supply, agricultural output, and intermediate production requirements ascertained through an input-output matrix. The best industrial structure is indicated in the first column of table 8.15. The actual produc-

Table 8.15. Production Structure with a Maximum Income, Rijnmond

Sector	Optimal production (fl, millions)	Gross production 1965 (fl, millions)
1. Agriculture	43.1	152.4
2. Oil and chemicals	36,993.4	4,714.5
3. Machinery	640.0	1,314.2
4. Other metals	314.8	371.2
5. Construction	1,740.8	1,242.5
6. Public utilities	455.7	252.6
7. Real estate	277.0	277.0
8. Transportation	197.4	2,682.9
9. Other industries	1,143.0	2,681.4
10. Other services	2,741.4	3,348.5
Associated total income	16,184.1	7,614.1

Source: Muller (1979).

Table 8.16. Emission Coefficients, Rijnmond

Sector	SO₂	CO	NOₓ	HF	Particulates
			Pollutant		
1. Agriculture	30.774	7.874	5.708		1.312
2. Oil and chemicals	16.617	21.945	11.079	0.089	0.856
3. Machinery	4.254	1.522	1.004		0.426
4. Other metals	28.287	727.371	17.457	1.751	13.470
5. Construction	4.140	1.402	0.948		4.124
6. Public utilities	128.483	61.830	45.342		12.861
7. Real estate	13.646	27.292	18.592		31.408
8. Transportation	0.242	1.211	0.485		3.709
9. Other industries	2.019	0.673	0.444		0.201
10. Other services	0.227	20.896	0.693		

Note: Figures are stated as metric tons per million guilders of product, 1965.
Source: Muller (1979).

tion levels in 1965 appear in the second column. The model suggests that a reallocation of labor in 1965 would have led to a more efficient program of production. Total income could have reached (fl)16,184 million (1 guilder equals US$0.40) instead of the actual income of (fl)7,614 million.

Emission coefficients are reproduced in table 8.16. These were multiplied into the economically optimal production structure in table 8.15 to obtain emissions of five pollutants. A dispersion model was then used to translate these emissions into ambient concentrations for different receptor points within in the region (table 8.17).

Ambient concentration standards were then introduced (table 8.18) and income was maximized subject to these and the original economic constraints. Because alternative residuals discharge technologies were not assumed, environmental quality constraints could be met only by changing the composition of production. The best economic-environmental quality solution is given

Table 8.17. Calculated Air Pollution Concentrations Implied by a Production Structure with Maximum Income (μg/m³), Rijnmond

Receptor point	SO₂	CO	NOₓ	HF	Particulates
1. Oostvoorne	822.8	2,180.4	1,022.6	7.9	196.3
2. Vlaardingen	863.0	2,276.4	1,097.6	8.7	210.7
3. Maassluis	926.7	2,471.3	1,181.0	9.4	207.3
4. Rotterdam	1,118.7	2,810.5	1,374.5	10.3	270.1
5. Hoek van Holland	1,075.6	2,877.6	1,381.9	11.0	242.8
Standard	350	10,300	100	3	240

Source: Muller (1979).

Table 8.18. Ambient Air Concentration Standards, Rijnmond (Averaging Time = 24 Hours)

Pollutant	Standards
Sulfur dioxide	350 $\mu g/m^3$ (National Health Council)
Nitrogen oxides	100 $\mu g/m^3$ (standard of NO_2, SWA Commission)
Carbon monoxide	10,300 $\mu g/m^3$ (one-third of the hourly standard, SWA Commission)
Hydrogen fluoride	3 $\mu g/m^3$ (Yocom 1970)
Small particulates	240 $\mu g/m^3$ (Rotterdam Council 1970)

Source: Muller (1979).

in table 8.19. The actual production levels in 1965 are shown again for comparative purposes. Regional income in the suggested optimum could be higher than actual income, but is much less than the income level associated with the best economic solution with no environmental quality constraints, as in table 8.15.

Another conclusion yielded by the model is that in moving from the actual 1965 production levels to the best economic-environmental quality solution, the labor force would still be fully used. Thus, simply by reallocating resources, an improvement in the quality of the environment could be obtained without creating unemployment or sustaining a decline in actual income. Shadow prices were computed to test the sensitivity of results to arbitrary changes in standards. It was discovered that the standard for nitrogen oxides at Rotterdam had a highly restrictive effect on income.

Reducing Discharges with Technical Means

Technical reduction of discharges is aptly illustrated by an air pollution emission control model developed by Kohn (1975) for the St. Louis, Missouri (United States) airshed. Kohn assumes that several discharge reduction pro-

Table 8.19. Optimal Production Structure within Environmental Quality Constraints Shown in Table 8.18

Sector	Optimal gross production (fl, millions)	Gross production 1965 (fl, millions)
1. Agriculture	152.4	152.4
2. Oil and chemicals	724.1	4,714.5
3. Machinery	447.5	1,314.2
4. Other metals	5,222.7	371.2
5. Construction	1,213.3	1,242.5
6. Public utilities	201.7	242.6
7. Real estate	277.0	277.0
8. Transportation	148.6	2,682.9
9. Other industries	6,900.0	2,681.4
10. Other services	1,969.6	3,348.5
Associated total income	7,889.1	7,614.1

Source: Muller (1979).

cesses, each with different costs and emissions, can normally be used in the production of any commodity. The steel production process can use electrostatic precipitators, scrubbers, or precipitators and scrubbers combined. Electric power plants may have precipitators or a combination of precipitators and a desulfurization plant. A set of variables $x_1, x_2, \ldots, x_n$ represents the activity levels of all alternative processes. Kohn's model minimizes the total annualized incremental cost of meeting prescribed limits on total emissions of various air pollutants (not ambient air quality standards) while simultaneously satisfying minimum total production levels. The objective function of the model, as a hypothetical example, takes the following form:

minimize

$$\$0.00x_1 + \$0.10x_2 + \$0.25x_3 + \$0.00x_4 + \$1.20x_5$$

subject to

$$
\begin{aligned}
7x_1 + 4x_2 + 3x_3 + 3x_4 + 2x_5 &\leq 8,000,000 \ (i), \\
13x_1 + 13x_2 + 13x_3 + 118x_4 + 12x_5 &\leq 40,000,000 \ (ii), \\
2x_1 + 2x_2 + 2x_3 + 20x_4 + 16x_5 &\leq 35,000,000 \ (iii), \\
x_1 + x_2 + x_3 &= 1,000,000 \ (iv), \\
x_4 + x_5 &= 2,000,000 \ (v).
\end{aligned}
\qquad (8-15)
$$

The first three activity levels (x_1, x_2, and x_3) are outputs of steel from different processes measured in tons per year. As shown in equation *(iv)*, 1,000,000 tons of steel must be produced from the three processes. The last two activities (x_4 and x_5) represent different processes for electric energy generation, measured in terms of annual coal consumption in tons. Altogether, 2,000,000 tons of coal must be used, as in equation *(v)*.

The coefficients in equations *(i)*, *(ii)*, and *(iii)* are emission coefficients, measured in pounds per unit of output. The first constraint is for particulates, restricting total annual emissions to 8,000,000 pounds. Constraints *(ii)* and *(iii)* limit total emissions of sulfur dioxide and nitrogen oxides, respectively.

Process x_1 is assumed to be already in use for steel production, as is process x_4 for electricity generation. These have zero incremental control costs, as is evident in the objective function. Extra costs would be incurred, however, if other processes were used. Process x_5 in the electricity sector, for example, would involve an incremental cost of $1.20 for every ton of coal used in that process.

The solution to the above problem is $x_1 = 0$, $x_2 = 971,698$, $x_3 = 28,302$, $x_4 = 28,302$, and $x_5 = 1,971,698$. In this solution, current methods of production in the steel industry would be discontinued, and process x_2 would be heavily used instead, with some production from process x_3. Electricity would be produced mainly with process x_5, but some is still desirable from the existing process, x_4. The total annualized incremental cost of meeting the standards (the value of the objective function) is $2,470,283.

Table 8.20. Shadow Prices for Air Pollutants

Pollutant constrained	Price ($ per pound)
Carbon monoxide	0.00428
Hydrocarbons	0.02476
NO_x	0.32639
SO_x	0.02193
Particulates	0.07748

Source: Kohn (1975).

The full-scale operational model developed by Kohn had twenty-three sectors and five air pollutants. As in Muller's model, estimates were made of ambient air quality levels under alternative sets of emission limits. Shadow prices for emission constraints were also computed (table 8.20). Note that, as in the Rijnmond study, the highest shadow price applies to nitrogen oxides.

Mixed Integer-Linear Programming

One of the limitations of the ordinary linear-programming approach to technical pollution abatement is that multiple processes may be selected to meet prescribed outputs. This may not be feasible in the real world from an engineering viewpoint. For both steel and electricity production in Kohn's hypothetical model, two processes appeared for each industry in the optimal solution. In reality, a given plant or industry often has to decide on only one process. This can be handled in modeling terms by integer programming. Assuming that other activities can be accurately represented by a linear-programming framework, a mixed-integer linear-programming model for a regional system can be constructed.

As a simple hypothetical example, consider a model designed to assist planning and management of the coal-electric cycle. Suppose coal is obtained from a single mine (output represented by x_1) and is put through a coal washery (output x_2). A total quantity of coal, (q), has to be transported, and this can be done by road, x_3, rail, x_4, or sea, x_5. These variables can be modeled by ordinary linear programming. Electric power may be produced by three different processes, but only one is permitted. The required output level for electricity is represented by s, and activity levels for the three alternative technologies by x_6, x_7, and x_8. The unit cost of each activity in the cycle is denoted c_j. There are m different types of residuals discharged by each activity, determined by a set of emission coefficients, e_{kj}. Emissions from the entire fuel cycle are not permitted to exceed levels denoted by e_k^*.

The programming model minimizes the total costs of production for the coal-electric cycle, subject to total emission constraints and specified output levels for mined coal, x_1^*, washed coal, x_2^*, transport, q, and electricity, s. Because these activities are interdependent, required activity levels in many situations can be specified as functions of the end product, electricity. The form of the model is as follows:

$$\text{minimize } c_1 x_1 + c_2 x_2 + \ldots + c_8 x_8$$

subject to

$$
\begin{aligned}
x_1 &= x_1^* , \\
x_2 &= x_2^* , \\
x_3 + x_4 + x_5 &= q , \\
x_6 - \delta_1 s &> 0 , \\
x_7 - \delta_2 s &> 0 , \\
x_8 - \delta_3 s &> 0 ,
\end{aligned}
$$

$$
\begin{aligned}
e_{11}x_1 + e_{12}x_2 + \ldots\ldots\ldots + e_{18}x_8 &< e_1^* , \\
e_{21}x_1 + e_{22}x_2 + \ldots\ldots\ldots + e_{28}x_8 &< e_2^* ,
\end{aligned}
$$

.
.
.

$$
\begin{aligned}
e_{m1}x_1 + e_{m2}x_2 + \ldots\ldots\ldots + e_{m8}x_8 &< e_m^* , \\
\delta_1 + \delta_2 + \delta_3 &= 1 , \\
0 < \delta_1 < 1 \qquad \delta_i \text{ an integer} , \\
x_1, x_2, \ldots\ldots\ldots, x_8 &> 0 .
\end{aligned}
\tag{8--16}
$$

An Application of Integer Programming. Burton and Sanjour (1970) used an integer-programming model to study cost-effective methods of controlling air quality in the Kansas City (United States) area. Attention was focused on reduction of SO_2 and particulates emissions from coal combustion. Various technical measures for residuals discharge reduction were examined. Four examples appear in table 8.21. Altogether, seventeen distinct discharge reduction strategies were modeled. Burton and Sanjour used a

Table 8.21. Alternative Emission Reduction Techniques and Levels

Alternative	Level
1. Substitute low-sulfur coal (reduces SO_2 emissions)	1. 2% sulfur 2. 1.5% sulfur 3. 1.0% sulfur
2. Install precipitator (reduces particulate emissions)	1. Low efficiency 2. Medium efficiency 3. High efficiency
3. Switch to oil (reduces SO_2 and particulates)	1. 2% sulfur 2. 1.5% sulfur 3. 1.0% sulfur
4. Switch to natural gas (reduces SO_2 and particulates)	1. Interruptible (95% gas, 5% light oil) 2. Firm (100% gas)

Source: Burton and Sanjour (1970).

computer search technique for examining all feasible combinations and their associated costs and emission levels.

A dispersion model was introduced to determine ambient concentrations in spatial terms. The least-cost method of reaching specified ambient air quality standards was ascertained and comparisons made with four other strategies: (1) a ban on fossil fuels with more than 1% sulfur; (2) equiproportional reduction of emissions; (3) maximum reduction of particulates alone; and (4) maximum reduction of particulates and sulfur oxides together. Maps were presented showing ambient concentrations of SO_2 and particulates under the alternative strategies. Although it was possible to calculate the costs of different strategies, shadow prices for levels of reduction were not ascertainable. This is a general characteristic of integer-programming models.

Some Limitations of Linear Programming

Like most general-equilibrium models, linear-programming models require much data gathering, information processing, and computing time. The planner must decide whether the problem is really so complex that an elaborate model needs to be constructed.

Another possible obstacle is the derivation of planners' and decision makers' values. These must be determined in a very specific way to be incorporated in a programming model. It may be quite confusing to decision makers if they are asked to place relative weights on economic and environmental quality variables. Cost-minimization exercises, subject to environmental quality constraints, could be the best approach if decision makers are reluctant to reveal their preferences. Expert assistance can be obtained from economists and engineers in estimating costs and from scientists and health authorities in establishing sensible environmental quality standards. Sensitivity analysis should provide a reasonable range of trade-offs from which a final option could be chosen.

The mathematical properties of linear-programming models often lead to unrealistic solutions. One characteristic of such models is "flip-flop" changes in solutions when weights in the objective function are changed. As shown in figure 8.2, for example, subtraction of damage costs from market values of tourism and electric power generation leads to an optimum at point A, where no electric power should be produced. This is quite an extreme result. In complex situations, major shifts in mixes of activities can occur. Further constraints can, of course, overcome this problem, but in a large model it may be difficult to tell where the extra constraints must be added.

Another feature of linear programming is that the number of variables in the final solution can never exceed the number of constraints. If only a few basic constraints are specified, either the solution may turn out to be overly simplistic, or further arbitrary constraints might need to be incorporated, thereby possibly invalidating true restrictions on the attainment of planning objectives. In addition, simplistic solutions to the primal problem create difficulties with shadow prices in the dual. Unless a constraint is binding, the associated factor has a zero shadow price. This occurred, for instance, in the dual problem corresponding to figure 8.4. At the optimal point, D, only the supply of labor and the constraint on particulates were responsible for the final solution. The SO_x and investment constraints were redundant, leading to zero shadow prices for w_1 and w_4.

Substitution possibilities and nonlinearities can be introduced into a model using linear approximation methods, but further data collection, estimation, and computing effort are required. A nonlinear simulation module for an aquatic ecosystem was, for example, used in the Delaware Valley model (Spofford, Russell, and Kelly 1976), but many difficulties were experienced. This module has since been replaced with a linear Streeter-Phelps dissolved oxygen module so that the entire model now has a strictly linear-programming form.

In addition, it is difficult to accommodate realistic situations involving joint costs and economies of scale in linear programming approaches.

Despite all of these drawbacks, the trouble and expense of constructing linear-programming models for regional environmental quality management may still be worthwhile. Better results are not likely to be achieved through ad hoc methods.

OTHER MODELS

Input-output analysis and linear programming are only two approaches to economic-environmental quality modeling. Nonlinear programming, in which a nonlinear objective function and/or a nonlinear constraint set is used, can be applied to certain problems (Olson et al. 1977). Optimization models can also be converted to dynamic forms whereby an objective function is maximized over time, subject to restrictions that define permissible rates of change of the variables in the system. Although these approaches may have strong theoretical appeal, data collection can be a serious problem. Moreover, if the model has a large number of variables, obtaining solutions usually involves a great deal of computer time. As with simpler optimization procedures, costs and benefits can be incorporated in nonlinear and dynamic optimization models. The Dynamic Energy System Optimization Model (DE-SOM), developed by Brookhaven National Laboratory (EPRI 1979) to analyze alternative energy technologies, minimizes the present value of a stream of costs incurred in various forms of energy production over time, subject to constraints on primary energy supplies, energy demands, energy conversion efficiencies, and environmental quality tolerances. DESOM was designed to guide energy system development planning at the national level but can also be applied in a regional setting.

Another technique that is frequently used as an environmental planning and management tool is dynamic simulation modeling. A set of equations describes the economic-environmental system. The equations are set up on an electronic computer, and the behavior of the system is simulated by arbitrarily varying the parameters of the model and recording the results. A new computer run must be carried out for each combination of initial assumptions. The technique is particularly useful in studying systems that have complex interactions, time lags, and nonlinear properties. It has been widely used to assist with the management of fisheries, forestry, and wildlife.

An interesting application of simulation modeling is the regional development study of the Rio Caroni Basin in the state of Bolivar, Venezuela (Holling 1978). The Rio Caroni Basin is a watershed for a large hydroelectric scheme (the Guri Hydroelectric Project). The first part of the Guri project was finished in 1977 and provided 2,650 MW of electricity to industry in the region. The second stage, scheduled to be completed in 1982, raises the generating capacity to 9,000 MW. Land use in the basin could affect the long-term efficiency of power generation. Vegetative cover is a major factor in controlling the absorption of rainwater, surface flows in wet and dry seasons, and the rate of soil loss and deposition in the reservoir through erosion. More than half of the catchment is covered with forests. Agriculture and logging are

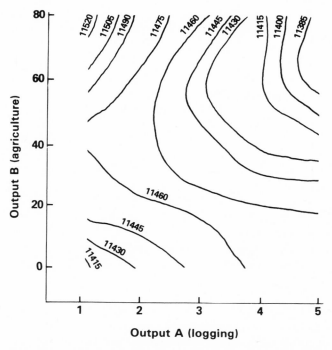

Figure 8.6 Total net benefits as a function of levels of agriculture and logging output: year fifty of simulation run of Guri hydroelectric project, Venezuela (millions of Bolivars [B]; US$1.0 = B4.3). (*Source:* Holling, 1978.)

expanding; both represent threats to the forested areas and, indirectly, to the successful operation of the hydroelectric scheme.

A mathematical model of the basin was constructed to describe the interactions of rainfall, soil, vegetation, water flows, and soil erosion. Two types of land-use activity affecting vegetative cover were then introduced: activity A, representing the rate of logging, measured as the area of forest subject to exploitation; and activity B, indicating the area of forest land replaced by agriculture. Simulations for twenty-five combinations of the two activities were then carried out, assessing the effects on timber production, crop yields, and electricity production over a period of fifty years.

Net benefits of each type of output (agriculture, timber, and electricity) were estimated. Total net benefits as a function of the two types of activity are described in diagrammatic form in figure 8.6. The highest level of net benefits arises with a low level of activity A (logging) combined with a high level of activity B (agriculture). Various constraints (on average rates of hydroelectric power generation and on ecological deterioration) were superimposed on this diagram to determine optimal feasible levels of activities A and B.

APPENDIX

Matrix Formulation of Input-Output Model

Total outputs must meet the condition

$$x_t = Ax_t + f_t, \tag{8A-1}$$

where x is the vector of total outputs by sector, A is the matrix of direct requirements coefficients, f is the vector of final demands, and t represents time periods.

The model is solved as follows, where I is an identity matrix:

$$(I - A) x_t = f_t, \tag{8A-2}$$

$$x_t = (I - A)^{-1} f_t. \tag{8A-3}$$

The Leontief inverse matrix is $(I - A)^{-1}$.

Economic inputs are represented by the vector q and determined by solving the equation system below, where B is the matrix of supplementary economic coefficients:

$$q_t = Bx_t. \tag{8A-4}$$

Environmental quality effects, summarized by the vector r, are obtained in the same way, making use of the environmental quality coefficients matrix E:

$$r_t = Ex_t, \tag{8A-5}$$

$$\text{since } x_t = (I - A)^{-1} f_t, \tag{8A-6}$$

$$r_t = E(I - A)^{-1} f_t.$$ (8A–7)

The cumulated environmental quality coefficient matrix is defined as

$$C = E(I - A)^{-1},$$ (8A–8)

permitting r to be determined as a function of final demands, as in the equation

$$r_t = Cf_t.$$ (8A–9)

REFERENCES

Ayres, R. U., and F. Gutmanis. "Technological Change, Pollution and Treatment Cost in Input-Output Analysis." In *Report,* U.S. Commission on Population, Resources and the Environment, Washington, D.C., 1972.

Bower, B. T., ed. *Regional Residuals Environmental Quality Management Modeling.* Washington, D.C.: Resources for the Future, 1975.

Burton, E., and W. Sanjour. "A Simulation Approach to Air Pollution Abatement Program Planning." *Socio-Economic Planning Sciences* 4, 1 (1970): 147–59.

Cumberland, J. H., and B. N. Stram. "Empirical Results from Application of Input-Output Models to Environmental Problems." Paper presented to Sixth International Conference on Input-Output Techniques, 1974, Vienna.

EPRI. *Dynamic Energy System Optimization Model.* Report No. EA1079. Palo Alto, Calif.: EPRI, 1979.

Försund, F. R., and S. Strom. "Industrial Structure, Growth and Residuals Flows." In *The Management of Water Quality and the Environment,* ed. J. G. Rothenberg and I. G. Heggie. London: Macmillan, 1976.

Hite, J. D., and E. A. Laurent. *Environmental Planning: An Economic Analysis.* New York: Praeger, 1972.

Holling, C. S., ed. *Adaptive Environmental Assessment and Management.* New York: Wiley-Interscience, 1978.

House, P. W. *Trading Off Environment, Economics and Energy.* Lexington, Mass.: Heath, 1977.

James, D. E. "A System of Energy Accounts for Australia." *Economic Record* 56, 153 (June 1980): 171–81.

————. "General-Equilibrium Modelling of Environmental Damage: Energy Use and Combustion Emissions in Australia." In *Economic Approaches to Natural Resource and Environmental Quality Analysis,* ed. M. M. Hufschmidt and E. L. Hyman. Dublin: Tycooly International, 1982.

James, D. E.; H.M.A. Jansen; and J. B. Opschoor. *Economic Approaches to Environmental Problems.* Amsterdam: Elsevier, 1978.

Jansen, H.M.A.; A. A. Olsthoorn; J. B. Opschoor; J.H.A. Stapel; J. B. Vos; and J. L. ten Broek. *Economic Structure and Environmental Pollution in the Netherlands.* Amsterdam: Institute for Environmental Problems, Free University, 1978.

Kneese, A. V., and B. T. Bower. *Environmental Quality and Residuals Management.* Baltimore: Johns Hopkins University Press, 1979.

Kohn, R. "Input-Output Analysis and Air Pollution Control." In *Economic Analysis of Environmental Problems,* ed. E. S. Mills. New York: Columbia University Press, 1975.

Leontief, W., and D. Ford. "Air Pollution and the Economic Structure: Empirical Results of

Input-Output Computations." In *Input-Output Techniques,* ed. A. Brody and A. P. Carter. Amsterdam: North Holland, 1972.

Macrakis, M. S., ed. *Energy: Demand, Conservation and Institutional Problems.* Cambridge, Mass.: MIT Press, 1976.

Meister, A. D.; E. O. Heady; K. J. Nicol; and R. W. Strohbehn. *U.S. Agricultural Production in Relation to Alternative Water, Environmental and Export Policies.* Ames, Iowa: Center for Agricultural and Rural Development, Iowa State University, 1976.

Miernyk, W. H., and J. T. Sears. *Air Pollution Abatement and Regional Economic Development.* Lexington, Mass.: Heath, 1974.

Muller, F. *Energy and Environment in Interregional Input-Output Models.* The Hague: Martinus Nijhoff, 1979.

Olson, K. D.; E. O. Heady; C. C. Chen; and A. D. Meister. "Estimated Impacts of Two Environmental Alternatives in Agriculture; a Quadratic Programming Analysis." *CARD Report 72.* Ames, Iowa: Center for Agricultural and Rural Development, Iowa State University, March 1977.

OECD. *Macro-economic Evaluation of Environmental Programmes.* Paris 1978.

Ridker, R. G. "The Economy, Resource Requirements and Pollution Levels." In *Report,* U.S. Commission on Population, Resources and the Environment, Washington, D.C., 1972.

Russell, C. S. *Residuals Management in Industry: A Case Study of Petroleum Refining.* Baltimore: Johns Hopkins University Press, 1973.

Russell, C. S., and W. J. Vaughan. *Steel Production: Processes, Products and Residuals.* Baltimore: Johns Hopkins University Press, 1976.

Shefer, D. "Forecasting Industrial Air Pollution in the Haifa Bay Area with an Input-Output Model." *Socio-Economic Planning Sciences* 7, 5 (1973): 397–406.

Spofford, W. O.; C. S. Russell; and R. A. Kelly. *Environmental Quality Management.* Washington, D.C.: Resources for the Future, 1976.

Victor, P. A. *Pollution: Economy and Environment.* London: Allen and Unwin, 1972.

Bibliography of
Key References

Basta, D. J.; J. L. Lounsbury; and B. T. Bower. *Analysis for Residuals-Environmental Quality Management: A Case Study of the Ljubljana Area of Yugoslavia*. Research Paper R–11. Washington, D.C.: Resources for the Future, 1978.

This is a report of an application of the RFF "regional residuals-environmental quality management" approach to a five-commune area of 350 square miles and population of about 250,000 in northwestern Yugoslavia. This area was selected because it would enable the REQM approach to be tested in a real-world context that was poor in data for analysis, and because it provided a test of the approach in a socioeconomic and political context that was significantly different from the United States, Canada, or Western Europe. The report first presents the conceptual framework of REQM and then describes how the method would be applied to the study area by (1) defining the conditions for analysis, (2) selecting an analytical methodology, (3) defining study outputs, and (4) allocating available resources for the study. Actual application is reported in terms of (1) analysis of activities that generate and discharge residuals, (2) natural-systems models used for estimating the effects of residuals on ambient environmental quality, and (3) alternative combinations of physical measures, with associated implementation incentives, developed to achieve selected environmental quality targets for the study area.

This report represents a good example of specific application of the analytical and planning methods set forth in Chapters 4 and 5 of the *Guide*.

Basta, D. J., and B. T. Bower, eds. *Analyzing Natural Systems: Analysis for Regional Residuals-Environmental Quality Management*. Washington, D.C.: Resources for the Future, 1982.

Within the framework of analysis for regional residuals-environmental quality management (REQM), this volume provides four types of useful information. The first is a general introduction to analyzing natural systems, particularly in terms of the two basic approaches to such analysis, namely, statistical and conservation of mass and energy. The second consists of three more detailed chapters on

321

analyzing land surface runoff, surface bodies of water, and the atmosphere. The third is a set of summary tables of the characteristics of operational models for the foregoing three types of natural systems. Finally, a procedure is presented for selecting one or more natural-systems models, as needed, in any given analytical context.

Bower, B. T. "Studies of Residuals Management in Industry." In *Economic Analysis of Environmental Problems*, ed. E. S. Mills. New York: National Bureau of Economic Research, 1975.

This paper reviews the analytical approaches used in a set of studies at Resources for the Future (RFF) of various industrial activities, in relation to the factors that affect the generation and discharge of residuals into the environment. Both individual activities and linked activities, e.g., coal mining, coal preparation, coal or energy transport, and coal combustion for energy generation, are included. These studies involve identifying the relevant unit processes and operations for each type of activity, estimating materials and energy balances for each of the unit processes and operations, estimating residuals generated for various combinations of prices of factor inputs, and estimating responses to various sets of effluent standards or effluent charges imposed on the given activity.

Bower, B. T., ed. *Regional Residuals Environmental Quality Management Modeling.* Research Paper R–7. Washington, D.C.: Resources for the Future, 1977.

This report contains summary descriptions of several regional environmental quality models developed with RFF leadership and support during the 1970s. Following two introductory chapters on the concepts and management issues of "Regional Residuals Environmental Quality Management Modeling," four case study applications are summarized. The most detailed and complex study is the "Lower Delaware Valley Integrated Residuals Management Model," in which regional airborne, waterborne, and solid residuals are handled in an integrated system. Summaries are also presented of the application of regional modeling to the Ljubljana area in Yugoslavia, the Ostrava area in Czechoslovakia, and the upper Colorado River Basin in the United States. Through the summaries of the four cases and the associated commentaries, this report highlights the opportunities, limitations, and problems of applying this regional approach to several different real-life settings.

Cooper, C. M. *Economic Evaluation and the Environment.* London: Hodder and Stoughton for the United Nations Environment Programme (UNEP), 1981.

This study forms part of UNEP's activities in developing techniques for evaluating the economic and social consequences of environmental effects of development. The book is aimed as much at policy makers and environmental scientists as at economists. As a result, economic jargon is consciously avoided wherever possible and considerable attention is devoted to questions that noneconomists frequently find of particular interest. Early parts of the book raise such issues as whether economic evaluation is objective and what are valid economic bases for evaluating environmental damages. Cooper provides answers to questions and complaints commonly heard from noneconomists when economic evaluation of the environment is being discussed. The chapters on risk and uncertainty, social rates of discount and long-run environmental costs, and alternatives to benefit-cost analysis are useful and complement areas not extensively covered in the *Guide*. In general, the exposition is clear and logical and relies on verbal and graphical explanations rather than on mathematical ones. The book does not provide a detailed listing of valuation techniques with examples; its main strength is its systematic discussion of how economic analysis can be used to value the environment. The assumptions behind economic analysis, as well as its potential and limitations, are explored to help noneconomists better understand what economic analysis can and cannot do.

Dorfman, R., and N. S. Dorfman, eds. *Economics of the Environment: Selected Readings,* 2d ed. New York: Norton, 1977.

The second edition of this popular reader contains most of the articles originally appearing in the 1972 edition. While the book is not suitable for use as a textbook or as a reference for individual valuation techniques, it presents a number of important and provocative articles on various aspects of the use of economics in valuing the environment. The wide range of interests and perspectives of the authors is reflected in the selected readings, and the divergence between opposing views is illuminating. The book is divided into five sections and covers an introductory overview, economic analysis and the environment, environmental protection policies, long-run dynamics of resource use, and the measurement of costs and benefits. While it does not provide a unified exposition of environmental economics, the book does present thought-provoking essays on important facets of the field by leading economists such as Arrow, Tobin, Mishan, Dorfman, and Solow.

Freeman, A. M. III. *The Benefits of Environmental Improvement: Theory and Practice.* Baltimore: Johns Hopkins University Press for Resources for the Future, 1979.

The measurement of benefits from environmental improvements is the topic of this book. The basic theory behind the measurement of welfare for individuals and society is covered, with a focus on compensating and equivalent measurements of welfare changes. Various approaches to benefit measurement are covered: techniques based on market data as well as on nonmarket data (surveys and voting). Property value approaches, including those based on hedonic prices, are covered in detail. Measurements based on health, recreation, and productivity benefits are also included. This book is well written, clearly organized and heavily referenced. It does not provide detailed examples of the techniques discussed but does give a good explanation of the theoretical bases of the various approaches and a lucid discussion of application within the policy framework. This book is closely related to the techniques outlined in Chapter 6 of the *Guide*.

Holling, C. S., ed. *Adaptive Environmental Assessment and Management*. New York: Wiley, 1978.

This book was written for policy makers and managers dissatisfied with the traditional procedures and principles used in environmental impact assessment and management. The first ten chapters describe the steps used in designing an adaptive environmental assessment and management (AEAM) project. The emphasis of the whole program is to affect decision making. To achieve this, a series of workshops is used for problem definition, model building, and communication with senior administrators. To create a sense of joint effort in model building leading to cooperation and acceptance of the results and recommendations, workshop participants must include disciplinary specialists, modeling experts, and decision makers. Although techniques dealing with multiple activity modeling such as the Leopold matrix are discussed, the main focus is on simulation models. Model structure emphasizes an understandable "comprehensible simplification" instead of detailed complexity. For communicating the results, instead of the conventional lengthy and detailed written reports the AEAM approach uses workshops, narrated slide presentations, and pictures and graphs including nomograms. In Part II, case studies of forest, fishery, and wildlife management and of regional resource development provide examples of simulation models used for analyzing situations involving multiple activities.

Hufschmidt, M. M., and E. L. Hyman, eds. *Economic Approaches to Natural Resource and Environmental Quality Analysis*. Dublin: Tycooly International, 1982.

This book is a compendium of papers presented at, and a report of proceedings of, a Conference on Extended Benefit-Cost Analysis held at the Environment and Policy Institute, East-West Center, in Honolulu in September 1979. The report of conference proceedings and the keynote paper present useful summaries of many different approaches and techniques for economic analysis of environmental and natural resource aspects of development. Nine papers deal with general theoretical and methodological issues of environmental and resource economics; three papers present national aspects of environmental economics and management in Malaysia, Indonesia, and Sri Lanka; two papers are concerned with international and global aspects of environmental analysis; and, finally, two papers present the results of case studies of watershed conservation in a reservoir project in Ecuador and bauxite mining and environmental protection in Western Australia.

This compendium contains much valuable background information on theory and applications of environmental and resource economics by a number of experienced scholars and practitioners. Of special interest are the findings and recommendations of the conference participants on future actions that the Environment and Policy Institute should take: actions that have led to the preparation of this *Guide* and of supporting case studies.

Hyman, E. L. "The Valuation of Extramarket Benefits and Costs in Environmental Impact Assessment." *Environmental Impact Assessment Review* 2, 3 (September 1981): 227–64.

This article presents a careful summary of currently available techniques used to value extramarket (unpriced) benefits and costs. The techniques are divided into five categories: (1) economic surrogates for unpriced benefits and costs, including the travel cost, property value, and wage differential approaches; (2) supply-side approaches such as replacement cost, defensive expenditure, and cost-effectiveness analysis; (3) hypothetical valuation based on willingness to pay or willingness to accept compensation as determined by bidding games and use estimation games; (4) trade-off analyses that rely on choices between packages of goods rather than the subjective placing of monetary values on various outcomes as is done in the hypothetical valuation approaches; and (5) human capital approaches that attempt to place monetary values on illness and death. For each set of techniques Hyman discusses their theoretical validity, ease of data collection, and problems of reliability and bias. The discussion of possible biases in bidding and use-estimation games is particularly interesting. While examples of the various techniques are not presented in the article, extensive references to the current literature are provided.

Krutilla, J. V., and A. C. Fisher. *The Economics of Natural Environments*. Baltimore: Johns Hopkins University Press for Resources for the Future, 1975.

The valuation, allocation, and management of the resources found in the natural environment are the topics of this book. Based on work done at Resources for the Future, this book is aimed at policy makers as well as economists. Part I introduces the institutional and theoretical considerations involved in managing and valuing natural environments. In particular, the concept of irreversibility as it relates to resources and to economic decisions is covered, including such important concerns as determining the appropriate discount rate, the problem of intertemporal equity, and uncertainty and option value. The second part of the book contains several case studies of actual development decisions involving natural environments. The environments involved range from undeveloped mountain and river canyon areas or prairie wetlands to the Alaskan wilderness. In each case a proposed development project—a hydroelectric dam, a mine and smelter, a ski resort, a pipeline—is evaluated with respect to its impact on a desirable natural environment. Both the environmental effects of the proposed development and the benefits and costs of the development are discussed. In particular, questions relating to the opportunity cost of foregone development are explicitly considered. The examples illustrate how economic analysis and environmental concerns can be combined to evaluate these difficult development decisions involving relatively untouched natural environments.

OECD. *Macro-economic Evaluation of Environmental Programmes*. Paris, 1978.

The need for macro-type evaluation is not always obvious because in most cases environmental programs are expressed in emission or similar standards; the implications for public and private expenditures, and their consequences for growth, employment, prices, and balance of payments are not explicit. Macro-econometric models make dynamic analysis possible and allow international comparisons to be made when the same model is used. Five macro-economic models applied in four countries (Italy, Japan, the Netherlands, and the United States) are presented and discussed. All five models use an interindustry input-output table to analyze the impacts of environmental policies on prices, consumption, and exports. Each also includes a number of macro-economic relationships to modify the effects of price rises at an aggregate level and to allow the multiplier effects of committed expenditure to be explicit. This report provides examples in which input-output models have been applied. These examples illustrate the usefulness and the difficulty in applying input-output analysis to environmental problems. Among the difficulties are lack of data and problems in understanding the relationship between environmental variables and macro-economic variables.

Pearce, D. W., ed. *The Valuation of Social Cost.* London: Allen and Unwin, 1978.

This is a collection of eight papers about the theory of social cost measurement, especially when market prices are not available or do not reflect "true" social costs. The economic approaches discussed and appraised include the compensation approach, the property value concept, exclusion facility or preventive expenditure, and the valuation of human life. Environmental issues discussed include air and water pollution, damage to health, and benefits of recreational land use. The final chapter discusses the reasons why GNP is not an appropriate measure of a nation's "welfare." The collection represents a good coverage of the economic approaches discussed in Chapters 6 and 7 of the *Guide.*

Sinden, J. A., and A. C. Worrell. *Unpriced Values: Decisions Without Market Prices.* New York: Wiley, 1979.

Divided into three parts, this book presents a comprehensive overview of the problems associated with placing monetary values on various benefits and costs for which there are no market prices. The first part discusses the concepts of valuation and the basic economic theory of individual and social valuation. The second part is the heart of the book—a detailed discussion of many of the techniques used to determine unpriced values with illustrations of their application. The discussion of valuation approaches based on direct questioning (survey techniques) and market and land values is of particular interest. The third part of the book discusses the application of these techniques in actual decision making and how difficulties in their use can be overcome.

This book is somewhat difficult to use because discussion of some techniques is scattered across several chapters and the overall organization is confusing. Nevertheless, it contains much useful information. In particular, there is considerable detail on the various valuation techniques presented in Chapters 6 and 7 of the *Guide.* The extensive bibliographic references are useful.

Squire, L., and H. G. van der Tak. *Economic Analysis of Projects*. Baltimore: Johns Hopkins University Press for the World Bank, 1975.

This book is an extremely useful follow-up to the economic analysis techniques presented in the UNIDO *Guidelines for Project Evaluation* (1972) and Little and Mirrlees, *Project Appraisal and Planning for Developing Countries* (1974). The general approach set forth has since been adopted by the World Bank for economic analysis of development projects. Although environmental concerns are not emphasized and case studies are not presented in the book, Squire and van der Tak provide a good, practical introduction to the use of social benefit-cost analysis in project appraisal. The first part of the book discusses the basic concepts of benefit-cost analysis, including the identification of relevant benefits and costs, valuation approaches, and investment criteria. The second and third parts contain extensive discussions of the derivation and estimation of shadow prices. Such topics as shadow wage rates, prices of traded and nontraded goods, and weighting systems are covered. The text is clearly written and well organized and, as such, is a very useful basic reference for the general area of economic analysis of projects. Although not overly technical, it is fairly rigorously presented and has a short, but useful, bibliography of standard references.

Indexes

AUTHOR INDEX

329

SUBJECT INDEX

The Johns Hopkins University Press

ENVIRONMENT, NATURAL SYSTEMS, AND DEVELOPMENT

This book was set in Times Roman text and News Gothic
Condensed display by The Composing Room of Michigan, Inc.,
from a design by Susan P. Fillion. It was printed on 50-lb.
Glatfelter Offset paper and bound by Thomson-Shore, Inc.